THE PILGRIM CHURCH

THE
PILGRIM CHURCH

E. H. BROADBENT

With a Foreword by
F. F. Bruce

A Pickering Classic

A Pickering Classic
Pickering & Inglis Ltd
3 Beggarwood Lane, Basingstoke, Hants, RG23 7LP, UK
Marshall Pickering
A subsidiary of the Zondervan Corporation

Copyright © 1931 by E. H. Broadbent

First published in 1931
Reprinted 1935, 1946, 1950, 1956, 1963, 1974, 1978, 1981
Reissued in new format 1985

British Library CIP data

Broadbent, E. H.
    The pilgrim church
    1. Church history
    I. Title
    270   BR 145.2

ISBN 0-7208-0677-1

Printed in Great Britain at
The Camelot Press Ltd, Southampton

Foreword

WHEN *The Pilgrim Church* first appeared in 1931, it was widely, and justly, hailed as a pioneer study of a phase of Christian history which had all too often been neglected or misrepresented. A month or two after its appearance the late Professor A. Rendle Short told me that in his judgment it was the best work that Pickering and Inglis had ever published.

The author, Edmund Hamer Broadbent (1861-1945), spent much time, during a period of nearly fifty years, travelling in Central and Eastern Europe, where he made the acquaintance of a number of Christian groups, gathered in separation from the established churches of those lands and sometimes enduring no little persecution on that account. As he enjoyed their fellowship, he conceived the desire to know more about their origin and history, and this led him to the course of intensive research which bore fruit in *The Pilgrim Church*. The works, both published and unpublished, which provided him with his main sources of information are listed in his preface and bibliography, not to mention his footnotes. The reviewer of the book in *The Evangelical Quarterly* remarked that 'it would be difficult to suggest a more helpful course of study than that laid down in these introductory pages'. In subsequent years others have engaged in further exploration of the field—we may think of Leonard Verduin's study of the Anabaptists, *The Reformers and their Stepchildren* (1964)—but the pioneer quality of *The Pilgrim Church* remains.

It has been held against it that it includes within its scope some groups whose orthodoxy was more than suspect —those, for instance, with whom Sir Steven Runciman has dealt in *The Medieval Manichee* (1947). This criticism was largely met in advance by the author when he pointed out that much of the information about these groups comes from their opponents, who had an interest in painting their beliefs and practices in the blackest hues. It should also be borne in mind that people who, whether by choice or by necessity, are severed from the mainstream of contemporary culture, inevitably develop eccentricities in attitude and conduct. Even Mr. Broadbent, for all his breadth of charity, drew the line at including the Dukhobors in his pilgrim succession!

But most of the groups described in this volume have a rightful place not only in the pilgrim succession but in the apostolic succession, because in them we can recognize the infallible tokens of that succession—the maintenance of of the apostolic gospel and the warmth of the apostolic fellowship. In the more ecumenical climate of today, the contribution that they made, and continue to make, to the church's witness in the world is more readily appreciated and acknowledged than it formerly was. If mainstream Christianity has accomplished what these 'separated brethren' could not have achieved, it must be said that the 'separated brethren' have at times borne a distinctive and indispensable testimony to essential aspects of Christian truth which, but for their faithfulness, might have been lost. This Paperback edition of *The Pilgrim Church* will ensure that this service of theirs will not be forgotten and that a new generation of readers will be reminded of the debt we owe them.

University of Manchester   F. F. BRUCE

Preface

THERE is one history, which, though it contains the darkest tragedy, yet by common consent is called "The Good News", "The Glad Tidings", or by a name which it has captured and made its own: *"The Gospel"*.

Its four historians are uniquely known as *"The Four Evangelists"*, or tellers forth of the Good News.

This history tells how, by a miraculous birth, God entered into a relationship to man which even creation had not established, and by a sacrificial death and mighty resurrection vanquished death, put away sin its cause, and to His glory as Creator added that of Redeemer.

The foundations of this history, the preparation for it, indeed the actual foretelling of it and evidences of its truth precede it in the Scriptures of the Old Testament. Interwoven with these, inseparable from them, is the *History of Israel*, which is therefore itself one of universal value.

The *History of the Church* or company of those who by faith have received Christ and become His followers, is still in the making, not yet complete. On this account and because of its immense extent, although it is of supreme importance, parts only of it can be written and from time to time. First one, then another, must relate what he has seen or has learned from trustworthy records, and this must be taken up and added to as stage after stage of the long pilgrimage is traversed.

The following pages are a contribution to the unfolding story. Much that others have searched out and related has been made use of, repeated, woven in, so that this book is a *compilation*, to which is added the writer's individual share in the growing narrative. It is hoped and expected that the frequent quotations from and references to the works of several authors will lead the readers of this volume to turn to the books from which so much has been derived, and thus come to share more fully in the fruits of the patient labours and able expositions of their authors.

An attempt is made in this book to introduce those who have not much time for reading or research, into some of the experiences of certain churches of God which, at different times and in various places, have endeavoured in their meetings, order, and testimony to make the Scriptures their guide and to act upon them as the Word of God, counting them as sufficient for all their needs in all their circumstances.

There have always been such churches; the records of most have disappeared, but what remain are of such volume that only a selection can be given.

General history is left out of account, except where the course of some of these churches requires reference to current events. Neither is any account given of what is usually understood by "ecclesiastical" history, except in its relation to the churches or congregations of believers carrying out the teachings of Scripture, which are the subject of this narrative.

Some spiritual movements are considered which only partially accepted the principle of taking the Scriptures as sufficient guide, because in their measure these too throw valuable light on the possibility of such a course.

In addition to the works mentioned below, and others also, advantage has been taken of the help so richly provided and placed within the reach of most by such works as the "Encyclopædia Britannica" and Hastings' "Encyclopaedia of Religion and Ethics".

A beginner may look up the subject in one of these standard works of reference, where he will be directed to some of the literature considered as authoritative. In reading a selection of this he will be referred to the original authorities and also (as these are not always available) to their most trustworthy expositors. In the present volume the books used and referred to are mostly well known and accessible; sometimes a popular work has been chosen in preference to one more erudite, so that anyone interested may get fuller information more easily. Where books written in languages other than English are made use of, translations are referred to if they are to be had, but sometimes there are none, and then the original works are named for the benefit of those who can read them.

In the beginning of the History, "The Ante-Nicene

Christian Library" provides a store of information, from which much has been drawn. When the time of Marcion is reached, "Marcion Das Evangelium vom Fremden Gott" by Ad. v. Harnack is used, and for matters connected with the Roman Empire, "East and West Through Fifteen Centuries" by Br.-Genl. G. F. Young C.B. For Augustine "A Select Library of the Nicene and Post Nicene Fathers of the Christian Church" translated and annotated by J. C. Pilkington, M.A. edited by Philip Schaff, is a guide. "Latin Christianity" by Dean Milman, helps in several periods. We are indebted to Georg Schepss for the true history of Priscillian and his teaching. His book, "Priscillian ein Neuaufgefundener Lat. Schriftsteller des 4 Jahrhunderts" describes his discovery in the Würzburg University, in 1886, of the important MS. of the Spanish Reformer. This MS. is examined and explained by Friedrich Paret in his "Priscillianus Ein Reformator des Vierten Jahrhunderts Eine Kirchengeschichtliche Studie zugleich ein Kommentar zu den Erhaltenen Schriften Priscillians", and much has been drawn from this valuable commentary. Important information as to those called Paulicians is given in "Die Paulikianer im Byzantischen Kaiserreiche etc." by Karapet Ter-Mkrttschian, Archdeacon of Edschmiatzin, the centre of the Armenian Church. An invaluable book for the period is "The Key of Truth A Manual of the Paulician Church of Armenia" translated and edited by F. C. Conybeare. The document was discovered by the translator in 1891 in the library of the Holy Synod at Edjmiatzin; his notes and comments are of the utmost interest and value. The discovery of the "Key of Truth" raises the hope that other documents illustrating the faith and teaching of the brethren may yet be found. The history of the Bogomils in the Balkan Peninsula is largely drawn from "An Official Tour Through Bosnia and Herzegovina" by J. de Asboth, Member of the Hungarian Parliament, and from "Through Bosnia and the Herzegovina on Foot etc." by A. J. Evans, the distinguished traveller and antiquarian, later Sir Arthur Evans. "Essays on the Latin Orient" by William Miller, has also been made use of. The chapter on the Eastern Churches, especially the Nestorian, owes very much to "Le Christianisme dans l'Empire Perse sous la Dynastie Sassanide" by J. Labourt; to "The Syrian Churches" by J. W. Etheridge; and to "Early Christianity Outside the Roman Empire" by F. C. Burkitt M.A. The account of the Synod of Seleucia is taken chiefly from "Das Buch des Synhados" by Oscar Braun, while "Nestorius and his Teachings" by J. Bethune-Baker, has supplied most of what is given about Nestorius, and "The Bazaar of Heraclides of Damascus" by the same author, has especially been quoted; these give a vivid picture of Nestorius and should be read in full if possible. For the description of the spread of the Nestorians into China, "Cathay and the Way Thither" by Col. Sir Henry Yule, published by the Hakluyt Society, is of great interest and has been freely drawn upon.

Coming to the times of the Waldenses and Albigenses, "The Ancient Vallenses and Albigenses" by G. S. Faber, and "Facts and Documents illustrative of the History Doctrine and Rites of the Ancient Albigenses and Waldenses" by S. R. Maitland, have been referred to very fully. Perhaps the largest use has been made of the works of Dr. Ludwig Keller, especially for the history and teaching of the Waldenses. His position as Keeper of State Archives, giving access as it does to most important documents, has been used by him to investigate the histories of those known as "heretics", and his publications are an invaluable contribution to the understanding of these much misunderstood people. Dr. Keller's book, "Die Reformation und die älteren Reformparteien" is a mine of information and all who can do so should read it. Use has also been made of his book "Ein Apostel der Wiedertäufer" and of a number of others written or issued by him. Of the time of the Reformation, the "Life and Letters of Erasmus" by J. A. Froude, gives a vivid picture, and "A Short History of the English People" by John Richard Green, is a constant help by giving in an interesting and reliable way the historical setting of the particular events related. "England in the Age of Wycliffe" by George Macaulay Trevelyan has been used, and much has been taken from "John Wycliffe and his English Precursors" by Lechler (translated). "The Dawn of the Reformation the Age of Hus" by H. B. Workman, has been used; his references to

authorities are valuable. Considerable quotations have been
made from Cheltschizki's "Das Netz des Glaubens" translated from Old Czech into German by Karl Vogel. The
description of the Moravian Church is based to a large
extent on the "History of the Moravian Church" by J. E.
Hutton, issued by the Moravian Publication Office, while
for Comenius "Das Testament der Sterbenden Mutter"
and "Stimme der Trauer", both translations into German
from Bohemian, the former by Dora Peřina, the latter by
Franz Slaměnik, are quoted. One of the books most used
is the very valuable one, "A History of the Reformation"
by Thos. M. Lindsay. "Die Taufe. Gedanken über die
urchristliche Taufe, ihre Geschichte und ihre Bedeutung
für die Gegenwart" by J. Warns, is of great value,
especially for the history of the Anabaptists, and its many
references to authorities are useful. The important and
deeply interesting records of the Anabaptists in Austria
are taken from "Fontes Rerum Austriacarum" and other
publications by Dr. J. Beck and Joh. Loserth, which
are referred to in more detail in the footnotes to the pages
where this part of the history is related. The history of
the Mennonites in Russia is chiefly found in "Geschichte
der Alt-Evangelischen Mennoniten Brüderschaft in Russland" by P. M. Friesen, who was appointed by the
"Mennoniten-Brüdergemeinde" as their historian, and
supplied by them with the documentary evidence they
possessed; use is also made of "Fundamente der Christlichen Lehre u. s. w." by Joh. Deknatel. Of the book by
Pilgram Marbeck, "Vermanung etc.", summarized, only
two copies are known to exist, one of which is in the
British Museum. Very considerable use has been made of
the valuable book by Karl Ecke, "Schwenckfeld, Luther
und der Gedanke einer Apostolischen Reformation".
The chapter on events in France is indebted to the "History
of the Reformation of the Sixteenth Century" by J. H.
Merle D'Aubigné, translated by H. White and for Farel,
to the "Life of William Farel" by Frances Bevan, one of
several interesting works of similar character by the same
authoress. Another work by Merle D'Aubigné here made
much use of is "The Reformation in Europe in the Time
of Calvin". "The Huguenots, their Settlements Churches
and Industries in England and Ireland" by Samuel Smiles,

gives much of value about the Huguenots. "Un Martyr du Désert Jacques Roger" by Daniel Benoit, tells of the "Churches of the Desert" after the Revocation of the Edict of Nantes.

Returning to England, the "Memoir of William Tyndale" by George Offor, is quoted and otherwise referred to. The book most used in the account of the Nonconformists in England is "A History of the Free Churches of England" by Herbert S. Skeats, which would well repay reading; and "A Popular History of the Free Churches" by C. Silvester Horne, gives an interesting account of these churches. The "Laws of Ecclesiastical Polity" of Richard Hooker, is referred to. The "Journal of George Fox" supplies the best information as to his life. Three books which give excellent histories of the spiritual movements in Germany and surrounding countries after the Reformation have been largely made use of: "Geschichte des Christlichen Lebens in der rheinisch-westphälischen Kirche" by Max Goebel; "Geschichte des Pietismus und der Mystik in der Reformirten Kirche u.s.w." by Heinr. Heppe; and "Geschichte des Pietismus in der reformirten Kirche" by Albrecht Ritschl. "John Wesley's Journal" is the best source for an account of his life. "The Life of William Carey Shoemaker and Missionary" by George Smith, supplies most of what is told here of him. The account of the brothers Haldane is taken chiefly from the "Lives of Robert and James Haldane" by Alexander Haldane. For Russia and the Stundists, in addition to the "Geschichte etc.," of P. M. Friesen, a useful book is "Russland und das Evangelium" by J. Warns. In the history of the rise of the German Baptists use is made of "Johann Gerhard Oncken, His Life and Work" by John Hunt Cook. For later movements in England etc., some MSS. have been available, and "A History of the Plymouth Brethren" by W. Blair Neatby, has been consulted. Extensive extracts have been made from the "Memoir of the late Anthony Norris Groves, containing Extracts from his Letters and Journals" compiled by his widow, illustrating the important part the teaching and example of Groves played in the history of churches of the New Testament type. "A Narrative of some of the Lord's Dealings with George Müller" has been used as the best account

of Müller's influential testimony; and details of the life
of R. C. Chapman have been taken from "Robert Cleaver
Chapman of Barnstaple" by W. H. Bennet, his personal
friend. "Collected Writings of J. N. Darby" edited by
William Kelly, is used to show Darby's teaching.
"Nazarenes in Jugoslavia" published in the United States
by the "Nazarenes", and various pamphlets, give information as to the movement connected with the people
bearing this name.

The tragedy and glory of *"The Pilgrim Church"* can
only be faintly indicated as yet, nor can they be fully known
until the time comes when the Word of the Lord is
fulfilled: "there is nothing covered, that shall not be
revealed; and hid, that shall not be known" (Matt. 10. 26).
At present, albeit through mists of our ignorance and
misunderstanding, we see her warring against the powers
of darkness, witnessing for her Lord in the world, suffering
as she follows in His footsteps. Her people are ever *pilgrims*, establishing no earthly institution, because having
in view the heavenly city. In their likeness to their
Master they might be called *Stones which the Builders
Rejected* (Luke 20. 17), and they are sustained in the confident hope that, when His kingdom is revealed, they will
be sharers in it with Him.

List of Some of the Books

OF WHICH USE HAS BEEN MADE. OTHERS NOT INCLUDED HERE ARE
REFERRED TO IN THE FOOTNOTES.

"The Ante-Nicene Christian Library"

"Marcion. Das Evangelium vom Fremden Gott" Ad. v. Harnack.

"East and West Through Fifteen Centuries" Br.-Genl. G. F. Young
C.B.

"A Select Library of the Nicene and Post Nicene Fathers of the Christian
Church" translated and annotated by J. C Pilkington M.A.
Edited by Philip Schaff.

"Latin Christianity" Dean Milman.

"Priscillian ein Neuaufgefundener Lat. Schriftsteller des 4 Jahrhunderts"
Dr. Georg. Schepss, who discovered the MS. in the Würzburg
University, 1886.

"Priscillianus Ein Reformator des Vierten Jahrhunderts" Friedrich
Paret.

"Die Paulikianer im Byzantischen Kaiserreiche etc." Karapet Ter-
Mkrttschian. Archidiakonus von Edschmiatzin.

"The Key of Truth A Manual of the Paulician Church of Armenia"
translated and edited by F. C. Conybeare. Document found
by the translator in 1891 in the library of the Holy Synod at
Edjmiatzin.

"An Official Tour through Bosnia and Herzegovina" J. de Asboth,
Member of Hungarian Parliament.

"Through Bosnia and the Herzegovina on Foot etc." A. J. Evans.

"Essays on the Latin Orient" William Miller.

"Le Christianisme dans l'Empire Perse sous la Dynastie Sassanide"
(224-632). J. Labourt.

"The Syrian Churches" J. W. Etheridge.

"Early Christianity outside the Roman Empire" F. C. Burkitt M.A

"Das Buch des Synhados" Oscar Braun.

"Nestorius and his teachings" J. Bethune-Baker.

"The Bazaar of Heraclides of Damascus" J. Bethune-Baker.

"Cathay and the Way Thither" Col. Sir Henry Yule. Hakluyt Society.

"Nestorian Missionary Enterprise. The Story of a Church on Fire"
Rev. John Stewart M.A., Ph.D. T. & T. Clark, Edinburgh.

"The Ancient Vallenses and Albigenses" G. S. Faber

"Facts and Documents illustrative of the History Doctrine and Rites
of the Ancient Albigenses and Waldenses" S. R. Maitland.

xiv LIST OF SOME BOOKS REFERRED TO

"Die Reformation und die älteren Reformparteien" Dr. Ludwig Keller K. Staatsarchivar.

"Life and Letters of Erasmus" J. A. Froude.

"A Short History of the English People" John Richard Green.

"England in the Age of Wycliffe" George Macaulay Trevelyan.

"John Wycliffe and his English Precursors" Lechler. translated by Lorimer.

"The Dawn of the Reformation the Age of Hus" H. B. Workman M.A.

"Das Netz des Glaubens" Peter Cheltschizki. translated from Old Czech to German by Dr. Karl Vogel.

"History of the Moravian Church" J. E. Hutton.

"Das Testament der Sterbenden Mutter" J. A. Comenius. translated into German by Dora Peřina.

"Stimme der Trauer" J. A. Comenius. trans. into German by Franz Slaměnik.

"Unum Necessarium" J. A. Comenius.

"A History of the Reformation" Thos. M. Lindsay.

"Die Taufe. Gedanken über die urchristliche Taufe, ihre Geschichte und ihre Bedeutung für die Gegenwart" J. Warns.

"Ein Apostel der Wiedertäufer" Dr. Ludwig Keller.

Vorträge und Aufsätze aus der Comenius Gesellschaft 7ter Jahrgang 1 u. 2 Stück. "Georg Blaurock und die Anfänge des Anabaptismus in Graubündten und Tirol" Aus dem Nachlasse des Hofrates Dr. Joseph R. von Beck. Herausgegeben von Joh. Loserth.

"Fontes Rerum Austriacarum" Oesterreichische Geschichts-Quellen. Abth. 2 Bd. 43. "Die Geschichts-Bücher der Wiedertäufer in Oesterreich-Ungarn u.s.w. in der Zeit von 1526 bis 1785" Gesammelt, Erläutert und Ergänzt durch Dr. Josef Beck.

Archiv für Oesterreichische Geschichte. 78 Band. "Der Anabaptismus in Tirol u.s.w." Aus dem Nachlasse des Hofrates Joseph R. von Beck. Herausgegeben von Joh. Loserth.

"Geschichte der Wiedertäufer und ihres Reichs zu Münster" Dr. Ludwig Keller.

"Geschichte der Alt-Evangelischen Mennoniten Brüderschaft in Russland" P. M. Friesen.

"Fundamente der Christlichen Lehre u.s.w." Joh. Deknatel.

"Vermanung u.s.w." Pilgram Marbeck.

"Schwenckfeld, Luther und der Gedanke einer Apostolischen Reformation" Karl Ecke.

"History of the Reformation of the Sixteenth Century" J. H. Merle D'Aubigné D.D. translated by H. White B.A.

"Life of William Farel" Frances Bevan.

"The Reformation in Europe in the Time of Calvin" J. H. Merle D'Aubigné, D.D.

"The Huguenots Their Settlements Churches and Industries in England and Ireland" Samuel Smiles.

"Un Martyr du Désert Jacques Roger" Daniel Benoit.

"Memoir of William Tyndale" George Offor.

A History of the Free Churches of England" Herbert S. Skeats.

"A Popular History of the Free Churches" C. Silvester Horne.

"Laws of Ecclesiastical Polity" Richard Hooker.

"Journal of George Fox"

"Geschichte des Christlichen Lebens in der rheinisch-westphälischen Kirche" Max Goebel.

"Geschichte des Pietismus und der Mystik in der Reformirten Kirche u.s.w." Heinr. Heppe.

"Geschichte des Pietismus in der reformirten Kirche" Albrecht Ritschl.

"John Wesley's Journal"

"The Life of William Carey Shoemaker and Missionary" George Smith C.I.E., LL.D.

"Lives of Robert and James Haldane" Alexander Haldane.

"Russland und das Evangelium" Joh. Warns.

"Johann Gerhard Oncken. His Life and Work" John Hunt Cooke.

"Memoirs of Alexander Campbell" Richardson. The Standard Press, Cincinnati, Ohio.

"Autobiography of B. W. Stone" The Standard Press, Cincinnati, Ohio. MSS. Ed. Cronin, J. G. Bellett, etc.

"A History of the Plymouth Brethren" W. Blair Neatby.

"Memoir of the late Anthony Norris Groves containing Extracts from his Letters and Journals" Compiled by his Widow.

"A Narrative of some of the Lord's Dealings with George Müller"

"Robert Cleaver Chapman of Barnstaple" W. H. Bennet.

"Collected Writings of J. N. Darby" Edited by William Kelly. Ecclesiastical Vol. 1.

"Nazarenes in Jugoslavia" Apostolic Christian Publishing Co. Syracuse N.Y., U.S.A.

"Einzelne Briefe und Betrachtungen aus dem Nachlasse von S. H Fröhlich"

Contents

CHAPTER I

BEGINNINGS .. ..

PAGE
1

29-313

The New Testament suited to present conditions—The Old Testament and the New—The Church of Christ and the churches of God—The Book of the Acts provides a pattern for present use—Plan of this account of later events—Pentecost and the formation of churches—Synagogues—Synagogues and churches—Jewish Diaspora spreads the knowledge of God—The earliest churches formed of Jews—Jews reject Christ—Jewish religion, Greek philosophy and Roman power oppose the churches—Close of the Holy Scriptures—Later writings—Clement to the Corinthians—Ignatius—Last links with New Testament times—Baptism and the Lord's Supper—Growth of a clerical caste—Origen—Cyprian—Novatian—Different kinds of churches—Montanists—Marcionites—Persistence of Primitive Churches — Cathars — Novatians — Donatists — Manichaeans—Epistle to Diognetus—The Roman Empire persecutes the Church—Constantine gives religious liberty—The Church overcomes the world.

CHAPTER II

CHRISTIANITY IN CHRISTENDOM 20

313-476, 300-850, 350-385

Church and State associated — Churches refusing union with the State—Donatists condemned—Council of Nicaea—Arianism restored—Athanasius—Creeds—Canon of Scripture—The Roman world and the Church—Break-up of the Western Roman Empire—Augustine—Pelagius—Change in the position of the Church—False doctrines: Manichaeism, Arianism, Pelagianism, Sacerdotalism—Monasticism—The Scriptures remain for guidance—Missions—Departure from New Testament Missionary principles—Irish and Scottish Missions on the Continent—Conflict between British and Roman Missions—Priscillian.

CHAPTER III

PAULICIANS AND BOGOMILS 41

50-1473

Growth of clerical domination—Persistence of Primitive churches—Their histories distorted by their enemies—

xvii

Early churches in Asia Minor—Armenia—Primitive churches in Asia Minor from Apostolic times—Unjustly described by their opponents as Manichaeans—The names Paulician and Thonrak—Continuity of New Testament churches—Constantine Silvanus—Simeon Titus—Veneration of relics, and image worship—Iconoclastic Emperors——John of Damascus—Restoration of images in Greek Church—Council of Frankfurt—Claudius Bishop of Turin—Mohammedanism — Sembat — Sergius — Leaders of the churches in Asia Minor—Persecution under Theodora—The Key of Truth—Carbeas and Chrysocheir—The Scriptures and the Koran—Character of the churches in Asia Minor—Removal of believers from Asia to Europe—Later history in Bulgaria—Bogomils—Basil—Opinions regarding Paulicians and Bogomils—Spread of Bogomils into Bosnia—Kulin Ban and Rome—Intercourse of Bogomils with Christians abroad—Bosnia invaded—Advance of Mohammedans—Persecution of Bogomils—Bosnia taken by the Turks—Friends of God in Bosnia a link between the Taurus and the Alps—Bogomil tombs.

CHAPTER IV

THE EAST 67

B.C. 4—A.D. 1400

The Gospel in the East—Syria and Persia—Churches in Persian Empire separated from those in Roman Empire—Eastern churches retained Scriptural character longer than those in the west—Papa ben Aggai federates churches—Zoroaster—Persecution under Sapor II—Homilies of Afrahat—Synod of Seleucia—Persecution renewed—Nestorius—The Bazaar of Heraclides—Toleration—Influx of western bishops—Increase of centralization—Wide spread of Syrian churches in Asia—Mohammedan invasion—Catholikos moved from Seleucia to Bagdad—Genghis Khan—Struggle between Nestorianism and Islam in Central Asia—Tamerlane—Franciscans and Jesuits find Nestorians in Cathay—Sixteenth century translation of part of Bible into Chinese—Disappearance of Nestorians from most of Asia—Causes of failure.

CHAPTER V

WALDENSES AND ALBIGENSES 85

1100-1230, 70-1700, 1160-1318, 1100-1500

Pierre de Brueys—Henri the Deacon—Sectarian names refused—The name Albigenses—Visits of brethren from the Balkans — The Perfect — Provence invaded — Inquisition established—Waldenses—Leonists—Names—Tradition in the valleys—Peter Waldo—Poor Men of Lyons—Increase of missionary activity—Francis of Assisi—Orders of Friars—Spread of the churches—Doctrine and practices of the Brethren—Waldensian valleys attacked—Beghards and Beghines.

CONTENTS

CHAPTER VI

CHURCHES AT THE CLOSE OF THE MIDDLE AGES 102

1300-1500

Influence of the Brethren in other circles—Marsiglio of
Padua—The Guilds—Cathedral builders—Protests of
the cities and guilds—Walther in Cologne—Thomas
Aquinas and Alvarus Pelagius—Literature of the brethren
destroyed—Master Eckhart—Tauler—The "Nine Rocks"
—The Friend of God from the Oberland—Renewal of
persecution—Strassburg document on persistence of the
churches—Book in Tepl—Old Translation of German
New Testament—Fanaticism—Capture of Constantinople
—Invention of Printing—Discoveries—Printing Bibles—
Colet, Reuchlin—Erasmus and the Greek New Testament—
Hope of peaceful Reformation—Resistance of Rome—
Staupitz discovers Luther.

CHAPTER VII

LOLLARDS, HUSSITES, THE UNITED BRETHREN, ... 117

1350-1670

Wycliff — Peasant Revolt — Persecution in England —
Sawtre, Badley, Cobham—Reading the Bible forbidden—
Congregations — Huss — Žižka — Tabor — Hussite wars—
Utraquists—Jakoubek—Nikolaus—Cheltschizki—The Net
of Faith—Rokycana, Gregor, Kunwald—Reichenau,
Lhota—United Brethren—Lukas of Prague—News of
German Reformation reaches Bohemia—John Augusta—
Smalkald war—Persecution and emigration—George Israel
and Poland—Return of brethren to Bohemia—Bohemian
Charter—Battle of the White Mountain—Comenius.

CHAPTER VIII

THE REFORMATION 141

1500-1550

A Catechism—Brethren of the Common Life—Luther—
Tetzel—The ninety-five Theses at Wittenberg—The Papal
Bull burnt—Diet of Worms—The Wartburg—Translation
of the Bible—Efforts of Erasmus for compromise—Develop-
ment of the Lutheran Church—Its reform and limitations—
Staupitz remonstrates—Luther's choice between New
Testament churches and National Church system—Loyola
and the Counter Reformation.

CHAPTER IX

THE ANABAPTISTS 153

1516-1566

The name Anabaptist—Not a new sect—Rapid increase—
Legislation against them—Balthazer Hubmeyer—Circle

of brethren in Basle—Activities and martyrdom of Hub-
mayer and his wife—Hans Denck—Balance of truth—
Parties — M. Sattler — Persecution increases — Landgraf
Philip of Hessen—Protest of Odenbach—Zwingli—
Persecution in Switzerland — Grebel, Manz, Blaurock —
Kirschner—Persecution in Austria—Chronicles of the Ana-
baptists in Austria Hungary—Ferocity of Ferdinand—
Huter—Mändl and his companions—Communities—
Münster—The Kingdom of the New Zion—Distorted use
of events in Münster to calumniate the brethren—Disciples
of Christ treated as He was—Menno Simon—Pilgram
Marbeck and his book—Sectarianism—Persecution in
West Germany—Hermann Archbishop of Cologne attempts
reform—Schwenckfeld.

CHAPTER X

FRANCE AND SWITZERLAND   208

1500-1800

Le Fèvre—Group of believers in Paris—Meaux—Farel's
preaching — Metz — Images destroyed — Executions —
Increased persecution in France—Farel in French Switzer-
land—Neuchâtel—The Vaudois and the Reformers meet
—Visit of Farel and Saunier to the valleys—Progress in
Neuchâtel—Breaking of bread in the South of France—
Jean Calvin—Breaking of bread in Poitiers—Evangelists
sent out—Froment in Geneva—Breaking of bread outside
Geneva—Calvin in Geneva—Socinianism—Servetus—In-
fluence of Calvinism—The Placards—Sturm to Melanch-
thon—Organization of churches in France—The Huguenots
—Massacre of St. Bartholomew—Edict of Nantes—The
Dragonnades—Revocation of the Edict of Nantes—Flight
from France—Prophets of the Cevennes—War of the
Camisards—Churches of the desert reorganized—Jacques
Roger—Antoine Court.

CHAPTER XI

ENGLISH NONCONFORMISTS   235

1525-1689

Tyndale—Reading of Scripture forbidden—Church of
England established—Persecution in the reign of Mary—
Baptist and Independent churches—Robert Browne—
Barrowe, Greenwood, Penry—Dissenters persecuted in
Elizabeth's reign—Privye church in London—Hooker's
Ecclesiastical Polity—Church of English exiles in Amster-
dam—Arminius—Emigration of brethren from England to
Holland—John Robinson—The Pilgrim Fathers sail to
America—Different kinds of churches in England and Scot-
land—Authorized Version of the Bible published—Civil
war—Cromwell's New Model Army—Religious liberty
—Missions—George Fox—Character of Friends' Movement
—Acts against Nonconformists—Literature—John Bunyan.

CONTENTS

CHAPTER XII

LABADIE, THE PIETISTS, ZINZENDORF, PHILADELPHIA　　..　255

1635-1750

Labadie—Forms a fellowship in the Roman Catholic
Church—Joins the Reformed Church—Goes to Orange—
To Geneva—Willem Teelinck—Gisbert Voet—van Loden-
steyn—Labadie goes to Holland—Difference between
Presbyterian and Independent ideals—Reforms in the
Middelburg church—Conflict with Synods of the Reformed
Church—Conflict on Rationalism—Labadie condemns
Synods—He is excluded from the Reformed Church—A
separate church formed in Middelburg—The new church
expelled from Middelburg—It removes to Veere—Then
to Amsterdam—Household church formed—Anna Maria
van Schürman—Difference with Voet—Household troubles
—Removal to Herford—Labadie dies in Altona—Removal
of household to Wieuwerd—Household broken up—Effects
of testimony—Spener—Pietists—Franke—Christian David
—Zinzendorf — Herrnhut — Dissensions — Zinzendorf's
Statutes accepted—Revival—Discovery of document in
Zittau—Determination to restore the Bohemian Church—
Question of relations with the Lutheran Church—The
negro Anthony—Moravian Missions—The Mission in Eng-
land—Cennick—Central control unsuited to expanding
work—Philadelphia Societies—Miguel de Molinos—
Madame Guyon—Gottfried Arnold—Wittgenstein—The
Marburg Bible—The Berleburg Bible—Philadelphian
Invitation—Hochmann von Hochenau—Tersteegen—Jung
Stilling—Primitive and Reformed and other churches—
Various ways of return to Scripture.

CHAPTER XIII

METHODIST AND MISSIONARY MOVEMENTS　　..　　..　285

1638-1820

Condition of England in the 18th century—Revivals in
Wales—Temporary schools—Societies formed—The Holy
Club at Oxford—Mrs. Wesley—John and Charles Wesley
sail to Georgia—John Wesley returns and meets Peter
Boehler—Accepts Christ by faith—Visits Herrnhut—
George Whitefield—He preaches to the colliers at Kings-
wood—John Wesley also begins preaching in the open air—
Lay preachers—Strange manifestations—Great revivals—
Charles Wesley's hymns—Separation between Moravian
and Methodist Societies—Divergence in doctrine of Wesley
and Whitefield—Conference—Separation of Methodist
Societies from the Church of England—Divisions—General
benefit from the movement—Need of missionary work—
William Carey—Andrew Fuller—Formation of Missionary
Societies—Difference between Mission Stations and churches
—The brothers Haldane—James Haldane preaches in

CONTENTS

Scotland—Opposition of Synods—Large numbers hear the Gospel—A church formed in Edinburgh—Liberty of ministry—Question of baptism—Robert Haldane visits Geneva—Bible Readings on Romans—The Lord's Supper in Geneva—A church formed.

CHAPTER XIV

THE WEST 305

1790-1890

Thomas Campbell—A "Declaration and Address"—Alexander Campbell—Church at Brush Run—Baptism—Sermon on the Law—Republican Methodists take the name "Christians"—Baptists take the name "Christians"—Barton Warren Stone—Strange revival scenes—The Springfield Presbytery formed and dissolved—Church at Cane Ridge—The Christian Connection—Separation of Reformers from Baptists—Union of Christian Connection and Reformers—Nature of Conversion—Walter Scott—Baptism for the remission of sins—Testimony of Isaac Errett.

CHAPTER XV

RUSSIA 318

1788-1914, 850-1650, 1812-1930, 1823-1930, 1828-1930

Mennonite and Lutheran emigration to Russia—Privileges change the character of the Mennonite churches—Wüst—Revival—Mennonite Brethren separate from Mennonite Church—Revival of Mennonite Church—Meetings among Russians forbidden—Circulation of Russian Scriptures allowed — Bible translation — Cyril Lucas — Stundists — Various avenues by which the Gospel came into Russia—Great increase of the churches—Political events in Russia lead to increased persecution—Exiles—Instances of exile and of the influence of the New Testament—Decree of the Holy Synod against stundists—Evangelical Christians and Baptists—General disorder in Russia—Edict of Toleration —Increase of churches—Toleration withdrawn—Revolution —Anarchy—Rise of Bolshevik Government—Efforts to abolish religion—Suffering and increase—Communists persecute believers—J. G. Oncken—A Baptist Church formed in Hamburg—Persecution—Tolerance—Bible School —Spread and division in Russia—Gifts from America—Nazarenes—Fröhlich—Revival through his preaching—Excluded from the Church—The Hungarian journeymen meet Fröhlich—Meetings in Budapest—Spread of the Nazarenes—Sufferings through refusal of military service—Fröhlich's teaching.

CHAPTER XVI

GROVES, MÜLLER, CHAPMAN   347

1825-1902

Churches formed in Dublin—A. N. Groves—Leaves with
party for Bagdad—Work begun—Plague and flood—Death
of Mrs. Groves—Arrival of helpers from England—Colonel
Cotton—Removal of Groves to India—Objects of his stay
there—To bring missionary work back to the New Testament pattern—To reunite the people of God—George
Müller—Henry Craik—Church formed at Bethesda Chapel,
Bristol, to carry out New Testament principles—Müller's
visit to Germany—Institutions and Orphanage carried on
for the encouragement of faith in God—Robert Chapman—
J. H. Evans—Chapman's conversion—His ministry in
Barnstaple and travels—Circles accepting the Scriptures
as their guide.

CHAPTER XVII

QUESTIONS OF FELLOWSHIP AND OF INSPIRATION   ..   372

1830-1930

Meeting in Plymouth—Conditions in French Switzerland—
Darby's visits—Development of his system—"The church
in ruins"—August Rochat—Difference between Darby's
teaching and that of brethren who took the New Testament
as the pattern for the churches—Change from Congregational
to Catholic principle—Spread of meetings—Letter from
Groves to Darby—Suggestion of a central authority—Darby
and Newton—Darby and the church at Bethesda, Bristol—
Darby excludes all who would not join him in excluding
the church at Bethesda—World-wide application of system
of excluding churches—Churches which did not accept the
exclusive system—Their influence in other circles—
Churches on the New Testament pattern formed in many
countries — Rationalism — Biblical Criticism — C. H.
Spurgeon—Increased circulation of the Scriptures.

CHAPTER XVIII

CONCLUSIONS   394

Can churches still follow New Testament teaching and
example? — Various answers — Ritualistic churches —
Rationalism — Reformers — Mystics and others — Evangelical Revival—Brethren who throughout all the centuries
have made the New Testament their guide—Spread of the
Gospel—Foreign Missions—Revival through return to the
teachings of Scripture—Every Christian a missionary,
each church a Missionary Society—Difference between a
church and a mission station—Difference between an
institution and a church—Unity of the churches and spread
of the Gospel—New Testament churches among all people
on the same basis—Conclusion.

CHAPTER I

Beginnings

29-313

THE New Testament suited to present conditions—The Old Testament and the New—The Church of Christ and the churches of God—The Book of the Acts provides a pattern for present use—Plan of this account of later events——Pentecost and the formation of churches—Synagogues—Synagogues and churches—Jewish Diaspora spreads the knowledge of God—The earliest churches formed of Jews—Jews reject Christ—Jewish religion, Greek philosophy and Roman power oppose the churches—Close of the Holy Scriptures—Later writings—Clement to the Corinthians—Ignatius—Last links with New Testament times—Baptism and the Lord's Supper—Growth of a clerical caste—Origen—Cyprian—Novatian—Different ' inds of churches—Montanists—Marcionites—Persistence of Primitive ʾurches—Cathars—Novatians—Donatists—Manichaeans—Epistle to ⸴ʌognetus—The Roman Empire persecutes the Church—Constantine gives religious liberty—The Church overcomes the world.

THE New Testament is the worthy completion of the Old. It is the only proper end to which the Law and the Prophets could have led. It does not do away with them but enriches, in fulfilling and replacing them. It has in itself the character of completeness, presenting, not the rudimentary beginning of a new era which requires constant modification and addition to meet the needs of changing times, but a revelation suited to all men in all times. Jesus Christ cannot be made known to us better than He is in the four Gospels, nor can the consequences, or doctrines, which flow from the facts of His death and resurrection be more truly taught than they are in the Epistles.

The Old Testament records the formation and history of Israel, the people through whom God revealed Himself in the world until Christ should come. The New Testament reveals the Church of Christ, consisting of all who are born again through faith in the Son of God and so made partakers of the Divine and Eternal Life (John 3. 16).

As this body, the whole Church of Christ, cannot be seen and cannot act in any one place, since many of its members

1

are already with Christ and others scattered throughout
the world, it is appointed to be actually known and to
bear its testimony in the form of churches of God in various
places and at different times. Each of these consists of
those disciples of the Lord Jesus Christ who, in the place
where they live, gather together in His Name. To such the
presence of the Lord in their midst is promised and the
manifestation of the Holy Spirit is given in different ways
through all the members (Matt. 18. 20; 1 Cor. 12. 7).

Each of these churches stands in direct relationship to
the Lord, draws its authority from Him and is responsible
to Him (Rev. 2 and 3). There is no suggestion that one
church should control another or that any organized union
of churches should exist, but an intimate personal fellowship unites them (Acts 15. 36).

The chief business of the churches is to make known
throughout the world the Gospel or Glad Tidings of Salvation. This the Lord commanded before His ascension,
promising to give the Holy Spirit as the power in which
it should be accomplished (Acts 1. 8).

Events in the history of the churches in the time of the
Apostles have been selected and recorded in the Book of
the Acts in such a way as to provide a permanent pattern
for the churches. Departure from this pattern has had
disastrous consequences, and all revival and restoration
have been due to some return to the pattern and principles
contained in the Scriptures.

The following account of some later events, compiled
from various writers, shows that there has been a continuous succession of churches composed of believers who
have made it their aim to act upon the teaching of the
New Testament. This succession is not necessarily to be
found in any one place, often such churches have been
dispersed or have degenerated, but similar ones have
appeared in other places. The pattern is so clearly
delineated in the Scriptures as to have made it possible for
churches of this character to spring up in fresh places
and among believers who did not know that disciples
before them had taken the same path, or that there were
some in their own time in other parts of the world. Points of
contact with more general history are noted where the connection helps to an understanding of the churches described

Some spiritual movements are referred to which, though they did not lead to the formation of churches on the New Testament pattern, nevertheless throw light on those which did result in the founding of such churches.

From Pentecost there was a rapid spread of the Gospel. The many Jews who heard it at the feast at Jerusalem when it was first preached, carried the news to the various countries of their dispersion. Although it is only of the missionary journeys of the Apostle Paul that the New Testament gives any detailed record, the other Apostles also travelled extensively, preaching and founding churches over wide areas. All who believed were witnesses for Christ, "they that were scattered abroad went everywhere preaching the word" (Acts 8. 4). The practice of founding churches where any, however few, believed, gave permanence to the work, and as each church was taught from the first its direct dependence on the Holy Spirit and responsibility to Christ, it became a centre for propagating the Word of Life. To the newly-founded church of the Thessalonians it was said, "from you sounded out the word of the Lord" (1 Thess. 1. 8). Although each church was independent of any organization or association of churches, yet intimate connection with other churches was maintained, a connection continually refreshed by frequent visits of brethren ministering the Word (Acts 15. 36). The meetings being held in private houses, or in any rooms that could be obtained, or in the open air, no special buildings were required.* This drawing of all the members into the service, this mobility and unorganized unity, permitting variety which only emphasized the bond of a common life in Christ and indwelling of the same Holy Spirit, fitted the churches to survive persecution and to carry out their commission of bringing to the whole world the message of salvation.

The first preaching of the Gospel was by Jews and to Jews, and in it frequent use was made of the synagogues. The synagogue system is the simple and effectual means by which the national sense and religious unity of the Jewish people have been preserved throughout the centuries of their dispersion among the nations. The centre of the

* "Mission und Ausbreitung des Christentums"   A. v. Harnack.

synagogue is the Scriptures of the Old Testament, and the
power of Scripture and synagogue is shown in the fact that
the Jewish Diaspora has neither been crushed by the
nations nor absorbed into them. The chief objects of the
synagogue were the reading of Scripture, the teaching of
its precepts, and prayer; and its beginnings go back to
ancient times. In the seventy-fourth Psalm is the complaint: "Thine enemies roar in the midst of Thy congregations . . . they have burned up all the synagogues of God
in the land" (Psa. 74. 4, 8). On the return from the captivity it is said that Ezra further organized the synagogues,
and the later dispersion of the Jews added to their
importance. When the Temple, the Jewish centre, was
destroyed by the Romans, the synagogues, widely distributed as they were, proved to be an indestructible bond,
surviving all the persecutions that followed. In the centre
of each synagogue is the ark in which the Scriptures are
kept, and beside it is the desk from which they are read.
An attempt under Barcochebas (A.D. 135), which was one
of many efforts made to deliver Judaea from the Roman
yoke and seemed for a short time to promise some success,
failed as did all others, and only brought terrible retribution
on the Jews. But though force failed to free them, the
gathering of the people round the Scriptures as their centre
preserved them from extinction.

The likeness and connection between the synagogues
and the churches is apparent. Jesus made Himself the
centre of each of the churches dispersed throughout the
world, saying, "where two or three are gathered together
in My name, there am I in the midst of them" (Matt.
18. 20), and He gave the Scriptures for their unchanging
guidance. For this reason it has proved impossible to
extinguish the churches; when in one place they have been
destroyed they have appeared again in others.

The Jews of the Diaspora* developed great zeal in making
the true God known among the heathen, and large numbers
were converted to God through their testimony. In the
third century B.C. the translation of the Hebrew Scriptures
into Greek was accomplished in the Septuagint Version,
and as Greek was, both at that time and long afterwards,

---

* "Das Judenthum in der vorchristlichen griechischen Welt"
M. Friedländer.

the chief medium of intercommunication among the peoples of various languages, an invaluable means was supplied by which the Gentile nations could be made acquainted with the Old Testament Scriptures. Equipped with this, the Jews used both synagogue and business opportunities in the good work. James, the Lord's brother, said: "Moses of old time hath in every city them that preach him, being read in the synagogues every sabbath day" (Acts 15. 21). Thither Greeks and others were brought in, burdened with the sins and oppressions of heathendom, confused and unsatisfied by its philosophies, and, listening to the Law and the Prophets, came to know the one true God. Business brought the Jews among all classes of people and they used this diligently to spread the knowledge of God. One Gentile seeker after truth writes that he had decided not to join any one of the leading philosophical systems since through a happy fortune a Jewish linen merchant who came to Rome had, in the simplest way, made known to him the one God.

There was liberty of ministry in the synagogues. Jesus habitually taught in them—"as His custom was, He went into the synagogue on the sabbath day, and stood up for to read" (Luke 4. 16). When Barnabas and Paul, travelling, came to Antioch in Pisidia, they went to the synagogue and sat down. "After the reading of the law and the prophets the rulers of the synagogue sent unto them, saying, Ye men and brethren, if ye have any word of exhortation for the people, say on" (Acts 13. 15).

When Christ the Messiah came, the fulfilment of all Israel's hope and testimony, large numbers of Jews and religious proselytes believed in Him, and the first churches were founded among them; but the rulers of the people, envious of Him who is the promised seed of Abraham, the greatest of David's sons, and jealous of a gathering in and blessing of the Gentiles such as the Gospel proclaimed, rejected their King and Redeemer, persecuted His disciples, and went on their way of sorrow without the Saviour who was, to them first, the very expression of the love and saving power of God toward man.

As the Church was first formed in Jewish circles the Jews were its first opponents, but it soon spread into wider surroundings and when Gentiles were converted to Christ

it came into conflict with Greek ideas and with Roman
power. Over the cross of Christ His accusation was written
in Hebrew, Greek, and Latin (John 19. 20), and it was in
the sphere of the spiritual and political power represented
by these languages that the Church was to begin to suffer,
and there also to gain her earliest trophies.

Jewish religion affected the Church, not only in the form
of physical attack, but also, and more permanently, by
bringing Christians under the Law, and we hear Paul in
the Epistle to the Galatians crying out against such retrogression: "a man is not justified by the works of the law,
but by the faith of Jesus Christ" (Gal. 2. 16). From the
book of the Acts and the Epistle to the Galatians it is seen
that the first serious danger that threatened the Christian
Church was that of being confined within the limits of a
Jewish sect and so losing its power and liberty to bring the
knowledge of God's salvation in Christ to the whole world.

Greek philosophy, seeking some theory of God, some
explanation of nature and guide to conduct, laid hold of all
religions and speculations, whether of Greece or Rome, of
Africa or Asia, and one *gnosis* or "knowledge", one system
of philosophy after another arose, and became a subject of
ardent discussion. Most of the Gnostic systems borrowed
from a variety of sources, combining Pagan and Jewish,
and later Christian teachings and practices. They
explored the "mysteries" which lay for the initiated behind
the outward forms of heathen religions. Frequently they
taught the existence of two gods or principles, the one
Light, the other Darkness, the one Good, the other Evil.
Matter and material things seemed to them to be products
of the Power of Darkness and under his control; what was
spiritual they attributed to the higher god. These speculations and philosophies formed the basis of many heresies
which from the earliest times invaded the Church, and are
already combated in the later New Testament writings,
especially in those of Paul and John. The means adopted
to counter these attacks and to preserve unity of doctrine
affected the Church even more than the heresies themselves,
for it was largely due to them that the episcopal power
and control grew up along with the clerical system which
began so soon and so seriously to modify the character of
the churches.

The Roman Empire was gradually drawn into an attack on the churches; an attack in which eventually its whole power and resources were put forth to crush and destroy them.

About the year 65 the Apostle Peter was put to death, and, some years later, the Apostle Paul. * The destruction of Jerusalem by the Romans (A.D. 70) emphasized the fact that to the churches no visible head or centre on earth is given. Later, the Apostle John brought the Scriptures of the Old and New Testaments to their close, a close worthy of all that had gone before, by writing his Gospel, his Epistles, and the Revelation.

There is a noticeable difference between the New Testament and the writings of the same period and later which are not included in the list or *canon* of the inspired Scriptures. The inferiority of the latter is unmistakeable even when the good in them is readily appreciated. While expounding the Scriptures, defending the truth, refuting errors, exhorting the disciples, they also manifest the increasing departure from the divine principles of the New Testament which had already begun in apostolic days and was rapidly accentuated afterwards.

Written in the lifetime of the Apostle John, the first Epistle of Clement to the Corinthians gives a view of the churches at the close of the Apostolic period.† Clement was an elder in the church at Rome. He had seen the Apostles Peter and Paul, to whose martyrdom he refers in this letter. It begins: "The church of God which sojourns at Rome to the church of God sojourning at Corinth". The persecutions they passed through are spoken of with a calm sense of victory: "women . . ." he writes, "being persecuted, after they had suffered unspeakable torments finished the course of their faith with steadfastness, and though weak in body received a noble reward." The tone is one of humility; the writer says: "we write unto you not merely to admonish you of your duty, but also to remind ourselves." Frequent allusions are made to the Old Testament and its typical value and many quotations

* "The Church in Rome in the First Century" George Edmundson M.A.

† "The Writings of the Apostolic Fathers" Vol.I of the Ante-Nicene Christian Library.

are given from the New Testament. The hope of the Lord's return is kept before his readers; he reminds them too of the way of salvation, that it is not of wisdom or works of ours, but by faith; adding that justification by faith should never make us slothful in good works. Yet even here the beginning of a distinction between clergy and laity is already evident, drawn from Old Testament ordinances.

In his last words to the elders of the church at Ephesus the Apostle Paul is described as sending for them and addressing them as those whom the Holy Spirit had made overseers (Acts 20). The word "elders" is the same as *presbyters* and the word "overseers" the same as *bishops*, and the whole passage shows that the two titles referred to the same men, and that there were several such in the one church. Ignatius,* however, writing some years after Clement, though he also had known several of the Apostles, gives to the bishop a prominence and authority, not only unknown in the New Testament, but also beyond what was claimed by Clement. Commenting on Acts 20,† he says that Paul sent from Miletus to Ephesus and called the bishops and presbyters, thus making two titles out of one description, and says that they were from Ephesus and neighbouring cities, thus obscuring the fact that one church, Ephesus, had several overseers or bishops.

One of the last of those who had personally known any of the Apostles was Polycarp, bishop of Smyrna, who was put to death in that city in the year 156. He had long been instructed by the Apostle John, and had been intimate with others who had seen the Lord. Irenaeus is another link in the chain of personal connection with the times of Christ. He was taught by Polycarp and was made bishop of Lyons in 177.

The practice of baptizing believers‡ on their confession of faith in the Lord Jesus Christ, as taught and exemplified in the New Testament, was continued in later times. The first clear reference to the baptism of infants is in a writing

* "The Writings of the Apostolic Fathers" Vol. I of the Ante-Nicene Christian Library.

† The Greek Testament, etc. Henry Alford D.D., Dean of Canterbury. Note on Acts 20. 17.

‡ "Die Taufe. Gedanken über die Urchristliche Taufe ihre Geschichte und ihre Bedeutung für die Gegenwart" Joh. Warns.

of Tertullian in 197, in which he condemns the practice beginning to be introduced of baptizing the dead and of baptizing infants. The way for this change, however, had been prepared by teaching concerning baptism, which was divergent from that in the New Testament; for early in the second century baptismal regeneration was already being taught. This, together with the equally striking change by which the remembrance of the Lord and His death (in the breaking of bread and drinking of wine among His disciples) was changed into an act miraculously performed, it was claimed, by a priest, intensified the growing distinction between clergy and laity. The growth of a clerical system under the domination of the bishops, who in turn were ruled by "Metropolitans" controlling extensive territories, substituted a human organization and religious forms for the power and working of the Holy Spirit and the guidance of the Scriptures in the separate churches.

This development was gradual,* and many were not carried away by it. At first there was no pretension that one church should control another, though a very small church might ask a larger one to send "chosen men" to help it in matters of importance. Local conferences of overseers were held at times, but until the end of the second century they appear to have been called only when some special occasion made it convenient that those interested should confer together. Tertullian wrote: "It is no part of religion to compel religion, which should be adopted freely, not by force."

Origen, one of the greatest teachers,† as well as one of the most spiritually-minded of the fathers, bore a clear testimony to the spiritual character of the Church. Born (185) in Alexandria, of Christian parents, he was one of those who, in early childhood, experience the workings of the Holy Spirit. His happy relations with his wise and godly father, Leonidas, his first teacher in the Scriptures, were strikingly shown when, on the imprisonment of his father because of the faith, Origen, then seventeen years old, tried to join him in prison, and was only hindered from doing so by a stratagem of his mother, who hid his clothes.

---

* "Early Church History" J. Venn Bartlett, M.A., D.D., Lecturer on Church History at Mansfield College, R.T.S., 1925.

† Ante-Nicene Christian Library. Writings of Origen

He wrote to his father in prison, encouraging him to constancy. When Leonidas was put to death and his property confiscated, the young Origen was left the chief support of his mother and six younger brothers. His unusual ability as a teacher quickly brought him into prominence, and while he treated himself with extreme severity, he showed such kindness to the persecuted brethren as involved him in their sufferings. He took refuge for a time in Palestine, where his learning and his writings led bishops to listen as scholars to his expositions of the Scripture. The bishop of Alexandria, Demetrius, indignant that Origen, a layman, should presume to instruct bishops, censured him and recalled him to Alexandria, and though Origen submitted, eventually excommunicated him (231). The peculiar charm of his character and the depth and insight of his teaching devotedly attached to him men who continued his teaching after his death. This took place in 254, as a result of the torture to which he had been subjected five years before in Tyre during the Decian persecution. Origen saw the Church as consisting of all those who have experienced in their lives the power of the eternal Gospel. These form the true spiritual Church, which does not always coincide with that which is called the Church by men. His eager, speculative mind carried him beyond what most apprehended, so that many looked upon him as heretical in his teaching, but he distinguished between those things that must be stated clearly and dogmatically and those that must be put forward with caution, for consideration. Of the latter he says: "how things will be, however, is known with certainty to God alone, and to those who are His friends through Christ and the Holy Spirit." His laborious life was devoted to the elucidation of the Scriptures. A great work of his, the *Hexapla*, made possible a ready comparison of different versions.

Very different from Origen was Cyprian,* bishop of Carthage, born about 200. He freely uses the term "the Catholic Church" and sees no salvation outside of it, so that in his time the "Old Catholic Church" was already formed, that is, the Church which, before the time of Constantine, claimed the name "Catholic" and excluded all who did not conform to it. Writing of Novatian and

* Ante-Nicene Christian Library.   Writings of Cyprian.

those who sympathized with him in their efforts to bring about greater purity in the churches, Cyprian denounces "the wickedness of an unlawful ordination made in opposition to the Catholic Church"; says that those who approved Novatian could not have communion with that Church because they endeavoured "to cut and tear the one body of the Catholic Church", having committed the impiety of forsaking their Mother, and must return to the Church, seeing that they have acted "contrary to Catholic unity". There are, he said, "tares in the wheat, yet we should not withdraw from the Church, but labour to be wheat in it, vessels of gold or silver in the great house." He commended the reading of his pamphlets as likely to help any in doubt, and referring to Novatian asserts, "He who is not in the Church of Christ is not a Christian . . . there is one Church . . . and also one episcopate."

As the churches increased, the first zeal flagged and conformity to the world and its ways increased also. This did not progress without protest. As the organization of the Catholic group of churches developed there were formed within it circles which aimed at reform. Also, some churches separated from it; and others, holding to the original New Testament doctrines and practices in a greater or less degree, gradually found themselves separated from the churches which had largely abandoned them. The fact that the Catholic Church system later became the dominant one puts us in possession of a great body of its literature, while the literature of those who differed from it has been suppressed, and they are chiefly known to us by what may be gleaned from the writings directed against them. It is thus easy to gain the erroneous impression that in the first three centuries there was one united Catholic Church and a variety of comparatively unimportant heretical bodies. On the contrary, however, there were then, as now, a number of divergent lines of testimony each marked by some special characteristic, and different groups of mutually-excluding churches.

The numerous circles that worked for reform in the Catholic churches while remaining in their communion, are often called Montanists. The use of the name of some prominent man to describe an extensive spiritual movement is misleading, and although it must sometimes be accepted for the sake of convenience, it should always be with the reservation that, however important a man may be as a leader and exponent, a spiritual movement affecting multitudes of people is something larger and more significant.

In view of the increasing worldliness in the Church, and the way in which among the leaders learning was taking the place of spiritual power, many believers were deeply impressed with the desire for a fuller experience of the indwelling and power of the Holy Spirit, and were looking for spiritual revival and return to apostolic teaching and practice. In Phrygia, Montanus* began to teach (156), he and those with him protesting against the prevailing laxity in the relations of the Church to the world. Some among them claimed to have special manifestations of the Spirit, in particular two women, Prisca and Maxmillia. The persecution ordered by the Emperor Marcus Aurelius (177) quickened the expectation of the Lord's coming and the spiritual aspirations of the believers. The Montanists hoped to raise up congregations that should return to primitive piety, live as those waiting for the Lord's return and, especially, give to the Holy Spirit His rightful place in the Church. Though there were exaggerations among them in the pretensions of some to spiritual revelations, yet they taught and practised needed reform. They accepted in a general way the organization that had developed in the Catholic churches and tried to remain in their communion; but while the Catholic bishops wished to include in the Church as many adherents as possible, the Montanists constantly pressed for definite evidences of Christianity in the lives of applicants for fellowship. The Catholic system obliged the bishops to take increasing control of the churches, while the Montanists resisted this, maintaining that the guidance of the churches was the prerogative of the Holy Spirit, and that room should be left for His workings. These differences soon led to the formation of separate churches in the East, but in the West the Montanists long remained as societies within the Catholic churches, and it was only after many years that they were excluded from, or left, them. In Carthage,

* "Encyclopædia Britannica" Article, Montanus.

Perpetua and Felicitas, the touching record of whose
martyrdom has preserved their memory, were still, though
Montanists, members of the Catholic church at the
time of their martyrdom (207), but early in the third
century the great leader in the African churches, the
eminent writer Tertullian, attaching himself to the
Montanists, separated from the Catholic body. He wrote:
"where but three are, and they of the laity also, yet there
is a church."

A very different movement, which spread so widely as
seriously to rival the Catholic system, was that of the
Marcionites,* of which Tertullian, an opponent of it,
wrote: "Marcion's heretical tradition has filled the whole
world." Born (85) at Sinope on the Black Sea, and brought
up among the churches in the Province of Pontus, where
the Apostle Peter had laboured (1 Peter 1. 1), and of which
Aquila (Acts 18. 2) was a native, Marcion gradually
developed his teaching, but it was not until he was nearly
sixty years of age that it was published and fully discussed
in Rome.

His soul was exercised as he faced the great problems of
evil in the world, of the difference between the revelation
of God in the Old Testament and that contained in the
New, of the opposition of wrath and judgement on the one
hand to love and mercy on the other, and of Law to Gospel.
Unable to reconcile these divergencies on the basis of
Scripture as generally understood in the churches, he
adopted a form of dualistic theory such as was prevalent
at the time; asserting that the world was not created by
the Highest God, but by a lower being, the god of the
Jews, that the Redeemer God is revealed in Christ, who,
having no previous connection with the world, yet out of
love, and in order to save a world that had failed and to
deliver man from his misery, came into the world. He
came as a stranger and unknown, and consequently was
assailed by the (supposed) creator and ruler of the world
as well as by the Jews and all servants of the god of this
world. Marcion taught that the duty of the true Christian
was to oppose Judaism and the usual form of Christianity,
which he considered as only an offshoot of Judaism. He

* "Marcion das Evangelium vom Fremden Gott" Ad. v. Harnack.

was not in agreement with the Gnostic sects for he did not preach salvation through the "mysteries", or attainment of knowledge, but through faith in Christ, and he aimed at first at the reformation of the Christian churches, though later they and his followers excluded each other.

As his views could not be maintained from Scripture, Marcion became a Bible critic of the most drastic kind. He applied his theory to the Scriptures and rejected all in them that was in manifest opposition to it, retaining only what seemed to him to support it, and interpreting that in accordance with his own views rather than with the general tenor of Scripture, even adding to it where that appeared to him desirable. Thus, although he had formerly accepted, he later rejected the whole of the Old Testament, as being a revelation of the god of the Jews and not of the Highest and Redeemer-God, as prophesying of a Jewish Messiah and not of Christ. He thought the disciples mistook Christ for the Jewish Messiah. Holding that the true Gospel had been revealed to Paul only, he refused also the New Testament, with the exception of certain of Paul's Epistles and the Gospel of Luke, which latter, however, he freely edited to get rid of what ran contrary to his theory. He taught that the remainder of the New Testament was the work of Judaizers bent on destroying the true Gospel and that they also had inter-polated, for the same purpose, the passages to which he objected in the books which he received. To this abridged New Testament Marcion added his own book, "Antitheses", which took the place of the Book of the Acts.

He was an enthusiast for his Gospel, which he declared was a wonder above all wonders; a rapture, power and astonishment such as nothing that could be said or thought could equal. When his doctrines were pronounced heretical he began to form separate churches, which rapidly spread. Baptism and the Lord's Supper were practised, there was a greater simplicity of worship than in the Catholic churches, and the development of clericalism and worldli-ness was checked. In accordance with their view of the material world they were severely ascetic, forbade marriage and only baptized those who took a vow of chastity. They considered the body of Jesus to have been not material, but a phantom, yet capable of feeling, as our bodies are.

Any error may be founded on parts of Scripture; the truth alone is based on the whole. Marcion's errors were the inevitable result of his accepting only what pleased him and rejecting the rest.

Departure from the original pattern given in the New Testament for the churches met very early with strenuous resistance, leading in some cases to the formation within the decadent churches of circles which kept themselves free from the evil and hoped to be a means of restoration to the whole. Some of them were cast out and met as separate congregations. Some, finding conformity to the prevailing conditions impossible, left and formed fresh companies. These would often reinforce those others which, from the beginning, had maintained primitive practice. There is frequent reference in later centuries to those churches that had adhered to Apostolic doctrine, and which claimed unbroken succession of testimony from the time of the Apostles. They often received, both before and after the time of Constantine, the name of Cathars, or Puritans, though it does not appear that they took this name themselves.

The name Novatians was also given to them, though Novatian was not their founder, but one who, in his day, was a leader among them. On the question which so much agitated the churches during times of persecution, as to whether or not persons should be received who had "lapsed", that is, had offered to idols since their baptism, Novatian took the stricter view. A martyred bishop in Rome named Fabian, who in his lifetime had ordained Novatian, was followed by one Cornelius, who was willing to receive the lapsed. A minority, objecting to this, chose Novatian as bishop and he accepted their choice, but he and his friends were excommunicated (251) by a synod at Rome. Novatian himself was martyred later, but his sympathizers, whether called Cathars, Novatians, or by other names, continued to spread widely. They ceased to recognize the Catholic churches or to acknowledge any value in their ordinances.

The Donatists* in North Africa were influenced by the teaching of Novatian. They separated from the Catholic Church on points of discipline, laying stress on the character

* "The Later Roman Empire" Professor J. B. Bury. Vol. I, c. 9.

of those who administered the sacraments, while the Catholics considered the sacraments themselves as more important. In their earlier years the Donatists, who were given this name after two leading men among them, both of the name of Donatus, were distinguished from the Catholics generally by their superior character and conduct. In parts of North Africa they became the most numerous of the different branches of the Church.

While Christian churches were developing in various forms there was also a new Gnostic religion, Manichaeism, which arose and spread widely and became a formidable opponent of Christianity. Its founder, Mani, was born in Babylonia (c. 216). His dualistic system drew from Persian, Christian, and Buddhist sources, and he announced his call to be the continuer and completer of the work begun and carried on by Noah, Abraham, Zoroaster, Buddha, and Jesus. He travelled and taught extensively, reaching even to China and India, and exercised a great influence on some of the Persian rulers, but at last was crucified. His writings continued to be revered and his followers, numerous in Babylon and in Samarcand, spread in the West also, and that in spite of violent persecution.

Amidst the confusion of conflicting parties there were true teachers, able and eloquent in directing souls in the way of salvation. One, whose name is unknown, writing in the second century to an inquirer named Diognetus,* sets himself to answer the questions asked as to the mode of worshipping God among the Christians, the reason of their faith and devotion towards God and love to one another, why they neither worshipped the gods of the Greeks nor followed the Jewish religion, and why this new practice of piety had only so late entered into the world.

He writes—"Christians are distinguished from other men neither by country, nor language", living in such places "as the lot of each of them has determined, and following the customs of the natives in respect to clothing, food, and the rest of their ordinary conduct, they display to us their wonderful and confessedly striking method of life. They

---

* The Ante-Nicene Christian Library, Vol. I, "Epistle to Diognetus". The Writings of the Apostolic Fathers.

dwell in their own countries, but simply as sojourners. As citizens, they share in all things with others, and yet endure all things as if foreigners. Every foreign land is to them as their native country, and every land of their birth as a land of strangers. ... They pass their days on earth, but they are citizens of heaven They obey the prescribed laws, and at the same time surpass the laws by their lives. ... they are reviled and bless". Then, speaking of God, he says, He, "who is almighty, the Creator of all things, ... has sent from heaven, and placed among men, Him who is the truth, and the holy and incomprehensible Word, and has firmly established Him in their hearts. He did not, as one might have imagined, send to men any ... angel, or ruler, ... but the very Creator and Fashioner of all things—by whom He made the heavens—by whom He enclosed the sea within its proper bounds"—whom the stars obey. "This messenger He sent to them. ... As a king sends his son, who is also a king, so sent He Him; as God He sent Him; as to men He sent Him; as a Saviour He sent Him." Not as judging us He sent Him, though "He will yet send Him to judge us, and who shall endure His appearing?" As to the delay in sending the Saviour, God has always been the same, but waited in His long-suffering. He had "formed in His mind a great and unspeakable conception, which He communicated to His Son alone." As long as He concealed His own wise counsel He appeared to neglect us, but this was to make it manifest that of ourselves we cannot enter into the kingdom of God. But when the appointed time had come, "He Himself took on Him the burden of our iniquities, He gave His own Son as a ransom for us, the Holy One for transgressors, the blameless One for the wicked, the righteous One for the unrighteous, the incorruptible One for the corruptible, the immortal One for them that are mortal. For what other thing was capable of covering our sins than His righteousness? By what other one was it possible that we, the wicked and ungodly, could be justified, than by the only Son of God? O sweet exchange! O unsearchable operation! O benefits surpassing all expectation! that the wickedness of many should be hid in a single righteous One, and that the righteousness of One should justify many transgressors!"

When the Church came into contact with the Roman Empire,* a conflict ensued in which all the resources of that mighty power were exhausted in a vain endeavour to vanquish those who never resisted or retaliated, but bore all for love of the Lord in whose footsteps they were following. However much the churches were divided in view and practice, they were united in suffering and victory. Although the Christians were admittedly good subjects, their faith forbade their offering incense or giving divine honours to the Emperor or to the idols. Thus they were looked upon as being disloyal to the Empire, and, as idol worship entered into the daily life of the people, into its religion and business and amusements, the Christians were hated for their separation from the world around them. Severe measures were directed against them, at first spasmodic and local, but by the end of the first century it had been made illegal to be a Christian; persecution became systematic, and extended over the whole Empire. There were considerable intervals of respite, but with each recurrence the attack became more violent; all the possessions of the confessors of Christ were confiscated, they were imprisoned, and not only were they put to death in countless numbers, but every imaginable torture was added to their punishment. Informers were rewarded; those who sheltered the believers shared their fate; and every portion of the Scriptures that could be found was destroyed. By the beginning of the fourth century this extraordinary warfare, between the mighty world-empire of Rome and these unresisting churches that were yet invincible because "they loved not their lives unto the death", seemed as though it could only end in the complete extinction of the Church.

Then an event happened which brought this long and dreadful conflict to an unexpected close. In the struggles that were going on in the Roman Empire, Constantine was victorious and, in 312, gained his decisive victory, entered Rome and immediately issued an edict bringing the persecution of Christians to an end. This was followed, a year later, by the Edict of Milan, by which all men were given freedom to follow whatever religion they chose.

Thus the Roman Empire was overcome by the devotion

* "East and West Through Fifteen Centuries" Br.-Genl. G. F. Young C.B. Vol. I.

to the Lord Jesus of those who knew Him. Their patient,
unresisting endurance had changed the bitter hostility and
hatred of the Roman world, first into pity, and then into
admiration.

Pagan religions were not at first persecuted, but, being
deprived of State support, steadily declined. The profession of Christianity was favoured. Laws abolishing
abuses and protecting the weak brought in a measure of
prosperity not known before. The churches, freed from
oppression from without, entered upon a new experience.
Many had preserved their primitive simplicity, but many
had been affected by the profound inward changes in their
constitution which have been noted, and were very different
from the New Testament churches of Apostolic days.
Their entry on a larger sphere will exhibit the effects of
these changes.

CHAPTER II

Christianity in Christendom

313-476   300-850   350-385

CHURCH and State associated—Churches refusing union with the State—
Donatists condemned—Council of Nicaea—Arianism restored—Athanasius—Creeds—Canon of Scripture—The Roman world and the Church—
Break up of the Western Roman Empire—Augustine—Pelagius—Change
in the position of the Church—False doctrines; Manichaeism, Arianism,
Pelagianism, Sacerdotalism—Monasticism—The Scriptures remain for
guidance—Missions—Departure from New Testament Missionary principles—Irish and Scottish Missions on the Continent—Conflict between
British and Roman Missions—Priscillian.

313-
476 THE prominence of the Bishops and especially of the
     Metropolitans in the Catholic churches made for
ease in communication between the Church and the civil
authorities. Constantine himself, while retaining the old
imperial dignity of chief priest of Pagan religion, assumed
that of arbitrator of the Christian churches. The Church
and the State quickly became closely associated, and it
was not long before the power of the State was at the
disposal of those who had the lead in the Church, to enforce
their decisions.   Thus the persecuted soon became persecutors.

In later times those churches which, faithful to the
Word of God, were persecuted by the dominant Church as
heretics and sects, frequently refer in their writings to their
entire dissent from the union of Church and State in the
time of Constantine and of Sylvester, then bishop in Rome.
They trace their continuance from primitive Scriptural
churches in unbroken succession from Apostolic times—
passing unscathed through the period when so many
churches associated themselves with the worldly power—
right down to their own day. For all such, persecution was
soon renewed, but instead of coming from the Pagan Roman
Empire it came from what claimed to be the Church
wielding the power of the Christianized State.

The Donatists being very numerous in North Africa and

having retained, or restored, much of the Catholic type of organization among themselves, were in a position to appeal to the Emperor in their strife with the Catholic party, and this they soon did. Constantine called together many bishops of both parties and gave his decision against the Donatists, who were then persecuted and punished; but this did not allay the strife, which continued until all together were blotted out by the Mohammedan invasion in the seventh century.

The first general council of the Catholic churches was summoned by Constantine and met at Nicaea in Bithynia (325). The principal question before it was that of the doctrine taught by Arius, a presbyter of Alexandria, who maintained that the Son of God was a created Being, the first and greatest, but yet, consequently, not on an equality with the Father. Over 300 bishops were present, with their numerous attendants, from all parts of the Empire, to examine this matter, and the Council was opened in great state by Constantine. A number of the bishops present bore in their bodies marks of the tortures which they had endured in the time of persecution. With two dissentients, the Council decided that the teaching of Arius was false, that it had not been the teaching of the Church from the beginning, and the Nicene creed was framed to express the truth of the real Divine Nature of the Son and His equality with the Father.

Although the decision reached was right, the way of reaching it, by the combined efforts of the Emperor and the bishops, and of enforcing it, by the power of the State, manifested the departure of the Catholic church from the Scripture. Two years after the Council of Nicaea Constantine, altering his view, received Arius back from exile, and in the reign of his son Constantius all the bishoprics were filled by Arian bishops; the Government, now become Arian, persecuted the Catholics as formerly it had done the Arians.

One of those in high places, moved neither by popular clamour nor by the threats or flatteries of the authorities was Athanasius. As a young man he had taken part in the Council of Nicaea and afterwards became Bishop of Alexandria. For nearly fifty years, though repeatedly exiled, he maintained a valiant witness to the true divinity of the Saviour. Slandered, brought up before tribunals, taking refuge in the desert, returning to the city, nothing shook his advocacy of the truth he believed.

Arianism lasted nearly three centuries as the state religion in a number of countries, especially in the later-established Northern kingdoms. The Lombards in Italy were the last to abandon it as the national religion.

Not only the first, but the first six General Councils, of which the last was held in 680, were occupied to a large extent with questions as to the Divine Nature, the relations of the Father, the Son, and the Holy Spirit. In the course of endless discussions, creeds were hammered out and dogmas enunciated in the hope that the truth would by them be fixed and could then be handed down to succeeding generations. It is noticeable that in the Scriptures this method is not used. From them we see that the mere letter cannot convey the truth, which is spiritually apprehended, neither can it be handed from one to another, but each one must receive and appropriate it for himself in his inward dealings with God, and be established in it by confessing and maintaining it in the conflict of daily life.

It is sometimes supposed that Scripture is not sufficient for the guidance of the churches without the addition of, at least, early tradition, on the ground that it was by the early Church councils that the canon of Scripture was fixed. This of course could only refer to the New Testament. The peculiar characteristics and unique history of the people of Israel fitted them to receive the Divine revelation, to recognize the inspired writings, and to preserve them with an invincible pertinacity and accuracy. And with regard to the New Testament, the canon of inspired books was not fixed by the Church councils, it was acknowledged by the councils because it had already been clearly indicated by the Holy Spirit, and accepted by the churches generally, and this indication and acceptance has ever since been confirmed by every comparison of the canonical with the apocryphal and non-canonical books, the difference in value and power being evident.

This second period of the history of some of the churches, beginning with Constantine's edict of toleration in 313, is of lasting importance because it exhibits the experiment on a large scale, of the union of Church and State. Could the Church, by union with the world, save it?

The Roman world* had reached its greatest power and glory. Civilization had attained to the utmost of which it was capable apart from the knowledge of God. Yet the misery of the world was extreme. The luxury and vice of the rich were boundless; a vast proportion of the people were slaves. The public exhibitions, where the sight of every kind of wickedness and cruelty amused the populace, deepened the degradation. There was still vigour at the extremities of the Empire, in conflict with surrounding enemies, but disease at the heart threatened the life of the whole body, and Rome was helplessly corrupt and vicious.

As long as the Church had remained separate it had been a powerful witness for Christ in the world, and was constantly drawing converts into its holy fellowship. When, however, already weakened by the adoption of human rule in place of the guidance of the Spirit, it was suddenly brought into partnership with the State, it became itself defiled and debased. Very soon the clergy were competing for lucrative positions and for power as shamelessly as the court officials, while, in congregations where a godless element predominated, the material advantages of a profession of Christianity changed the purity of the persecuted churches into worldliness. The Church was thus powerless to stem the downward course of the civilized world into corruption.

Ominous clouds, threatening judgment, were gathering. In distant China movements of the population, setting westward, led to a great migration of the Huns, who crossed the Volga, and, pressing upon the Goths in what is now Russia, forced them on to the frontiers of the Empire, which was by this time divided; the Eastern part, or Byzantine Empire, having Constantinople as its capital, and the Western, Rome. The Germanic or Teutonic nations came out of their forests. Pressed by the Mongol hordes from the East, and attracted by the wealth and weakness of the Empire, Goths (divided into Eastern and Western under the names of Ostrogoths and Visigoths) and

---

* "East and West Through Fifteen Centuries"   Br.-General G. F. Young C.B.

Germanic peoples such as the Franks, Vandals, Burgundians, Suevi, Heruli, and others, broke like the waves of some resistless flood over the doomed civilization of Rome. In one year great provinces such as Spain and Gaul were destroyed. The inhabitants, long accustomed to peace, congregated mostly in the cities for the sake of the ease and pleasure afforded there, saw the armies which had so long guarded their frontiers disappear; the cities were wiped out, and a cultivated and luxurious population, which had avoided the discipline of military training, was massacred or enslaved by Pagan barbarians. Rome itself was captured by the Goths under Alaric (410), and that great city was plundered and desolated by barbarian hosts. In 476 the Western Roman Empire came to an end, and in the vast regions where it had so long reigned, new kingdoms began to grow up. The Eastern part of the Empire continued, until, in 1453, nearly a thousand years later, Constantinople was captured by the Mohammedan Turks.

One of the great figures of history meets us at this period, Augustine (354-430),* whose teachings have left an indelible mark on all succeeding ages. In his voluminous writings and especially in his "Confessions", Augustine reveals himself in so intimate a way as to give the impression of being an acquaintance and a friend. A native of Numidia, he describes his early surroundings, thoughts, and impressions. His saintly mother, Monica, lives again in his pages as we read of her prayers for him, of her early hopes, and of her later sorrow as he grew up in a sinful manner of life, of her faith in his eventual salvation, strengthened by a vision and by the wise counsel of Ambrose, Bishop of Milan. His father was more concerned for his material, worldly advancement.

Though seeking light he found himself hopelessly bound by a sinful, self-indulgent life. For a time he thought he had found deliverance in Manichaeism, but soon perceived its inconsistency and weakness. He was affected by the preaching of Ambrose, but yet found no peace. When he was 32 years of age and was employed as a teacher of

* "A Select Library of the Nicene and Post-Nicene Fathers of the Christian Church" translated and annotated by J. C. Pilkington M.A. Edited by Philip Schaff.

rhetoric in Milan, he had reached a desperate state of distress, and then, to use his own words: "I flung myself down, how I know not, under a certain fig-tree, giving free course to my tears. . . . I sent up these sorrowful cries, 'How long, how long? To-morrow and to-morrow? Why not now? Why is there not this hour an end to my uncleanness?' I was saying these things and weeping in the most bitter contrition of my heart, when lo, I heard the voice as of a boy or girl, I know not which, coming from a neighbouring house and oft repeating, 'Take up and read, take up and read.' Immediately my countenance was changed, and I began most earnestly to consider whether it was usual for children in any kind of game to sing such words, nor could I remember ever to have heard the like. So, restraining the torrent of my tears, I rose up, interpreting it no other way than as a command to me from Heaven to open the book, and to read the first chapter I should light upon. . . . I grasped, opened, and in silence read that paragraph on which my eyes first fell—'Not in rioting and drunkenness, not in chambering and wantonness, not in strife and envying, but put ye on the Lord Jesus Christ and make not provision for the flesh, to fulfil the lusts thereof.' No further would I read, nor did I need, for instantly, as the sentence ended—by a light, as it were, of security infused into my heart—all gloom of doubt vanished away."

This, his conversion, caused the greatest joy, but no surprise, to his praying mother Monica, who, as they were returning to Africa a year later, died in peace. Augustine was baptized by Ambrose in Milan (387) and became later Bishop of Hippo (now Bona) in North Africa (395). His busy life was one of constant controversy. He lived at the time when the Western Roman Empire was breaking up; indeed a barbarian army was besieging his city of Hippo when he passed away. It was the fall of the Western Empire that led him to write his famous book the "City of God". Its full title explains its aim: "Though the greatest city of the world has fallen, the City of God abideth for ever". His view, however, of what the City of God is led him into teachings that have given rise to unspeakable misery, the very greatness of his name accentuating the harmful effects of the error he taught. He, beyond others, formulated the doctrine of salvation by the Church only, by means of her sacraments. To take salvation out of the hands of the Saviour and put it into the hands of men; to interpose a system of man's devising between the Saviour and the sinner, is the very opposite of the Gospel revelation. Christ says: "Come unto Me" and no priest or church has authority to intervene.

Augustine in his zeal for the unity of the Church and his genuine abhorrence of all divergence in doctrine and difference in form, lost sight of the spiritual, living, and indestructible unity of the Church and Body of Christ, uniting all who are sharers, by the new birth, in the life of God. Consequently he did not see the practical possibility of the existence of churches of God in various places and in all times, each retaining its immediate relation with the Lord and with the Spirit, yet having fellowship with the others, and that in spite of human weakness, of varying degrees of knowledge, of divergent apprehensions of Scripture and differences of practice.

His outward view of the Church as an earthly organization, naturally led him to seek outward, material means for preserving, and even compelling, visible unity. In controversy with the Donatists he wrote: "It is indeed better . . . that men should be led to worship God by teaching, than that they should be driven to it by fear of punishment or pain; but it does not follow that because the former course produces the better men, therefore those who do not yield to it should be neglected. For many have found advantage (as we have proved and are daily proving by actual experiment) in being first compelled by fear or pain, so that they might afterwards be influenced by teaching, or might follow out in act what they had already learned in word . . . whilst those are better who are guided aright by love, those are certainly more numerous who are corrected by fear. For who can possibly love us more than Christ, who laid down His life for the sheep? And yet, after calling Peter and the other Apostles by His words alone, when He came to summon Paul . . . He not only constrained him with His voice, but even dashed him to the earth with His power; and that He might forcibly bring one who was raging amid the darkness of infidelity, to desire the light of the heart, He first struck him with physical blindness of the eyes. Why therefore should not the Church use force in compelling her lost sons to return? . . . The Lord Himself said 'Go out into the highways and hedges and compel them to come in' . . . Wherefore if the power which the Church has received by divine appointment in its due season, through the religious character and faith of kings, be the instrument by which those who are found in the highways and hedges—that is, in heresies and schisms—are compelled to come in, then let them not find fault with being compelled."

Such teaching, from such an authority, incited and justified those methods of persecution by which Papal Rome equalled the cruelties of Pagan Rome. So a man of strong affections and quick and tender sympathies, departing from the principles of Scripture, though with good intentions, became implicated in a vast and ruthless system of persecution.

One with whom Augustine had much controversy was Pelagius.* He was a native of the British Isles, came to Rome at the very beginning of the fifth century, when about thirty years of age, and, although a layman, soon came to be recognized as a writer of ability on the Scriptures and as a man of excellent uprightness of life. Augustine, though later his great doctrinal antagonist, bears witness to this. Derogatory reports published afterwards by Jerome appear to have had their origin less in matters of fact than in the heat of controversy. In Rome Pelagius met Celestinus, who became the most active exponent of his teachings. Pelagius was a reformer; the laxity and self-indulgence of the lives of most profemssing Christians deeply grieved him and he became a strenuous preacher of practical righteousness and sanctification.

Too exclusive occupation with this aspect of truth led him to over-emphasize the freedom of the human will and to minimize the operations of Divine grace. He taught that men are not affected by Adam's transgression, unless it be by his example; that Adam must have died even if he had not sinned; that there is no original sin, and that the actions of every man are in accordance with his own choice. Therefore perfect righteousness is possible to every man. Infants, he said, are born without sin. Here he came into direct conflict with Catholic teaching. He taught infant

* "Dictionary of Christian Biography" Smith & Wace.

baptism but denied that it was the means of regeneration, affirming rather that it introduces the child into a state of grace, into the Kingdom of God, into a condition where it is capable of obtaining salvation and life, sanctification and union with Christ. Augustine in opposing this teaching read to his congregation an extract from a work of Cyprian written a hundred and fifty years before, in which it is stated that infants are baptized for the remission of sin, and he then entreated Pelagius to abstain from a teaching which was divergent from so fundamental a doctrine and practice of the Church. Pelagians would not use the prayer, "forgive us our sins," regarding it as unsuitable for Christians, seeing that we need not sin; if we do, it is of our own will and choice, and such a prayer could only be the expression of an unreal humility.

The conflict as to the doctrines of Pelagius and Celestinus became wide-spread and it occupied much of the time and energies of Augustine, who wrote voluminously on the subject. Councils were held; those in the east acquitted Pelagius; those in the west condemned him, a result due to the influence of Augustine in the Latin churches, which had led to their accepting more definite, dogmatic statements concerning the relation between the will of God and the will of man than those in the east. The Pope in Rome, Innocent, was appealed to, and welcomed the opportunity of emphasizing his authority. He excommunicated Pelagius and all his followers, but his successor, Zozimus, reinstated them. The western bishops, meeting in Carthage, were able to win the support of the civil power, and Pelagius and his supporters were banished and their goods confiscated. Pope Zozimus seeing this, changed his view and also condemned Pelagius. Eighteen Italian bishops refused submission to the Imperial decree, one of whom, Julian, Bishop of Eclanum, contended with Augustine with ability and unusual moderation, pointing out that the use of force and the change of mind of a Pope are not the right weapons with which to deal with matters of doctrine.

Pelagius taught much that was true and salutary, but the characteristic doctrine of Pelagianism is not only contrary to Scripture, but also to the facts of human nature. Men are aware of their corrupt and fallen nature

and of their bondage under sin, and the facts of life manifest
it. Our real partaking of the life and nature of one man,
the first Adam, sharing his sin, subjected as he to death,
makes it possible for our whole race to be brought into a
real relationship with the one Man, the second Adam,
Jesus Christ, opening the way for any man, by his own
choice and faith, to become a partaker of His eternal life
and Divine nature.

The first three centuries of the Church's history prove
that no earthly power can crush it. It is invincible to
attacks from without. The witnesses of its sufferings, and
even its persecutors, become its converts and it grows
more rapidly than it can be destroyed. The following
period of nearly two hundred years shows that the union
of the Church and the State, even when the powers of the
mightiest Empire are put into the Church's hands, do not
enable her to save the State from destruction, for, in
abandoning the position which her very name implies, of
being "called out" of the world, and of separation to
Christ, she loses the power that comes from subjection to
her Lord, exchanging it for an earthly authority that is
fatal to herself.

The Church of Christ has been subjected not only to the
violence of outward persecution and the seductions of
earthly power, but also to the assaults of false doctrines.
From the third century to the fifth, four such forms of
doctrine were developed, of so fundamental a character
that their workings have never ceased to affect the Church
and the world.

1. *Manichaeism* assails alike the teaching of Scripture
and the testimony of Nature that God is the Creator of
all things. The opening words of the Bible are: "In the
beginning God created the heaven and the earth" (Gen.
1. 1); and it reveals man as the crown of Creation, in the
words, "So God created man in His own image" (Gen.
1. 27). Reviewing everything that He had made, God
saw that it was "very good" (Gen. 1. 31). Manichaeism,
by attributing the visible and corporeal to the work of a
dark and evil power and only that which is spiritual to
the true God, struck at the roots of the Divine revelation,
of which Creation, the Fall, and Redemption are essential

and indivisible parts. From the erroneous view of the body spring, on the one side, the excesses of asceticism, regarding the body as only evil; on the other side many degrading practices and doctrines encouraged by failure to see in the body anything but that which is animal, losing sight of its Divine origin and consequent capacity for redemption and restoration to the likeness of the Son of God.

2. The most glorious revelation, that in which all Scripture culminates, is that Jesus Christ is God manifest in the flesh, made known to us by becoming man, and by His sacrificial death making propitiation for the sin of the world. *Arianism*, by denying the divinity of Christ, declaring Him to be, though the first and highest, yet a created Being, keeps man immeasurably distant from God, prevents us from knowing Him as God our Saviour, and would leave us to the vague hope of attaining to something higher than we now experience, by improvement of our own character.

3. *Pelagianism* denies the teaching of Scripture as to the implication of all mankind in Adam's transgression. Affirming that Adam's sin only affected himself and his own relations with God, and that each human being born into the world is originally without sin, it weakens man's sense of his need of a Saviour, prevents his coming to a true knowledge of himself, and leads him to seek salvation, partly at least, in himself. The recognition of our share in the Fall is intimately connected in Scripture with our share in the atoning work of Christ, the second Adam; and, while individual responsibility and free will are insisted upon, this is not to the exclusion of, but in conjunction with, the teaching as to the will of God and the racial connection of mankind. This, while involving all in the same condemnation, includes all in the same salvation.

4. *Sacerdotalism* would make salvation to be found only in the Church and by means of its sacraments administered by its priests. At this time, of course, the Church meant the Roman Church, but the doctrine has been applied to themselves, and still is, by many other systems, larger and smaller. Nothing is taught more clearly and insistently by the Lord and the Apostles than that the sinner's salvation is by faith in the Son of God, in His atoning

death and resurrection. A church or circle which claims that
in it alone salvation is to be found; men who arrogate to
themselves the power of admission to or exclusion from
the Kingdom of God; sacraments or forms that are made
into necessary means of salvation, give rise to tyrannies
that bring untold miseries on mankind and obscure the
true way of salvation that Christ has opened to all men
through faith in Him.

The decline of the churches in spirituality, their
departure from the New Testament pattern, and their
consequent growing worldliness, subjection to human
system, and toleration of sin, not only provoked efforts
to reform them, or to establish reformed churches, as seen
in the Montanist and Donatist movements, but also
led some seekers after holiness and communion with God
to withdraw themselves from all intercourse with men.*
Circumstances in the world, devastated by barbarians,
and in the Church, deflected from its proper testimony in
the world, made them hopeless either of intercourse with
God in daily life or of fellowship with the saints in the
churches. So they retired into desert places and lived as
hermits, in order that, freed from the distractions and
temptations of ordinary life, they might by contemplation
attain to that vision and knowledge of God for which their
souls craved. Influenced by the prevalent teaching as to
the evil of matter, they counted on an extreme simplicity
of living and ascetic practices to overcome the hindrances
which they judged the body to present to spiritual life.

In the fourth century the hermit Anthony in Egypt
became celebrated for his solitary life, and many, stirred
to emulate his piety, established themselves near to him,
imitating his manner of living, and he was persuaded to
lay down a rule of life for them. Hermits increased in
number, and some practised great severities on themselves;
Simeon Stylites was one who gained renown by living for
years on the top of a pillar. Soon a further development
took place, and Pachomius, in Southern Egypt, early in
the fourth century founded a monastery where those who
retired from the world lived no longer alone, but as a community. Spreading both into the Eastern and Western

* "Monasticism" Ad. v. Harnack.

churches, such communities came to be an important part
of the life of the peoples. About the beginning of the sixth
century, Benedict of Nursia, in Italy, gave a great impetus
to this movement, and his rule of life for the monastic
bodies prevailed beyond all others. He occupied the
monks less exclusively with personal austerities and turned
their activities into the performance of religious ceremonies and into the service of men, giving especial attention
to agriculture. The monasteries of the Benedictine order
were one of the principal means by which Christianity was
spread among the Teutonic nations during the seventh and
eighth centuries. From Ireland also, by way of the Isle
of Iona and through Scotland, the Columban monasteries
and settlements prepared and sent out devoted missionaries into Northern and Central Europe.

As the Popes of Rome gradually came to dominate the
Church and to occupy themselves in intriguing and
fighting for temporal power, the monastic system drew to
itself many of those who were spiritual and who had desires
after God and after holiness. A monastery, however,
differed widely from a church, in the New Testament sense
of the word, so that those souls that felt themselves impelled to flee from the worldly Roman Church did not find
in the monastery what a true church would have provided.
They were bound under the rules of an institution instead
of experiencing the free workings of the Holy Spirit.

The various monastic orders that arose followed one
course of development.* Beginning with poverty and
severest self-denial, they became rich and powerful,
relaxed their discipline and grew into self-indulgence and
worldliness. Then a reaction would induce some to begin
a new order, of absolute self-humiliation, which in its
turn traced the same cycle. Of such reformers were Bernard of Cluny, early in the tenth century, and Stephen
Harding of Citeaux in the eleventh. It was in the Cister-
cian monastery at Citeaux that Bernard, afterwards Abbot
of Clairvaux, spent some of his earlier years; he came to
exercise an influence above that of kings and Popes, but
a more lasting and happier memorial of him remains in
some of the hymns which he wrote.

Many women also sought refuge from the world in the

"Latin Christianity" Dean Milman. Vol. 4.

nunneries which grew up. These religious houses, both for men and women, were, during dark and turbulent times, sanctuaries for the weak and centres where learning was preserved amid the prevailing barbarism, and where the Scriptures were copied, translated, and read. Yet they were a fruitful soil for idleness and oppression, and the religious orders came to be active instruments in Papal hands for the persecution of all who endeavoured to restore the churches of God on their original foundation.

The gradual transformation of the New Testament churches from their original pattern into organizations so different from it that its relation to them came to be scarcely recognizable, seemed as though it might continue until all was lost. The effort to save the churches from disunion and heresy by means of the episcopal and clerical system not only failed, but brought great evils in its train. The expectation that the persecuted churches would gain by union with the State was disappointed. Monasticism proved unable to provide a substitute for the churches as a refuge from the world, becoming itself worldly. There remained, however, through all these times one thing capable of bringing about restoration. The presence of the Scriptures in the world supplied the means which the Holy Spirit could use in the hearts of men with a power able to overcome error and bring them back to Divine truth, and there never ceased to be congregations, true churches, which adhered to the Scriptures as the guide of faith and doctrine, and the pattern both for individual conduct and for the order of the Church. These, though hidden and despised, yet exercised an influence that did not fail to bear fruit.

During these troubled times, missionary activity did not cease, but was carried on with zeal and devotion. Indeed, until in the eleventh century the Crusades absorbed the enthusiasm of the Catholic nations, there was a constant testimony, which gradually subdued the barbarian conquerors and carried the knowledge of Christ to the distant lands from which they came. Nestorian missionaries travelled as far as China and Siberia and established churches from Samarcand to Ceylon. Greeks from Constantinople passed through Bulgaria and penetrated the depths of Russia, while the heathen nations of Central and Northern Europe were reached by missionaries both from the British and Roman Churches. In North Africa and in Western Asia there were more who professed Christianity than there are to-day.

The errors, however, which prevailed in the professing churches were reflected in their missionary work. There was no longer the simple preaching of Christ and founding of churches as in the early days, but, with a measure of the truth there was also insistence on ritual and on legal observances; and when kings came to confess Christianity, the principle of Church and State led to the forcible outward conversion of multitudes of their subjects to the new State religion. Instead of churches being founded in the different towns and countries, independent of any central organization and having direct relations with the Lord, as in Apostolic days, all were drawn into one of the great organizations which had its centre in Rome or Constantinople or elsewhere. What is true on a large scale applies also on a small, and the harmful workings of this system are seen wherever, instead of sinners' being led to Christ and given the Scriptures as their guide, they are pressed into membership of some foreign denomination or taught to look to some Mission for guidance and supplies, the development of the gifts of the Holy Spirit among them being hindered, and the spread of the Gospel among their countrymen retarded.

300-850

A purer form of missionary work, however, than that which went out from Rome, spread from Ireland, through Scotland to Northern and Central Europe. Ireland* first received the Gospel in the third or fourth century, through merchants and soldiers, and by the sixth century it was a Christianized country and had developed such missionary activity that its missions were working from the shores of the North Sea and the Baltic to those of the Lake of Constance.

Monks from Ireland seeking places of retirement from the world, established themselves on some of the islands between Ireland and Scotland. Iona (Hy), called the "Isle of Saints", where Columba settled, was one point from which missions went into Scotland, and the Irish and

* "Irland in der Kirchengeschichte" Kattenbusch.

Scottish monks preached in England and among the heathen on the Continent.

Their method was to visit a country and, where it seemed suitable, found a missionary village. In the centre they built a simple wooden church, around which were clustered school-rooms and huts for the monks, who were the builders, preachers, and teachers. Outside this circle, as required, dwellings were built for the students and their families, who gradually gathered around them. The whole was enclosed by a wall, but the colony often spread beyond the original enclosure. Groups of twelve monks would go out, each under the leadership of an abbot, to open up fresh fields for the Gospel. Those who remained taught in the school, and, as soon as they had sufficiently learned the language of the people among whom they were, translated and wrote out portions of Scripture, and also hymns, which they taught to their scholars. They were free to marry or to remain single; many remained single so that they might have greater liberty for the work. When some converts were made, the missionaries chose from among them small groups of young men who had ability, trained them specially in some handicraft and in languages, and taught them the Bible and how to explain it to others, so that they might be able to work among their own people. They delayed baptism until those professing faith had received a certain amount of instruction and had given some proof of steadfastness. They avoided attacking the religions of the people, counting it more profitable to preach the truth to them than to expose their errors. They accepted the Holy Scriptures as the source of faith and life and preached justification by faith. They did not take part in politics or appeal to the State for aid. All this work, in its origin and progress, though it had developed some features alien to New Testament teaching and Apostolic example, was independent of Rome and different in important respects from the Roman Catholic system.

In 596, Augustine, with 40 Benedictine monks, sent by Pope Gregory I, landed in Kent and began the missionary work among the heathen in England which was to bear such abundant fruit. The two forms of missionary activity in the country, the older, British, and the newer, Roman, soon came into conflict. The Pope appointed

Augustine Archbishop of Canterbury, giving him supremacy over all British bishops already in the land. A national element accentuated the struggle between the two missions, the British, Celts, and Welsh being opposed to the Anglo-Saxons. The Church of Rome insisted that its form of Church government should be the only one permitted in the country, but the British order continued its resistance, until in the 13th century its remaining elements were absorbed into the Lollard movement.

On the Continent the wide-spread and established mission work of the Irish and Scottish missionaries was attacked by the Roman system under the active leadership of the English Benedictine Boniface, whose policy was to compel the British missionaries to submit, at least outwardly, to Rome, or be destroyed. He obtained State aid, under the direction of Rome, for the enforcement of his design. Boniface was killed by the Friesians in 755. The system he inaugurated gradually extinguished the earlier missions, but their influence strengthened many of the movements of reform which followed.

A Harmony of the four Gospels called *"Heliand"* (*i.e.*, "the Saviour"), written about 830 or earlier, an alliterative epic in the old Saxon language, was doubtless written in the circles of the British mission on the Continent. It contains the Gospel narrative in a form calculated to appeal to the people for whom it was written, and is remarkable for being free from any adoration of the Virgin or the saints, and from most of the characteristic features of the Roman Church at that period.

350-
385   In the fourth century a Reformer appeared, and a work of Reformation was wrought which affected wide circles in Spain, spread into Lusitania (Portugal) and to Aquitania in France, making itself felt in Rome also.

Priscillian was a Spaniard of wealth and position, a learned and eloquent man of unusual attainments. In common with many of his class he was unable to believe the old heathen religions, yet was not attracted by Christianity, and preferred classic literature to the Scriptures, so he had sought refuge for his soul in the prevalent philosophies, such as Neo-Platonism and Manichaeism. He was converted to Christ, was baptised, and began a new life of devotion to God and separation from the world. He became an enthusiastic student and lover of the Scriptures, lived an ascetic life as a help towards fuller union with Christ by making his body more fit to be a dwelling-place of the Holy Spirit, and though a layman, preached and taught diligently. Soon conventicles were organized and meetings held with a view to making religion a reality which should affect the character, and large numbers of persons, especially of the educated class, were drawn into the movement. Priscillian was made Bishop of Avila, but it was not long before he encountered the hostility of a part of the Spanish clergy. Bishop Hydatius, Metropolitan of Lusitania, led the opposition, and at a Synod held in 380 at Caesaraugusta (Saragossa) accused him of Manichaean and Gnostic heresy. The proceedings were not successful until political necessities led the Emperor Maximus, who had murdered Gratian and usurped his place, to desire the aid of the Spanish clergy; but then, at a Synod in Burdigala (Bordeaux) in 384, Bishop Ithacus, a man of evil repute, joined the attack, accusing Priscillian and those to whom they attached the title "Priscillianists", of witchcraft and immorality, and the accused were brought to Treves (Trier), condemned by the Church, and handed over to the civil power for execution (385). The eminent bishops, Martin of Tours and Ambrose of Milan, protested in vain against this; Priscillian and six others were beheaded, among them a distinguished lady, Euchrotia, widow of a well-known poet and orator. This was the first instance of the execution of Christians by the Church, an example to be followed afterwards with such terrible frequency. After this Martin and Ambrose refused to have any fellowship whatever with Hydatius and the other bishops who were responsible, and when the Emperor Maximus fell, the cruel torture and murder of these saintly persons was recorded with abhorrence and Ithacus was deprived of his bishopric. The bodies of Priscillian and his companions were brought to Spain and they were honoured as martyrs. Nevertheless a Synod in Treves approved what had been done, thus giving the official sanction of the Roman Church to the execution, and this was confirmed by the Synod of Braga held 176 years later, so that the ruling Church not only persecuted those whom it called Priscillianists, but handed down as history that Priscillian and those who believed as he did were punished for holding Manichaean and Gnostic doctrine and because of the wickedness of their lives and this continued for centuries to be the generally received opinion of them.

Although Priscillian had written voluminously, it was thought that all his writings had disappeared, so diligently had they been destroyed. In 1886 Georg Schepss discovered in the library of the University of Würzburg eleven of Priscillian's works, which he describes as being "contained in a precious Uncial M.S. . . . which until now had remained unknown."* It is written in very old Latin and is one of the oldest Latin MSS. known to exist. It consists of eleven tracts (some parts are missing) of which the first four contain details of the trial, and the remaining seven his teaching. The reading of these, Priscillian's own writings, shows that the account handed down of him was wholly untrue, that he was a man of saintly character, sound in doctrine, and an energetic reformer, and that those associated with him were companies of men and women who were true and devoted followers of Christ. Not content with murdering these people, exiling them, confiscating their goods, the Church authorities have persistently calumniated their memory.

The style of Priscillian's writing is vivid and telling, he constantly quotes Scripture† in support of what he advances and shows an intimate acquaintance with the whole of the Old and New Testaments. He maintained, however, the right of the Christian to read other literature, and this was made the occasion of accusing him of wishing to include the Apocrypha in the Canon of Scripture, which he did not do. He defends himself and his friends for their habit of holding Bible readings in which laymen were active and women took part, also for their objection

*Priscillian ein Neuaufgefundener Lat. Schriftsteller des 4 Jahrhunderts. Vortrag gehalten am 18 Mai, 1886, in der Philologisch-Historischen Gesellschaft zu Würzburg von Dr. Georg Schepss K. Studienlehrer am Humanist. Gymnasium Mit einem Blatt in Originalgrosse Faksimiledruck des Manuscriptes, Würzburg. A. Stuber's Verlagbuchhandlung, 1886.

† The quotations are from a translation earlier than that of Jerome (the Vulgate).

to taking the Lord's Supper with frivolous and worldly-
minded persons. For Priscillian the theological disputations in the Church had little value, for he knew the gift
of God, and had accepted it by a living faith. He would
not dispute as to the Trinity, being content to know that
in Christ the true One God is laid hold of by the help of the
Divine Spirit.* He taught that the object of redemption
is that we should be turned to God and therefore an energetic turning from the world is needed, lest anything might
hinder fellowship with God. This salvation is not a
magical event brought about by some sacrament, but a
spiritual act. The Church indeed publishes the confession, and baptizes, and conveys the commands or Word
of God, to men, but each one must decide for himself and
believe for himself. If communion with Christ should be
broken it is for each one to restore it by personal repentance.
There is no special official grace, laymen have the Spirit
as much as clergy. He exposes at length the evil and
falsity of Manichaeism, and his teaching, from the Scriptures, is entirely opposed to it. Asceticism he regarded
not as a chief thing in itself, but as a help towards that
entire union of the whole person with God or Christ, from
which the body cannot be excepted, because of its being
the habitation of the Spirit. This is rest in Christ, experience of Divine love and leading, incorruptible blessing.
Faith in God, who has revealed Himself, is a personal act
which involves the whole being in acknowledgment of
dependence on God for life and for all things. It brings
with it the desire and the decision to be wholly consecrated
to Him. Moral works follow of themselves because in
receiving the new life the believer has received into himself
that which contains the very essence of morality. Scripture is not only historical truth, but is at the same time
a means of grace. The spirit feeds upon it and finds that
every portion of it contains revelation, instruction, and
guidance for daily life. To see the allegorical meaning of
Scripture requires no technical training, but faith. The
Messianic-typical meaning of the Old Testament and the

* "Priscillianus Ein Reformator des Vierten Jahrhunderts. Eine
Kirchengeschichtliche Studie zugleich ein Kommentar zu den Erhaltenen Schriften Priscillians" von Friedrich Paret Dr. Phil. Repetent
am Evang.-Theol. Seminar in Tübingen. Würzburg A. Stuber's
Verlagsbuchhandlung. 1891.

historical progress of the New are pointed out, and this not only for the sake of knowledge, but as showing that not some only, but all the saints are called to complete sanctification.

Such teachings soon brought these circles into conflict with those of the Roman Church, especially as represented by such a scheming, political bishop as Hydatius. The clergy saw in the holy life of the ordinary believer that which assailed their peculiar position. The power of "apostolic succession" and of the priestly office was shaken by teaching which insisted on holiness and constant renewal of life by the Holy Spirit and communion with God. The distinction between clergy and laity was broken down by this, especially when the magical working of the sacraments was exchanged for a living possession of salvation through faith.

The breach was irreparable because due to two distinct views of the Church. It was not only a question of suppressing conventicles or of opposing what threatened to become an order of monks apart from the Church, but of a complete difference of principle. The policy of Hydatius was to strengthen the power of the Metropolitan as representing the See of Rome, with a view to carrying out the *Roman centralizing organization* which was as yet unpopular in Spain and incomplete and was opposed by the lesser bishops. The circles with which Priscillian was associated were in principle diametrically opposed to this; their occupation with Scripture and acceptance of it as their guide in all things led them to desire the *independence of each congregation*, and this they were already putting into practice.

After the death of Priscillian and his companions the circles of those who shared their faith increased rapidly, but, although Martin of Tours succeeded in modifying the first burst of persecution which followed that tragic event, persecution was continued and severe; nevertheless it was not until some two centuries later that the meetings were finally dispersed.

CHAPTER III

Paulicians and Bogomils

50-1473

Growth of clerical domination—Persistence of Primitive churches—
Their histories distorted by their enemies—Early churches in Asia
Minor—Armenia—Primitive churches in Asia Minor from Apostolic
times—Unjustly described by their opponents as Manichaeans—The
names Paulician and Thonrak—Continuity of New Testament churches—
Constantine Silvanus—Simeon Titus—Veneration of relics, and image
worship—Iconoclastic Emperors—John of Damascus—Restoration of
images in Greek Church—Council of Frankfurt—Claudius Bishop of
Turin—Mohammedanism—Sembat—Sergius—Leaders of the churches
in Asia Minor—Persecution under Theodora—The Key of Truth—
Carbeas and Chrysocheir—The Scriptures and the Koran—Character of
the churches in Asia Minor—Removal of believers from Asia to Europe—
Later history in Bulgaria—Bogomils—Basil—Opinions regarding Paulicians and Bogomils—Spread of Bogomils into Bosnia—Kulin Ban and
Rome—Intercourse of Bogomils with Christians abroad—Bosnia invaded
—Advance of Mohammedans—Persecution of Bogomils—Bosnia taken
by the Turks—Friends of God in Bosnia a link between the Taurus and
the Alps—Bogomil tombs.

THE union of Church and State was in all times looked
upon by many of the Lord's disciples as contrary to
His teaching; but whenever the Church had the power
of the State at its command, it used it for the forcible
suppression of any who dissented from its system or in
any way refused compliance with its demands, and great
numbers through indifference or interest or fear yielded at
least an outward obedience. There were, however, always
some who could not be induced to do this, but who still
endeavoured to follow Christ and keep the teachings of His
Word and the doctrine of the Apostles. These were continually objects of persecution.

The history of the centuries which followed Constantine
unfolds the growth in worldliness and ambition of the
clergy, both of the Eastern and Western Catholic churches,
until they claimed entire dominion over the possessions
and consciences of mankind, enforcing these claims with

a violence and guile that knew no limits. It also reveals
vistas here and there of the path of tribulation trodden by
countless saints who, at all times, and in various places,
have suffered all things at the hands of the dominant
World-Church, rather than deny Christ or be turned back
from following Him.

The true histories of these have been obliterated as far as
possible; their writings, sharing the fate of the writers,
have been destroyed to the full extent of the power allowed
to their persecutors. Not only so, but histories of them have
been promulgated by those to whose interest it was to disseminate the worst inventions against them in order to
justify their own cruelties. In such accounts they are depicted as heretics, and evil doctrines are ascribed to them
which they repudiated. They are called "sects", and labels
are attached to them which they themselves would not
acknowledge. They usually called themselves Christians,
or Brethren, but numerous names were given to them by
others in order to create the impression that they represented many new, strange, and unconnected sects, oppro-
brious epithets being applied to them to bring them into
disrepute. It is therefore difficult to trace their history;
what their adversaries have written of them must be
suspected; words from their own lips wrung out by
torture are valueless. There is, however, in spite of these
hindrances, a large body of trustworthy evidence, continually being added to by further investigation, which
shows what they were and did, what they believed and
taught; and these their own records afford a safe guide
to their faith and practice.

Even in the first three centuries there were numerous
bodies of Christians who protested against the growing
laxity and worldliness in the Church, and against its
departure from the teachings of Scripture. Movements of
revival have never ceased to be repeated, and even when no
connection between one and another is visible, the underlying cause is the same—a desire to return to the practice
of some New Testament truth. In the early centuries
Asia Minor and Armenia were frequently the scene of such
revivings, as well as being the refuge of churches that had
from the first, in varying degree, maintained purity of
doctrine and godliness of life.

The Gospel had spread northward from Antioch in its earliest days. The Apostles Barnabas and Paul, and many others, had preached and founded churches throughout Asia Minor. The Epistles to the Galatians, Ephesians, and Colossians give a vivid picture of the powerful, enlightening, and sanctifying effects of the Apostles' doctrine on the Christians of those early congregations, as well as of the strength of the opposing teachings which had to be combated. The *Catholic* system (so called because of its claim to be the entire and exclusive Church) with its clerical rule, developed rapidly there, but there never ceased to be those who resisted it. In the third century the kingdom of Armenia anticipated the union of Church and State under Constantine the Great, by making Christianity the state religion of Armenia. Yet the continuity of churches maintaining New Testament principles remained unbroken.

From the time of Mani the churches of believers who called themselves Christians, thus distinguishing themselves from others whom they called "Romans", had always been accused of being Manichaeans, though they declared that they were not and complained of the injustice of attributing to them doctrines they did not hold. The frequency with which anything is repeated is no proof that it is true, and since such writings as remain of these Christians contain no trace of Manichaeism, it is only reasonable to believe that they did not hold it. So far from accepting the sectarian names so lavishly given to them, these people not only spoke of themselves individually as "christian" or "brother", but also claimed to be collectively the "holy, universal, and Apostolic Church of our Lord Jesus Christ", and as the departure from the Scriptures of the worldly churches, Greek, Latin, or Armenian, became increasingly flagrant, they denied to them the title of churches, declaring they had forfeited it by their union with the State, by the introduction of unbelievers into their circles through the system of infant baptism, by their giving the Lord's Supper to unbelievers, and by various other evils they had introduced. The name Paulician was frequently given to these churches. The reason is not clear. They were also called Thonraks, after a place where they were at one time numerous. The persecutions to which they were subjected and the systematic destruction of their literature, hide from us all but occasional glimpses of their history, though what remains is sufficient to show that there were in those wide regions of Asia Minor and Armenia, around Mount Ararat and beyond the Euphrates, churches of baptized believers, disciples of the Lord Jesus Christ, who kept the teaching of the Apostles received from Christ and contained in the Scriptures, in an unbroken testimony from the first.

The claim of these numerous congregations to be the true descendants of the Apostolic churches (not necessarily in a natural sense from father to son, though that might often be the case, but as having maintained in unbroken succession their spiritual characteristics) is not invalidated by the large gaps in their history of which at present we possess no account. These are the natural consequence of the determined efforts that were unceasingly made, first by the Pagan Roman Empire and then by the State Churches, to destroy the people and their histories. These efforts had, to a large extent, their intended effect. There can be no doubt that in many districts, and at different times, such efforts were entirely successful, and that priceless testimonies of saints and churches have been utterly wiped out, never to be known again until the Day of Judgment comes. Rather is it a matter for surprise that so much has been preserved, and the existence of these numerous bodies of Christians of primitive doctrine and practice can be accounted for only in the way they themselves explain it, namely, by their adherence to the New Testament teaching. The absence of organization among them and of any earthly controlling centre, with the fact that they recognized the independence of each congregation, would lead to variety in the different churches. Then the characteristics of prominent leaders among them would also cause one generation to differ to some extent from another in spirituality or in the particular line of teaching emphasized. But they all claimed to draw their doctrine from the Scripture and to continue the Apostolic tradition, and this claim must be allowed, since nothing sufficient can be urged against it, nor can the contrary be proved.

Some accounts have been preserved of men who devoted their lives to visiting and strengthening such churches and to preaching the Gospel,* men of Apostolic spirit, strong, patient, humble-minded and of an undaunted courage. One who attached himself to these companies was Constantine, later called Silvanus. About the year 653 an Armenian, who had been held captive by the Saracens, was released, and on his homeward journey was received and kindly entertained by Constantine in his house. The conversation between them showed the observant Armenian that he had been led to a man of unusual capacity, and seeing how deeply interested his host had become in the Scriptures which they had read together, the grateful and far-seeing traveller left with his new friend a very precious gift—a MS. which contained the four Gospels and the Epistles of Paul. This book became the absorbing study of Constantine, and was the means of bringing about a radical change of life in him. He soon began to bear witness to what he had received, changed his name to that of Silvanus, the companion of the Apostle Paul, and, by attaching himself to the believers who rejected the image worship and other superstitions of the Byzantine Church, drew upon himself the anger of those in authority. He made Kibossa in Armenia his dwelling place, and from there as a centre he worked among the various peoples round about for some thirty years, many being converted, both from among the Catholics and the heathen. His journeys brought him along the Euphrates valley, across the Taurus Mountains, and into the western parts of Asia Minor, where his successful activities attracted the attention of the Byzantine Emperor, Constantine Pogonatus.

This Emperor issued a decree (684) against the congregations of believers and against Constantine in particular, sending one of his officers, named Simeon, to put it into effect. In order to give special significance to the execution of Constantine, Simeon supplied a number of his personal friends with stones and ordered them to stone the teacher whom they had so long revered and loved.

* "Die Paulikianer im Byzantischen Kaiserreiche etc." Karapet Ter-Mkrttschian Archidiakonus von Edschmiatzin.
"The Key of Truth A Manual of the Paulician Church of Armenia" F. C. Conybeare.
"The History of the Decline and Fall of the Roman Empire" Edward Gibbon.
"The Later Roman Empire" Prof. J. B. Bury, Vol. II, c. 14.

Risking their own lives by their refusal, they dropped the stones, but there was a young man present named Justus, who had been brought up by Constantine as his adopted son and treated with especial kindness; he flung a stone at his benefactor and killed him, thus earning high praise and reward from the authorities, who compared him to David slaying Goliath. Simeon was profoundly moved by all that he saw and heard at Kibossa, and, conversing with the Christians there, was convinced of the truth of their doctrines and the rightness of their practice. Returning to Constantinople, he could find no peace of soul at the court, and after three years of inward conflict, abandoned everything, escaped to Kibossa, and there, adopting the name of Titus, took up and continued the work of the man whom he had caused to be put to death. It was not long before he, too, joined the great company of martyrs, for, two years later, Justus, making use of his knowledge of the ways of the brethren, gave to the bishop—and he to the Emperor Justinian II—information which led to the capture of a large number of them. Expecting to terrorize the rest of the "heretics" into submission, the Emperor had these, including Simeon, all burnt together at one time. The fortitude of the sufferers, however, defeated his plan, fanning the faith and courage of many into a flame of devotion and testimony, so that more preachers and teachers were raised up and the congregations increased. They endured affliction with courage, unresisting, until a time of respite came to them through circumstances which took place in the Catholic world.

Veneration of relics began at an early stage of the Church's history. Helena, the mother of Constantine the Great, brought from Jerusalem wood supposed to be part of the cross, and nails which she believed had been used at the crucifixion. Pictures, images, and ikons began to be valued. Churches were built to receive relics or to commemorate the death of martyrs. Insensibly the meetings of the disciples of the Lord, in simple houses and rooms, changed to the gathering of all, willing or unwilling, believers or not, in consecrated buildings dedicated to the Virgin or one of the saints, filled with images, pictures, and relics, which became objects of worship. Prayer was diverted from God to the Virgin and the saints, and the idolatry of Paganism was reproduced in the gross superstitions that grew up around the images, the priests, and the forms of religion. It is a mark of the power of the revelation of Christ contained in the Scriptures, that even when Pagan idolatry and superstition had succeeded in gaining possession of the Catholic churches, there were to be found in them, then as now, great numbers of believers, whose hope of salvation was in Christ and whose lives were pious and godly. They, however, were a remnant, hidden in the mass of those who had been misled into the system of idolatry with its accompanying sin and ignorance, and their protests were raised in vain.

Such companies as those called Paulicians and other names, denounced the prevailing idolatry, and this was one of the chief reasons for the bitter persecution they suffered. In the regions where they were numerous, in the Taurus Mountains, Leo was born, who became Emperor of the Eastern, or Byzantine Empire, and is known as Leo the Isaurian. He was one of the best and most successful of the Byzantine Emperors, defending Constantinople from the Saracens and strengthening the Empire internally by his vigorous and wise reforms. Perceiving that the prevalent idolatry and superstition were among the chief causes of the miseries that were so evident in both East and West, he set himself to root out the evil. In 726 he issued his first edict against the worship of images, and followed it by a campaign of forcible destruction of images, and persecution of those who held to them. This initiated a struggle which lasted for more than a century. Leo found that he had stirred up a host of adversaries, of whom the most eloquent was the learned John of Damascus.

He taught,* ". . . since some find fault with us for worshipping and honouring the image of our Saviour and that of our Lady and those too of the rest of the saints and servants of Christ, let them remember that in the beginning God created man after His own image. . . . in the Old Testament the use of images was not common. But after

* A Select Library of Nicene and Post-Nicene Fathers of the Christian Church Edited by the Rev. N. Sanday, D.D., LL.D., Oxford. "John of Damascus, Exposition of the Orthodox Faith" translated by the Rev. S. D. F. Salmond D.D., F.E.I.S., Aberdeen.

God in His bowels of pity became in truth man for our salvation . . . lived upon the earth, worked miracles, suffered, was crucified, rose again and was taken back to heaven, since all these things actually took place and were seen by men, they were written for the remembrance and instruction of us who were not alive at that time in order that though we saw not we may still, hearing and believing, obtain the blessing of the Lord. But seeing that not every one has a knowledge of letters nor time for reading, the Fathers gave their sanction to depicting these events on images as being acts of great heroism in order that they should form a concise memorial of them. Often doubtless, when we have not the Lord's passion in mind and see the image of Christ's crucifixion His saving passion is brought back to remembrance, and we fall down and worship, not the material, but that which is imaged. . . . But this is an unwritten tradition, just as is also the worshipping towards the East and the worship of the Cross and very many other similar things. "

Almost all the priests and monks were against Leo; the aged Pope of Constantinople refused submission to his order and was replaced by another; the Pope of Rome, Gregory II, and his successor, Gregory III, were implacable opponents. In Greece a rival Emperor was chosen and attacked Constantinople, but was defeated. In Italy the orders were condemned and disobeyed. Leo, called *"the Iconoclast"* because of his destruction of images, was succeeded by his son Constantine and by his grandson Leo IV, who followed out his policy with even greator rigour than he. On the death of the last, his widow, Irene, reversed his policy, but for several reigns the conflict was continued with varying result, until (842) the death of the Emperor Theophilus, an opponent of image worship, left his widow, Theodora, regent during the minority of her son Michael III. Under the influence of the priests a secret supporter of image worship, Theodora, as soon as she was able, re-established the images. In the church of St. Sophia in Constantinople a great celebration of their restoration was solemnized. Images and pictures that had been kept in concealment were brought out and the dignitaries of the Church and of the State did reverence before them.

The question of images had an important place in the Council called and presided over by Charlemagne at Frankfurt (794).* Both civil and ecclesiastical rulers were present, so that it legislated on all matters. The Pope sent his representatives. The decisions of the Second Council of Nicaea, which had established the service and adoration of the images, were set aside, though they had been confirmed by the Pope and accepted in the East. In their zeal for images, those who favoured their use went so far as to call their opponents, not only iconoclasts, but also Mohammedans. Nevertheless it was laid down in Frankfurt that all worship of images was to be rejected; there was to be no adoration, worship, reverence, veneration of them; no kneeling, burning of lights or offering of incense before them, nor any kissing of lifeless images, even though representing the Virgin and the Child; but images might be allowed in churches as ornaments and as memorials of pious men and pious deeds. Also the teaching that God can only be worshipped in the three languages, Latin, Greek, and Hebrew, was controverted, and it was affirmed that "there is no tongue in which prayer may not be offered." The representatives of the Pope were not then in a position to protest. The general feeling of the Franks, in their wars against, and missions to, the heathen Saxons, was not favourable to idolatry.

Louis, the third son of Charlemagne, who was at that time King of Aquitaine, succeeded his father as Emperor (813). He was an admirer of a Spaniard named Claudius, a diligent student of the Scriptures, who had become renowned for his Commentaries on the Bible. As soon as he became Emperor, Louis appointed Claudius Bishop of Turin. The new bishop, with his knowledge and love of Scripture, took immediate advantage of the favourable circumstances created by the Council of Frankfurt, going even beyond its decrees in removing from the churches of Turin all images, which he called idols, not excepting the crosses. So many approved that no effective resistance could be made in Turin. Claudius also taught publicly that the Apostolic office of St. Peter ceased with his life, that "the power of the keys" passed to the whole Episcopal Order, and that the Bishop of Rome had Apostolic power

* "Latin Christianity"   Dean Milman   Vol. III.

only so far as he led an Apostolic life. There were naturally many who opposed this. Prominent among them was the abbot of a monastery near Nîmes, yet even he admitted that most of the Transalpine prelates thought with the Bishop of Turin.

Greater events, but also connected with the question of images, arose from small beginnings in Arabia. In 571 Mohammed was born in Mecca, and at his death in 632 the religion of Islam, of which he was the founder and prophet, had spread over the greater part of Arabia. *Islam*, or "submission to the will of God", had as its creed: "There is no God but God and Mohammed is His Prophet". It utterly repudiated images or pictures of any kind. Its book, the Koran, contains many confused references to persons and events spoken of in the Bible. Abraham as the Friend of God, Moses the Law of God, Jesus the Spirit of God, are all venerated, but are excelled by Mohammed the Prophet of God. This religion was mercilessly spread by the sword, and such was the resistless energy of the new enthusiasm that in less than a hundred years from the death of Mohammed, the dominion and religion of his followers stretched from India to Spain. The choice of conversion to Mohammedanism or death constantly reinforced the armies of Islam, but untold numbers died rather than deny Christ. In North Africa especially, where the churches were so numerous and had such traditions and records of the faith unto death of those who had suffered there during the persecution by the Pagan Roman Empire, a great proportion of the population was blotted out. Mohammedanism was a judgement on idolatry, whether Pagan or Christian.

The iconoclastic movement* had brought respite to the persecuted brethren in Asia Minor, but when (842), under the Empress Theodora, the supporters of images had triumphed, it was determined to exterminate the "heretics" who had so consistently and powerfully proclaimed that images, pictures, and relics were valueless, and had maintained a spiritual worship and the priesthood of all believers.

"Die Paulikianer im Byzantischen Kaiserreiche etc." Karapet Ter-Mkrttschian. Archidiakonus von Edschmiatzin.

For the testing time that was to come they were prepared
by the devoted labours of able men, such as Sembat, born
at the end of the eighth century, who was of a noble
Armenian family and so prominent in ministry that long
after his death Catholics spoke of him as the founder of
the Paulicians.

Another leader was Sergius (Armenian, *Sarkis*). "For
thirty-four years" (800-834), he says, "I have run from
east to west and from north to south, preaching the Gospel
of Christ, until my knees were weary". He had a strong conviction of his call to the ministry, and with great authority
healed divisions, and united and instructed the saints;
yet he could appeal to those who knew him and ask, with
a clear conscience, whether he had despoiled any one, or
had ever acted in an overbearing manner. Though he
worked as a carpenter, yet he visited almost every part of
the central Highlands of Asia Minor. His conversion
came about through his being persuaded to read the Scriptures. A believing woman asked him why he did not read
the Divine Gospels. He explained that only priests might
do this and not the laity. She replied that God is no
respecter of persons, but desires that all be saved and
come to a knowledge of the truth, and that it is a trick
of the priests to deprive the people of their share in
the Gospels. He read and believed, and long testified
most effectually for Christ. His epistles were widely
circulated and greatly valued, his activities being ended
only by his death, when he was cut in two with an axe by
his pursuers.

He was one of the most distinguished of a series of men
whose godly character and devoted service enshrined their
names in the memory of an heroic people. Constantine,
Simeon, Genesios, Joseph, Zacharias, Baanes, Sembat,
Sergius, are names that survive the wreckage of the persecutions that followed. So imbued were these brethren
with the spirit of the Acts and the Epistles, so desirous of
continuing unaltered the traditions of the New Testament,
and especially of preserving in their own countries the
remembrance that there apostles had laboured and founded
the first churches, that they habitually took the names
of men and of churches from the inspired records. Thus
Constantine was called Silvanus; Simeon, Titus; Genesios,

Timotheus; Joseph, Epaphroditus. Very different were the names given them by their adversaries, who called Zacharias the "hireling shepherd", and Baanes the "filthy one". Similarly the "true Christians", as they called themselves by way of distinction from the "Romans", gave memorial names to churches that were centres of their activities. So Kibossa, where Constantine and Simeon laboured, was their Macedonia; the village of Mananalis, around which Genesios worked, was their Achaia; while other churches were named after Philippi, Laodicea, Colosse, and so on.

These men laboured during 200 years, from the middle of the seventh to the middle of the ninth century. It was in their time, and possibly by one of them, that a book, "The Key of Truth", was written, which gives a vivid picture of them. The persecutions under the Empress Theodora at the close of this period, and the wars which followed, scattered the churches, and many of the believers crossed over to the Balkans. The churches were not without periods of internal trouble as well as attacks from without. In the time of Genesios divisions caused such disturbance that he was summoned to Constantinople to give account. The well-disposed Emperor, Leo the Isaurian, found no fault with his doctrines, nor did the Patriarch Germanus, and Genesios was sent back with letters ordering protection for the "Paulicians". But the Government did not permanently help the churches; its forcible suppression of the worship of images failed to loosen their hold, and it was liable to be actuated by motives of political expediency; thus Leo the Armenian, though an iconoclast Emperor, in order to please the Greek Church allowed an attack to be made on the "Paulicians", so weakening and alienating those who were his real strength.

Systematic slaughter, beheading, burning, drowning, began afresh under the Empress Theodora's orders, and continued for many years; but it failed to shake the stead-fastness of the believers. It was claimed that between the years 842 and 867 the zeal of Theodora and her inquisitors had brought about the death of 100,000 persons. This time is described by Gregory Magistros, who, 200 years later, was in charge of the persecution of similar people in the same district. He writes: "Prior to us many generals and magistrates have given them over to the sword and, without pity, have spared neither old men nor children, and quite rightly. What is more, our patriarchs have branded their foreheads and burned into them the image of a fox. . . . others again have put their eyes out, saying, 'you are blind to spiritual things therefore you shall not look on sensible things'".

The Armenian book entitled "The Key of Truth"*, mentioned above as having been written between the seventh and ninth centuries, describes the beliefs and practices of those called Paulicians, of Thonrak, at that time; and although there were doubtless many differences in the numerous scattered churches, yet this authentic account given by one of themselves, is applicable to most of them. The author is unknown, but writes with power and eloquence as well as with deep feeling and earnestness. He writes to give to the new born children of the Universal and Apostolic Church of our Lord Jesus Christ the holy milk whereby they may be nourished in the faith. Our Lord, he says, asks first for repentance and faith and then gives baptism, so we must follow Him and not do after the deceitful arguments of others, who baptize the unbelieving, the reasonless, and the unrepentant. When a child is born the elders of the church should give counsel to the parents that they may train the child in godliness and faith. This should be accompanied by prayer, the reading of the Scriptures, and giving the child a name. When anyone is baptized it should be at his or her earnest request. Baptism should be in rivers, or other water in the open air. The one to be baptized should, on his knees in the midst of the water, confess his faith before the congregation present, with great love and tears. The one who baptizes should be of blameless character. Prayer and the reading of Scripture should accompany the act. Again, the ordaining of an elder requires great care lest anyone unworthy be chosen. It must be ascertained whether he has perfect wisdom, love, which is chief of all, prudence, gentleness, humility, justice, courage, sobriety,

---

* "The Key of Truth" translated and edited by F. C. Conybeare. This document was found by the translator in 1891 in the library of the Holy Synod at Edjmiatzin, and he has added valuable annotations.

eloquence. In laying hands on him, which is to be done
with prayer and the reading of suitable Scriptures, he is to
be asked, "Art thou then able to drink the cup which I
am about to drink, or to be baptized with the baptism with
which I am about to be baptized?" The answer required
of him shows the dangers and responsibilities that such
men accepted, which none would take on themselves
unless there were an earnest love and a will to suffer to the
uttermost in the following of Christ and caring for His
flock. The reply is: "...I take on myself scourgings, imprisonment, tortures, reproaches, crosses, blows, tribulation and all temptations of the world, which our Lord and
Intercessor and the Universal and Apostolic Holy Church
took upon themselves, and lovingly accepted them. So even
do I, an unworthy servant of Jesus Christ, with great love
and ready will, take upon myself all these until the hour
of my death". Then, with the reading of many Scriptures,
he was solemnly and earnestly commended to the Lord,
the elders saying: "We humbly supplicate, entreat and
beseech Thee, . . . bestow Thy holy grace on this one, who
now is come and asks of Thee the grace of Thy holy authority
. . . make him resplendently pure from all evil thoughts . . .
open his mind to understand the Scriptures". Writing of
images and relics the author says: "...Concerning the mediation of our Lord Jesus Christ, and not of any other holy
ones, either of the dead, or of stones or of crosses and
images. In this matter some have denied the precious
mediation and intercession of the beloved Son of God, and
have followed after dead things, and in especial after
images, stones, crosses, waters, trees, fountains, and all
other vain things; as they admit and worship them, so
they offer incense and candles, and present victims, all
of which are contrary to the Godhead".

The conflict which these churches of God in the Taurus
Mountains and adjacent countries maintained with their
persecutors in Constantinople led to their laying more
emphasis on some portions of Scripture than on others.
The great professing Church had incorporated Paganism with
its system by the gradual introduction of the worship of the
Virgin Mary, and had brought the world into its ranks by
its practice of infant baptism. This caused the primitive
churches to lay great stress on the Lord's perfect humanity

at His birth, showing that Mary, though the Lord's mother, cannot properly be called the mother of God, and to emphasize the importance of the baptism of Jesus, when the Holy Spirit descended upon Him and the voice from heaven declared: "This is My beloved Son, in whom I am well pleased". In the many controversies as to the Divine and human nature of Christ, which after all efforts at explanation still remains a mystery, they used expressions which their adversaries construed as implying their disbelief in the Divinity of Christ before His baptism. They seem, rather, to have held that His Divine attributes were not in exercise from His birth to His baptism. They taught that it was at His baptism, when 30 years old, that our Lord Jesus Christ received authority, the high-priesthood, the kingdom; then He was chosen and won lordship; it was then that He became the Saviour of sinners, was filled with the Godhead, ordained king of beings in heaven and on earth and under the earth, even as He Himself said in Matthew 28. 18, "All authority is given unto Me in heaven and on earth".

These churches, carrying out the New Testament principles in a large measure, though no doubt in varying degree in different places, called by their adversaries Manichaeans, Paulicians, and other names, suffered for centuries with patience and without retaliation the dreadful wrongs inflicted on them. During the reigns of the iconoclastic Byzantine Emperors they had a respite, but the extraordinary persecutions carried on by the Empress Theodora goaded some of them to desperation, so that they took up arms against their oppressors.

In pursuance of her cruel orders the Imperial executioners had impaled a man whose son, Carbeas, held high rank in the Imperial service. On hearing this, Carbeas, in flaming indignation, renounced all allegiance to Byzantium; five thousand others joined him, and they established themselves at Tephrice, near Trebizond, which they fortified, and, in alliance with the Saracen Caliph, made it the centre of attacks on the Greek countries of Asia Minor. With this Mohammedan help they defeated the Emperor Michael, son of Theodora, captured the cities as far as Ephesus and destroyed the images they found there.

Carbeas was succeeded by Chrysocheir, whose raids

reached the western coast of Asia Minor and even threatened Constantinople. Ancyra, Ephesus, Nicaea, and Nicomedia were captured. In Ephesus horses were stabled in the cathedral, and the utmost contempt was shown for the pictures and relics, the building being considered as an idol temple. The Emperor, Basil I, was obliged to sue for peace, but Chrysocheir refused any terms short of the abandonment of Asia by the Greeks. Basil, compelled to fight, surprised his enemy; Chrysocheir was killed and his army defeated. The Byzantine army took Tephrice and scattered its inhabitants, who maintained themselves thereafter in the mountains.

As these revolted Paulicians saw on the one side the worshippers of images inflicting on them the most wicked oppression, and on the other the Mohammedans, free from any taint of idolatry, offering them liberty and help, it must have been difficult for them to judge which of the two systems was nearer to, or rather which was further from, the Divine revelation given in Christ. The Mohammedans, however, were incapable of progress, for they entirely rejected the Scriptures, and, by placing themselves under bondage to the *Koran*, a book of human origin, were necessarily prevented from advancing beyond that to which its originator had himself attained. The Greek and Roman Churches, though they had departed from the truth, yet retained the Scriptures, and thus there remained among them that which, by the Holy Spirit's power, was capable of bringing about revival.

In extracting some details of the history of these churches from the writings of their enemies, it cannot but be observed that these writings are so violent in abuse as to become manifest folly. To found accusations upon them, therefore, is to put trust in untrustworthy evidence, whereas any good that they may admit is likely to be an unwilling acceptance of what could not be denied, especially as we find that this good is usually explained to have been based on some evil motive. The constant accusation of Manichaeism is not credible in the face of its equally constant denial by the accused, and by their consistent teaching of, and suffering for, the contrary doctrines of Scripture. The admitted fact that they had the Scriptures, or a large portion of them, in pure, unaltered form, and diligently studied them, is not compatible with their being Manichaeans, as the doctrines of Mani could only be held by such as rejected the Scriptures or altered them. Accounts of unnaturally wicked behaviour do not agree with the admission that they were pious and of excellent conduct, superior to those among whom they lived, and it is unreasonable to explain that all their good behaviour was nothing but hypocrisy. The character of the somewhat voluminous witness of their enemies, combined with the few records of their own which have survived, gives confidence in rejecting the legend of Manichaeism and wickedness and in recognizing in these persecuted churches a people of the Lord who in their day maintained the testimony of Jesus Christ with faith and indomitable courage.

By scattering and alienating these brave and pious mountaineers, and driving them into alliance with the Mohammedans, the Byzantine Government destroyed its own natural defence against the threatening Mohammedan power and prepared the way for the fall of Constantinople.

In the middle of the eighth century the Emperor Constantine, son of Leo the Isaurian, who sympathized with the refusal of the brethren to attach any value to images, transferred a number of them to Constantinople and to Thrace, and later, about the middle of the tenth century, another Emperor, John Zimisces, an Armenian, who delivered Bulgaria from the Russians but afterwards added it to his own empire, moved a larger number to the West. These came among the Bulgarians, who in the ninth century had accepted Christianity through the Byzantine missionaries Cyril and Methodius and belonged to the Greek Orthodox Church.

There the immigrants from Asia Minor made converts and founded churches which spread rapidly. They came, over wide areas to be called, *Bogomili**, a Slav name meaning

* Some derive the name Bogomil from the name of a man prominent in the reign of the Bulgarian Czar Peter (927-968); sometimes they are called Bulgarians. Bogomili is a Slav plural form, hence the usual form in the West, Bogomils. Analagous names are still to be found in daily use in Slav countries; in Yugoslavia, for instance, the *Bogomolici*, *i.e.*, those who pray to God (from *Bogu*, "to God" and *moliti*, "to pray"). There is little doubt that the Bogomili were so called because they did

"Friends of God", derived from the phrase, *"Bogu mili"*, those dear or acceptable to God.

Out of a multitude whose very names have been forgotten the memory of a few has been preserved. One of them is Basil, who, though continuing to practise as a physician in order, by earning his living, to set a good example and so rebuke the lazy lives of those who made religion an excuse for begging, was, for some forty years of his life (1070-1111) indefatigable in preaching and teaching.

After this long period of uninterrupted ministry, he at last received a message from the Emperor Alexius himself, telling him that he admired his character, was deeply interested in his teaching, and had become desirous of conversion. With it there came an invitation to a private interview in the palace in Constantinople. Basil was entertained at table by the Emperor and a full discussion of doctrine took place, in which Basil spoke with the freedom of one addressing an anxious inquirer. Suddenly the Emperor, drawing aside a curtain, revealed a shorthand writer who had taken down the conversation (afterwards used as evidence), and ordered servants to put his guest in chains and cast him into prison. There he remained for years, until (1119), having refused to recant any of the doctrines he had taught, he was publicly burnt in the Hippodrome in Constantinople. The Emperor's daughter, the accomplished Princess Anna Comnena, describes these events with satisfaction; the preparation for the great day in the Hippodrome, the appearance of Basil, "a lanky man, with a sparse beard, tall and thin"; notes the crackling of the fire, how Basil turned his eyes from the sight of the flame and how his limbs quivered as he approached it. At this time many "Friends of God" were "ferreted out" and burnt, or imprisoned for life. The Princess laughed at their low origin, uncouth appearance, and habit of bowing their heads and muttering something between their lips. (They surely had need of prayer

strike their contemporaries as men and women who enjoyed a certain peace and communion with God.

"An official tour through Bosnia and Herzegovina" J. de Asboth. Member of Hungarian Parliament.

"Through Bosnia and the Herzegovina on Foot" etc. A. J. Evans.

"Essays on the Latin Orient" William Miller.

"Encyclopaedia of Religion and Ethics" Hastings. Article, Bogomils

at such times!) She was horrified at their doctrines and at
their disdain of the churches and church ceremonies. The
document drawn up as the result of the entrapping of Basil
by the Emperor has not much value owing to the fact that
there was no check on what those who published it liked
to put in it.

The opinions expressed by outsiders about these Christian congregations, both in Asia Minor and in Bulgaria,
vary greatly, for while it was usual to speak of them and
their doctrine as being indescribably wicked, there were
those who judged differently. The earliest writers appear
to have written more as partisans than as historians.
They accuse the "heretics" of practising vile and unnatural
fleshly sins, repeat from hearsay what was current about
them and include much from Mani and from what was
written against him. The writer Euthymius (died after
1118), says: "They bid those who listen to their doctrines
to keep the commandments of the Gospel, and to be meek
and merciful and of brotherly love. Thus they entice men
on by teaching all good things and useful doctrines, but
they poison by degrees and draw to perdition." Cosmas,
a Bulgarian Presbyter, writing at the end of the tenth
century, describes Bogomils as "worse and more horrible
than demons", denies their belief in the Old Testament
or the Gospels, says they pay no honour to the Mother of
God nor to the cross, they revile the ceremonies of the
Church and all Church dignitaries, call orthodox priests
"blind Pharisees", say that the Lord's Supper is not kept
according to God's commandment, and that the bread is
not the body of God, but ordinary bread. He attributes
their asceticism to their belief that the Devil created all
material things and says: "You will see heretics quiet and
peaceful as lambs . . . wan with hypocritical fasting, who
do not speak much nor laugh loud", and again, "when men
see their lowly behaviour, they think that they are of true
belief; they approach them therefore and consult them
about their soul's health. But they, like wolves that will
swallow up a lamb, bow their head, sigh, and answer full
of humility, and set themselves up as if they knew how it
is ordered in heaven." The Church Father, Gregory of
Narek, said of the Thonraks that they were not accused of
wickedness of life, but of free thought and of not acknow-

ledging authority. "From a negative position as regards the Church this sect has taken up a positive line of things and has begun to search out the foundation itself, the Holy Scriptures, seeking there pure teaching, sound guidance for the moral life. " A learned writer of the tenth century, Muschag, was greatly impressed by the teaching of the Thonraks, regarding it as unchristian and unworthy merely to condemn such people. He thought he found true Apostolic Christianity among them. Hearing of a case of persecution which they suffered, he said the lot of these persecuted ones was to be envied.

There is no evidence to support the charge that these Christians, whether called Paulicians, Thonraks, Bulgarians, Bogomils or otherwise, were guilty of wicked practices, and the accounts of their doctrines given by their enemies are unreliable. It was generally admitted even by these that their standard of life, their morals, their industry, were superior to those which prevailed round about them; and it was largely this which attracted to them many who failed to find in the State Church that which satisfied them.

Byzantine persecution drove many of the believers westward into Serbia, and the strength of the Orthodox Church in Serbia pushed them further, into Bosnia. They continued active on the eastern side of the Peninsula and in Asia Minor. In 1140 supposed Bogomil error was found in the writings of Constantine Chrysomalus and condemned at a synod held in Constantinople. The teaching objected to was, that Church baptism is not efficacious, that nothing done by unconverted persons, though baptized, is of any value, that God's grace is received by the laying on of hands, but only in accordance with the measure of faith. In 1143 a synod at Constantinople deposed two Cappadocian bishops on the charge of being Bogomils, and in the following century the Patriarch Gemadius complained of their spread in Constantinople itself, where, it was said, they got into private houses and made converts. Their churches continued in Bulgaria.

As late as the 17th century congregations known as "Pavlicani" (Paulicians)* remained in Philippopolis and

* "Das Fürstenthum Bulgarien" Dr. Constantin Jirecek, Wien. 1891 F Tempsky

other parts of Bulgaria reaching even North of the Danube, who were described by the Orthodox Church as "convinced heretics" and who condemned the Orthodox Church as idolatrous.   Then came Franciscan missionaries from Bosnia and laboured with much zeal among them, in spite of many dangers from the wrath of the Orthodox clergy. Taking advantage of the persecution suffered by the Paulicians at the hands of the Orthodox Church, the missionaries gradually persuaded them to put themselves under the protection of the Roman Catholic Church and so won them for Rome.   Long after this, however, they continued some of their former practices, especially their custom of meeting together for a meal in common, but they were little by little assimilated to the Roman practice, received images into their churches, and are now known as Bulgarian Catholics in contradistinction to the Bulgarians generally, who are either Orthodox, or Pomaks, that is, descended from ancestors forcibly converted to Mohammedanism.

It was, however, in Bosnia that their greatest development took place.   In the twelfth century they were already very numerous there, and spread to Spalato and Dalmatia. Here they came into conflict with the Roman Catholic Church.   The title of the rulers of Bosnia was *Ban*, the most eminent of these being Kulin Ban.   In 1180 this ruler was addressed by the Pope as a faithful adherent of the Church, but by 1199 it was acknowledged that he and his wife and family and ten thousand Bosnians had joined the Bogomil or Patarene heresy, otherwise churches of believers, in Bosnia.   Minoslav, Prince of the Herzegovina, took the same stand, as did also the Roman Catholic Bishop of Bosnia.   The country ceased to be Catholic and experienced a time of prosperity that has remained proverbial ever since.   There were no priests, or rather the priesthood of all believers was acknowledged.   The churches were guided by elders who were chosen by lot, several in each church, an overseer (called grandfather), and ministering brethren called leaders and elders. Meetings could be held in any house and the regular meeting-places were quite plain, no bells, no altar, only a table, on which might be a white cloth and a copy of the Gospels.   A part of the earnings of the brethren was set aside for the relief of sick believers and of the poor and for the support of those who travelled to preach the Gospel among the unconverted.

Pope Innocent III, with the help of the King of Hungary, brought such pressure to bear on Kulin Ban that, at a meeting (1203) between the Pope's envoys and the Ban, accompanied by the magnates of Bosnia, at Bjelopolje, "the White Plain", where Kulin held his court, the Bosnian leaders agreed to submit to the Roman Church, promised never again to relapse into heresy, but to erect an altar and a cross in each of their places of worship, and to have priests who should read the Mass and listen to Confession, and administer the Sacrament twice a year. They agreed to observe fasts and holy days, that the laity should cease to undertake spiritual functions, and that those who ministered in spiritual matters should be the clergy only, who would be distinguished from the laity by wearing cowls and being called brothers, and that when these elected a Prior, they would apply to the Pope for confirmation. Heretics were never again to be tolerated in Bosnia. Though, under pressure of the threat of war, the Ban and rulers of the country made such an agreement, the people entirely refused to accept it or to be bound by it in any way.

Brethren in Bosnia had intercourse with their fellow-believers in Italy, in the South of France, in Bohemia, on the Rhine, and in other parts, reaching even to Flanders and England. When the Pope declared a crusade against the Albigenses, and Provence was being wasted, fugitives found refuge in Bosnia. Bosnian and Provençal elders consulted together on matters of doctrine. Rumours were current that the spiritual movements in Italy, France, and Bohemia, were all connected with a "heretical Pope" in Bosnia. This was only imaginary, as no such person existed, but it showed that a strong influence went out from Bosnia. An Italian Inquisitor, Reniero Sacconi, living in the reign of Kulin, who, having been himself a "heretic", knew more about them than most, calls them the Church of the *Cathari*, or pure-living, a name used from before the time of the Emperor Constantine, and says they extended from the Black Sea to the Atlantic.

The peace which Kulin Ban purchased by yielding to

Rome was not of long duration, for he could not compel his people to observe its terms. On his death (1216) the Pope appointed a Roman Catholic Ban, and sent a mission to convert the Bosnians. The churches of the country, however, increased the more, and spread into Croatia, Dalmatia, Istria, Carniola and Slavonia. Some six years later the Pope, despairing of converting the Bosnians by other than forcible methods, and encouraged by the success of his crusade in Provence, ordered the King of Hungary to invade Bosnia. The Bosnians deposed their Roman Catholic Ban and elected a Bogomil, Ninoslav. For years the war went on, with varying fortune. Ninoslav yielded to circumstances and became a Roman Catholic, but no change in their rulers affected the faith and confession of the great bulk of the people. The country was devastated, but whenever the invading armies withdrew, the churches were found still existing, and the industry of the people quickly restored prosperity. Fortresses were erected throughout the country "for the protection of the Roman Catholic Church and religion"; the Pope gave the land to Hungary, which long ruled it, but its people still holding to their faith, he at length called a crusade of "all the Christian world" against it; the Inquisition was established (1291), and Dominican and Franciscan brothers competed in applying its terrors to the devoted churches.

Meanwhile, the constant pressure of Islam was becoming an increasing danger for Europe, and Hungary was in the forefront of the fight; yet this did not awaken the Catholic countries to see the folly of destroying a barrier between them and their most dangerous foe, and the Pope wrote (1325) to the Ban of Bosnia: "Knowing that thou art a faithful son of the Church, we therefore charge thee to exterminate the heretics in thy dominions, and to render aid and assistance unto Fabian, our Inquisitor, forasmuch as a large multitude of heretics from many and divers parts collected, have flowed together into the Principality of Bosnia, trusting there to sow their obscene errors and to dwell there in safety. These men, imbued with the cunning of the Old Fiend, and armed with the venom of their falseness, corrupt the minds of Catholics by outward show of simplicity and lying assumption of the name of Christians; their speech crawleth like a crab, and they creep in with humility, but in secret they kill, and are wolves in sheep's clothing, covering their bestial fury as a means whereby they may deceive the simple sheep of Christ. "

Bosnia experienced a period of political revival during the reign of Tvrtko, the first Ban to take the title of King. He and Kulin are the two most prominent of Bosnian rulers. Tvrtko tolerated the Bogomils, large numbers of whom served in his armies, and he greatly extended his kingdom. Towards the close of his reign the battle of Kossovo (1389) extended the Turkish rule over Serbia and made the Mohammedan menace to Europe more serious than ever. Even this did not suffice to stop persecution, and the Pope again encouraged the King of Hungary, promising him aid against the Turks and the "Bosnian Manichaeans and Arians. " King Sigismund of Hungary was successful in destroying the Bosnian army under the successors of Tvrtko, and caused 126 Bosnian magnates, whom he had captured, to be beheaded and thrown from the rocks of Doboj into the river Bosna (1408).

Then the Bosnians, driven to desperation, turned to the Turks for protection. Their chief magnate, Hrvoja, warned the King of Hungary—"so far I have sought no other protection, as my sole refuge has been the king; but if matters remain as they are I shall seek protection in that quarter where I shall find it, whether I thereby stand or fall. The Bosnians wish to hold out their hand to the Turks, and have already taken steps towards this. " Soon afterwards the Turks and Bogomil Bosnians, for the first time united, inflicted a heavy defeat on Hungary at the battle of Usora, a few miles from Doboj (1415).

The struggle between Christendom and Islam swayed to and fro on its long battle-front. But whenever the Papal party prevailed, persecution in Bosnia began afresh, so that (1450) some 40,000 Bogomils, with their leaders, crossed the frontier into Herzegovina, where the Prince Stefan Vuktchitch protected them. The capture of Constantinople in 1453 by Mohammed II, which led to the speedy subjection of Greece, Albania and Serbia under the hands of the Turks, did not cause the negotiations and intrigues for the conversion of the Bosnian Bogomils to cease. Sometimes their rulers were won over to Rome, but the people never. Therefore, as the end drew near. we find

Bosnian kings appealing to the Pope for help against the Turks, which was only given on condition of fresh persecution of the Bogomils, till at last (1463) when the Turks, who had been driven back for a time, advanced again on Bosnia, the people refused their king any aid, and preferring the Turk to the Inquisition, made no resistance to the invader, with the result that within a week the Sultan took possession of seventy towns and fortresses, in a country naturally strong for defence, and Bosnia passed permanently into Moslem hands, to stagnate for four centuries under a deadening system destructive of life and progress.

These *"Friends of God"* in Bosnia have left but little literature behind them, so that there remains much to be discovered of their doctrines and practices, which must have varied in different circles and at different periods. But it is evident that they made a vigorous protest against the prevailing evils in Christendom, and endeavoured with the utmost energy to hold fast to the teachings and example of the primitive churches, as portrayed in the Scriptures. Their relations with the older churches in Armenia and Asia Minor, with the Albigenses in France, Waldenses and others in Italy, and Hussites in Bohemia, show that there was a common ground of faith and practice which united them all. Their heroic stand for four centuries against overwhelming adversity, though unrecorded, must have yielded examples of faith and courage, of love unto death, second to none in the world's histories. They formed a link, connecting the Primitive churches in the Taurus Mountains of Asia Minor with similar ones in the Alps of Italy and France. Their land and nation were lost to Christendom because of the inveterate persecution to which they were subjected.

Scattered over the country, within the confines of the old Kingdom of Bosnia,* but nowhere else, are numerous stone monuments, often of great size—Bogomil tombstones. Sometimes one stone stands alone, sometimes they are in groups, which in places may number hundreds. It is estimated that there might be some 150,000 such monuments. The people call them *"Mramor"*, *i.e.*, marble, or

---

* "An Official Tour Through Bosnia and Herzegovina"   J. de Asboth, Member of Hungarian Parliament.

"Stetshak", that which stands, or *"Bilek"*, a sign or land-mark, or *"Gomile"*, an ancient tomb or mound. The very few inscriptions on them are in the Glagolitic character. They are remarkable for the absence of crosses or any symbols associated either with Christianity or Moham-medanism. Where, as occasionally, such symbols are found, it is evident that they have been added at a later date. The great majority of the stones are entirely without inscription of any kind, the few inscriptions there are give the names of the persons buried there. A few are elaborately carved with figures illustrating the life of the people at that time, warriors, hunters, animals, and varied ornamental designs. They are most numerous in the neighbourhood of Sarajevo, an immense group being found above the fortress, on the road to Rogatitza. One of the largest tombs stands alone on the Paslovatz Hill, near the ruins of Kotorsko, a giant sarcophagus of white limestone, hewn out of one solid block, together with the yet larger flag upon which it rests; at a distance if looks like a com-plete building.

Though they had so long resisted both the Greek and Latin churches, many of the Bosnians yielded to the Turks (who were at once their deliverers and their conquerors) and submitted to Mohammedanism. Some rose to the highest positions in the Turkish service. The family names of the present Mohammedan population of Bosnia preserve the record of their origin, while testifying also to the steady process of subjugation to Islam. Over the window of many a shop in Bosnia the traveller will find the Bosnian or "Southern Slav" name united with a purely Arabic or Turkish name which is generally placed before it. There are two distinct words in daily use throughout Bosnia to signify *Turk* or *Moslem*, the one meaning a Moslem of real Turkish or Anatolian origin, and the other a person of Slav race who has adopted the religion of Islam.

CHAPTER IV

The East

B.C. 4—A.D. 1400

The Gospel in the East—Syria and Persia—Churches in Persian Empire separated from those in Roman Empire—Eastern churches retained Scriptural character longer than those in the west—Papa ben Aggai federates churches—Zoroaster—Persecution under Sapor II—Homilies of Afrahat—Synod of Seleucia—Persecution renewed —Nestorius—The Bazaar of Heraclides—Toleration—Influx of western bishops—Increase of centralization—Wide spread of Syrian churches in Asia—Mohammedan invasion—Catholikos moved from Seleucia to Bagdad—Genghis Khan —Struggle between Nestorianism and Islam in Central Asia—Tamerlane—Franciscans and Jesuits find Nestorians in Cathay—Sixteenth century translation of part of Bible into Chinese—Disappearance of Nestorians from most of Asia—Causes of failure.

THE "wise men from the east" led by the star to Bethlehem, worshipped the Child newly "born King of the Jews"; presented to Him "gifts, gold and frankincense and myrrh", and "departed into their own country" (Matt. 2), where they doubtless related what they had seen and heard.   Among the multitude assembled at Jerusalem at Pentecost were "Parthians and Medes and Elamites and the dwellers in Mesopotamia", who were witnesses of the outpouring of the Holy Spirit and of the signs and wonders that accompanied it, and heard Peter preach that "God hath made that same Jesus, whom ye have crucified, both Lord and Christ" (Acts 2).   By them the Gospel was carried in its earliest days to the synagogues of the East.

Eusebius, writing of events which took place in the second century,* relates that many of the disciples at that time "whose souls were inflamed by the Divine Word and with a more ardent desire of wisdom, first fulfilled our Saviour's commandment by distributing their substance to those that were necessitous; then after that, travelling abroad, they performed the work of evangelists to those who had not yet at all heard the word of faith, being very ambitious to preach Christ and to deliver the books of the

* "The Syriac Churches"   J. W. Etheridge.

Divine Gospels. And these persons, having only laid the foundations of faith in remote and barbarous places and constituted other pastors, committed to them the culture of those they had perfectly introduced to the faith, and departed again to other regions. " Thus churches were founded and the evangelists pressed further afield, and that, not only within the wide bounds of the Roman Empire, but within the borders of its greatest neighbour, the Persian Empire, and beyond. A writer in the third century says: "That new power which has arisen from the works wrought by the Lord and His Apostles has subdued the flame of human passions and brought into the hearty acceptance of one faith a vast variety of races and nations the most different in their manners. For we can count up in our reckoning things achieved in India, among the Seres, Persians and Medes; in Arabia, Egypt, Asia and Syria; among the Galatians, the Parthians and the Phrygians; in Achaia, Macedonia and Epirus; in all the islands and provinces which the rising or the setting sun looks down upon. "

The churches which spread so rapidly in Syria and the Persian Empire were shut off from many of the influences which affected the Western churches by difference of language and by political circumstances, Aramaic being spoken in Palestine and Palmyra and used as the commercial language down the Euphrates valley, and the mutual jealousy and mistrust of the Roman and Persian Empires acting as a further bar to intercourse.

The Eastern churches kept their simple and Scriptural character longer than those of the West.* Even in the third century there was no definite organization of the separate churches into one system, the country was not divided into dioceses (there might be several bishops in one church at the same time), and the churches were active and successful in spreading the testimony continually into new regions.

Early in the fourth century Papa ben Aggai propounded a scheme for the federation of all the churches in Persia, including those in Syria and Mesopotamia, under the rule

* "Le Christianisme dans l'Empire Perse sous la Dynastie Sassanide" (224-632). J. Labourt.

of the bishop of the capital city, Seleucia-Ctesiphon, a position which he himself then occupied. This proposition was strenuously opposed, but continued to be pressed, and the bishop came to be called the *Catholikos*, and in time (498) the title Patriarch of the East was adopted.

The prevalent religion in Persia was derived from that introduced some eight centuries B.C. by Zoroaster. He, in his day, protested against the prevailing idolatry and wickedness, teaching that there is only one God, the Creator; that He is good, and alone to be worshipped. Zoroaster would use no compulsion in matters of religion, but trusted to the truth of what he taught to spread it. He made use of fire and light to represent the works of God, and employed darkness and charred wood to illustrate the powers of evil. He believed that God would bring about that which is good, and gave an epitome of conduct in the words, "Perform good actions, and refrain from evil ones." From the sixth to the third century B.C. Zoroastrianism prevailed generally among the Persians, but then its profession declined until it was revived by the Sassanid dynasty, which was the reigning dynasty at the time here considered.

When Constantine made Christianity the state religion in the Roman Empire the Kings of Persia began to suspect those in their own country, whom they called Nazarenes, of having sympathies with, and leanings towards, the rival Empire, which they hated and feared. In the long reign of the Persian King, Sapor II, this suspicion broke out into violent persecution, which was fanned by the magi, the Zoroastrian priests, unmindful both of their founder's precepts and of the testimony of those magi, their predecessors, who had been led by the star to Bethlehem. This persecution lasted for forty years, during which period the Christians suffered every imaginable torment. Some 16,000 are supposed to have lost their lives, and indescribable loss and misery was inflicted on countless confessors of Christ. By their patience and faith the churches in Persia came through this long and terrible trial victorious, and after a generation of suffering (339-379) considerable liberty of worship was restored to them.

Among the writings which remain from that time are the

Homilies of Afrahat, called "The Persian Sage."* The sharp dividing line between the Roman Empire and the countries outside of it is illustrated by the fact that these "Homilies", which contain an exposition of doctrine and practice, do not even mention the Council of Nicaea nor Arius nor Athanasius, though written at the very time when there was such violent agitation about them among the churches of the West. The first homily is on Faith, and teaches: "For this is Faith: When a man shall believe in God the Lord of all, that made the heaven and the earth and the seas and all that in them is, Who made Adam in His image. Who gave the Law to Moses. Who sent of His Spirit in the Prophets. Who sent moreover His Messiah into the world. And that a man should believe in the coming to life of the dead. And believe also in the mystery of baptism. This is the Faith of the Church of God. And that a man should separate himself from observing hours and sabbaths and months and seasons and enchantments and divinations and chaldaism and magic and from fornication and from revelling and from vain doctrines, the weapons of the Evil One, and from the blandishment of honeyed words, and from blasphemy and from adultery. And that no man should bear false witness and that none should speak with double tongue. These are the works of the Faith that is laid on the true Rock, which is the Messiah, upon whom all the building doth rise. " Afrahat condemns the teachings of Marcion and of Mani; he points out that there are many things which we are not able to understand, acknowledges the mystery of the Trinity but deprecates curious questions, saying: "Above the heavens, what is there—who doth suffice to tell? Beneath the earth, what is laid? There is none to say! The firmament— upon what is it stretched out, or the heavens—upon what are they hung? The earth—on what is it pillowed, or the deep—in what is it fixed? We are of Adam, and here, with our senses, we perceive little. Only this we know: that God is One, and His Messiah One, and One the Spirit, and one the Faith and one Baptism. More than thus far it doth not help us to speak; and if we say more we fall short, and. if we investigate we are helpless. " Afrahat's

* "Early Christianity Outside the Roman Empire"   F. C. Burkitt M.A.

study of prophecy led him to the conclusion that the attacks of Persia on the Roman Empire must of necessity fail.

The persecution of Christians in Persia, when Christianity was the state religion of the Roman Empire, strained to the utmost the relations between the two Empires, and when (399) Yezdegerd I succeeded to the Persian throne, the Roman Emperor sent to him the Bishop Maruta to negotiate for relief for the believers. He proved to be a skilful diplomat and, in conjunction with Isaak, who had been ordained Grand Metropolitan of Seleucia-Ctesiphon, obtained permission from the Persian king to call a Synod at Seleucia (410), to reorganize the Persian Church, so largely destroyed by persecution. At this Synod two royal officials presented Isaak as "Head of the Christians". *

Maruta had brought a letter from the bishops of the West, which, having been translated from Greek into Persian and shown to the king, was approved by him and ordered to be read before the assembled bishops. Its requirements were accepted by all. Coming as they did out of great tribulation, the Persian Christians were willing to concede much to those who promised them peace. In the account of the Synod it is said that it was held in the eleventh year of Yezdegerd the victorious Great King, after the churches of the Lord had found peace and quiet, after he had given to assemblies of Christ liberation and help to glorify Christ boldly in their bodies in life and death, after he had removed the cloud of persecution from all the churches of God and the night of oppression from all the flocks of Christ. For he had given commandment that in all his empire the temples destroyed by his ancestors should be beautifully restored, that the altars thrown down should be carefully served, that those who had been tested and tried by blows and bonds for God's sake should be set at liberty. This took place on the occasion of the election of our honourable great Father before God, Mar Isaak, Bishop of Seleucia, and head of the bishops of all the East, who before God was worthy of the grace of the rule of all the East, whose presence and government opened the door of mercy to rest and peace of the people and of the Church of God, whose humility and

* "Das Buch des Synhados"   Oscar Braun.

great honourableness was brighter than all bishops of
the East before him. . . . and through the messenger of
peace sent to the East in the mercy of God, the wise Father
and honourable Head, Mar Maruta, the bishop, who
brought about peace and unity between East and West.
He took pains to build up the churches of Christ so that the
godly laws and right true canons which were established
by our honourable fathers the bishops in the West should
be set up in the East for the edifying of the truth and of the
whole people of God. And through the care of various
bishops of the Roman lands all our churches and assemblies in the East received, though they be far from us in
body, compassionate love and gifts.

There was genuine rejoicing in deliverance from oppression, and thanksgiving to God for His great work on their
behalf; prayer also for the king that God might add days
to his days, that he might live for ever. They said that
in this glorious moment of the Synod their souls were as
though they had stood before the throne of Christ's glory;
"We forty bishops", they said, "gathered from various
parts, listened with great desire, to hear what was written in
the letter from the bishops of the West." The letter laid
down that there should not be, unnecessarily, two or three
bishops in one town, but one bishop in each town and its
district. Bishops were not to be appointed by less than
three bishops acting with the authority of the Metropolitan.
The dates of feasts were settled. All the canons of the
Council of Nicaea in the time of Constantine were read
and were signed by all present. Mar Isaak said: "Anyone
who does not agree with these praiseworthy laws and
excellent canons and does not accept them, may he be
accursed from all the people of God and may he have no
power in the Church of Christ." It is recorded further:
"All we bishops together confirmed it after him with
Amen, and we all spake as he." Then Mar Maruta said:
"All these explanations, laws, and canons, shall be written,
and at the close we will all sign them and confirm it in an
everlasting covenant." Mar Isaak said: "I subscribe at
the head of all." Then all the bishops from different
places promised after him: "We also all accept it with joy
and confirm what has been written above by our signature
at the foot." Having brought all this before the king,

Isaak and Maruta addressed the bishops again, saying: "Formerly you were in great trouble and went about in secret. But now the Great King has procured you great peace. And as Isaak went in and out before the Great King, he, according to his good pleasure, has made him Head of all Christians in the East. Especially since the day when Bishop Maruta came has the favour of the Great King brought much peace and quietness to you." The regulations were then given for the appointment of future Heads by Isaak and Maruta or their successors, with the approval of the reigning king. Further, of the Head they said: "And no one shall form a party against him. If anyone shall rise against him and contradict his will it must be told to us. We will then tell the Great King and the evil that he has done, whoever it may be, shall be judged by him." Then we left, Isaak and Maruta saying to us that all these things should be written, all that is useful for the service of the Catholic Church. This was gladly accepted, and it was agreed that anyone who set his own will against these ordinances should be utterly excluded from the Church of Christ, and his wound should never be healed, also the king should bring bitter punishment upon him.

There were many other ordinances, as, that the clergy should be celibate and not married as before; that bishops unable to be present on account of distance should be bound by what had been agreed upon; while some bishops, who from the beginning had opposed Isaak, were condemned as rebels. Meetings in private houses were forbidden, the boundaries of parishes were fixed, and only one church was to be permitted in each.

Thus were East and West united, bishops being sent to various parts to regulate all differences. Parties and divisions were to exist no more.

The death of Isaak revealed the uncertainty of such arrangements, depending, as they did, upon the will of the king. Numbers of the nobility having joined the churches, the jealousy of the magi was stirred and the king, remaining attached to his old religion, was influenced by his priests. Isaak was no longer there to mediate, and when some of the Christian priests, puffed up with the importance of their new official positions, defied the king to his face, he, impatient of contradiction, executed several of them on the spot. On the death of the king general and severe persecution ensued under his successors, Yezdegerd II and Bahram V.

A change of far-reaching consequence was meanwhile being prepared for the Syrian and Persian churches by events that were happening in the West.

Nestorius,* a preacher in Antioch, born at the foot of Mount Taurus in Syria, was appointed (428) by the Byzantine Emperor Theodosius II to the bishopric of Constantinople, where his lively eloquence and energy added to the importance of his high position. He had been influenced by the teaching of Theodore of Mopsuestia, who, opposing the growing tendency to make the Virgin Mary an object of worship, had insisted on the impropriety of giving her the title "Mother of God". Theodore's teaching had not been generally condemned, but when Nestorius taught the same, likewise running counter to the popular desire to exalt Mary, he was accused of denying the real Divinity of the Lord. The rivalry between the bishoprics of Alexandria and Constantinople, and between the schools of Alexandria and Antioch, made Cyril, bishop of Alexandria, more than willing to take advantage of the opportunity to attack Nestorius. A council was called at Ephesus. This was entirely dominated by Cyril who, without waiting for the bishops favourable to Nestorius to arrive, condemned him. Bitter quarrelling ensued, and the Emperor, for the sake of peace, though he had at first refused to confirm the decision of the Council, eventually deposed and then banished Nestorius, who passed the remainder of his life in circumstances of privation and danger, exchanging his activity and popularity in Constantinople for poverty and isolation in an oasis of the Egyptian desert.

He did not hold or teach the doctrine attributed to him, and his exclusion, though nominally on a point of doctrine, was really due to personal jealousy on the part of his episcopal colleague Cyril. A considerable number of the bishops, refusing assent to the judgement pronounced on Nestorius, were finally expelled and took refuge in Persia,

* "Nestorius and his Teachings" J. Bethune-Baker.

where they were well received, the influx of so many capable and experienced men being the means of reviving the churches and giving fresh impetus to the spreading of them into still more distant regions.   The name Nestorian was then applied to all the Eastern churches (though they did not themselves accept it, but protested against it) and they were supposed to hold the doctrine improperly attributed to Nestorius and equally unacceptable to them. They were distinct from, and opposed to, both the Byzantine and the Roman churches, and one of themselves wrote of them: "They are unjustly and injuriously called Nestorians; whereas Nestorius was never their patriarch, nor did they even understand the language in which he wrote; but when they heard how he defended the orthodox truth of two natures and two persons in one Son of God and one Christ, they gave their confirmation to his testimony because they themselves had entertained the same doctrine.   So that it may rather be said, that Nestorius followed them, than that they were led by him. "

While in exile Nestorius wrote his own account of his belief,* and the following is from "The Bazaar of Heraclides" a title concealing his name in order that the book might escape destruction.

Writing on the obedience of Christ, he says: "And therefore He took the form of a servant, a lowly form, a form that had lost the likeness of God.   He took not honour and glory, nor worship, nor yet authority, though He was Son, but the form of a servant was acting with obedience in the person of the Son, according to the mind of God; having His mind and not its own.   Nor did it do anything that it wished, but only what God the Word wished.   For this is the meaning of the 'form of God,' that the form of the servant should not have a mind or will of its own, but of Him whose the person is and the form.   Wherefore the form of God took the form of a servant, and it did not avoid aught of the lowliness of the form of a servant, but received all, that the (Divine) form might be in all; that without stint it might make it to be its own form.   For because He took this form, that He might take away the guilt of the first man and give to his nature that original image which he had lost

* "The Bazaar of Heraclides of Damascus"   J. Bethune-Baker

by his guilt, it was right that He should take that which had incurred the guilt and was held under subjection and servitude, together with all its bonds of dishonour and disgrace; since, apart from His person it had nothing divine or honourable or independent. . . . Now when a man is saved from all the causes from which disobedience arises, then truly and without doubt is he seen to be without sins. And therefore He took of the nature that had sinned, lest by taking of a nature which is incapable of sins, it should be thought that it was by nature that He could not sin, and not through His obedience. But though He had all those things that belong to our nature— anger and desire and thought—and these things also were developing as He grew gradually in age; yet they were made firm in the purpose of obedience. . . . Nor did He undertake obedience in the matter of those things in which there is a certain incentive of honour, of power, of renown, but rather in those that are poor and beggarly and contemptible and weak, and might well baulk the purpose of obedience: things which have absolutely no incentive to obedience, but rather to slackness and remissness. And He received no sort of encouragement; but from Himself alone came His desire of obedience to God and of loving what God wills. And therefore He was needy in all things. But though He was forcibly drawn by contrary things, in nothing did He decline from the mind of God; although Satan employed all these means to withdraw Him from the mind of God. And Satan sought to do this the more because he saw that He was in no wise anxious, for He was not seen at first to work any miracles, nor did He appear to have a charge to teach, but only to be in subjection and keep all the commandments. While He was consorting with all men, and surrounded on all sides by all the commandments, which showed that He had the power to disobey, in the midst of them all He behaved manfully, using nothing peculiar or different from others for His sustenance, but availing Himself of such things as were usual, like other men; that it might not be supposed that he was preserved from sin by aids of this sort, and that He could not be preserved without these things. And therefore in eating and drinking He observed all the commandments. And through fatigue and sweat He remained firm in His purpose, having His will fixed to the will of God. And there was nothing that could withdraw or separate Him therefrom; for He lived not for Himself but for Him whose own the person was; and He kept the person without stain and without scar; and by its means He gave victory to the human nature." After speaking then of Christ's baptism and temptation and telling how He was sent to preach salvation, Nestorius continues: "For God did not by means of death compass man's destruction, but brought him to a better mind and gave him helps . . ." After showing then that it was the purpose of Satan to bring man a second time, and this time utterly, to destruction, by inducing him to put Christ to death, he continues: "And He died for us erring ones; and He brought Death into the midst because it was necessary that he should be destroyed. And He did not hold back even from this, that He Himself should submit to Death; for by this He won the hope of Death's undoing . . . and it was with this same hope that He undertook obedience with immense love—not that He Himself should be cleared of guilt, but that He might pay the penalty for us, and not that He should gain the victory for Himself, but for all men. For as the guilt of Adam established all under guilt, so did His victory acquit all."

When the Eastern Churches, outside the Roman Empire, came under the stigma of "Nestorianism" and were branded as heretics, the Persian rulers saw that there was no longer any danger of their becoming allies of Constantinople or Rome, so there was given to them a liberty greater than they had ever before enjoyed. This, with the impetus given by the exiles from the West who had found a refuge among them, led to a further development of energy and zeal in preaching the Gospel among the heathen round about and beyond them. At the same time the influence was strengthened which aimed at organizing the churches under one head, so that not only were churches founded further and further afield, but bishoprics also were formed and bishops appointed to take charge of the new churches and keep them in touch with the central organization. Thus love to the Lord and compassion for the heathen carried these messengers of the Gospel to the most remote parts, accomplishing extraordinary journeys, and their word was accompanied by the saving power of the Holy Spirit, but at the same time the centralization that had developed caused the increasing departure of the centre from the teachings of Scripture to be reproduced in the new churches, introducing from the beginning an element of weakness which bore its fruit later.

So many were turned to the Lord that bishoprics were established in Merv, Herat, and Samarcand, in China, and elsewhere. Near Madras and at Kattayam in Travancore tablets have been found on which are inscriptions of the seventh or eighth century, one of which reads: "In punishment by the cross (was) the suffering of this One; He who is the true Christ, and God alone, and Guide ever pure". Churches were numerous in various parts of India; in the eighth century a certain David was appointed metropolitan of the bishoprics in China. In a list of metropolitans in the ninth century, those of India, Persia, Merv, Syria, Arabia, Herat, Samarcand, are named, and others are mentioned who, on account of being so far away from the centre, are excused from attending the quadrennial synods and instructed to send in reports every six years and not to neglect the collection for the support of the Patriarchate. These ardent missionaries reached all parts of the Continent of Asia; their bishoprics were established in Kambaluk (Pekin), Kashgar and Ceylon; they penetrated also into Tartary and Arabia. Their churches came to include the greater part of the population in Syria, Irak, and Khorasan, in some districts adjoining the Caspian, and among some of the Mongol tribes. They translated the Scriptures into several languages. There is a record from the ninth or tenth century of their having translated the New Testament into Sogdianese, an Indo-Iranian language. Near Singan-fu* a slab was found containing a long inscription in Syriac and Chinese, dating from the reign of Te Tsung (780-3). At the top is a cross and the heading "Monument commemorating the introduction and propagation of the noble law of Ta Ts'in in the Middle Kingdom". Among other things it records the coming of a missionary, Olopun,

* "Cathay and the Way Thither" Col. Sir Henry Yule Hakluyt Society.

from the Empire of Ta Ts' in in 635, bringing sacred books and images, tells how the books were translated, the doctrine approved by the imperial authority and permission given to teach it publicly.   It describes the spread of the doctrine, and how, later, Buddhism made more progress, but under Hiuan Tsung (713-755) a new missionary, Kiho, came and the Church was revived.   The mention of the images shows what declension there had been from the original purity of the Gospel and this departure prepared the way for the triumphs of Mohammedanism that were to come.   Moreover, as numbers increased so greatly the moral character and testimony of the Nestorians, or Chaldeans, degenerated.   About 845 the Chinese Emperor Wu Tsung dissolved many religious houses, both Christian and Buddhist, and compelled their numerous inmates to return to normal, secular life, special stress being laid on their rejoining the ranks of those who paid ground rent, and taking their places again in the family circles to which they belonged.   Foreigners among them were to be sent back to their native country.

As the great Mohammedan invasion swept over Persia large numbers of the Chaldean, or Nestorian, Christians were either scattered or absorbed into Islam, especially in Arabia and southern Persia.   When order was restored, however, and the Abbaside Caliphs were reigning in Bagdad, Syrian Christians became prominent at the court as doctors and as teachers of philosophy, science and literature.   In 762 the Catholikos removed from Seleucia, which was ruined, to the new capital of the conquerors, at Bagdad.   The rise of Genghis Khan and his immense conquests, leading (1258) to the capture of Bagdad by the Mongols, did not greatly affect the Syrian Church.   The heathen Mongol rulers were tolerant, and they employed Nestorians in important political negotiations with the western powers, with the object of combining with them for the destruction of Islam.   Active in these negotiations was a Chinese Nestorian, Yabh-alaha III, who rose from lowly rank to be Catholikos of the Syrian Church (1281-1317).

From the seventh century to the thirteenth the Syrian Church was as important in the East as the Roman and Greek Churches were in the West.   It covered immense territories and included very large populations.   From

Persia and Syria it had spread until it had numerous and long established missions in India and China. The majority of the peoples of Turkestan, with their rulers, had accepted Christianity, and in the chief centres of Asia the Christian church was to be found along with the heathen temple and the Mohammedan mosque.

In the neighbourhood of the hot salt-lake Issyk-kul, high among the mountains of Russian Turkestan, two cemeteries have been found.* On hundreds of the tombstones are crosses and inscriptions which show that they mark Nestorian graves. They cover the period from the middle of the thirteenth to the middle of the fourteenth century. The names of most of the Christians buried there show them to have been of Tartar race, then as now, the prevailing nationality of that country. The inscriptions are in Syriac and in Turkish. Among the many natives of the country there are also some Christians from other lands—a Chinese woman, a Mongol, an Indian, a Uigur,—showing that the believers in the different countries of Central Asia had communications with each other. There are references to the learning and gifts of some and to their devoted service among the churches, often the word "believer" is added to the name, and there are expressions of affection and of hope. Among the inscriptions are the following: "This is the grave of Pasak. The aim of life is Jesus our Redeemer"—"This is the grave of the charming maiden Julia"—"This is the grave of the priest and general, Zuma. A blessed old man, a famous Emir, the son of General Giwargis. May our Lord unite his spirit with the spirits of the fathers and saints in eternity"—"This is the grave of the church visitor Pag-Mangku, the humble believer"— "This is the grave of Shliha the celebrated commentator and teacher, who illuminated all the monasteries with light; son of Peter the august commentator of wisdom. His voice rang as high as the sound of a trumpet. May our Lord mix his pure soul with the just men and the fathers. May he participate in all heavenly joys"—"This is the grave of the priest Take who was very zealous for the church '.

* "Nestorian Missionary Enterprise" by the Rev. John Stewart, M.A., Ph.D. (T. & T. Clark, Edinburgh, 1928). A valuable work in itself, and also for the references to authorities given, including Chwolson, the translator of the inscriptions quoted.

There was great rivalry between the Nestorian missionaries and those of Islam for the favour of the Mongol khans.   In this struggle Islam was victorious and Syrian Christianity began to wane.   In the beginning of the fifteenth century, Timur, or Tamerlane, had already established his Empire, making Samarcand its centre.   Although a Mohammedan, he sacked Bagdad, and generally wrought such unparalleled devastation that great parts of Asia never recovered from it, and Christianity rapidly diminished in western Asia.

When the Franciscan and Jesuit missionaries* of the thirteenth and following centuries, in the course of their arduous travels, discovered the lost country of Cathay to be the same as newly-discovered China, they found numerous Syrian Christians there.   The Franciscan, John of Monte Corvino, a missionary who died in China about 1328, wrote: "I departed from Tauris, a city of the Persians, in the year of the Lord 1291 and proceeded to India . . . for thirteen months, and in that region baptized in different places about one hundred persons. . . . I proceeded on my journey and made my way to Cathay, the realm of the Emperor of the Tartars, who is called the Grand Cham. To him I presented a letter of our Lord the Pope, and invited him to adopt the Catholic Faith of our Lord Jesus Christ, but he had grown too old in idolatry.   However, he bestows many kindnesses upon the Christians, and these two years past I am abiding with him.   The Nestorians, a certain body who profess to bear the Christian name, but who deviate sadly from the Christian religion, have grown so powerful in these parts that they will not allow a Christian of another ritual to have ever so small a chapel, or to publish any doctrine different from their own. " The Archbishop of Soltania, writing about 1330, refers to John of Monte Corvino: "He was a man of very upright life, pleasing to God and men . . . he would have converted that whole country to the Christian Catholic faith, if the Nestorians, those false Christians and real miscreants, had not hindered him. . . . (He) was at great pains with those Nestorians to bring them under the obedience of our mother

* "Cathay and the Way Thither"   Col. Sir Henry Yule.   Hakluyt Society.

the holy church of Rome; for without this obedience, he told them, they could not be saved. And for this cause those Nestorian schismatics held him in great hate." The Nestorians were said to number more than 30,000 in Cathay and to be very rich, having handsome and devoutly ordered churches, with crosses and images in honour of God and the saints. "It is believed that if they would agree and be at one with the Minor Friars, and with other good Christians who dwell in that country, they would convert the whole country and the emperor likewise to the true faith." John of Monte Corvino himself, describing his methods of work, complains that his brethren do not write to him and is much concerned at the news that comes through from Europe—tells of a travelling doctor "who", he says, "spread abroad in these parts the most incredible blasphemies about the Court of Rome and our Order and the state of things in the West, and on this account I exceedingly desire to obtain true intelligence . . ." He begs for suitable helpers and says that he has already translated the New Testament and Psalter into the language of the country, "and have caused them", he adds, "to be written out in the finest penmanship they have; and so, by writing, reading, and preaching, I bear open and public testimony to the law of Christ."

When Robert Morrison was learning Chinese in London before going out for the London Missionary Society to his great work of translating the Bible into Chinese, he was shown and studied a Chinese manuscript that had been found in the British Museum, which contained a Harmony of the Gospels, the Book of the Acts, and the Pauline Epistles and also a Latin-Chinese Dictionary, supposed to be the work of an unknown Roman Catholic missionary of the 16th century. In the Chinese annals, after a description of the close of the Mongol and the rise of the Ming Dynasty (1368), this comment is made: ". . . a native from the Great Western Ocean came to the capital, who said that the Lord of Heaven, Ye-su, was born in Ju-tê-a which is identical with the old country of Ta Ts'in (Rome); that this country is known in the historical books to have existed since the creation of the world for the last 6000 years; that it is beyond dispute the sacred ground of history and the origin of all worldly affairs; that it should be considered as the country where the Lord of Heaven created the human race. This account looks somewhat exaggerated and should not be trusted . . . "

With the exception of a numerous and interesting body of Syrian Christians on the Malabar coast of South India, and some remnants around Urumiah, near their original home, these Persian and Syrian churches have disappeared from Asia where they were once so widely spread.

Until the end of the third century they retained a large measure of Scriptural simplicity in the ordering of their churches. Separated to some extent from the theological discussions that occupied the West, the apostolic messengers who went out from these churches threw their energies into incessant travelling, and were successful in spreading the Gospel and founding churches as far as the most remote parts of Asia. In the fourth century, when the churches in the Roman world had respite from the persecution they had suffered, those in Persia and the East entered into a time of fiery testing such as they had not hitherto experienced. This they endured, and their faith and patience prevailed. They were weakened more at this time by the federating scheme of Papa ben Aggai than by the losses they had suffered through persecution, and this prepared the way for the introduction of the Roman church system at the Synod of Seleucia at the beginning of the fifth century. The system here was necessarily modified by the fact that in the Persian Empire and in further Asia the rulers remained Pagan, and those who had seen in the union of Church and State in the time of Constantine one chief reason of the corruption of the churches in the West, might have expected better things in the East, where such a union could not take place. But the Roman organization of parishes, clergy, bishops, and metropolitans prevailed, and, abandoning the simple Scriptural order of the churches and their elders, the Syrian churches diverted their energies into the strifes and intrigues and divisions which continually took place among them, owing to the efforts of various men to obtain the influential post of bishop or catholikos. Even the important revivals which occurred at times were unable to stem their downward course seeing that they were the work of dominating persons aiming at strengthening episcopal authority rather than movements of the Spirit among the people, drawing them back through the Word to obedience to the commandments of the Lord.

The Nestorian division, by separating the Eastern Church from the Western, might have been an occasion of reviving, had it led to a return to the pattern of Scripture, but though it stimulated missionary zeal for a time, it did not shake the dominance of the clergy nor faith in the efficacy for salvation of the sacraments they administered. The churches lost much of the benefit of separation from the State when they had a Catholikos or Patriarch who could obtain the help of the secular arm in enforcing his decrees, and through whom the State could exercise an influence on them.   They were taught to look to Seleucia or to Bagdad rather than to Christ as their centre; to send their reports to them rather than bring their matters direct to Him "who walketh in the midst of the seven golden candle-sticks", to receive from them bishops for their guidance rather than count on the Holy Spirit to distribute among them the gifts needed for their edifying and for the further preaching of the Gospel.   By this channel, too, the use of images was introduced and extended, weakening the testimony of the Gospel among the heathen idol-worshippers, and destroying its power to resist the incoming tide of Mohammedanism, which overwhelmed and still holds vast territories where once there were the brightest hopes that the knowledge of Christ would prevail.

CHAPTER V

Waldenses and Albigenses

1100–1230   70–1700   1160–1318   1100–1500

Pierre de Brueys—Henri the Deacon—Sectarian names refused—The name Albigenses—Visits of brethren from the Balkans—The Perfect—Provence invaded—Inquisition established—Waldenses—Leonists—Names—Tradition in the valleys—Peter Waldo—Poor Men of Lyons—Increase of missionary activity—Francis of Assisi—Orders of Friars—Spread of the churches—Doctrine and practices of the Brethren—Waldensian valleys attacked—Beghards and Beghines.

BRETHREN from Bosnia and other Balkan countries, 1100–1230 making their way through Italy, came into the South of France, finding everywhere those who shared their faith. The teaching they brought with them found ready acceptance. The Roman clergy called them Bulgarians, Cathars, Patarenes, and other names, and, following the habit of centuries in Asia Minor and in the Balkan countries, affirmed that they were Manichaeans.

In addition to the circles to which these belonged, others were formed within the Church of Rome,* the result of spiritual movements which developed in such a way as to bring multitudes of persons, who belonged nominally to that communion, to leave the religious services to which they had been accustomed, and to gather round those who read and expounded to them the Word of God. Prominent among such teachers was Pierre de Brueys, an able and diligent preacher who for twenty years, braving all dangers, travelled throughout Dauphiny, Provence, Languedoc, and Gascony, drawing multitudes from the superstitions in which they had been brought up, back to the teachings of Scripture, until he was burned at St. Gilles (1126). He showed from Scripture that none should be baptized until they had attained to the full use of their reason; that it is useless to build churches, as God accepts sincere worship wherever offered; that crucifixes should not be venerated, but rather looked upon with horror, as representing the instrument on which our Lord suffered; that the bread and wine are not changed into the body and blood of Christ, but are symbols com-

* "Latin Christianity"   Dean Milman

memorative of His death; and that the prayers and good works of the living cannot benefit the dead.

He was joined by Henri, a monk of Cluny in deacon's orders, whose striking appearance, powerful voice, and great gift of oratory compelled attention, while his denunciation of the crying evils that abounded, his convincing expositions of Scripture, and his zeal and devotion, turned very many to repentance and faith, among them notorious sinners, who were converted and became changed in life. Priests who tried to oppose were terrified by the power of his preaching and at the sight of the multitudes that followed him. Undeterred by the violent death of his elder and admired brother and fellow-worker, he continued his testimony until Bernard of Clairvaux, at that time the most powerful man in Europe, was called to oppose him, as being the only one who could hope to do so successfully. Bernard found the churches deserted and the people wholly turned from the clergy, and although Henri was obliged to flee from his powerful opponent, all Bernard's oratory and authority could only put a temporary check on the movement, which was not dependent on any individual but was a spiritual one affecting the whole population. Henri was able to elude capture for a long time and continue his fearless work, but falling at last into the hands of the clergy he was imprisoned and either died in prison or was put to death there (1147).

In accordance with the inveterate habit of attaching some sectarian name to any who endeavoured to return to the teaching of Scripture, many were called at this time Petrobrussians, or Henricians, names which they themselves never acknowledged. Bernard of Clairvaux complained bitterly of their objection to taking the name of anyone as their founder. He said: "Inquire of them the author of their sect and they will assign none. What heresy is there, which, from among men, has not had its own heresiarch? The Manichaeans had Manes for their prince and preceptor, the Sabellians Sabellius, the Arians Arius, the Eunomians Eunomius, the Nestorians Nestorius. Thus all other pests of this stamp are known to have had each a man, as their several founders, whence they have at once derived both their origin and their name. But by what appellation or by what title will you enrol these

heretics? Truly by none. For their heresy is not derived
from man, neither through man have they received it . . ."
He then comes to the conclusion that they had received it
from demons.

The name Albigenses* does not appear until after the
Council held at Lombers near Albi about the middle
of the twelfth century. The people brought for trial
then made a confession of faith which did not differ
much from what a Roman Catholic might have made;
but as they had a conscientious objection to taking an
oath in confirmation of what they had said they were
condemned. This confession, including as it did a
declaration of belief in infant baptism, shows that those
affected by the religious movements of the time differed
among themselves in their degree of divergence from the
teachings of the dominant Church. In a time of such
spiritual unrest, all kinds of strange and fanciful ideas
took root, and both truth and error found fruitful ground.
Some persons who were examined and punished appear to
have been Mystics, and although many who were accused
of being Manichaeans had no sort of connection with them,
yet instances were found of those who held Manichaean
doctrine, and these were readily confounded with others
innocent of such teaching.

Among the people the brethren were most frequently
called "Good Men", and there is general testimony to the
fact that their manner of life was a pattern to all, and
especially that their simplicity and piety were a contrast
to the self-indulgence of the clergy.

At St. Félix de Caraman, near Toulouse, in 1167, a
conference of teachers of these churches was held at which
an elder from Constantinople took a leading part; he brought
good news of the progress of the churches in his own district
and also in Roumania, Bulgaria, and Dalmatia. In 1201
the visit of another leader, from Albania, was the occasion
of widespread revival in the South of France.

Some among the brethren devoted themselves entirely
to travelling and ministering the Word, and were called
"the Perfect," and, in accordance with the Lord's words

---

* "The Ancient Vallenses and Albigenses" G. S. Faber.
  "Facts and Documents illustrative of the History, Doctrine and Rites
of the Ancient Albigenses and Waldenses" S. R. Maitland.

in Matthew 19. 21, "If thou wilt be perfect, go and sell that thou hast, and give to the poor, and thou shalt have treasure in heaven: and come and follow Me", they possessed nothing, had no home, and literally acted upon this command. It was recognized that all are not called to such a path, and that the majority of believers, while acknowledging that they and all they have belong to Christ, should serve Him while remaining in their families and continuing in their usual occupations.

In Languedoc and Provence in the South of France, there was a civilization in advance of that in other countries. The pretensions of the Roman Church to rule had been generally opposed and set aside there. The congregations of believers who met apart from the Catholic Church were numerous and increasing. They are often called Albigenses, a name taken from Albi, a district where there were many of them, but this name was never used by them, nor of them until a later period. They had intimate connections with the brethren—whether called Waldenses, Poor Men of Lyons, Bogomils, or otherwise—in the surrounding countries, where churches spread among the various peoples. Pope Innocent III required of the Count of Toulouse, Raymond VI, who ruled in Provence, and of the other rulers and prelates in the South of France, that the heretics should be banished. This would have meant the ruin of the country. Raymond temporized, but was soon involved in a hopeless quarrel with the Pope, who in 1209 proclaimed a crusade against him and his people. Indulgences, such as had been given to the Crusaders who went at great risk to themselves to rescue the Holy Places in Palestine from the Mohammedan Saracens, were now offered to all who would take part in the easier work of destroying the most fruitful provinces of France. This, and the prospect of booty and licence of every kind attracted hundreds of thousands of men. Under the presidence of high clercial dignitaries and led by Simon de Montfort, a military leader of great ability and a man of boundless ambition and ruthless cruelty, the most beautiful and cultivated part of Europe at that time was ravaged, became for twenty years the scene of unspeakable wickedness and cruelty and was reduced to desolation. When the town of

Beziers was summoned to surrender, the Catholic inhabitants joined with the Dissenters in refusing, though warned that if the place were taken no soul should be left alive. The town was captured, and of the tens of thousands who had taken refuge there, none were spared. After the capture of another place, La Minerve, about 140 believers were found, women in one house, men in another, engaged in prayer as they awaited their doom. De Montfort had a great pile of wood prepared, and told them to be converted to the Catholic faith or mount that pile. They answered that they owned no papal or priestly authority, only that of Christ and His Word. The fire was lighted and the confessors, without hesitation, entered the flames.

It was near this spot, in the neighbourhood of Narbonne, that the Inquisition was established (1210), under the superintendence of Dominic, the founder of the Dominican order. When, at the Council of Toulouse (1229) it was made a permanent institution, the Bible, excepting only the Latin Psalter, was forbidden to the laity, and it was decreed that they might have no part of it translated into their own languages. The Inquisition finished what the crusade had left undone. Many of the brethren fled to the Balkan countries, others were scattered throughout the neighbouring lands, the civilization of Provence disappeared and the independent provinces of the south were incorporated into the kingdom of France.

In the Alpine valleys of Piedmont there had been for centuries congregations of believers calling themselves brethren, who came later to be widely known as Waldenses, or Vaudois, though they did not themselves accept the name. They traced their origin in those parts back to Apostolic times. Like many of the so-called Cathar, Paulician, and other churches, these were not 'reformed', never having degenerated from the New Testament pattern as had the Roman, Greek, and some others, but having always maintained, in varying degree, the Apostolic tradition. From the time of Constantine there had continued to be a succession of those who preached the Gospel and founded churches, uninfluenced by the relations between Church and State existing at the time. This accounts for the large bodies of Christians, well established in the

70–1700

Scriptures and free from idolatry and the other evils prevailing in the dominant, professing Church, to be found in
the Taurus Mountains and the Alpine valleys.

These latter, in the quiet seclusion of their mountains,
had remained unaffected by the development of the Roman
Church. They considered the Scriptures, both for doctrine
and church order, to be binding for their time, and not
rendered obsolete by change of circumstances.   It was
said of them that their whole manner of thought and action
was an endeavour to hold fast the character of original
Christianity.   One mark of their not being "reformers"
is to be observed in their comparative tolerance of the
Roman Catholic Church, a reformer almost inevitably
emphasizing the evil of that from which he has separated,
in order to justify his action.   In their dealings with
contemporaries who seceded from the Church of Rome, as
well as later in their negotiations with the reformers of
the Reformation, this acknowledgment of what was good
in the Church that persecuted them is repeatedly seen.

The inquisitor Reinerius, who died in 1259, has left it
on record: "Concerning the sects of ancient heretics,
observe, that there have been more than seventy: all of
which, except the sects of the Manichaeans and the Arians
and the Runcarians and the Leonists which have infected
Germany, have through the favour of God, been destroyed.
Among all these sects, which either still exist or which have
formerly existed, there is not one more pernicious to the
Church than that of the Leonists: and this for three reasons.
The first reason is; because it has been of longer continuance, for some say that it has lasted from the time of
Sylvester, others, from the time of the Apostles.   The
second reason is: because it is more general, for there is
scarcely any land, in which this sect does not exist.   The
third reason is; because, while all other sects, through the
enormity of their blasphemies against God, strike horror
into the hearers, this of the Leonists has a great semblance
of piety, inasmuch as they live justly before men, and
believe every point well respecting God together with all
the articles contained in the creed: only they blaspheme
the Roman Church and clergy, to which the multitude of
the laity are ready enough to give credence." A later
writer, Pilichdorf, also a bitter opponent, says that the

persons who claimed to have thus existed from the time of Pope Sylvester were the Waldenses.

Some have suggested that Claudius, Bishop of Turin, was the founder of the Waldenses in the mountains of Piedmont. He and they had much in common, and must have strengthened and encouraged one another, but the brethren called Waldenses were of much older origin. A Prior of St. Roch at Turin, Marco Aurelio Rorenco, was ordered in 1630 to write an account of the history and opinions of the Waldenses. He wrote that the Waldenses are so ancient as to afford no absolute certainty in regard to the precise time of their origin, but that, at all events, in the ninth and tenth centuries they were even then not a new sect. And he adds that in the ninth century so far from being a new sect, they were rather to be deemed a race of fomenters and encouragers of opinions which had preceded them. Further, he wrote that Claudius of Turin was to be reckoned among these fomenters and encouragers, inasmuch as he was a person who denied the reverence due to the holy cross, who rejected the veneration and invocation of saints, and who was a principal destroyer of images. In his commentary on the Epistle to the Galatians, Claudius plainly teaches justification by faith, and points out the error of the Church in departing from that truth.

The brethren in the valleys never lost the knowledge and consciousness of their origin and unbroken history there. When from the fourteenth century onward the valleys were invaded and the people had to negotiate with surrounding rulers, they always emphasized this. To the Princes of Savoy, who had had the longest dealings with them, they could always assert without fear of contradiction the uniformity of their faith, from father to son, through time immemorial, even from the very age of the Apostles. To Francis I of France they said, in 1544: "This Confession is that which we have received from our ancestors, even from hand to hand, according as their predecessors in all time and in every age have taught and delivered." A few years later, to the Prince of Savoy they said: "Let your Highness consider, that this religion in which we live is not merely our religion of the present day, or a religion discovered for the first time only a few years ago, as our enemies falsely pretend, but it is the religion

of our fathers and of our grandfathers, yea, of our fore-
fathers and of our predecessors still more remote. It is
the religion of the Saints and of the Martyrs, of the Confessors and of the Apostles. " When they came into contact
with the Reformers in the sixteenth century they said:
"Our ancestors have often recounted to us that we have
existed from the time of the Apostles. In all matters
nevertheless we agree with you, and thinking as you think,
from the very days of the Apostles themselves, we have
ever been consistent respecting the faith. " On the return
of the Vaudois to their valleys, their leader, Henri Arnold,
in 1689 said: "That their religion is as primitive as their
name is venerable is attested even by their adversaries, "
and then quotes Reinarius the Inquisitor who, in a report
made by him to the Pope on the subject of their faith,
admits, "they have existed from time immemorial. " "It
would not, " Arnold continues, "be difficult to prove that
this poor band of the faithful were in the valleys of Piedmont more than four centuries before the appearance of
those extraordinary personages, Luther and Calvin and
the subsequent lights of the Reformation. Neither has
their Church ever been reformed, whence arises its title of
Evangelic. The Vaudois are in fact descended from those
refugees from Italy, who, after St. Paul had there preached
the Gospel, abandoned their beautiful country and fled,
like the woman mentioned in the Apocalypse, to these wild
mountains, where they have to this day handed down the
Gospel, from father to son, in the same purity and simplicity as it was preached by St. Paul".

1160-
1318   Peter Waldo of Lyons, a successful merchant and banker,
was aroused to see his need of salvation by the sudden death
of one of the guests at a feast he had given. He became so
much interested in the Scriptures that (1160) he employed
clerks to translate parts into the Romance dialect. He had
been touched by the story of St. Alexius, of whom it was
related that he sold all that he had and went on a pilgrimage
to the Holy Land. A theologian directed Waldo to the
Lord's words in Matthew 19. 21: "If thou wilt be perfect,
go and sell that thou hast, and give to the poor, and thou
shalt have treasure in heaven: and come and follow Me. "
He therefore (1173) made over his landed property to his
wife, sold the remainder and distributed it among the poor.

For a time he devoted himself to the study of the Scriptures
and then (1180) gave himself to travelling and preaching,
taking as a guide the Lord's words: "He sent His disciples
two and two before His face into every city and place
whither He Himself would come.   Therefore said He unto
them, The harvest truly is great but the labourers are few:
pray ye therefore the Lord of the harvest, that He would
send forth labourers into His harvest.   Go your ways:
behold I send you forth as lambs among wolves.   Carry
neither purse nor scrip nor shoes: and salute no man by
the way."   Companions joined him, and, travelling and
preaching in this way, came to be known as the "Poor
Men of Lyons".   Their appeal for recognition (1179) to the
third Lateran Council, under Pope Alexander III, had already
been scornfully refused.   They were driven out of Lyons
by Imperial edict and (1184) excommunicated.   Scattered
over the surrounding countries, their preaching proved
very effectual, and "Poor Men of Lyons" became one of the
many names attached to those who followed Christ and His
teaching.

An inquisitor, David of Augsburg, says: "The sect of the
Poor Men of Lyons and similar ones are the more dangerous
the more they adorn themselves with the appearance of
piety . . . their manner of life is, to outward appearance,
humble and modest, but pride is in their hearts"; they say
they have pious men among them, but do not see, he continues,
"that we have infinitely more and better than they, and such
as do not clothe themselves in mere appearance, whereas
among the heretics all is wickedness covered by hypocrisy."
An old chronicle tells how as early as the year 1177
"disciples of Peter Waldo came from Lyons to Germany
and began to preach in Frankfurt and in Nüremberg, but
because the Council in Nüremberg was warned that they
should seize and burn them, they disappeared into
Bohemia."

The relations of Peter Waldo with the Waldenses were
so intimate that many call him the founder of a sect of
that name, though others derive the name from the Alpine
valleys, Vallenses, in which so many of those believers lived.
It is true that Waldo was highly esteemed among them,
but not possible that he should have been their founder,
since they founded their faith and practice on the Scrip-

tures and were followers of those who from the earliest times had done the same. For outsiders to give them the name of a man prominent among them was only to follow the usual habit of their opponents, who did not like to admit their right to call. themselves, as they did, "Christians" or "brethren". Peter Waldo continued his travels and eventually reached Bohemia, where he died (1217), having laboured there for years and sown much seed, the fruit of which was seen in the spiritual harvest in that country at the time of Huss and later. The accession of Peter Waldo and his band of preachers gave an extraordinary impetus to the missionary activities of the Waldenses, who until this time. had been somewhat isolated in their remote valleys, but now went everywhere preaching the Word.

Within the Roman Catholic Church there were many souls suffering under the prevailing worldliness, who desired a revival of spiritual life yet did not come out of that system and join themselves to these churches of believers which, outside of it, were endeavouring to act on the principles of Scripture. In the same year (1209) in which Pope Innocent III inaugurated the crusade against the South of France, Francis of Assisi, then 25 years old, hearing at mass one winter morning the words of Jesus from the tenth chapter of Matthew, in which He gave commands to the twelve apostles as He sent them out to preach, saw in this the way of the reformation he had desired and felt himself called to preach in utmost poverty and humility. From this sprang the order of Franciscan Friars which so quickly spread over the world. Francis was a wonderful preacher, and his sincerity and devotion and joyous nature drew multitudes to hear him. In 1210 he went to Rome with the little company of his earliest followers, and obtained from the Pope a somewhat reluctant verbal approval of their 'Rule', with permission to preach. The numbers wishing to join were soon so great that to meet the needs of those who desired to keep the Rule, and yet continue in their usual avocations, the "Third Order" was formed, the Tertiaries, who continued their secular occupations while submitting themselves to a prescribed rule of life, the pattern of which is chiefly found in the instructions of the Lord Jesus to the Apostles.

They vowed to restore ill-gotten gains, be reconciled to enemies, live in peace with all, live a life of prayer and works of charity, keep fasts and vigils, pay tithes to the church, take no oaths, nor bear arms, use no bad language, practise piety to the dead. The spirit of Francis burned for the conversion of heathen and Mohammedans, as well as for that of his own Italians, and twice he suffered almost to death in endeavouring to reach and preach to the infidels in Palestine and Morocco. In 1219 the second Chapter General of the Order was held and numerous friars were sent out to all countries, from Germany to North Africa, and later to England also. Five who went to Morocco suffered martyrdom. The Order soon grew beyond the power of Francis to control it, came under the organizing authority of men of different ideals, and, to his great grief, the Rule of Poverty was modified. After his death (1226) the division, which had begun earlier, between the strict and the lax friars, became more acute; the stricter ones, or *Spirituali*, were persecuted, four of them being burnt in Marseilles (1318), and in the same year the Pope formally declared to be heresy the teaching that Christ and His Apostles possessed nothing.

These new orders of Friars, the Dominicans and Franciscans, like the older orders of monks, arose from a sincere desire for deliverance from intolerable evils prevailing in the Church and the world, and from the soul's quest after God. While the older monastic orders were chiefly occupied with personal salvation and sanctification, the later orders of friars devoted themselves more to helping in their needs and miseries the men and women around them. Both institutions, the Monastic and the Preaching Orders, for a time exercised a widespread influence for good, yet both, being founded on the ideas of men, quickly degenerated, and became instruments of evil—active agents in opposing those who sought revival by carrying out and making known the Scriptures.

The histories of the monks and of the friars show that if a spiritual movement can be kept within the confines of the Roman Catholic Church or any similar system it is doomed, and must inevitably be dragged down to the level of that which it sought originally to reform. It purchases exemption from persecution at the cost of its life.

Francis of Assisi and Peter Waldo were both laid hold of
by the same teaching of the Lord, and yielded themselves
to Him with uttermost devotion. In each case the example
set and the teaching given gained the hearts of large numbers
and affected their whole manner of life. The likeness
turned to contrast when the one was accepted and the
other rejected by the organized religion of Rome. The
inward relation to the Lord may have remained the same,
but the working out of the two lives differed widely.
The Franciscans being absorbed into the Roman system,
helped to bind men to it, while Waldo and his band of
preachers directed multitudes of souls to the Scriptures,
where they learned to draw for themselves fresh and in-
exhaustible supplies from the "wells of salvation."

1100-
1300
In 1163 a Council of the Romish Church at Tours,*
called together by Pope Alexander III, forbade any intercourse with Waldenses because they taught "a damnable
heresy, long since sprung up in the territory of Toulouse."
Before the close of the 12th century there was a numerous
Waldensian church in Metz, which had translations of
the Bible in use. The church in Cologne had long been
in existence in 1150 when a number of its members were
executed, of whom their judge said "They went to their
death not only with patience but with enthusiasm."
In Spain in 1192 King Alfonso of Aragon issued an edict
against them and stated that in doing so he was acting
according to the example of his predecessors. They were
numerous in France, Italy, Austria, and many other
countries. In the Diocese of Passau, in 1260, they were
to be found in forty-two parishes, and a priest of Passau
wrote at that time: "In Lombardy, Provence, and elsewhere the heretics had more schools than the theologians,
and far more hearers. They disputed openly, and called
the people to solemn meetings in the Market places or in
the open fields. No one dared to hinder them, on account
of the power and number of their admirers." In Strassburg in 1212 the Dominicans had already arrested 500
persons who belonged to churches of the Waldenses.
They were of all classes, nobles, priests, rich and poor,

* "Die Reformation und die älteren Reformparteien" Dr. Ludwig
Keller.

men and women.   The prisoners said that there were many like them in Switzerland, Italy, Germany, Bohemia, etc.   Eighty of them, including 12 priests and 23 women were given over to the flames.   Their leader and elder, named John, declared as he was about to die, "We are all sinners, but it is not our faith that makes us so, nor are we guilty of the blasphemy of which we are accused without reason; but we expect the forgiveness of our sins, and that without the help of men, and not through the merit of our own works. "   The goods of those executed were divided between the Church and the civil authority, which placed its power at the disposition of the Church.   A decretal of Pope Gregory IX, in 1263, declared—"We excommunicate and anathematize all heretics, Cathars, Patarenes, Poor Men of Lyons, Passagini, Josepini, Arnaldistae, Speronistae, and others, by whatever names they may be known, having indeed different faces, but being united by their tails, and meeting in the same point through their vanity. "   The inquisitor, David of Augsburg, admitted that formerly "the sects were one sect" and that now they hold together in the presence of their enemies.   These scattered notices, taken from among many, are sufficient to show that primitive churches were widespread in Europe in the twelfth and thirteenth centuries, that in some parts they were so numerous and influential as to have a large measure of liberty, though elsewhere they were subjected to the most cruel persecution, and that, although many names were given to them, and there must have been variety of view among so many, yet they were essentially one, and had constant communication and fellowship with one another.

The doctrines and practices of these brethren, known as Waldenses, and also by other names, were of such a character that it is evident they were not the fruits of an effort to reform the Roman and Greek churches and bring them back to more Scriptural ways.   Bearing no traces of the influence of those churches, they indicate, on the contrary, the continuance of an old tradition, handed down from quite another source—the teaching of Scripture and the practice of the primitive Church.   Their existence proves that there had always been men of faith, men of spiritual power and understanding, who had maintained in the churches a tradition close to that of apostolic days, and far removed from that which the dominant Churches had developed.

Apart from the Holy Scriptures they had no special confession of faith or religion, nor any rules, and no authority of any man, however eminent, was allowed to set aside the authority of Scripture. Yet, throughout the centuries, and in all countries, they confessed the same truths and had the same practices. They valued Christ's own words, in the Gospels, as being the highest revelation, and if ever they were unable to reconcile any of His words with other portions of Scripture, while they accepted all, they acted on what seemed to them the plain meaning of the Gospels. Following Christ was their chief theme and aim, keeping His words, imitating His example. The Spirit of Christ, they said, is effective in any man in the measure in which he obeys the words of Christ and is His true follower. It is only Christ who can give the ability to understand His words. If anyone love Him he will keep His words. A few great truths were looked upon as essential to fellowship, but otherwise, in matters open to doubt or to difference of view, large liberty was allowed. They maintained that the inner testimony of the indwelling Spirit of Christ is of great importance, since the highest truths come from the heart to the mind; not that new revelation is given, but a clearer understanding of the Word. The portion of Scripture most dwelt upon was the Sermon on the Mount, this being looked upon as the rule of life for the children of God. The brethren were opposed to the shedding of blood, even to capital punishment, to any use of force in matters of faith and to taking any proceedings against such as harmed them. Yet most of them allowed self-defence, even with weapons; so the inhabitants of the valleys defended themselves and their families when attacked. They would take no oaths nor use the Name of God or of Divine things lightly, though on certain occasions they might allow themselves to be put on oath. They did not admit the claim of the great professing Church to open or close the way of salvation, nor did they believe that salvation was through any sacraments or by anything but faith in Christ, which showed itself in the activities of love. They held the doctrine of the sovereignty of God in election, together with that of man's free will. They considered that in all times and in all forms of churches there were enlightened men of God. They therefore made use of the writings of Ambrose, Augustine, Chrysostom, Bernard of Clairvaux and others, not accepting, however, all they wrote, but only that which corresponded with the older, purer teaching of Scripture. The love of theological disputation and pamphlet war was not developed among them, as among so many others; yet they were ready to die for the truth, laid great stress on the value of practical piety and desired in quietness to serve God and to do good.

In matters of church order they practised simplicity, and there was nothing among them corresponding to that which had grown up in the Church of Rome. Yet the churches and elders accepted their responsibilities with the utmost seriousness. In matters of discipline, appointment of elders, and other acts, the whole church took part, in conjunction with its elders. The Lord's Supper was in both kinds and for all believers, and was looked upon as a remembrance of the Lord's body given for them and at the same time as a strong exhortation to yield themselves to be broken and poured out for His sake. "As to baptism," writes an opponent, Pseudo-Reimer (1260), "some err, claiming that little children are not saved by baptism, for, they declare, the Lord says 'He that believeth and is baptized shall be saved', but a child does not yet believe."

They believed in Apostolic succession through the laying on of the hands of such as had it on those really called to receive this grace. They taught that the Church of Rome had lost this when Pope Sylvester accepted the union of Church and State, but that it remained among themselves. When, however, through circumstances, it was not possible of application, God could convey the needed grace without it.

Those whom they called "Apostles" played an important part in their testimony. While the elders and overseers remained in their homes and churches, the "Apostles" travelled continually, visiting the churches. A distinction was made between those called to be "Perfect," and others of the followers of Christ, based on the fact that in the Gospels some were called to sell all that they had and follow Christ, while others of His disciples were equally called to serve Him in the surroundings in which He found them. The Waldensian Apostles had no property or goods or home or family; if they had had these they left them. Their life was one of self-denial, hardship and danger. They travelled in utmost simplicity, without money, without a second suit, their needs being supplied by the believers among whom they ministered the Word. They always went two and two, an elder and a younger man, of whom the latter waited on his older companion. Their visits were highly esteemed, and they were treated with every token of respect and affection. Owing to the dangers of the times they usually travelled as business men and often the younger men carried light wares, as knives, needles, etc., for sale. They never asked for anything; indeed, many undertook serious medical studies that they might be able to care for the bodies of those they met with. The name "Friends of God" was often given to them. Great care was used in commending men to such service, since it was felt that one devoted man was worth more than a hundred whose call to this ministry was less evident.

The Apostles chose poverty, but otherwise it was considered a principal duty of each church to provide for its poor. Often, when private houses were insufficient and simple meeting rooms were built, there would be houses attached to these where their poor or aged could live and be cared for.

Regular individual reading of the Scriptures, regular daily family worship, and frequent Conferences were among the most highly-prized means of maintaining spiritual life.

These saints would take no part in government; they said the Apostles were often brought before tribunals, but it is not ever said that they sat as judges.

They valued education as well as spirituality; many who ministered the Word among them had taken a degree at one of the Universities. Pope Innocent III (1198-1216) bore a double testimony to them when he said that among the Waldenses educated laymen undertook the functions of preachers, and again, that the Waldenses would only listen to a man who had God in him.

The comparative peace of the Waldensian valleys was broken when, in 1380, Pope Clement VII sent a monk as inquisitor to deal with heretics in certain parts. In the next thirteen years about 230 persons were burnt, the goods of the sufferers being divided between the inquisitors and the rulers of the country. In the winter of 1400 the scope of the persecution was enlarged, and many families took refuge in the higher mountains, where most of the children and women and many men died of cold and hunger. In 1486 a Bull of Innocent VIII gave authority to the Archdeacon of Cremona to extirpate the heretics, and eighteen thousand men invaded the valleys. Then the peasants began to defend themselves, and, taking advantage of the mountainous nature of the country, and their knowledge of it, drove back the attacking force, but for more than a hundred years the conflict continued.

From the twelfth century there begin to be records of houses where poor and old and infirm people lived together, doing such work as they could, and helped by the gifts of wealthy benefactors. Though the members of such households took no vows, and never begged, and so the houses differed from convents, yet they were of a religious character. They were called "workhouses" and those in them called themselves "Christ's Paupers". Frequently an "Infirmary" was attached to the house, and many of the sisters devoted themselves to nursing the sick, while the brethren often held schools and taught in them. They liked to call such an institution "God's House". Later the names of Beghard and Beghine were used to describe them, the former name being given to the men's and the latter to the women's houses. From the beginning they were suspected of "heretical" tendencies, and, indeed, there is no doubt that they were constantly a refuge for brethren who, in times of persecution, lived quietly under their shelter. In course of time they came to be looked upon as always heretical institutions, and numbers of their members were put to death. In the latter part of the 14th century they were taken possession of by the Papal authorities and transferred, for the most part, to the Franciscan Tertiaries.

CHAPTER VI

Churches at the Close of the Middle Ages

1300–1500

Influence of the brethren in other circles—Marsiglio of Padua—The
Guilds—Cathedral builders—Protest of the cities and guilds—Walther
in Cologne—Thomas Aquinas and Alvarus Pelagius—Literature of the
brethren destroyed—Master Eckart—Tauler—The "Nine Rocks"—The
Friend of God from the Oberland—Renewal of persecution—Strassburg
document on persistence of the churches—Book in Tepl—Old Translation
of German New Testament—Fanaticism—Capture of Constantinople—
Invention of Printing—Discoveries—Printing Bibles—Colet, Reuchlin—
Erasmus and the Greek New Testament—Hope of peaceful Reformation—
Resistance of Rome—Staupitz discovers Luther.

THE influence of the Waldensian Apostles and the
testimony of the "brethren" affected circles far
wider than those with which they were definitely associated,
and in the first half of the fourteenth century their
teachings prevailed to an extent never known before.

In 1302 Pope Boniface VIII issued a Bull declaring that
submission to the Roman Pope was, for every human being,
necessary to his soul's salvation. From this the consequence
was deduced that there is no God-given authority in the
world apart from that which is derived from the Pope. The
Emperor, Ludwig of Bavaria, headed the protests that
such claims aroused, and the Pope placed the greater part
of the empire under an interdict.

An important factor in the conflict was the writings of
Marsiglio of Padua,* whom the Emperor protected and
trusted, in spite of the Pope's declaring him to be the worst
heretic he had ever read. Born in Padua (1270), Marsiglio
studied at the University in Paris, where he greatly distinguished himself. In 1324 he published his "Defensor
Pacis", in which he shows very clearly, according to
Scripture, the relations between the State and the Church.
He says it has become usual to apply the word Church to
the ministers of the Church, bishops, priests and deacons.
This is opposed to the Apostolic use of the word, according

* "Die Reformation und die älteren Reformparteien" Dr. Ludwig Keller,

to which the Church is the assembly, or the total of those who believe in Christ. In this sense Paul writes to the Corinthians, "Unto the church of God which is at Corinth" (1 Cor. 1. 2). It is not by an oversight, he points out, that an improper use of the word has been adopted, but on well-considered grounds, which have great value for the priesthood but destructive consequences for Christianity. It is with the help of this false assumption, and the special passages of Scripture which are misused to support it, that that hierarchical system has been built up, which now, contrary to the Holy Scriptures and the commands of Christ, takes to itself the highest judicial power, not only in spiritual but also in earthly matters, whereas the highest authority, from which bishops and priests must receive theirs, is the Christian church, and no teacher or shepherd has the right to compel obedience by force or by punishment in this world. Who then has the right to appoint bishops, pastors and ministers generally? For the Apostles, Christ was the source of authority; for their successors, the Apostles; after the death of the Apostles the right of choice went over to the congregations of the believers. The Book of the Acts gives an example in the choice of Stephen and Philip. If in the presence of the Apostles it was the church that chose, how much more must this way be observed after their death?

The Christian churches and their teachings spread most rapidly among the people of the great cities, and especially among the members of the different workmen's and trade guilds. In Italy and France the brethren were often called "Weavers", it being said as a reproach that they were mostly hand-workers and even their teachers were weavers and shoemakers. These guilds were very powerful, and had their ramifications in all countries, from Portugal to Bohemia and from England to Sicily. Each had its own elaborate organization and they were also inter-related. They had a religious as well as a technical character, and the reading of Scripture and prayer had an important place in their functions. One of the most powerful was that of the Masons, which included the many kinds of workers connected with building. We have evidence of the power and importance of this guild in the wonderful beauty, grace, and strength of the numerous cathedrals and churches, town halls and houses, which were built in the 12th, 13th, and 14th centuries, and still give to Europe an inimitable interest and charm. In the builders' huts around the cathedrals that were growing up, the Master would read the Scriptures, even in times when elsewhere the mere possession of a Bible was punishable with death. Large numbers of people who had nothing to do with building—ladies, shopkeepers, and others— became members of the guild on payment of a nominal contribution, it might be but a pot of honey or a bottle of wine. Such members were sometimes more numerous than the actual workpeople, finding in the guild a refuge from persecution, and opportunity for hearing the Word of God. The artistic value and varied beauty of most handiwork at that time was largely inspired by the spiritual passion which lay behind the patient technical skill of the worker.

The cities of the Empire and the guilds supported the Emperor Ludwig in his conflict with the Pope, and they suffered severely under the Interdict. In 1332 a number of cities addressed a letter to the Archbishop of Treves. They declared that the Emperor Ludwig of all the princes of the world lived most according to the teaching of Christ, and that in faith, as well as in modest resignation, he shone as an example to others. "We shall at all times", they said, "unto death, hold to him in firm and unchangeable fidelity, springing from faith, attachment and sincere obedience to him as our true Emperor and natural lord. No sufferings, no changes, no circumstances of any kind will ever separate us from him." They go on to illustrate the right relations between Church and State by the sun and moon, express the most painful regret that ambition of earthly honour had disturbed these relations, deny the Papal claim to be the only source of authority, and as "poor Christians" beg and pray that no further harm may be done to the Christian faith.

Strassburg and Cologne were, for centuries, chief centres of the brethren; the churches of God there were large, and influenced many beyond their own circles. A chronicle relates that in 1322 a certain Walther came to Cologne from Mainz. He was "a leader of the Brethren and a dangerous heresiarch, who for many years had remained hidden and

had involved many in his dangerous errors, he was seized
near Cologne and by court of justice given over to the fire
and burnt. He was a man full of the Devil, more able than
any other, constant in his error, clever in his answers,
corrupt in faith, and no promises, no threats, not even the
most terrible tortures could bring him to betray his fellow-
culprits, of whom there were many. This Lollard, Walther,
of Netherland origin, had little knowledge of the Latin
language, and wrote the numerous works of his false faith
in the German tongue, as he could not do it in the Roman
speech, and distrubuted them very secretly to those whom
he had deceived and led astray. As he refused all repentance and recantation, and defended his error most steadfastly, not to say obstinately, he was thrown into the fire
and left nothing but his ashes behind. "

The writings of Thomas Aquinas had proved effective
in establishing the doctrine that since all power in heaven
and on earth was given to Christ, His representative, the
Pope, had the same authority. Alvarus Pelagius, a
Spanish Franciscan, supported the same view in writings
which gained him great consideration. "The Pope", he
wrote, "seems to those who view him with the spiritual
eye, to be, not a man but a God. There are no bounds to
his authority. He can declare to be right what he will and
can take away from any their rights as he sees fit. To doubt
this universal power leads to being shut out from salvation.
The great enemies of the Church are the heretics, who will
not wear the yoke of true obedience. These are extremely
numerous in Italy and Germany, and in Provence, where
they are called Beghards and Beghines. Some call them
'Brethren', others 'the Poor in Life', others 'Apostles' ".
"The Apostles and Beghards", he continues, "have no fixed
dwelling, take nothing with them on their journeys, never
beg, and do no work. This is the worse in their case
because they were formerly builders, smiths, etc. " Another
writer (1317) says that heresy had spread so much among
the priests and monks that all Alsace was full of it.

Special efforts were made to destroy heretical literature.
In 1374 an edict was published in Strassburg condemning
all such works as well as their authors, and ordering that
all who possessed any should give them up within 14
days, that they might be burnt. Later, the Emperor

Charles IV (1369) instructed inquisitors to examine the books both of laymen and clergy, because the laity are not allowed to use books about the Holy Scripture in the German language, lest they should fall into the heresies in which the Beghards and Beghines live. This led to much destruction of such literature.

In 1307 the Vice-General of the Dominican Order in Saxony was the celebrated Master Eckart who, when at the University of Paris, had gained the reputation of being the most learned man of his day. His enlightened preaching and teaching led to the loss of his dignities, but after a period of seclusion he was found again in Strassburg, where his power as a preacher soon gathered a large following around him. Eckart's writings were made so much use of by the Beghards in Strassburg that he himself came under suspicion and moved to Cologne, where, after he had preached for some years, he was cited to appear before the Archbishop upon a charge of heresy. The matter was brought before the Pope, and Eckarts' writings were condemned and forbidden, but in spite of this his teaching continued to prevail because of his holiness of life and high character. Suso was one who found peace through him, and in Cologne he met and influenced Tauler when he was still a young man.

In the struggle between the Emperor Ludwig of Bavaria and the Pope, the well-known Dominican, Dr. Johannes Tauler, boldly took the side of the Emperor. Not only was he greatly esteemed and loved in Strassburg, where his sermons drew large numbers, but his fame as a preacher and teacher spread into other countries. When (1338), on account of the Interdict, most of the clergy left Strassburg, Tauler remained, finding in the greater need of the city greater opportunity of service. He also visited other places which were suffering in the same way as Strassburg, spending some time in Basle and in Cologne. Ten years later the plague devastated Strassburg and again Tauler stood to his post, and, with two friends, one an Augustinian and the other a Carthusian monk, served the suffering and terrified people. These three published letters, in which they justified their ministries to those who lay under the ban, arguing that, since Christ died for all, the Pope could not close the way of salvation to any because they denied his authority and were loyal to their rightful King. For this the three friends were driven from Strassburg and retiring to the neighbouring convent of which the Carthusian was Prior, from there continued to send out their writings. Afterwards Tauler lived in Cologne, preaching in the church of St. Gertrude, but was able later to return to Strassburg, where he died (1361), at seventy years of age, after a painful illness, during which he was cared for by his sister in the convent of which she was a nun.

In his own lifetime Tauler was accused of belonging to the "sects" and defended himself, taking the place of belonging to the "Friends of God." He said: "The Prince of this world has nowadays been sowing weeds among the roses, insomuch that the roses are often choked, or sorely torn by the brambles. Children, there must needs be a flight or a distinction; some sort of a separation, whether within the cloisters or without, and it does not make them into a sect, that the 'Friends of God' profess to be unlike the world's friends." When his teaching was called Beghard teaching, he replied by warning the "cold and sleepy people" whose trust was their having done all "that the Holy Church had commanded," that "when they had done all this, they would have no peace in their hearts for ever unless the uncreated, eternal Word of the Heavenly Father should inwardly renew them and really make a new creature of them. Instead of this they rock themselves in a false security and say, 'We belong to a holy order and have the holy fellowship and pray and read'. These blind people think that the precious sufferings of our Lord Jesus Christ and His costly blood may thus be played with and remain without fruit. No, children, no, it cannot be so . . . and if someone comes and warns them as to the dreadful danger in which they live and that they will die in fear, they mock him and say 'That is the way the Beghards talk'. This they do to those who cannot bear to see the miseries of their neighbours, and so point out to them the right way." He said it is the clergy, who think everything of themselves and consider their own ways as being necessarily perfection, who are the "Pharisees", and it is they who destroy the "Friends of God". The General of the Jesuits ordered (1576) that the books of Tauler should not be read, and

(1590) Pope Sixtus V placed his sermons on the Index of prohibited books. Those writings of Tauler that were considered to be especially heretical were destroyed, and what remain have been altered. On the other hand, writings have been attributed both to Eckart and to Tauler which evidently were not written by them. Owing to the circumstances of persecution that prevailed, the true authorship of many books was concealed. What we possess of Tauler's teaching shows his intimate sympathy with the brethren and the Christian churches.

The book which, under the title of "History of Tauler's Conversion" has always been attached to his sermons, has been shown not to have been written by him nor of him, but it is one which well deserves the wide circulation it has had. It recounts the conversion of a priest and eminent preacher through the counsels of a godly layman. It has connections with another book of unknown authorship called the "Nine Rocks" which had a great influence. This latter was long supposed to have been written by Suso, but his edition was taken from a copy made by the wealthy Strassburg citizen Rulman Merswin, one of Tauler's most intimate friends. Suso omits a passage which would have offended Roman Catholic susceptibilities , but was characteristic of the teaching of the brethren. It runs as follows: "I tell thee thou art right when thou prayest God to have mercy upon poor Christendom; for know that for many hundred years Christendom has never been so poor or so wicked as in these times; but I tell thee, whereas thou sayest that the wicked Jews and heathen are all lost, that is not true. I tell thee, in these days, there is a portion of the heathen and the Jews whom God preferreth greatly to many who bear the Christian name and yet live contrary to all Christian order . . . where a Jew or heathen, in any part of the world, hath a good, God-fearing mind in him, in simplicity and honesty, and in his reason and judgement knoweth no better faith than that in which he was born, but were minded and willing to cast that off if he were given to know any other faith that were more acceptable to God, and would obey God, if he ventured body and goods therefor; I tell thee, where there is a Jew or heathen thus earnest in his life, say, ought he not to be much dearer to God than the evil, false Christian men who have received baptism, and act contrary to God, knowing that they do so?" Suso also alters a passage where the persecution of the Jews is attributed to the covetousness of the Christians, and makes it the covetousness of the Jews, a change agreeable to his general readers.

Among the most interesting of the many godly people with whom Tauler was in touch was one whose name is not known, but who is called the Friend of God from the Oberland.* He is first heard of in 1340, when he was already one of those 'Apostles' hidden from the world on account of persecution, yet exercising an extraordinary influence and authority. He spoke Italian and German, visited the brethren in Italy and Hungary, and, about 1350, came to Strassburg, and two years later repeated the visit. Here he met Rulman Merswin and gave him the "Book of the Nine Rocks" to copy. In 1356, after an earthquake in Basle, he wrote a Letter to Christendom, commending the following of Christ as the only remedy for all evils. After this he and some companions established themselves in a remote place in the mountains, and from there corresponded with the brethren in various parts. The Friend of God from the Oberland had been a man in a good position, but when he decided to forsake the world he gave up all his possessions. He did not at once distribute all his money, but for a time used it as borrowed from God, and gradually applied it all to godly purposes. He remained unmarried. Writing to a "House of God" founded by Rulman Merswin near Strassburg, he describes the little settlement in the mountains as one of "simple, good, modest Christian brethren", and says they were all persuaded that God was about to do something that was as yet hidden, and that until it was revealed they were to remain where they were, but then they would have to separate to the ends of Christendom. He asks their prayers, for, he says, "the Friends of God are somewhat in distress". Writing of being dead to the world, he explains: "Our meaning is, not that a man should go out of the world and become a monk, our meaning is that he should stay in the world, but that he should not consume his heart and feelings on friends and earthly honours. Acknowledging

---

* "Nicolaus von Basel Leben und Ausgewählte Schriften"   Dr. Karl Schmidt. (Wien 1866).

that when he was in that way of life he sought his own
things and his own honour more than God's, let him give
up this worldly honour and seek God's honour in all his
doings, as God Himself has so often counselled him; then
I am sure, God in His Divine wisdom will enlighten him,
and with this wisdom he will know better in an hour how
to give good counsel than formerly in a year." Consulted
by Merswin as to the use of his money, he said: "Would it
not be better to help the poor than to build a convent?"
In 1380 thirteen of the Friends of God met in the hidden
place in the mountains. Among them was a brother from
Milan and one from Genoa, a merchant who had given up
all his wealth for Christ's sake, also two from Hungary.
After long-continued prayer they took the Lord's Supper
together. Then they began to consult as to what was best
to be done in the circumstances of renewed persecution that
had come upon the believers, and afterwards they sent out
their recommendations to the secret Friends in different
lands; such as Merswin in Strassburg, and others. Eventually they dispersed, going their different ways, and, as far
as they can be traced, suffered death for their testimony.

The death of the Emperor Ludwig* and the election of
Charles IV (1348) brought about a disastrous change in the
circumstances of the Christian congregations. The new
Emperor was entirely under the influence of the Pope and
his party, and advantage of this was taken to make a more
determined effort than before to crush all dissent. During
the former half of the 14th century the churches of believers
had increased abundantly and the influence of their teaching
had profoundly affected many people who did not formally
attach themselves to them; but from the middle of that
century fiery trial tested them. Inquisitors were sent in
increasing numbers into the Empire, and the Emperor gave
them all the power the Popes desired. The greater part of
Europe became the scene of the cruel execution of many of
its best citizens. Records of burnings abound. In 1391,
400 persons were brought before the courts in Pomerania
and Brandenburg accused of heresy; in 1393, 280 were
imprisoned in Augsburg; in 1395, about 1000 persons were

* "Die Reformation und die älteren Reformparteien"   Dr. Ludwig
Keller.

"converted" to the Catholic faith in Thuringia, Bohemia, and Moravia; the same year 36 were burnt in Mainz; in 1397, in Steier, about 100 men and women were burnt; two years later 6 women and one man were burnt in Nüremberg. The Swiss cities suffered similar atrocities. During this time Pope Boniface IX issued an edict ordering that all suitable means should be used to destroy the plague of heretical wickedness. He quotes from a report in which those whom he calls his "beloved sons the inquisitors" in Germany, describe the Beghards, Lollards and Schwestrionen, who call themselves "the Poor" and "Brethren" and say that for more than 100 years this heresy has been forbidden under the same forms, and that in different towns several of this obstinate sect have been burnt almost every year. In 1395 an inquisitor, Peter Pilichdorf, boasted that it had been possible to master these heretics. Bohemia and England were places of refuge for many who fled to them, the teaching of Wycliff in England and of Jerome and Huss in Bohemia having powerfully influenced those countries.

A document of the year 1404, preserved in Strassburg, though written by an adversary, contains a quotation from one of the brethren, who says: "for 200 years our fellowship has enjoyed good times and the brethren became so numerous that in their councils 700 and more persons were present. God did great things for the fellowship. Then severe persecution broke over the servants of Christ, they were driven from land to land, and to the present time this cruelty continues. But, since the Church of Christ was founded, the true Christians have never been so far reduced that in the world, or at least in some countries, some of the saints have not been found. Also our brethren, on account of persecution, have at times crossed the sea, and in a certain district have found brethren, but because they did not understand the language of the country, intercourse with them was difficult and they have returned. The face of the Church changes like the phases of the moon. Often the Church blossoms on account of the number of the saints and is strong on this earth, and again she seems to fall and to pass away entirely. But if she disappears in one place we know that she is to be seen in other lands, even if the saints are only few who lead a good life and remain in the holy fellowship. And we believe that the Church will be raised up again in greater numbers and strength. The founder of our covenant is Christ and the Head of our Church is Jesus the Son of God." The same document accuses the brethren of destroying the unity of the Church by teaching that a man who lives virtuously will yet only obtain salvation by his faith; blames them that they condemn such men as Augustine and Jerome; also that they have no written prayers, but that an elder among them will begin to pray and continue for a longer or shorter time as it may seem suitable to him; also that they have the Holy Scriptures in their mother tongue in their memories and repeat it in this language in their meetings. It is further stated in this document that the brethren confessed seven points of the Holy Christian faith: (1) the Triune God; (2) that this God is the Creator of all things, visible and invisible; (3) that He gave the Law of Moses; (4) that He let His Son become man; (5) that He has chosen for Himself a spotless Church; (6) that there is a resurrection; (7) that He will come to judge the living and the dead.

These seven points reappear, but in German instead of Latin (they are in Latin in the Strassburg document) in a well-worn 14th century book found in the abbey at Tepl, near the mountainous district of the Böhmerwald, so long a refuge of persecuted brethren. This is a production of the brethren themselves, and was evidently used by one or more of them. Passages of Scripture for reading on Sundays and some other days are arranged, from which it is evident that the Roman Catholic feasts, with few exceptions, were not observed. The importance of regular reading of the Scriptures is pointed out, and also that each father of a family should be a priest in his own household. The chief part of the book, however, consists of a German translation of the New Testament. This translation differs considerably from the Vulgate, used by the Roman Church, and resembles the German translations in use from the introduction of printing to the making of Luther's translation, which latter shows many signs of its influence, as does still more a later translation again, used for about a century by those then called Anabaptists and Mennonites.

The troubles of the times in which these people lived, and the persecutions suffered, led to no little fanaticism. Some, calling themselves brethren and sisters of the Free

Spirit, acted on the assumption that their own feelings were the leadings of the Holy Spirit, and gave themselves over to outrageous folly and sin. Some good people carried ascetic practices to extremes, and some, driven into isolation by persecution, became narrow in outlook and developed views on equality which made them suspicious of learning and disposed to consider ignorance as a virtue.

About the middle of the 15th century a series of events began which transformed Europe.

The capture of Constantinople by the Turks (1453) caused the flight of learned Greeks to the West. These carried with them priceless manuscripts containing the old Greek literature, long forgotten in the darkened West. Soon Greek Professors were teaching in the Universities of Italy the language which gave the key to these treasures of knowledge, and from there to Oxford the study of Greek spread rapidly. From this arose such a reviving of literature as deserved the name given to it of the *Renaissance*, New Birth, or New Learning, but the restoration and publication of the text of the Greek New Testament had more powerful results than were produced by the recovery of any other of the restored literature.

At the same time the invention of printing provided the means by which the new knowledge could be disseminated, and it was in printing the Bible that the first printing presses were chiefly occupied.

The discovery of America by Columbus, and the discovery of the Solar System by Copernicus, also gave great enlargement to men's minds and activities.

The study of the New Testament in countless circles showed the absolute contrast between Christ and His teaching on the one hand, and an utterly corrupt Christendom on the other. By the end of the 15th century 98 complete editions of the Latin Bible had been printed, and much larger numbers of Portions. The Archbishop of Mainz renewed the edicts forbidding the use of German Bibles, but in about 12 years 14 editions of the German Bible had been printed, 4 editions of the Dutch Bible, and large numbers of Portions. These were all taken from the same text as the Testament found in the abbey at Tepl.

Among the students of Greek in Florence was John

Colet, who afterwards lectured on the New Testament in Oxford; he seemed to his hearers like one inspired, as, discarding accepted religion, he revealed Christ to the students, and expounded the Epistles of Paul. Reuchlin, a Jew, did equally valuable work in reviving the study of the Hebrew language in Germany.

In all the groups of distinguished scholars and printers forming over Europe, Erasmus* became the best known scholar. He was born in Rotterdam and his early life, as an orphan, was a constant struggle against poverty, but his exceptional abilities could not be hidden and he came to be admired, not only in learned circles, but also in all the Courts, from London to Rome. His greatest work was the publication of the Greek Testament, with a new Latin translation, accompanied by many notes and paraphrases. Edition after edition was called for. In France alone 100,000 copies were sold in a short time. People were able to read the very words that had brought salvation into the world; Christ and the Apostles became known to them, and they saw that the religious tyranny and wickedness that had so long oppressed them had no resemblance to the revelation of God given in Christ. As in his notes Erasmus contrasted the teaching of the Scriptures with the practices of the Roman Church, indignation against the clergy became vocal. Sarcasms were freely published which expressed in unmeasured terms the contempt in which they were held. Erasmus, writing of the mendicant friars, says: "Those wretches in the disguise of poverty are the tyrants of the Christian world;" of bishops, they "destroy the Gospel . . . make laws at their will, tyrannize over the laity, and measure right and wrong with rules constructed by themselves . . . who sit, not in the seat of the Gospel, but in the seat of Caiaphas and Simon Magus, prelates of evil"; of priests, he wrote: "There are priests now in vast numbers, enormous herds of them, seculars and regulars, and it is notorious that very few of them are chaste"; of the Pope: "I saw with my own eyes Pope Julius II . . . marching at the head of a triumphal procession as if he were Pompey or Caesar. St. Peter subdued the world with faith, not with arms or soldiers or military engines; St. Peter's successors would win as many victories as St. Peter won

* "Life and Letters of Erasmus" J. A. Froude.

if they had Peter's spirit"; of the singing of choristers in the churches: "Modern church music is so constructed that the congregation cannot hear one distinct word. . . . A set of creatures who ought to be lamenting their sins, fancy they can please God by gurgling in their throats".

In introducing his Greek New Testament Erasmus writes of Christ and the Scriptures: "Were we to have seen Him with our eyes, we should not have so intimate a knowledge as they give us of Christ, speaking, healing, dying, rising again, as it were, in our very presence." "If the footprints of Christ are shown us in any place, we kneel down and adore them. Why do we not rather venerate the living and breathing picture of Him in these books?" "I wish that even the weakest woman might read the Gospels and the Epistles of St. Paul. I wish that they were translated into all languages, so as to be read and understood, not only by Scots and Irishmen, but even by Saracens and Turks. But the first step to their being read is to make them intelligible to the reader. I long for the day when the husbandman shall sing portions of them to himself as he follows the plough, when the weaver shall hum them to the time of his shuttle, when the traveller shall while away with their stories the weariness of his journey."

Erasmus was one of many who hoped for a peaceful reformation of Christendom. Conditions seemed favourable. The sanguinary Pope Julius had been succeeded by Leo X of the famous Medici family, irreligious, but devoted to art and literature, who gave his approbation to the Greek New Testament of Erasmus. Francis I, King of France, had resisted all Europe rather than yield the liberties of France to Pope Julian. Henry VIII of England was enthusiastically in favour of reform, and had surrounded himself with the best and most able men of the same mind, Colet, Sir Thomas More, Archbishop Warham, Dr. Fisher. The other rulers of Europe, in the Empire and in Spain, were favourable. But great institutions are not easily changed. They resent criticism and resist reform. There was never any real prospect that the Roman Court would be brought into line with the teaching and example of Christ.

Some new and powerful agency was needed to bring about reform, and this was being quietly prepared in the very midst of the monkish circles. The discovery was made by one considered as a leader of the movement of reform, Johann von Staupitz. He was Vicar General of the Augustinians, and (1505) on a journey of inspection of the houses of this Order, found in Erfurt a young monk, Martin Luther, deeply exercised as to his soul's salvation. Staupitz won his confidence, being genuinely concerned to help him, and advised him to study the Holy Scriptures and also to read Augustine and the writings of Tauler and the Mystics. As he followed this counsel the Light broke in upon him and the doctrine of justification by faith became the experience of his soul.

CHAPTER VII

Lollards, Hussites, The United Brethren
1350-1670

Wycliff—Peasant Revolt—Persecution in England—Sawtre, Badley, Cobham—Reading the Bible forbidden—Congregations—Huss—Žižka — Tabor — Hussite wars — Utraquists —Jakoubek — Nikolaus — Cheltschizki—The Net of Faith—Rokycana, Gregor, Kunwald—Reichenau, Lhota—United Brethren—Lukas of Prague—News of German Reformation reaches Bohemia—John Augusta—Smalkald war—Persecution and emigration—George Israel and Poland—Return of brethren to Bohemia—Bohemian Charter—Battle of the White Mountain—Comenius.

SIMILAR conditions to those which on the Continent led many to see the wrong of the practices of the prevailing Church, and, further, to question the doctrines which gave rise to them, operated also in England, where the derisive name of *Lollard** (babbler) was given to many earnest people who spoke of a better way. Political and economic wrongs were mixed with religious questions, specially in the earlier days of the movement, and it was the wealth and corruption of the clergy which were first attacked, but as time went on it was seen that doctrine was at the root of practice, and the former came to be the centre of conflict. It had not been the habit in England to persecute what was deemed heresy so violently as on the Continent, but early in the reign of Henry IV, at the beginning of the 15th century, the progress of Lollardry was such that the sovereign, in order to please the clerical party, introduced death by burning as its punishment.

John Wycliff, the most eminent scholar in Oxford, became prominent in this conflict. His attacks on the corrupt practices of the Church drew him at first into the political struggle then so fiercely raging; but those who thought to use him as an important ally for their own purposes, fell from him as they came to see the consequences of the principles he taught, and he became the leader of those who sought deliverance in a return to

---

* "Foxe's Book of Martyrs"
"A Short History of the English People" John Richard Green.
"England in the Age of Wycliffe" George Macaulay Trevelyan.

Scripture and in the following of Christ. In his treatise, "The Kingdom of God" and in other writings, he shows that "the Gospel of Jesus Christ is the only source of true religion," and that "the Scripture alone is truth". The doctrine he called "Dominion" established the fact of the personal relation and direct responsibility of each man to God. All authority, he taught, is from God, and all who exercise authority are responsible to God for the use of what He has committed to them. Such doctrine, directly denying the prevailing ideas as to the irresponsible authority of Popes and Kings, and the necessity for the mediatory powers of the priesthood, aroused violent opposition, which was intensified when in 1381 Wycliff published his denial of the doctrine of Transubstantiation, thus striking at the root of that supposed miraculous power of the priests which had so long enabled them to dominate Christendom. Here his political supporters, and even his own University, forsook him. But his most important work was that which gave the people of England access to the source of true doctrine. His translation of the Bible wrought a revolution in English thought and the English Bible has proved one of the most effectual powers for righteousness that the world has known. Writing and circulating popular tracts and organizing bands of travelling preachers, Wycliff found to be the most effective means of spreading the teachings of Scripture. So great was his influence that all the power of his bitter enemies could not accomplish more than to drive him from Oxford to his retreat in Lutterworth, which became a centre from which instruction and encouragement went out over the country.

Among the scholastics in Wycliff's[*] day the teachings of the Fathers, decisions of Councils and decrees of Popes, were considered, together with the Scriptures, as constituting authority in matters of religion, the last not holding a higher position than the others. Gradually, as he grew intimately acquainted with the Scriptures, Wycliff came to acknowledge their exclusive authority and to value the others only in so far as they were in agreement with the Scriptures. He saw a double source of Christian knowledge, reason and revelation, and found that these are

[*] "John Wycliff and his English Precursors" Lechler translated by Lorimer.

not opposed to each other, but that reason, or natural light, has been weakened by the Fall, and therefore labours under a degree of imperfection, which God in His grace heals by imparting revealed knowledge through the Scriptures, and these, therefore, come to be apprehended as the exclusive authority. The unconditional, binding authority of the Holy Scripture was the great truth to which Wycliff bore witness and which was attacked by his opponents, both sides recognizing how far-reaching were the consequences involved. This he expounded in his book, "Of the Truth of Holy Scripture" (1378), in which he taught that the Bible is the Word of God or Will and Testament of the Father; God and His Word are one. Christ is the Author of Holy Scripture, which is His law, He Himself is in the Scriptures, to be ignorant of them is to be ignorant of Him. More detail would have made the Scriptures inapplicable to some circumstances, but being what they are, the Scriptures are applicable to all, and nothing impossible of observance is enjoined in them. The effects of Scripture show its Divine source and authority; the experience of the Church at large speaks for the sufficiency and efficacy of the Bible. By the observance of the pure law of Christ, without mixture of human tradition, the Church very rapidly grew, but since the admission of tradition into it the Church has steadily declined. Other forms of wisdom vanish away; the wisdom imparted by the Holy Spirit to the Apostles at Pentecost remains. Scripture is infallible; other teachers, even one so great as Augustine, are liable to lead into error. To place above Scripture and prefer to it, human traditions, doctrines, and ordinances, is nothing but an act of blind presumption. It is no justification of a doctrine that it contains, in a collateral way, much that is good and reasonable, for so is it even now with the behests and the whole life of the Devil himself, otherwise God would not suffer him to exercise such power. The history of the Church shows that departure from evangelical law and mixture of later tradition was at first slight and almost imperceptible, but as time went on the corruption grew ever ranker. As to the interpretation of Scripture, the theological doctors cannot have the power of interpretation for us, but the Holy Spirit teaches us the meaning of Scripture, as Christ opened the Scriptures to the Apostles. It would be dangerous for anyone to assume that he had the right meaning of Scripture by illumination of the Holy Spirit, but it is only by His enlightening that anyone can understand the Scriptures. No one can understand who is not enlightened by Christ. A devout, virtuous, and humble spirit is necessary. Scripture is to be interpreted by Scripture, so that the general tenor may be ascertained; tearing the Scriptures in pieces, as heretics do, is to be avoided. First its primary and literal sense is to be taken, and then its further and figurative meanings. It is important to use right words; Paul was careful in the use of prepositions and adverbs. Christ is true man and true God, existing from all eternity, at His incarnation He united both natures in His one Person. His grandeur is incomparable as the only Mediator between God and men, the Centre of humanity, our one, only Head. The personal application of the salvation wrought by Christ is by conversion and sanctification; conversion is a turning away from sin and a believing appropriation of the saving grace of Christ, that is, repentance and faith. Repentance is necessary and must be fruitful. Wycliff puts faith and sanctification together, and does not see faith apart from works. He viewed the Church not as the visible Catholic Church, or organized community of the hierarchy, but as Christ's Body and Bride, consisting of the whole number of the elect, having, in the visible world, only its temporary manifestation and pilgrimage; its home, origin, and end being in the invisible world, in Eternity. Salvation, he said, is not dependent on connection with the official Church or the mediation of the clergy. There is free, immediate access of all believers to the grace of God in Christ, and every believer is a priest. The ground of the Church, Wycliff taught, was the Divine election, and a man cannot have assurance of his own standing in grace, only an opinion, but a godly life is the evidence.

Summoned to appear before the Pope, he refused and said, "Christ during His life upon earth was of all men the poorest, casting from Him all worldly authority. I deduce from these premises, as a simple counsel of my own, that the Pope should surrender all temporal authority to the civil power and advise his clergy to do the same."

He died quietly in Lutterworth on the last day of the year 1384.

The Peasant Revolt (1377-1381), which took place in the last years of Wycliff's life, hindered the religious revival at the time by uniting against it the nobility and clergy, who laid on those they called Wycliffites the blame for the excesses and losses of the insurrection. Although this was unjust, yet there is an undeniable and intimate connection between true Christianity and the deliverance of the oppressed. Christ declared at the outset of His ministry that He was sent "to preach the gospel to the poor . . . to heal the broken-hearted, to preach deliverance to the captives, and recovering of sight to the blind, to set at liberty them that are bruised" (Luke 4. 18). This fitly described the workers on the land at this time, and the coming among them of the Scriptures helped to awaken in them the sense that "God is no respecter of persons" (Acts 10. 34), and that their enslavement under their luxurious rulers was irreligious because it was unjust. Wycliff's scholarly sermons, coming from the stately surroundings of Oxford, appealed to them less than the rough rhymes and open-air preaching of John Ball, one of themselves, crying out from amidst the misery in which they lived—"By what right are they whom we call lords greater folk than we? On what grounds have they deserved it? Why do they hold us in serfage? If we all came of the same father and mother, of Adam and Eve, how can they say or prove that they are better than we, if it be not that they make us gain for them by our toil what they spend in their pride?" His rhyme went everywhere—"When Adam delved and Eve span, Who was then the gentleman?" The revolt was crushed and iniquitous laws enacted to keep down the labourers on the land, but by slow and painful stages their liberties were gained, and the most potent influence in bringing this about was the effect of the Scriptures on the consciences of men.

The translation of the Bible had its due effect, and great numbers of the people came to acknowledge it as the only guide for faith and conduct. Various views prevailed as to different points, but there was general agreement as to the authority of Scripture, and the ruling Church was denounced as apostate and idolatrous. It was said that two men could not be found together and one not be a Lollard or a Wycliffite, and that Scripture had "become a vulgar thing, and more open to lay folk and women that know how to read than it is wont to be to clerks themselves."

The first to suffer at the stake after the law was enacted for burning heretics was William Sawtre (1401), a Norfolk rector. The House of Commons presented petitions to Henry IV praying for the diversion of the surplus revenues of the Church to useful purposes, and the modification of the laws against Lollards. His answer was to sign a warrant for burning Thomas Badly, a tailor of Evesham. This man, accused of denying transubstantiation, after giving a courageous defence of his belief before the Bishop of Worcester, was tried in St. Paul's Church before the Archbishops of Canterbury and York and many of the clergy and nobility, and was burnt at Smithfield.

A leader among the Lollards was Sir John Oldcastle, Lord Cobham, a distinguished soldier. His castle of Cowling was a refuge for the travelling preachers, and meetings were held there, in spite of their being forbidden under severe penalties. Henry IV did not venture to interfere with him, but as soon as Henry V came to the throne he besieged and captured the castle and took its owner prisoner. He escaped from the Tower, however, and was able for some years to elude pursuit, though many others were taken and executed, including thirty-nine of the Lollard leaders. When Sir John was finally captured in Wales he was burnt, the first English nobleman to die for the faith.

After his death a law was passed that whoever read the Scriptures in English should forfeit land, chattels, goods and life, and be condemned as a heretic to God, an enemy to the crown, and a traitor to the kingdom; that he should not have any benefit of sanctuary; and that, if he continued obstinate, or relapsed after being pardoned, he should first be hanged for treason against the king, and then burned for heresy against God.

Yet the brethren, though driven into obscurity or exile, were not extinguished, and some congregations, even, continued to exist. They were most numerous in East Anglia and in London. Large churches were to be found in the neighbourhood of Beccles at the time of the accession of Henry VI (1422). Though the congregations were often broken up and re-formed, yet some were in continuous existence over considerable periods; some, for instance, in Buckinghamshire, for 60 or 70 years, which maintained fellowship with those in Norfolk and Suffolk and with others in other parts of the country. The Bishop of London, writing to Erasmus in 1523, said: "It is no question of some pernicious novelty, it is only that new arms are being added to the great band of Wycliffite heretics."

One of the foreign students who listened to Wycliff in Oxford was Jerome of Prague.* He returned to his own city full of zeal for the truths he had learned in England, and taught boldly that the Roman Church had fallen away from the doctrine of Christ and that every one who sought salvation must come back to the teachings of the Gospel. Among many on whose hearts such words fell with power was Jan Hus (John Huss)†, theological doctor and preacher in Prague, and confessor to the Queen of Bohemia. His sincere faith and striking abilities, with his eloquence and charm of manner, wrought mightily among people already prepared by the labours of the Waldenses who had been before him. He wrote and spoke in the Czech language, and the long rivalry between Teuton and Slav, represented in Bohemia by the Germans and the Czechs respectively, soon gave a political aspect to the movement, the German element supporting the Romish power, and the Czech the teachings of Wycliff. The Pope, through the Archbishop of Prague, excommunicated Huss and had Wycliff's writings publicly burned, but the king of Bohemia, the nobility, the University, and the majority of the people supported Huss and his teaching. At Constance, on the beautiful lake of that name, a Council was opened (1414),‡ which lasted for

* "The Dawn of the Reformation the Age of Hus" H. B. Workman M.A.

† "John Huss and his Followers" Jan Herben (1926).

‡ Ulrich von Richental. "Chronik des Konzils zu Konstanz" 1414-1418. Herausgegeben von Dr. Otto H. Brandt. R. Voigtländers Verlag in Leipzig mit 18 Nachbildungen nach der Aulendorfer Handschrift. (Voigtländers Quellenbücher Bd. 48).

three and a half years and drew together an extraordinary assemblage of ecclesiastical dignitaries and of the princes and rulers of the various states, besides a vast throng of people of all kinds. During this time the city was the scene of elaborate entertainments and of unabashed wickedness. There were then three rival Popes, and one object of the Council was to remedy the confusion and schisms which such a state of things implied. The three reigning Popes were dethroned and another chosen in their place, Martin V.

Another object of the Council was to combat the teachings associated with the names of Wycliff and Huss. Huss was invited to be present and the Emperor Sigismund gave him a safe conduct, assuring him of security from molestation if he would come. Relying on the Emperor's word, he came to Constance in time for the opening of the General Council, willing to use the opportunity of expounding the doctrines of Scripture before such a company. But, in spite of the Imperial promise, he was seized and cast into a foul dungeon on an island in the lake. To justify this action the Council promulgated a solemn decree (1415), claimed as a decision given by the Holy Spirit and infallible, for ever binding, that the Church is not bound to keep faith with a heretic. Huss was subjected to every kind of persuasion and ill-treatment to induce him to retract what he had taught, namely that salvation is by grace, through faith, and apart from the works of the law, and that no title or position, however exalted, can make a man acceptable to God without godliness of life. With humility and a rare courage and ability, he steadfastly maintained that he was ready to retract anything he had taught provided it could be shown from Holy Scripture that he was wrong, but that he would withdraw nothing that he saw to be taught in the Word of God. Also he refused to retract opinions which he had never held, but which had been falsely attributed to him. The accusation of being "infected with the leprosy of the Waldenses" and of having preached Wycliffite doctrines shows that the unity of the truth held in these various circles was recognized by their enemies. After a solemn service of degradation Huss was burned. A fortnight before, he had written: "I am greatly consoled by that saying of Christ, 'Blessed are ye when men shall hate you' . . . a good, nay the best of greetings, but difficult, I do not say to understand, but to live up to, for it bids us rejoice in these tribulations. . . . It is easy to read it aloud and expound it, but difficult to live out. Even that bravest Soldier, though He knew that He should rise again on the third day, after supper was depressed in spirit. . . . On this account the soldiers of Christ, looking to their leader, the King of Glory, have had a great fight. They have passed through fire and water, yet have not perished, but have received the crown of life, that glorious crown which the Lord, I firmly believe, will grant to me—to you also, earnest defenders of the truth, and to all who steadfastly love the Lord Jesus. . . . O most Holy Christ, draw me, weak as I am, after Thyself, for if Thou dost not draw us we cannot follow Thee. Strengthen my spirit, that it may be willing. If the flesh is weak, let Thy grace prevent us; come between and follow, for without Thee we cannot go for Thy sake to a cruel death. Give me a fearless heart, a right faith, a firm hope, a perfect love, that for Thy sake I may lay down my life with patience and joy. Amen. Written in prison, in chains, on the eve of St. John the Baptist. "

Jerome of Prague soon followed the same fiery way, and the course of Hussite Bohemia was divided into three principal streams; those who fought; those who endeavoured to compromise, called Utraquists or Calixtines; and those who elected to suffer.

The first, under the leadership of Jan Žižka carried on a vigorous and successful warfare. The little town of Tabor, on a steep hill in the heart of Bohemia, was a military and spiritual centre. In its market place may still be seen remains of the stone tables where tens of thousands of people met to celebrate the Lord's Supper, taking both the bread and the wine, which latter had been reserved by the Church of Rome for the use of her clergy only, and refused to the laity. The cup became the symbol of the Taborites. At the foot of Tabor hill is a pool, still called Jordan, where great numbers were baptized on the confession of their faith. Žižka led not only the nobility but the nation. The free peasantry were affected by the common spirit of irresistible enthusiasm. Their agricultural implements were turned into formidable weapons, and Žižka taught them to use their farm wagons both for transport and as movable entrenchments. The Pope raised crusades against them, but the invading armies were utterly routed and the Hussites penetrated and devastated all the surrounding countries, great excesses being committed on both sides. The Church was forced to make terms with the Hussites, and at the Council of Basle (1433) acknowledged their right to free preaching of the Word of God, to taking the Lord's Supper in both kinds, to abolishing the worldly possessions of the clergy, and to the rescinding of many oppressive laws. Yet wars continued, the country was exhausted and demoralized by its efforts, laws which enslaved the peasantry weakened the power of the nation, and (1434) at the battle of Lipan the Taborites were defeated. An agreement, the "Compacts of Basle", was made which divided the Bohemians. The Utraquists being the most favourable to the Roman Catholic Church, were acknowledged by the Pope as the National Church of Bohemia, the privilege of the use of the Cup was granted them, their leader, Rokycana, was made archbishop, and everything passed back again into the hands of Rome.

While these conflicts were going on, and while the Hussite successes were at their height, there were always some who, in matters of faith and testimony, did not rely on material force, but as they had learned from the Waldensian preachers earlier, continued to seek and find guidance in the Scriptures as to their church order and Gospel witness, to follow Christ in their willingness to suffer wrong and in putting their trust in God.

Prominent among these was Jakoubek,* a colleague of Huss at the Prague University, who, as early as 1410, lecturing there, had contrasted the false, antichristian Church of Rome, with the true Church or communion of the saints, and exhorted all Christians to return to the primitive Church. Also Nikolaus, a German, who had been expelled from Dresden for heresy, and who was well acquainted with the Scriptures and with Church history, influenced the Taborites as he showed them what had been the teaching of the Apostles and the order of the early

*"Jahrbücher für Kultur und Geschichte der Slaven" N. F. Band v. Heft 1, 1929. E. Perfeckij.

Church and how errors had gradually crept in. The question of the right of Christians to use the sword was much discussed in Prague. The Taborites considered that even though its use must do harm, yet the unavoidable necessity of defence obliged it. Under the force of circumstances it might also be right to attack and despoil the enemy. Before long Jakoubek found himself in direct opposition to the Taborites on this point. The most influential and able opponent of the use of war, even for defence, was Peter Cheltschizki, who, though in many ways in sympathy with the Taborites, was untiring in opposing them and Žižka in their appeal to arms.

Although the writings of the brethren were frequently burned with their authors, some escaped, among them a book by Peter Cheltschizki, entitled *"The Net of Faith"** written in 1440, which preserves much of their teaching and exercised a great influence. He writes: "Nothing else is sought in this book but that we, who come last, desire to see the first things and wish to return to them in so far as God enables us. We are like people who have come to a house that has been burnt down and try to find the original foundations. This is the more difficult in that the ruins are grown over with all sorts of growths, and many think that these growths are the foundation, and say, 'This is the foundation' and 'This is the way in which all must go,' and others repeat it after them. So that in the novelties that have grown up they think to have found the foundation, whereas they have found something quite different from, and contrary to, the true foundation. This makes the search more difficult, for if all said, 'the old foundation has been lost among the ruins', then many would begin to dig and search for it and really to begin a true work of building upon it, as Nehemiah and Zerubbabel did after the destruction of the temple. It is much more difficult now to restore the spiritual ruins, so long fallen down, and get back to the former state, for which no other foundation can be laid than Jesus Christ, from whom the many have wandered away and turned to other gods and made foundations of them." And again: "I do not say that everywhere

*"Das Netz des Glaubens" by Peter Cheltschizki, translated from Old Czech into German by Dr. Karl Vogel. (Einhorn Verlag in Dachau bei München.)

where the Apostles preached all believed, but some, whom God had chosen; here more, there fewer. In the Apostles' times the churches of believers were named according to the towns, villages and districts, they were churches and assemblies of believers, of one faith. These churches were separated by the Apostles from the unbelievers. I do not pretend that the believers could, in a material, local sense, all be separated into a particular street of the town, rather, they were united in an association of faith and came together in local gatherings where they had fellowship with each other in spiritual things and in the Word of God. And in accordance with such association in faith and in spiritual things they were called churches of believers. " He relates how "in Basle in 1433 the Papal representative said that though there was much to praise in the early Church, yet it was very simple and poor, and as the temple followed the tabernacle, so the present beauty and glory of the Church has followed its first simplicity. Also many things unknown in the early Church are now made known. " Cheltschizki's comment on this is: "The song would be good if it were not a lie. "

He taught that the "great priest" (*i.e.*, the Pope) dishonours the Saviour by taking to himself the Divine power to forgive sins, which God has reserved for Himself alone. "God has borne witness that He Himself remits sins and blots out men's iniquities through Christ who died for the sins of men. As to this, the testimony of faith is that He is the Lamb of God who took away sins and forgives the world, possessing in Himself the unique right of forgiving sins, because He is Himself at once God and man. And on this account He died as a man for sins and gave Himself to God on the cross as an offering for sins. Thus God obtained by Him and His pains the forgiveness of the sins of the world. So He alone has the power and right to forgive men their sins. Therefore, the great priest, in utmost pomp with which he raises himself above all that is called God, as a robber has laid hands on these rights of Christ. He has instituted the pilgrimage to Rome through which sins are to be cleansed away. Therefore, drunken crowds run together from all lands, and he, the father of all evil, distributes his blessing from a high place to the crowds that they may have the forgiveness of all sins and deliverance from all judgement. He saves from hell and purgatory, and there is no reason why anyone should go there. Also he sends into all lands tickets, for money, which ensure deliverance from all sins and pains; they do not even need to take the trouble to come to him, they have only to send the money and all is forgiven them. What belongs to the Lord alone, this official has taken to himself, and he draws the praise which belongs to his Lord, and becomes rich through the sale of these things. What is left for Christ to do for us when His official frees us from all sins and judgement and can make us just and holy? It is only our sins that stand in the way of our salvation. If the great priest remits all these what shall the poor Lord Jesus do? Why does the world neglect Him so and does not seek salvation from Him? Simply on this account that the great priest overshadows Him with his majesty and makes Him darkness in the world, while he, the great priest, has a great name in the world and unexampled renown. So that the Lord Jesus, already crucified, is held up to the world's laughter, and the great priest only is in everyone's mouth, and the world seeks and finds salvation in him. "

The Utraquist archbishop, Rokycana,* preaching in the famous Tyn Church in Prague, eloquently commended Cheltschizki's teachings and denounced the evils in the Church of Rome. He did not, however, act upon what he preached. But many of his hearers determined to carry out the principles they had learned, and, gathering around a man of good report, named Gregory, known as the Patriarch, withdrew from Rokycana and founded (1457) a community in North East Bohemia, in the village of Kunwald, where was the castle of Lititz. Many joined them there, some, followers of Cheltschizki and some from Waldensian churches, also students from Prague, and others. Though maintaining a connection with the Utraquist Church they returned in many things to the teaching of Scripture and to the practice of the early churches. They had a Utraquist priest as pastor, but elected elders; there were also those among them who, after the old Waldensian custom, were called "the Perfect" and gave up the whole of their property. They were not long left in peace. In a few years the settle-

* "History of the Moravian Church" J. E. Hutton.

ment at Kunwald was broken up, the Utraquist Church persecuting them as bitterly as the Roman Catholic had done; Gregory was imprisoned and tortured, one Jakob Hulava was burnt, and the brethren hid themselves in the mountains and forests. Yet their numbers increased, and gradually the persecution died down.

In 1463, in the mountains of Reichenau,† and again in 1467 at Lhota, there were general gatherings of brethren, at which many persons of rank and influence were present, where they considered afresh the principles of the Church. One of the first things they did was to baptize those present, for the baptism of believers by immersion was common to the Waldenses and to most of the brethren in different parts, though it had been interrupted by pressure of persecution. They also formally declared their separation from the Church of Rome. They called themselves Jednota Bratrská (Church of the Brotherhood), or Unitas Fratrum, the United Brethren. They did not wish by this to found a new party or to separate in any way from the other numerous churches of brethren in many lands; but they hoped that their example might encourage them to make known more definitely their separation from the Roman Church system. Before the close of their meetings, nine men were chosen from among those present, of whom there were about sixty, and from these nine three were chosen by lot, and from these, one, Matthias of Kunwald, whom they sent to be ordained by the Waldensian bishop Stephen in Austria, thus marking their continued connection with the Waldensian brethren. They did not consider this ordination as essential, but desirable; they thought that the Roman Church at the time of Sylvester had lost any Apostolic succession there might ever have been, but that if any still existed it must have been among Cathars, Paulicians and Waldenses that it had been preserved.

They communicated their decisions to the Archbishop Rokycana; and when he, from the pulpit, denounced them, they wrote further, showing that their action was not the formation of something new, but a return to the true Church of the first Christians which had always been maintained among the Waldenses. Reproached that by their

†"Die Reformation und die älteren Reformparteien" Dr. Ludwig Keller.

separation they condemned all outside their circle, and
denied the possibility of salvation to them, they replied
that they never held that true Christianity was bound to
particular views and forms; that they recognized true
Christians among those who did not belong to their assemblies, and counted it a sin on the part of the Church of Rome
that it denied salvation to those who did not submit to the
Pope. A nephew of the Archbishop, who was among the
brethren, wrote: "No one can say that we condemn and
exclude all who remain obedient to the Romish Church. . .
That is by no means our persuasion. . . . As we do not
exclude the elect in the Indian and Greek Churches, even
so we do not condemn the elect among the Romans. . ."

They laid stress on holiness of life as taught by the Lord
and the Apostles, helped by church discipline as shown in
the Scriptures, but combined with the fullest liberty of
conscience. Simplicity in living was commended; there
should be no suffering through poverty among the brethren,
the rich being ready in helping the poor.

As numbers increased changes took place, persons of
education and position and of wealth became members, and
the leadership passed out of the hands of the simpler
brethren into those of men of wider education. Lukas of
Prague was for forty years, until his death (1528), the most
prominent and active man among them. He was a voluminous and effective writer, indeed, the works produced by the
brethren at this time and their use of the printing press far
exceeded what was done by the much more numerous
Roman Catholic party. Hymn-writing and music flourished
among them. It was no longer thought wrong to occupy
positions of authority in the State, or to make honest profits
in business beyond the supply of actual needs, and the
objection to taking oaths ceased. Education was cultivated and the Brethren's schools came to be generally
sought after. The doctrine of justification by faith was
more clearly taught than before. Lukas also developed
organization for the government of the Church, and introduced no little ritual into its formerly simple worship.
Not all followed, a few held aloof, clinging to their old ways.

After a time the Pope, Alexander VI, succeeded in persuading the King of Bohemia that the growing power of
the Brethren endangered his throne, and in 1507 the Edict

of St. James was issued requiring all to be attached to the
Roman Catholic or to the Utraquist Church, or to leave the
country. The Brethren were once more the objects of
persecution, their meetings were closed, their books burned,
and they themselves imprisoned, exiled, or put to cruel
deaths. This lasted some years, during which time Lukas
was indefatigable in comforting and encouraging his people,
until he himself was captured and imprisoned. Gradually
the good report of the Brethren wore down the persecution,
some of their bitterest enemies died strange and sudden
deaths, which made others fear to continue their work.
The King of Bohemia himself died, and quarrels between
the Roman Catholics and the Utraquists diverted their
attention from the Brethren, who again began to enjoy quiet.

At the same time news came from Germany of Luther's
great doings at Wittenberg, and as soon as possible the
Brethren sent representatives and put themselves in touch
with the Reformers. Lukas, now liberated, had some
doubts as he heard of what seemed to him the boisterous
ways of Luther and the Wittenberg students, so different
from the precise life he had introduced in the Brethren's
Communities, where some rule ordered every act, but the
Brethren generally hailed with enthusiasm such unexpected allies. Luther, for his part, was doubtful about the
Brethren, but in 1520 he wrote to Spalatin: "Thus far I
have, although unconsciously, proclaimed all that Huss
preached and maintained; Johann Staupitz did unconsciously maintain the same—in a word, we are all Hussites,
without having known it; Paul and Augustine themselves
are Hussites—in the full sense of the word! Behold the
horrible misery which came over us because we did not
accept the Bohemian doctor for our leader. . . ."

The next great leader of the United Brethren, John
Augusta, who at thirty-two was made a bishop, and was
recognised as their most capable guide, favoured the fullest
co-operation with the Protestants in Germany. In 1526
the old Bohemian royal house came to an end, and the
kingdom fell to the Roman Catholic family of Hapsburg,
Ferdinand I adding it to his many other territories. Many
of the Bohemian nobility had befriended, and some belonged to, the Brethren. Their help in giving them places
of refuge on their estates in times of trouble had been

invaluable. John Augusta made use of one of them,
Konrad Krajek (who had built one of the principal centres
of the Brethren at Jungbunzlau), in his negotiations with
the new and very ill-disposed king. These negotiations were
successful, and there followed a further time of prosperity.

In 1546 war broke out between the Smalcald League, or
League of the Protestant Princes of Germany, under the
leadership of the Elector of Saxony, and the Emperor
Charles V, brother of the King of Bohemia; the Protestant
against the Roman Catholic powers. Ferdinand summoned
the nobles and people of Bohemia to support him, as his
subjects; the Elector of Saxony called on the United
Brethren to aid in the struggle for the Protestant faith.
Some of the most powerful of the Bohemian nobility
belonged to the Brethren, who were very numerous and
influential throughout the land. A meeting was held in the
house of one of the nobles, and it was decided to fight on
the Protestant side. At the battle of Mühlberg (1547) the
Protestants were defeated, Ferdinand returned to Prague
victorious, and began the intended extirpation of the
Brethren. Four of the nobles were publicly executed in
Prague, the possessions of others were confiscated, meetings
were closed, and an order was issued that any who refused to
join the Roman Catholic or Utraquist Church must leave
the country within six weeks.

Then began a great emigration. From all sides the
exiles, with their long trails of wagons, followed the roads
leading towards Poland. The people on the way sympathized
with the wanderers, let them pass toll-free, fed and entertained them. They were refused permission to settle in
Poland or Polish Prussia, and only after six months'
travelling were they given a resting place in the city of
Königsberg, in East Prussia, which was Lutheran. A young
blacksmith among them, George Israel, a man of extraordinary vigour both of faith and of physical strength,
overcame all obstacles and obtained for the Brethren a
place in Poland, in the town of Ostrorog. Settling in
Ostrorog, they made it a centre from which their work
spread over the country. They not only preached the
Gospel there, but did much to draw together the different
sections of Protestants in the country.

In 1556, Ferdinand becoming Emperor, the throne of

Bohemia passed to his son, Maximilian, and under his rule
the Brethren were allowed to return, to rebuild their
meeting-places, and resume their meetings. They had by
no means all been rooted out of Bohemia, and soon their
churches were re-established in Bohemia and Moravia, with
Poland now added. John Augusta, long imprisoned, frequently tortured, eventually joined the Utraquist Church,
believing that he could in this way bring about its union
with the Brethren. Indeed, many of the Utraquists had
become Protestants, and Bohemia and Moravia were for
the most part Protestant countries.

The chief leaders among the Brethren were two noblemen,
Wenzel of Budowa, and Charles of Žerotín. These had
large estates, keeping almost regal state, and were godly
men in whose households the reading of the Word and
prayer had their important place. The country prospered,
education became general. A Polish noble coming in 1571
to one of the settlements of the Brethren, said: "O immortal
God, what joy was then kindled in my heart! Verily it
seemed to me, when I observed and inquired about everything, that I was in the church of Ephesus or Thessalonica,
or some other apostolic church; here I saw with my own
eyes and heard with my own ears such things as we read in
apostolic letters. ... " From 1579 to 1593 the great work was
accomplished of translating the Bible from the original
tongues into the Czech language, and this "Kralitz Bible"
is the basis of the translation still in use; it became the
foundation of Czech literature.

It was the ambition of the nobles that the Church of the
United Brethren should cease to be merely tolerated and
liable at any time to renewed persecution; they aspired to
making it the National Church of Bohemia. When (1603)
the Emperor Rudolph II asked the Bohemian Diet, or
Parliament, for money for his projected campaign against
the Turks, Wenzel of Budowa demanded the repeal of the
Edict of St. James, and that complete religious liberty
should be given to the people. Only then would money be
voted. The Protestant nobles of all shades supported him,
and the people were enthusiastically on his side. The
Emperor, between the Protestants and the Jesuits, promised and retracted repeatedly, and no progress was made.
Then Wenzel called the nobles together, they collected

men and supplies and swore to resort to force if their demands should not be granted. The Emperor yielded, signed the Bohemian Charter giving full religious liberty, and there was general rejoicing among the people. A Board of twenty-four "Defenders" was formed to attend to the proper carrying out of the terms of the Charter. All the Protestant parties and the United Brethren signed the general Bohemian National Protestant Confession. In 1616 Ferdinand II became King of Bohemia. He was entirely under the influence of the Jesuits and though at his coronation he took an oath to observe the Charter, he began immediately to break it. His two principal ministers Martinitz and Slawata took forcible measures against the liberties of Protestants, and the attitude of the two religious parties towards each other became most threatening. The inevitable crisis was reached in connection with a quarrel about Church property, A church in possession of the Protestants was, by order of the King, seized and destroyed, whereupon the Defenders forced their way into the Royal Castle in Prague, where the King's Council was assembled. An angry altercation ended in Martinitz and Slawata being thrown out of the window, only a dung-heap which broke their sixty-foot fall saving them from serious harm. The Defenders raised an army, deposed King Ferdinand, and made Frederick, the Elector Palatine, son-in-law of James I of England, king. The Jesuits were expelled and the Roman Catholics mass was held up to derision.

The decisive battle between the two parties, the battle of the White Mountain, was fought (1620) on a hill outside Prague, and resulted in the complete defeat of the Defenders. On the 21st of June, 1621, in the Great Square in Prague on one side of which stands the Tyn Church, and on the other the Council House, 27 Protestant noblemen, including Wenzel of Budowa, were publicly beheaded. Each was offered his life on condition of accepting the Roman Catholic faith, and each refused it. Murder and violence of every kind were let loose on the land. Thirty-six thousand families left Bohemia and Moravia, the population of Bohemia being reduced from three millions to one. Thus, the Hussite religion and Bohemian independence disappeared together.

Over large parts of Europe the Thirty Years War had begun its devastating course.

Jan Amos Comenius (b. 1592), known later the world over for his reform of education, is a heroic figure in this time of distress. He did not approve of the way in which the Brethren had engaged in politics and war. At the time of the great disaster he had only been three years settled as minister of the congregation of brethren at Fulneck in Moravia, and this place was sacked and destroyed by Spanish soldiers, compelling him to fly. He took refuge in the castle of Charles of Žerotín, where he became leader of the band of refugees that gathered there. While there he wrote a book, *"The Labyrinth of the World and the Paradise of the Heart"* in which, in allegorical form, he taught that peace is not to be found in the world, but in the indwelling of Christ in the heart. Driven from Žerotín, Comenius led the last band of fugitives from Moravia. He had lost everything. His wife and child died of the privations of the way. As they said farewell to their native land, he encouraged their faith to believe that God would preserve there a "hidden seed" which would afterwards grow and bear fruit.

At last a resting place was found at Lissa (Lesno) in Poland (1628), where Comenius became Director of the School, and from whence he visited England (1641), being invited to re-organize education there. The Civil War in England drove him to further journeys, in Sweden and elsewhere. In 1656 a defeat of the Swedes by the Poles resulted in the burning of the "heretics' nest" in Lissa by the Poles, and Comenius again lost everything, including MSS. he had prepared for publication, the fruit of years of labour. The Peace of Westphalia in 1648 had already destroyed the last hope of a re-establishment of the Bohemian Brethren, the Catholic and Protestant Powers alike refusing them any toleration. Under these circumstances of utter loss Comenius wrote, giving such counsel to the Brethren and to the world as exhibits the experience of the soul which continues to trust God when all earthly help has failed.

In Lissa in 1650 he wrote "The Testament of the Dying Mother"* in which he counsels preachers of the Moravian

* "Das Testament der Sterbenden Mutter" von J. A. Comenius. written in Bohemian, 1650, at Lissa. translated into German by Dora Peřina

Church left without any circle of fellowship, to accept invitations to minister the Word in Evangelical churches; not to flatter their hearers nor strengthen divisions, but to aim at kindling love and oneness of mind. He advised those of the "orphans" who were not preachers, if they found congregations where they were not forced to follow men but rather instructed to follow Christ, where they saw the truth of the Gospel of Jesus, to join them, to pray for their peace and to seek their growth and progress in that which is good, giving them a shining example, leading them in warmth and prayer, so that, from them at least the wrath of Almighty God which must come over Christendom might be averted.

Adding more general exhortation, he says: "Even you I cannot forget, dear sisters, evangelical churches; nor thee our mother from whom we sprang, Roman Church. Thou wast a mother to us but art become a . . . vampire who sucks the children's blood. Therefore, I wish that in thy misery thou mightest be converted to repentance and forsake the Babylon of thy blasphemy. . . . To all Christian assemblies together I bequeath my longing for unity and reconciliation, for union in faith and in love, for the Unity of the Spirit. O may this spirit which the Father of spirits gave me from the beginning come over you so that you may long as utterly as I have done for the uniting and fellowship in the truth of Christianity of all those who call on the Name of Jesus in truth. May God bring you to the ground of what is essential and useful, as He taught me, that you may all come to see what you ought to be zealous for and what not, and how you should avoid all zeal that is without knowledge and does not further the progress of the Church, but rather tends to its destruction; and then, further, that you may see where flaming zeal is needful so that you may be happily zealous for the praise of God, even to the yielding of your lives. O that you might all be carried away by longing for the mercy of our God, the worthiness of Jesus and the delightful sweet inward gifts of the Holy Spirit, which are communicated through true faith, true love, and true hope in God. In this the nature of true Christianity is contained."

in Leitmeritz. Monatsschriften der C.G. XVI Band, Heft 1. Herausgegeben von Ludwig Keller, Berlin. Weidmannsche Buchhandlung.

The *"Voice of Mourning"* was written in 1660 in Amster·
dam, Comenius' last dwelling place, where he died ten
years later.* In it he says: "We hear that the Lord
heals only the wounded, gives life only to the dead, and
redeems from hell only those cast down into it (1 Sam. 2),
then let us be willing for Him to do as He will with us, and
if His will is first to wound us and slay us and cast us down
into hell, let His will be done; meantime, we expect that
without fail, here or in eternity, we shall be healed, made
alive again, and brought to heaven! Even our Lord who
had to endure a measureless painful, shameful, and sorrowful death, comforted Himself with this that the corn of
wheat, if it does not die, remains alone, but if it dies brings
forth a rich harvest. If, therefore, out of His wounds healing
has sprung up, out of His death life, out of His hell heaven
and salvation, why should not we, the little grains of corn,
die according to the will of God? If the blood of the martyrs
and also our blood shall be the seed of the Church for the
increase later of those who fear God, ah, let us, weeping,
scatter the precious seed that we may bring in the sheaves
with rejoicing. God will not destroy without building
again. He makes all things new. God knows what He is
doing, we must trust Him to pull down and to build up as
He will. He does not do these things for no purpose,
something great lies hidden under it all. The whole
Creation is subject to the will of God and we also, whether
we understand what He does or not. He does not need
our advice as to what He does. "

When he was 77 years of age and his fame was established
throughout Europe as having revolutionized in the best
sense the spirit and methods of teaching, Comenius wrote
the *"One Thing Needful"*.† He compares the world to a
laybrinth, and shows that the way out is by leaving what is
needless, and choosing the *one thing needful*—Christ. "The
great number of teachers" he says "is the reason of the
multitude of sects, for which we shall soon have no names
left. Each church reckons itself as the true one, or at least
as the purest, truest part of it, while among themselves they

* "Stimme der Trauer" von J. A. Comenius. Translated from Bohemian
into German by Franz Slaměnik. Monatschriften der Comenius-Gesell-
schaft XVII Band, Heft 3. Herausgegeben von Ludwig Keller. Verlag
von Eugen Diederichs, Jena, 1908.
† "Unum Necessarium" J. A. Comenius.

persecute each other with the bitterest hatred. No reconciliation is to be hoped for between them; they meet enmity
with irreconcilable enmity. Out of the Bible they forge
their different creeds; these are their fortresses and bulwarks behind which they entrench themselves and resist
all attacks. I will not say that these confessions of faith—
for that they are so we can admit in most cases—are bad
in themselves. They become so, however, in that they feed
the fire of enmity; only by putting them away altogether
would it be possible to set to work on healing the wounds
of the Church". " . . . To this *labyrinth of sects* and various
confessions another belongs; the love of disputation. . . .
What is attained by it? Has a single learned strife ever
been settled? Never. Their number has only been increased. Satan is the greatest sophist; he has never been
overcome in a strife of words" . . . "In Divine service the
words of men are usually heard more than the Word of
God. Each one chatters as he pleases, or kills time by
learned disquisitions and disproving the views of others.
Of the new birth and how a man must be changed into the
likeness of Christ to become partaker of the Divine Nature
(2 Peter 1. 4), scarcely anything is said. Of the power
of the keys the Church has almost lost the power of binding,
only the power of loosing remains. . . . The sacraments,
given as symbols of unity, of love, and of our life in Christ,
have been made the occasion of bitterest conflict, a cause of
mutual hatred, a centre of sectarianism. . . . In short,
Christendom has become a labyrinth. The faith has been
split into a thousand little parts and you are made a heretic
if there is one of them you do not accept. " . . . "What can
help? Only the *one thing needful*, return to Christ, looking
to Christ as the only Leader, and walking in His footsteps,
setting aside all other ways until we all reach the goal,
and have come to the unity of the faith (Eph. 4. 13). As
the Heavenly Master built everything on the ground of the
Scriptures so should we leave all particularities of our
special confessions and be satisfied with the revealed Word
of God which belongs to us all. With the Bible in our
hand we should cry: I believe what God has revealed in this
Book; I will obediently keep His commands; I hope for
that which He has promised. Christians, give ear! There
is only one Life, but Death comes to us in a thousand forms.

There is only one Truth, but Error has a thousand forms. There is only one Christ, but a thousand Antichrists. . . So thou knowest, O Christendom, what is the one thing needful. Either thou turnest back to Christ or thou goest to destruction like the Antichrist. If thou art wise and wilt live, follow the Leader of Life. "

"But you, Christians, rejoice in your being caught up, . . . hear the words of your Heavenly Leader, 'Come unto Me.' . . . Answer with one voice, 'Even so, we come' ".

CHAPTER VIII

The Reformation
1500–1550

A Catechism—Brethren of the Common Life—Luther—Tetzel—The ninety-five theses at Wittenberg—The Papal Bull burnt—Diet of Worms —The Wartburg—Translation of the Bible—Efforts of Erasmus for compromise—Development of the Lutheran Church—Its reform and limitations—Staupitz remonstrates—Luther's choice between New Testament churches and National Church system—Loyola and the Counter Reformation.

THE connection between the brethren in different countries is illustrated by the fact that the same catechism for the instruction of their children was used by the Waldenses in the valleys, in France, and in Italy, also by the various brethren in the German lands, and in Bohemia by the United Brethren.* It was a small book and was published in Italian, French, German and Bohemian. Different editions are known, printed at intervals from 1498 to 1530.

Closely connected with these brethren were the "Brethren of the Common Life" who in the 15th and early 16th centuries established a network of schools throughout the Netherlands and North-West Germany. Their founder was Gerhard Groote of Deventer, in Holland, who, in consultation with Jan van Rysbroeck, formed the brotherhood and established the first school, at Deventer. Groote expressed his principle of teaching when he said: "the root of study and the mirror of life must be in the first instance the Gospel of Christ." He thought that learning without piety was likely to be more of a curse than a blessing. The teaching was excellent, the school at Deventer under the famous schoolmaster Alexander Hegius had 2000 pupils. Thomas à Kempis, who afterwards wrote the *"Imitation of Christ"* went to school there; and Erasmus also was a pupil. The schools spread widely, Latin and some Greek were taught and the children learned to sing

* "A History of the Reformation" Thos. M. Lindsay. (T. & T. Clark Edinburgh. 1906-7. 2 Vols.)

evangelical Latin hymns. Adult classes were carried on
in which the Gospels were read in the language of the
country. Money was earned by copying MSS. of the New
Testament, and, later, by printing it. Tracts of the
Brethren and of the Friends of God were multiplied. In
this way a sound education was provided, based on the
Holy Scriptures.

A hymn book, published in Ulm in 1538, shows the
provision made for praise and worship in the congregations
of the brethren. The end of its long title states that it
was for "the Christian Brotherhood, the Picards, until
now considered as Unchristian and Heretics, used and sung
daily to the honour of God. "

It was the Bible which had the first place in enlightening
and developing Luther; he was helped by Staupitz also, and
found in the writings of Tauler and some of the brethren,
more Divine doctrine,* he said, than in all the Universities and teachings of the schoolmen; nothing was sounder
and corresponded more with the Gospel. He soon became
active as a writer and his early pamphlets (1517-20)† were
written in the spirit of the brethren, showing how salvation
is not through the intervention of the Church, but that
every man has direct access to God and finds salvation
through faith in Christ and obedience to His Word. He
was laid hold of by the teaching of Scripture that salvation
is of the grace of God, through faith in Jesus Christ, and
not obtained by our own works. The ability and zeal with
which Luther preached these truths not only awakened
hope and expectation in the circles where they were already
known, but also powerfully affected others who had hitherto
been ignorant of them.

In 1517 a prominent salesman of Papal indulgences,
Tetzel, showed a shamelessness and buffoonery in his
business which, more perhaps than anything else, impressed on people its inherent charlatanry. When he came
to Wittenberg, Luther, failing to arouse the Elector of Saxony
to action, and encouraged by Staupitz, himself nailed on
the church door the Ninety-five Theses which set Europe

* "Die Reformation und die älteren Reform Parteien"   Dr. Ludwig
Keller.

† "Life and Letters of Erasmus" J. A. Froude.

in a blaze, as men realized that a voice had at last been raised to utter what most felt—that the whole system of indulgences was a fraud and had no place in the Gospel. A poor monk now faced and fought the whole vast Papal power; his "Address to the Nobility of the German Nation on the Liberty of the Christian Man" and his "Babylonian Captivity of the Church" appealed to all Europe.   The Pope issued a Bull excommunicating him; he burnt it publicly at Wittenberg (1520).   Summoned to Worms before the Papal authorities, he braved all dangers and went, and none was able to harm him.   When he left, his life being threatened, his friends carried him off secretly to a castle, the Wartburg, and let it be supposed that he was dead. There he translated the New Testament into German, following it later by the Old Testament.   The effect of increased reading of the Scriptures, and that in a time when questions of religion were violently agitating masses of the population, was to change the whole aspect of Christendom. The dull hopelessness with which men had seen the ever-increasing corruption and rapacity of the Church, was exchanged for a vivid hope that now, at last, the time of revival had come, the time of a return to Apostolic, primitive Christianity; Christ Himself was seen afresh, revealed in the Scriptures as the Redeemer and immediate Saviour of sinners and the Way to God for suffering humanity.

With such radical divergence of view and interest, however, conflict was inevitable.   Luther's following and band of sympathizers grew enormously, but the old system of the Roman Church was not to be changed without a struggle. There were some who, with Erasmus, hoped for compromise and peace, but the monks, who saw their position and privileges vanishing, were violent beyond measure, and the Papal authorities decided to use the old weapons of cursing and killing to crush the new movement, while Luther, leaving his early humility, grew to be as dogmatic as the Pope.

Political rivalries made the situation more dangerous. Oppression of the land workers led to the Peasants' War (1524-5), for which Luther and his party were blamed by the other side.   A general conflagration threatened the nations.   Erasmus wrote (1520): "I wish Luther . . . would be quiet for a while. . . . what he says may be true, but there are times and seasons. " Again, to Duke George of Saxony (1524) : "When Luther first spoke the whole world applauded, and your Highness among the rest. Divines who are now his bitterest opponents were then on his side. Cardinals, even monks, encouraged him. He had taken up an excellent cause. He was attacking practices which every honest man condemned, and contending with a set of harpies, under whose tyranny Christendom was groaning. Who could then dream how far the movement would go ? . . . Luther himself never expected to produce such an effect. After his Theses had come out I persuaded him to go no further. . . . I was afraid of riots. . . . I cautioned him to be moderate. . . . The Pope put out a Bull, the Emperor put out an Edict, and there were prisons, faggots and burnings. Yet all was in vain. The mischief only grew. . . . I did see, however, that the world was besotted with ritual. Scandalous monks were ensnaring and strangling consciences. Theology had become sophistry. Dogmatism had grown to madness, and, besides there were the unspeakable priests and Bishops and Roman officials. . . . I considered that it was a case for compromise and agreement. . . . Luther's patrons were stubborn and would not yield a step. The Catholic divines breathed only fire and fury. . . . I trust, I hope, that Luther will make a few concessions and that the Pope and princes may still consent to peace. May Christ's Dove come among us, or else Minerva's owl. Luther has administered an acrid dose to a diseased body. God grant it may prove salutary!" Again (1525) he wrote "I regard Luther as a good man, raised up by Providence to correct the depravity of the age. Whence have all these troubles arisen? From the audacious and open immorality of the priesthood, from the arrogance of the theologians and the tyranny of the monks. " He advised abolishing what was manifestly wrong but retaining all that could be kept without harm, exercising tolerance, allowing liberty of conscience, and he wrote, "Indulgences, with which the monks so long fooled the world, with the connivance of the theologians, are now exploded. Well, then, let those who have no faith in saints' merits, pray to Father, Son and Holy Ghost, imitate Christ in their lives, and leave those alone who do believe in saints. . . . Let men think as they please of purgatory, without quarrelling with others who do not think as they do. . . . Whether works justify or faith justifies matters little, since all allow that faith will not save without works. "

The conflict was too bitter for such moderate counsels to prevail. They were few who saw any possibility of toler-ance. The development of Luther himself under the influence of such extraordinary circumstances, in its turn influenced them. From having been a devoted Roman Catholic in his earlier years, he had by his meeting with Staupitz and occupation with the Scriptures been brought into sympathy with the Brethren and with the Mystics, but his conflict with the Romish clergy now drew him into close relations with a number of the German Princes; and this association, together with the returning influence of his old training, led him gradually to the formation of the Lutheran Church. The stages of this development were marked by a drawing away from the old congregations of brethren and, side by side with the revival of much Scrip-ture truth, an incorporation in the new Lutheran Church of much also that was taken over from the Romish system. Luther emphasized the teachings of the Apostle Paul more, those of the Gospels less, than the old churches of believers; he pressed the doctrine of justification by faith, without a sufficiency of the balancing truth of the following of Christ which was so prominent in their preaching. His teaching as to the absence of any freedom of will or choice in man, and of salvation as being solely by the grace of God, went so far as to lead to the neglect of right conduct as a part of the Gospel. Among the doctrines carried over from the Church of Rome was that of baptismal regeneration, and, with this, the general practice of baptising infants. While reviving the teaching of Scripture as to individual salva-tion by faith in Christ Jesus and His perfect work, Luther did not go on to accept the New Testament teaching as to the churches, separate from the world, yet maintained in it as witnesses to it of the saving Gospel of Jesus Christ; he adopted the Roman Catholic system of parishes, with their clerical administration of a world considered as Christianized. Having a number of rulers on his side, he maintained the principle of the union of Church and State, and accepted the sword of the State as the proper means of converting or punishing those who dissented from the new

ecclesiastical authority. It was at the Diet, or Council, of
Speyer (1529) that the Reform party presented the pro-
test to the Roman Catholic representatives, from which the
name Protestant came to be applied to the Reformers.
The League of Smalcald in 1531, bound together nine
Princes and eleven free cities as Protestant Powers.

In view of Luther's development, Staupitz warned him:
"Christ help us that we may come at last to live according
to the Gospel which now sounds in our ears and which many
have on their lips, for I see that multitudes misuse the
Gospel to give liberty to the flesh. Let my entreaty affect
you, for I was once the pioneer of holy evangelical teaching. " In finally declaring the divergence of his way from
that which Luther was taking, he contrasts nominal
Christians with real Christians, and writes: "It is the
fashion now to separate faith from evangelical life, as
though it were possible to have real faith in Christ and yet
remain unlike Him in life. Oh, cunning of the foe! Oh,
misleading of the people! Hear the speech of fools: Whoever believes in Christ requires no works. Listen to the
saying of truth: Let him who serves Me follow Me. The
evil spirit tells his fleshly Christians that a man is justified
without works and that Paul preached this. This is false.
He did indeed speak against those legal works and outward
observances in which, through fear, men put their trust for
salvation, and he strove against them as useless and leading
to condemnation, but he never thought evil or did anything
but praise those works which are the fruits of faith and love
and obedience to the heavenly commandments, and
he proclaimed and preached their necessity in all his
epistles."

Luther taught: "Learn from St. Paul that the Gospel
teaches of Christ that He came, not to give a new law by
which we should walk, but that He might give Himself
an offering for the sins of the whole world. " The old
churches had always taught that a true Christian was one
who, having received the life of Christ by faith, constantly
desired and endeavoured, by the help of His indwelling
life, to walk according to His example and word.

Luther by his mighty strokes hewed a way through long
consecrated privileges and abuses, so that reform became
possible. He revealed Christ to countless sinners as the

Saviour to whom each one was invited to come, without intervention of priest or saint or church or sacrament, not on account of any goodness in himself, but as a sinner in all his needs, to find in Christ, through faith in Him, perfect salvation, founded in the perfect work of the Son of God. Instead, however, of continuing in the way of the Word, Luther then built up a church, in which some abuses were reformed, but which in many respects was a reproduction of the old system. Multitudes who looked to him for guidance accepted that form in which he moulded the Lutheran Church; many, seeing that he did not continue in the way of return to the Scriptures which they had hoped for, remained where they were, in the Roman Catholic Church, and the hopes awakened among the brethren gradually faded away as they saw themselves placed between two ecclesiastical systems, each of which was ready to enforce conformity in matters of conscience, by the sword.

Luther had seen the Divine pattern for the churches, and it was not without an inward struggle that he abandoned the New Testament teaching of independent assemblies of real believers, in favour of the National or State Church system which outward circumstances pressed upon him. The irreconcilable difference between these two ideals was the essential ground of conflict. Baptism and the Lord's Supper took on such importance in the fight only because in the true Church they mark the gulf dividing the Church from the world, whereas in a National Church they are used to bridge it, infant baptism and the general administration of the Lord's Supper doing away with the necessity for personal faith in the recipients. Moreover, the powers arrogated to a priesthood alone competent to perform these rites bring the nation under a domination in matters of faith and conscience, which, when working in unison with the State, or civil Government, make free churches impossible, and religion a matter of nationality. Such a National Church is very comprehensive. It can include a great variety of views. It can take in unbelievers, and condone much wickedness, and can allow even its clergy to express disbelief in the Scriptures; but, if it has power to prevent it, it will not tolerate those who baptize believers, or who take the Lord's Supper among themselves as disciples of Christ; because these things strike at the foundations of its character as a national church, though it is not the rites themselves which are the fundamental cause of difference, but the Church question.

With unprecedented power and courage Luther had brought to light the Scripture truths as to the individual salvation of the sinner by faith, but failed when he might have shown the way to a return to Scripture in all things, including its teaching as to the Church. He had taught: "I say it a hundred thousand times, God will have no forced service." "No one can or ought to be forced to believe." In 1526 he had written: "The right kind of evangelical order cannot be exhibited among all sorts of people, but those who are seriously determined to be Christians and confess the Gospel with hand and mouth, must enrol themselves by name and meet apart, in one house, for prayer, for reading, to baptize, to take the Sacrament, and exercise other Christian works. With such order it would be possible for those who did not behave in a Christian manner to be known, reproved, restored, or excluded, according to the rule of Christ (Matt. 18. 15). Here also they could, in common, subscribe alms, which would be willingly given and distributed among the poor, according to the example of Paul (2 Cor. 9. 1-12). Here it would not be necessary to have much or fine singing. Here a short and simple way of baptism and the Sacrament could be practised, and all would be according to the Word and in love. But I cannot yet order and establish such an assembly, for I have not yet the right people for it. If, however, it should come about that I must do it, and am driven to it, I will willingly do my part. In the meantime I will call, excite, preach, help, forward it, until the Christians take the Word so in earnest that they will themselves find how to do it and continue in it." Yet Luther knew that the "right people" were there; people whom he described as "true, pious, holy children of God." After much hesitation he came at last to oppose any attempt to put into practice what he had so excellently portrayed. He did not, however, as did many of his followers, look upon the Lutheran Church as being the best possible form of religion that could be devised; he described it as "provisional", as the "outer court" and not the "Sanctuary" and he did not cease to exhort and warn the people. He said: "If we look aright at what people now do who reckon themselves as Evangelical and know how to talk much about Christ, there is nothing behind it. Most of them deceive themselves. The number of those who began with us and had pleasure in our teaching was ten times greater, now not a tenth part of them remains steadfast. They learn indeed to speak words, as a parrot repeats what people say, but their hearts do not experience them; they remain just as they are, they neither taste nor feel how true and faithful God is. They boast much of the Gospel and at first seek it earnestly, yet afterwards nothing remains; for they do what they like, follow their lusts, become worse than they were before and are much more undisciplined and presumptuous . . . than other people, for peasants, citizens, nobles, all are more covetous and undisciplined than they were under the Papacy." "Ah, Lord God, if we only practised this doctrine aright, Thou shouldst see, that where now a thousand go to the Sacrament scarcely a hundred of them would go. Then the horrible sins would be less with which the Pope with his hellish law has flooded the world: then at last we should come to be a Christian assembly, where now we are almost utter heathen with the name of Christian; then we could separate from ourselves those of whom we know by their works that they never believed and never had life, a thing that now is impossible to us."

Once the new Church was put under the power of the State it could not be altered, but Luther never pretended that the churches which he had established were ordered after the pattern of the Scriptures. While Melanchthon spoke of the Protestant Princes as "chief members of the Church", Luther called them "makeshift Bishops" and frequently expressed his regret for the lost liberty of the Christian man and independence of the Chrstian congregations that had once been his aim.

At the time when Luther burnt the Pope's Bull* and the Reformation began its course, another man was preparing himself for the work which was to be the chief means of

* "A History of the Reformation" Thomas M. Lindsay M.A., D.D.

checking the progress of Protestantism, and of organizing the counter-Reformation which won back to the Church of Rome large districts where the movement of Reform had already prevailed.

Ignatius Loyola,* of noble Spanish ancestry, was born in 1491, became a page at the court of Ferdinand and Isabella, and then a soldier, distinguished from the first by his intrepid courage, but a wound which he received when he was thirty years of age, and which made him permanently lame, changed the whole course of his life.

During the long illness following his wound he read some of the books of the Mystics and became passionately desirous of being delivered from the lusts of his former life and of doing great things, not now for military glory in the service of an earthly king, but for God and as a soldier of Jesus Christ. "Show me O Lord" he prayed, "where I can find Thee: I will follow like a dog, if I can only learn the way of salvation." After long conflict he yielded himself to God, found peace in the assurance that his sins were forgiven, and was delivered from the power of carnal desire. At the famous monastery of Montserrat, among the mountain peaks which look as though leaping flames had suddenly been turned to stone, after a night's watch and confession, Loyola hung up his weapons before the ancient wooden image of the Virgin and dedicated himself to her service and that of Christ, gave away his very clothes, and, taking the rough garb of a pilgrim, limped to the neighbouring Dominican monastery of Manresa. There he not only followed the methods of self-examination common to the Mystics, but set himself to note with minute exactness all that he observed in himself, meditations, visions, and also outward postures and positions, to find out which were most favourable to the development of spiritual ecstasies. There he wrote a great part of his book, "Spiritual Exercises" which was afterwards to have so powerful an influence.

The quest of the Mystics for immediate communion with God, without priestly or other intervention, constantly brought them into conflict with the priests. Suspected of being of this mind, Loyola was more than once imprisoned

* "Encyclopaedia Britannica" Article, Loyola.

by the Inquisition and by the Dominicans, but was always able to show them that he was not what they thought, and to obtain release.   Indeed, although at first so strongly affected by the writings of the Mystics, Loyola evolved a system which was the very contrary of their teaching. Instead of seeking experiences of direct communion with Christ, he placed each member of his Society under the guidance of a man, his confessor, to whom he was pledged to make known the most intimate secrets of his life and to yield implicit obedience.   The plan was that of a soldier, each one was subject to the will of one above him, and even the highest was controlled by those appointed to observe every act and judge every motive.   In the course of years of study and travel, of teaching and charitable activities, during which there were unavailing efforts to get to Jerusalem, and also interviews with the Pope, that company gradually gathered round Loyola, which was organized by him as the "Company of Jesus" in Paris in 1534.   He and six others, including Francis Xavier, took vows of poverty and chastity and of missionary activity, and in 1540 the Pope recognized the "Society of Jesus", to which the name of "Jesuit" was first given by Calvin and others, its opponents.   The careful choice and the long and special training of its members, during which they were taught entire submission of their own will to that of their superiors, made of them a weapon by which not only was the Reformation checked, but a "Counter Reformation" was organized which regained for Rome much that she had lost.

The Society worked consistently and skilfully for reaction.   Its rapid growth in power and its unscrupulous methods raised many enemies against it even in the Church of Rome, as well as in various countries where its interference not only in religious, but also in civil matters, was resented.   Its history was a stormy one.   At times it rose to the point of entirely dominating the policy of a nation; then it would be driven out and forbidden altogether—only to return when circumstances once more became favourable.   The attempt of Hermann von Wied, Archbishop Elector of Cologne, to bring about a Catholic Reformation and a reconciliation with the Reformers, was frustrated by Canisius, the able representative whom

the Society had won in Germany, while in countless instances movements of reform were repressed or rendered
nugatory and the dominion of Rome strengthened, by its
activities. Diligent and devoted members went out as
missionaries and brought the form of religion which they
represented, to the heathen peoples of India, China, and
America.

CHAPTER IX

The Anabaptists

1516–1566

The name Anabaptist—Not a new sect—Rapid increase—Legislation against them—Balthazer Hubmeyer—Circle of brethren in Basle—Activities and martyrdom of Hubmeyer and his wife—Hans Denck—Balance of truth—Parties—M. Sattler—Persecution increases—Landgraf Philip of Hessen—Protest of Odenbach—Zwingli—Persecution in Switzerland—Grebel, Manz, Blaurock—Kirschner—Persecution in Austria—Chronicles of the Anabaptists in Austria Hungary—Ferocity of Ferdinand—Huter—Mändl and his companions—Communities—Münster—The Kingdom of the New Zion—Distorted use of events in Münster to calumniate the brethren—Disciples of Christ treated as He was—Menno Simon—Pilgram Marbeck and his book—Sectarianism—Persecution in West Germany—Hermann Archbishop of Cologne attempts reform—Schwenckfeld.

ABOUT 1524, in Germany, many of the churches of brethren, such as had existed from the earliest times, and in many lands, repeated what had been done at Lhota in 1467; they declared their independence as congregations of believers and their determination to observe and to carry out as churches the teachings of Scripture. As formerly at Lhota, so now on these occasions those present who had not yet as believers received baptism by immersion were baptized.* This gave rise to a new name, a name which they themselves repudiated, for it was attached to them as an offensive epithet in order to convey the impression that they had founded a new sect; the new name was *Anabaptist* (baptized again). As time went on this name was applied also to certain violent people of Communistic practices and principles subversive of order and morality. With these the brethren had no sort of connection; but by branding them with the same name, those who persecuted the brethren obtained an appearance of justification, as though they were suppressing dangerous disorder. As in earlier times the literature of the Christians had been destroyed, and their histories written by

*"Die Reformation und die älteren Reformparteien"   Dr. Ludwig Keller, who gives authorities,

their enemies, so in the 16th century the same thing was done again, and in view of the unbridled violence of language common at that time in religious controversy, it is more than ever necessary to search out whatever remains of their own writings and records.

In the report of the Council of the Archbishop of Cologne* about the "Anabaptist movement", to the Emperor Charles V, it is said that the Anabaptists call themselves "true Christians", that they desire community of goods, "which has been the way of Anabaptists for more than a thousand years, as the old histories and imperial laws testify." At the dissolution of the Parliament at Speyer it was stated that the "new sect of the Anabaptists" had already been condemned many hundred years ago and "by common law forbidden." It is a fact that for more than twelve centuries baptism in the way taught and described in the New Testament had been made an offence against the law, punishable by death.

The general reviving stirred by the Renaissance brought many of the assemblies of believers who had been driven into hiding by persecution to show themselves again. An ecclesiastical edict issued in Lyons against one of the brethren said, "Out of the ashes of Waldo many new shoots arise and it is necessary to impose a severe and heavy punishment as an example." Many believers emerged, too, from the Swiss valleys; they called each other brethren and sisters, and were well aware that they were not founding anything new, but were continuing the testimony of those who for centuries had been persecuted as "heretics", as the records of their martyrs showed.

In Switzerland the refuge of persecuted believers was mostly in the mountains, while in Germany it was frequently in the powerful shelter afforded by the Trade Guilds. The time of the Reformation brought out here also many hidden brethren, who, joining themselves to the existing churches, and forming fresh ones, quickly grew to such numbers and developed such activity as alarmed the State Churches, Roman Catholic and Lutheran. A sympathetic observer, not one of themselves, wrote of them that in

*"Die Taufe. Gedanken über die urchristliche Taufe, ihre Geschichte und ihre Bedeutung für die Gegenwart" J. Warns, who also gives authorities and sources.

1526 a new party arose, which spread so quickly that
their doctrine soon permeated the whole country and they
obtained a great following; many who were sincere of heart
and zealous toward God, joined them. They seemed to
teach nothing but love, faith, and the Cross, showed themselves patient and humble in many sufferings, broke bread
with each other as a sign of unity and love, and faithfully
helped one another. They held together and increased so
rapidly that the world was afraid they might cause revolution, but they were always found to be guiltless of
such thoughts, though in many places they were tyranni-
cally treated.

Although the brethren were careful to take the Word
as their guide and would not willingly come under
the domination of man, they thankfully recognized
as elders and overseers in the different churches the
men among them who had those gifts of the Spirit which
fitted them to be guides. Among them at this time
Dr. Balthazar Hubmeyer was pre-eminent.* After a
brilliant career as a student at the Freiburg University
and as Professor of Theology at Ingoldstadt, he was appointed (1516) preacher at the cathedral at Regensburg,
where his preaching attracted crowds of hearers. Three
years later he moved to Waldshut, and while there experienced a spiritual change, accepting Luther's teaching,
and came also to be looked upon as being influenced
by "Bohemian heresy", that is, the teaching of the assemblies of brethren in Bohemia. His Invitation to Brethren,
of 11th Jan., 1524, requests those interested to meet
at his house, with their Bibles. He explains that the
object of the meeting is that they might be helped
together by acquaintance with the Word of God to
continue to feed Christ's lambs, and reminds them
that it was a custom from the times of the Apostles
that those who were called to minister the Divine Word
should meet together and collect Christian counsel for
dealing with matters of difficulty concerning the Faith.
A number of questions were suggested which they were

*"Neue Studien zur Geschichte der Theologie und der Kirche"
Herausgegeben von N. Bonwetsch, Göttingen und R. Seeberg, Berlin.
Zwanzigstes Stück.
  "D. Balthasar Hubmeier als Theologe" (Berlin, Trowitzch & Sohn,
1914) von Carl Sachsse.

earnestly and affectionately exhorted to consider in the light of the Scriptures, and he promised that according to his ability, he would provide them with a brotherly meal at his own expense. He expressed his own thoughts and teachings thus: "the holy universal Christian Church is a fellowship of the saints and a brotherhood of many pious and believing men who with one accord honour one Lord, one God, one faith and one baptism." It is, he said, "the assembly of all Christian men on earth wherever they may be in the whole circle of the world"; or again, "a separated communion of a number of men that believe in Christ", and explained, — "there are two churches, which in fact cover each other, the general and the local church, . . . the local church is a part of the general Church which includes all men who show that they are Christians." As to community of goods, he said it consists in our always helping those brethren who are in need, for what we have is not our own but is entrusted to us as stewards for God. He considered that on account of sin the power of the sword had been committed to earthly Governments, and that therefore it was to be submitted to in the fear of God. Such gatherings were frequently held in Basle, where Hubmeyer and his friends zealously searched the Holy Scriptures and considered the questions brought before them.

Basle was a great centre of spiritual activity. The printers were not afraid to issue books branded as heretical, and from their presses such works as those of Marsiglio of Padua and of John Wycliff went out into the world. Brethren of striking gift and ability were among those who met with Hubmeyer for the consideration of Scripture. Of one, Wilhelm Reublin, it is recorded that he expounded the Holy Scriptures in so Christian and excellent a way that nothing like it had ever been heard before, so that he gained great numbers. He had been a priest in Basle and, during that time, at the celebration of the feast of Corpus Christi, had carried a Bible in procession instead of the monstrance. He was baptized, and later, when living near Zürich, was expelled from the country, so continued his preaching in Germany and Moravia. There were often brethren present from abroad, through whose visits connections with churches in other lands were maintained.

Among these was Richard Crocus from England, a learned man who exercised great influence among students, and many came also from France and from Holland.

In 1527 another Conference of brethren was called, in Moravia, at which Hubmeyer was present. It was held under the protection of Count Leonhard and Hans von Lichtenstein; the former was baptized on this occasion by Hubmeyer, who himself had been baptized two years earlier by Reublin. At that time 110 others had been baptized, and another 300 were baptized afterwards by Hubmeyer, among them his own wife, the daugher of a citizen of Waldshut. The same year Hubmeyer and his wife escaped, with the loss of everything, from an advancing Austrian army and reached Zürich, but there he was soon discovered by Zwingli's party and thrown into prison.

The city and Canton of Zürich were at this time completely under the influence of Ulrich Zwingli, who had begun the work of Reformation in Switzerland even earlier than Luther in Germany. The doctrine of the Swiss Reformers, differing in some respects from those taught by Luther, had spread over many of the Cantons and far into the German States.

The Zürich Council arranged a disputation between Hubmeyer and Zwingli in which the former, broken by imprisonment, was overwhelmed by his robust opponent. Afraid of being delivered into the hands of the Emperor, he went so far as to retract some of his teaching, but immediately repented bitterly of this fear of man and besought God to forgive and restore him. From there he went to Constance, then to Augsburg, where he baptized Hans Denck. In Nikolsburg, in Moravia, Hubmeyer was very active as a writer, printing some sixteen books. During his short stay in the district about 6000 persons were baptized and the numbers in the churches rose to 15,000 members. The brethren were by no means of one mind on all points, and when the enthusiastic preacher Hans Hut came to Nikolsburg and taught that it was not Scriptural for a believer to bear arms in the service of his country or for self-defence, or to pay taxes for carrying on war, Hubmeyer opposed him. In 1527 King Ferdinand forced the authorities to give Hubmeyer up to him, and brought him to Vienna, where he insisted on his being tortured and executed.   Hubmeyer's wife encouraged him to remain firm, and a few months after his arrival in Vienna he was brought to the scaffold set up in the Market Place.   He prayed with a loud voice: "Oh, my gracious God, give me patience in my martyrdom! Oh, my Father, I thank Thee that Thou wilt take me to-day out of this vale of sorrow. Oh Lamb, Lamb, who takest away the sin of the world! Oh my God, into Thy hands I commit my spirit!"   From the flames he was heard to cry out, "Jesus, Jesus!"   Three days later his heroic wife was drowned in the Danube, thrown from the bridge with a stone around her neck.

One of the most influential of the brethren, who helped to guide the churches in the agitated times of the Reformation, was Hans Denck.*   A native of Bavaria, he had studied in Basle, where he took his degree, and must have come into contact with Erasmus and the brilliant circle of scholars and printers gathered there.   Being appointed to the charge of one of the most important schools in Nüremberg he moved to that city (1523), where the Lutheran movement had already prevailed for a year, led by the young and gifted Osiander.   Denck, also a young man, of about 25, hoped and expected to find that the new religion had brought morality and uprightness and godliness of life among the people.   He was disappointed to find that this was not so, and inquiring into the cause, was forced to the conclusion that it was due to a defect in the Lutheran teaching, which, while insisting on the doctrine of justification by faith, apart from works, and on the abolition of many abuses that had prevailed in the Catholic Church, neglected to press the necessity of obedience, self-denial, and the following of Christ, as being an essential part of true faith.   Perceiving these things by degrees, Osiander showed (1551) how experience only proved that the Wittenberg teaching made men "safe and careless." "Most men" he said, "dislike a teaching which lays upon them strict moral requirements that check their natural desires.   Yet they like to be considered as Christians, and listen willingly to the hypocrites who preach that our righteousness is only that God holds us to be righteous, even if we are bad people, and that our righteousness is without us and not in us, for, according to such teaching,

* "Ein Apostel der Wiedertäufer" Dr. Ludwig Keller.

they can be counted as holy people. Woe to those who preach that men of sinful walk cannot be considered pious; most are furious when they hear this, as we see and experience, and would like all such preachers to be driven away or even killed, but where that cannot be done, they strengthen their hypocrite preachers with praise, comfort, presents and protection, so that they may go on happily and give no place to the truth, however clear it may be, and thus the false saints and hypocritical preachers are one the same as the other; as the people so their priest. " Denck had perceived all this while Osiander was far from doing so, and was still calling Denck's teaching "horrible error. " Osiander, in fact, denounced Denck to the city magistrates, who invited him to appear before them and his Lutheran opponents. In the disputation which followed, Denck, according to one of the other side, "showed himself so able that it was seen to be useless to contend with him by word of mouth. " So it was decided that he should be required to give a written confession of his beliefs on seven important points that were indicated, Osiander declaring himself willing to reply to this in writing. When Denck's answers were presented, however, the Nüremberg preachers said it would not be wise that Osiander's promise should be fulfilled, nor did they deem themselves capable of convincing Denck, and accordingly preferred to give their reply to the City Council. The result was that (1525) Denck was required to quit Nüremberg before that night and get ten miles away from the city, with the threat that if he did not pledge himself on oath to do this he would be imprisoned. The reason given was that he had introduced unchristian errors and ventured to defend them, that he would not accept any instruction, and that his answers were so crooked and cunning that it was evidently useless to attempt to teach him. By the next morning Denck had said farewell to his family, left his situation, and set out on a wanderer's path, which lasted for the rest of his life.

In his "confession" Denck acknowledged the wretchedness of his natural state, but said that he was aware of something within him which was against sin and awakened desire after life and blessedness. He was told that these were to be obtained by faith, but saw that faith must mean something more than a mere acceptance of what he had heard or read. A natural resistance to reading the Scriptures was overcome by that voice of conscience within him which impelled him to do so, and he found that Christ revealed in the Scriptures corresponded to that which had been revealed of Him in his own heart. He found that he could not understand the Scriptures by a mere outward reading of them, but only as the Holy Spirit revealed them to his heart and conscience.

The document of the Lutheran ministers which led to Denck's exile stated that he "meant well", that "his words were written in such a way and with such Christian understanding that his thoughts and meaning might well be allowed", yet consideration for the unity of the Lutheran Church required them to act otherwise. In spite of this, wherever he came, Denck found that calumnies had preceded him, and that all kinds of evil doctrines were attributed to him which caused him to be avoided as a dangerous man. He never allowed himself to requite his adversaries as they had treated him; and although, according to the fashion of that time, the most violent denunciations of him were written, his own writings are free from any such spirit. He said, on an occasion of especial provocation: "Some have misrepresented and accused me to such an extent, that even a meek and humble heart is with difficulty held in check", and again: "it grieves me to my heart that I should be in disunion with many a one whom I cannot otherwise regard than as my brother, for he worships the God whom I worship and honours the Father whom I honour." "Therefore I will, if God will, as far as is possible, not make an adversary of my brother, nor of my Father a Judge, but, on the way, be reconciled with all my adversaries."

After a time spent in the hospitable home of one of the brethren in St. Gallen, Denck had to leave, as his host came into conflict with the authorities, and he found a place in Augsburg, through the influence of friends. In Augsburg there was at that time not only strife between the Lutherans and Zwinglians and between each of these and the Catholics, but a general depravity of morals, seriously affecting the people. Having compassion on the many distracted souls, Denck began to gather together such of the citizens as were willing to meet as a church of believers, who would combine faith in the atoning work of Christ with following in His footsteps in the conduct of their daily life. He had not yet joined himself to the companies of believers called by those outside, Baptists or Anabaptists, but he found himself doing in Augsburg what they were doing elsewhere, and what he had seen intimately at St. Gallen. A visit of Dr. Hubmeyer brought him to the decision to throw in his lot with the brethren and to be baptized. There were before Denck's arrival many baptized believers in Augsburg, and the church grew rapidly. Most were poor people, but there were also some of wealth and position. The writings and zeal of Eitelhans Langenmantel drew many. He was a son of one of the most eminent of Augsburg's citizens, a man who had been fourteen times Mayor, and had also occupied higher positions in the State. In 1527 the members of the church had increased to about eleven hundred, and their activities in the surrounding country helped in the founding and strengthening of churches in all the chief centres.

A writer well acquainted with the sources of information says:* "it may be believed that many, from a real need of the hea t, sickened by the recriminations and the mutual accusations of heresy from the different pulpits, sought refuge in being edified, quietly, and apart from all sectarianism. . . . It was a beautiful ideal which floated before the eyes of the purer spirits among the Anabaptists. They looked back with longing gaze to that glorious time when the pilgrim Apostles, going from town to town, founded the first Christian churches, where all came together in a spirit of love, as members of one body. "

Many hymns were written at this time in which the disciples expressed their worship and their experience.

As persecution began to be directed particularly against Denck he left Augsburg and took refuge in Strassburg, where there was a large assembly of baptized believers. The leaders of the Protestant party were two men of ability, Capito and Bucer, who had not attached themselves definitely either to Wittenberg or Zürich, though their relations with Zwingli and the Swiss Reformers were the

*"Reformations Geschichte Augsburg"   Friedrich Roth.   (München 1881).

more intimate. Capito hoped it might be possible to remain connected with both parties and so be a means of happier relations between them. He was also undecided on the question of baptism, and had friendly connections with many of the brethren. The presence among the brethren of some extreme men, of whom they failed to rid themselves, injured their influence and kept some from coming among them who would otherwise have done so. Zwingli's introduction of capital punishment for those who differed from him on points of doctrine weakened his influence with Capito. When Denck arrived, conditions were such and the brethren so numerous and influential that it seemed as though they might come to be the dominant factor in the religious life of the city. He soon became intimate with Capito, and his godliness, ability and personal charm drew to him, as to a trustworthy leader, not only the brethren who were looked upon as Baptists, but many others who were undecided as to the course they should take in such confusing conditions. Bucer regarded these circumstances with alarm, and, judging that there was no future for any party that could not fall back on the civil power to support it, he, in conjunction with Zwingli, worked so successfully on the fears of the City Council that within a few weeks of his arrival Denck received an order of expulsion. His sympathizers were so many that they could probably have resisted it and prevented his being exiled, but he, on the principle he always upheld, of submission to the authorities, left the city (1526).

In many dangers Denck wandered from place to place. In Worms, where there was a large congregation, he stayed for a time and had the translation of the Prophets printed which he and Ludwig Hetzer had made (1527). In three years thirteen editions of this translation were published. The first edition had to be printed five times, and in the following year six times more. The Augsburg edition was reprinted five times in nine months. Soon after this, Denck took a leading part in a Conference of brethren from many districts, in Augsburg, where he opposed some who were inclined to use force against the growing persecutions. This was called "the martyrs' conference", because so many who took part in it were later put to death. Reaching Basle, broken down in health through his many wanderings and privations, he came into touch with his friend of early days, the Reformer Hausschein, called Œcolampadius, who, finding him in a dying condition, provided for him a safe and quiet retreat, where he passed away in peace. Shortly before his death he wrote: "Hard and painful is for me my homelessness, but what presses upon me more is that my zeal has brought so little result and fruit. God knows I value no other fruit than that very many, with one heart and mind, should glorify the Father of our Lord Jesus Christ, whether they be circumcised or baptised or neither. For I think quite otherwise than those who bind the Kingdom of God too much to ceremonies and the elements of this world, whatever they may be." In days when tolerance was little practised he said: "in matters of faith all should be free, willing, and from conviction."

Disputes as to doctrine have not always been founded on the defence of truth by one party and of error by the other. Frequently dissension has arisen because one side has emphasized one aspect of the truth, while the other side has laid stress on a different aspect of the same truth. Each side has then made much of those portions of Scripture which support the view it favoured, and minimized or explained away those parts which the other side has considered important. Thus the reproach has arisen that anything can be proved from Scripture, which on this account has been looked upon as an unsafe guide. This characteristic of Scripture, on the contrary, exhibits its completeness. It is not one-sided, but presents in its turn every phase of truth. Thus the doctrine of justification by faith alone, without works, is plainly taught, but so, in its own place, is the balancing doctrine of the necessity of good works, and that they are the consequence and proof of faith. It is plainly taught that fallen man is incapable of any good, of any motion or will towards God, that salvation originates in the love and grace of God towards men; but, also, that there is in man a capacity for salvation, a conscience which responds to the Divine Light and Word, condemning sin and approving righteousness. Indeed, every great doctrine revealed in Scripture has a balancing truth and both are necessary to a knowledge of the whole truth.   In this the Word of God resembles the work of God in Creation, in which opposing forces work together to bring about the intended end.

It is often thought that when the Reformation was established, Europe was divided into Protestants (whether Lutheran or Swiss) on the one hand, and Roman Catholics on the other.   The large numbers of Christians are over-looked who did not belong to either party, but who, most of them, met as independent churches, not relying, as the others did, on the support of the civil power, but endeavour-ing to carry out the principles of Scripture as in New Testa-ment times.   They were so numerous that both the State Church parties feared they might come to threaten their own power and even existence.   The reason that so important a movement occupies so small a place in the history of those times is, that by the relentless use of the power of the State, the great Churches, Catholic and Pro-testant, were able almost to destroy it, the few adherents who were left being driven abroad or remaining only as weakened and comparatively unimportant companies.   The victorious party was also able to destroy much of the literature of the brethren, and, writing their history, to represent them as holding doctrines which they repudiated, and to give them names to which an odious significance was attached.

In 1527, under the guidance of Michael Sattler and others, a Conference was held in Baden, where it was agreed (1) that only believers should be baptized, (2) that discipline should be exercised in the churches, (3) that the Lord's Supper should be kept in remembrance of His death, (4) that members of the church should not have fellowship with the world, (5) that it is the duty of the shepherds of the church to teach and exhort, etc., (6) that a Christian should not use the sword or go to law, (7) that a Christian must not take an oath.   Sattler was active in preaching the Word in many districts, and came, in the Spring of 1527, from Strassburg to Württemberg.   In Rottenburg he was arrested and condemned to death for his doctrines. In accordance with the sentence of the Court, he was shame-fully mutilated in different parts of the town, then brought to the gate, and what remained of him thrown on the fire.

His wife and some other Christian women were drowned, and a number of brethren who were with him in prison were beheaded. These were the first of a terrible series of such executions in Rottenburg. The large meeting in Augsburg was scattered by similar means. The first to die was Hans Leupold, an elder of the church, who was arrested in a meeting, with 87 others, and beheaded (1528). He composed a hymn in prison which was included in the collection of the brethren. Many of the hymns of these Baptists were written in prison, and exhibit the deep experiences of suffering and of love to the Lord through which they passed. They spread rapidly among the suffering saints, to whom they brought strong consolation and encouragement. Two weeks later the gifted Eitelhans Langenmantel, in spite of his connections with the most influential families, was executed, along with four others. Large numbers were beaten out of the town, often branded with a cross on the forehead. In Worms the congregation of believers was so large that all efforts to disperse it failed; it continued to exist in secret.

Landgraf Philip of Hessen was a noble exception to the rulers of the time. He alone braved all the consequences of refusing to sign or obey the mandate of the Emperor Charles V, issued from Speyer, which solemnly commanded all rulers and officers in the Empire " . . . that all and every one baptized again or baptizing again, man or woman, of an age to understand, shall be judged and brought from natural life to death with fire and sword or the like according to individual ˙circumstance, without previous inquisition of the spiritual judge", also that any failing to bring their children to be baptized should come under the same law, also that none should receive or conceal or fail to give up any who might endeavour to escape from these regulations. The Elector of Saxony, counselled by the Wittenberg theologians, forced Landgraf Philip to banish or imprison some of the Baptists, but he could not be compelled to go beyond this and was able to boast that he had never had one put to death. He stood to it, that in times where one had one opinion and another another, those in error should be converted by instruction and not by force. He said he saw better lives among those called "fanatics" than among the Lutherans, and he could not bring his conscience to allow him to punish or put to death anyone for his faith, when there was not otherwise sufficient cause for doing so.

In the Palatinate there were many brethren in the districts of Heidelberg, Alzey, and Kreuznach. In the year 1529 alone, 350 were executed. Some especially cruel persecutions at Alzey drew from a brave Evangelical pastor, Johann Odenbach, a protest which does him honour. It is addressed to the "appointed judges of the poor prisoners in Alzey whom people call Anabaptists" and reads as follows—"You, as poor ignorant and unlearned people, ought to cry diligently and earnestly to the true Judge and pray for His Divine help and for wisdom and grace. Then you would not lightly stain your hands with innocent blood, even though Imperial Majesty and all the Princes in the world had commanded you thus to judge. These poor prisoners, with their baptism, have not so deeply sinned against God that He will damn their souls on that account, nor have they acted so criminally against the Government and against mankind as to forfeit their lives. For right baptism or second baptism is not such a power as that it can either save a man or condemn him. We must allow baptism to be just a sign by which we acknowledge that we are Christians, dead to the world, enemies of the Devil, wretched, crucified people, who seek not temporal but eternal blessings; striving unceasingly against flesh, sin and Devil, and living a Christian life. Not many of you judges would know what to say about right or wrong baptism if it came to being bound and questioned under torture. Ought you on that account to be put to the sword? No! I do not say this to support second baptism, which should be done away with by Holy Scripture and not by the hangman's hands. Therefore, dear friends, do not usurp that which belongs to the Divine Majesty, lest the wrath of God should overwhelm you worse than the Sodomites and all evil-doers on earth. You have had many thieves, murderers and scoundrels more mercifully treated in prison than these poor creatures who have neither stolen nor murdered, are not incendiaries or traitors, nor have committed any shameful sin, but who are against all such things and with sincere and simple intention, through a small error, have been baptized again to the honour of God, and not to

injure anyone. How can you possibly find it in your heart
or conscience to say or acknowledge that for this they should
be beheaded or that they will be damned for it? If you
would deal with them as Christian judges ought to do, and
if you knew how to instruct them out of the Gospel, there
would be no need of a hangman; in this way the truth
would doubtless prevail and imprisonment would be
sufficient punishment. In the same way your priests
ought to act, carrying them on their shoulders as erring
sheep to the fold of Christ and proving to them henceforth
that their office is to show them favour and brotherly love,
to comfort, sustain, and restore them with sweet evangelical doctrine. Do not let yourselves be deceived into
condemning these poor people to death. You ought to be
terrified in this matter, you ought to sweat blood for agony,
for you do not know wherein the error lies. You should not
just pay no heed when these poor creatures say: 'We desire
better instruction out of the Holy Scripture and are willing
to obey if a better way can be shown us out of the Gospel.'
Think of your eternal shame through such an error! Think
of the contempt and fury of the ordinary man when these
poor people are slaughtered! It will come to be said of
them: 'See with what great patience, love and worship
these pious people have died, how knightly have they
striven against the world!' Oh, that we might be as
guiltless before God as they, indeed, they have not been
overcome, they have suffered outrage: they are God's
holy martyrs. Everyone will say that it was not to do
away with the error of the poor Anabaptists that you gave
such a bloody judgment, but that you might destroy by
force the holy Gospel and the pure truth of God..."

The effect of this was that those judges refused to pronounce judgement in matters of faith.

Zwingli wrought his great Reformation work chiefly in
German Switzerland. In the city and Canton of Zürich
he came to exercise a predominant authority. In 1523
he introduced the State Church system into Zürich, and
the Great Council received the responsibility of giving
decisions in cases affecting the Church and doctrine.
This power was at once directed against the brethren.
A believer named Müller, brought before the Council

said: "Do not oppress my conscience, for faith is a free gift of God's mercy and is not to be interfered with by anyone. The mystery of God lies hidden, and is like a treasure in the field which no one can find unless the Spirit of the Lord show it to him. So I beg of you, you servants of God, leave me my faith free." This was not allowed. The new State Church accepted the principle of the old Church, that it is right to act against "heretics" by imprisonment and even death.

In his earlier years Zwingli had had close relations with the brethren. He had seriously considered the question of baptism and had stated that there was no Scripture for infant baptism. As he developed the movement of reform, however, on the lines of a State Church, depending on the civil power to enforce its decisions, he necessarily drew away from the brethren.

They were numerous and active in Zürich, * three of their number being especially prominent, and one of these formerly an intimate friend of Zwingli. This was Konrad Grebel, son of a member of the Zürich Council. He had distinguished himself in the Universities both of Paris and Vienna, and when he returned to Zürich attached himself to the congregation of believers there. Another was Felix Manz, an eminent Hebrew scholar, whose mother was also an ardent Christian and opened her house for meetings. The third had been a monk, who, being affected by the Reformation, came out of the Church of Rome. He was given the name of "Blaurock" or "Bluecoat" and was often called "Strong George" on account of his size and vigour.

These three were untiring, travelling, visiting from house to house, preaching, exhorting, and great numbers accepted the Gospel and were baptized and gathered as churches. In Zürich there were frequent public baptisms, and the believers met regularly for the Lord's Supper, which they called the Breaking of Bread. They spoke of themselves as the assembly of the true children of God, and kept themselves separate from the world, in

*Vorträge und Aufsätze aus der Comenius Gesellschaft. 7ter Jahrgang, 1 u 2 Stück. "Georg Blaurock und die Anfänge des Anabaptismus in Graubündten und Tirol" Aus dem Nachlasse des Hofrates Dr. Joseph R. von Beck. Herausgegeben von Joh. Loserth.

which they included both the Reformed and the Roman Catholic Churches. The Council forbade all these things, and a public disputation was ordered, but as the Council had power to decide the result, it only ended in an order that all who had not done so should have their children baptized within eight days, and the baptisms by the brethren were forbidden under heavy penalties. Grebel, Manz and Blaurock, however, only increased their activities, and people came by hundreds to hear the Word and to be baptized. While Grebel and Manz were moderate and persuasive in their ways, Blaurock was of an uncontrollable zeal and would at times go into the churches and interrupt the service, preaching there himself. The people were devoted to him, but the conflict with the authorities became rapidly more bitter, and many of the brethren were severely punished. Blaurock did not hesitate to say to Zwingli himself: "Thou hast, my Zwingli, constantly met the Papists with the statement that what is not founded in God's Word is of no value, and now thou sayest there is much that is not in God's Word and yet it is done in communion with God. Where is now the powerful word with which thou hast contradicted Bishop Faber and all the monks?" At last the three preachers and fifteen others, including six women, were condemned to imprisonment, with water, bread and straw, there to die and rot, and any persons baptizing or being baptized were ordered to be punished by drowning (1526). The prisoners escaped in various ways, they had many sympathizers, but persecution became relentless, and the Cantons of Bern and St. Gallen among others joined Zürich in endeavouring to exterminate the churches. In the Canton of Bern 34 persons were executed, and some who fled to Biel, where there was a large assembly of brethren, were followed there. The meetings, which were held secretly at night in a forest, were discovered and scattered, and fresh places of gathering had to be found. At this time Grebel died of the plague (1526), Blaurock was captured and condemned to be stripped and beaten with rods through the town "so that the blood should flow", and banished. Manz also was secured and was drowned.

All this did not check the spread of the churches,

which continued to increase, but it had the effect of driving into the neighbouring Austrian province of the Tyrol those whose preaching and testimony quickly established churches there. Among these was "Strong George" who travelled all over the Tyrol braving all dangers, and great numbers were won through his preaching, especially in and around Klausen, where the believers became very numerous and active in spreading the Word further. After many escapes Blaurock and a companion, Hansen Langegger, were caught and burnt in Klausen (1529).

In the same year Michael Kirschner, who had borne a good testimony for the Lord in Innsbruck, was publicly burnt in that town. Blaurock's dangerous service was taken up by Jakob Huter, among others. In the year Blaurock was burnt Huter was in a meeting for breaking bread, when it was surprised by soldiers; 14 brethren and sisters were arrested, but the rest escaped and Huter among them. In constant danger he went about, reconciling differences, encouraging the suffering, preaching the Word. Persecution was so severe that many fled into Moravia, where, for a time, they had liberty, but the frontiers were closely watched to prevent any from getting away, and arrangements were made with the Venetian Government, on the other side, to prevent the hunted men and women from escaping in that direction. All over Austria there was a great spread of the Gospel and numerous churches were founded, which, after long and heroic suffering, were scattered and crushed by persecution. In Tyrol and Görz a thousand persons were burnt, beheaded, or drowned. In Salzburg a meeting was surprised in the house of a pastor and a large number put to death. One girl of sixteen stirred such pity by her youth and beauty that all begged for her life, but as she would not recant, the executioner carried her in his arms to a horse-trough, held her under water until she was dead, and then laid the lifeless body on the flames. Ambrosius Spittelmeyer of Linz, after an active and fruitful testimony, was martyred at Nüremberg. The Church in Linz had a faithful overseer in Wolfgang Brandhuber, who, together with seventy members of the assembly, was put to death (1528). So, in place after place, the Lord's witnesses were raised up by the preaching of Jesus Christ and Him crucified, and in the most literal way followed in His footsteps. Troops of soldiers were sent through these countries to search out and kill those called "heretics", without trial.

Though they were called *Anabaptists*,* it was not the form of baptism that gave them courage to suffer as they did. They were aware of immediate communion with their Redeemer; no man and no religious form came between their souls and Him. With those called Mystics, they found that abiding in Christ and He in them, they shared His victory over the world. This fellowship with Him enabled them to understand their communion with those who shared it with them, and in their churches to realize the fellowship of saints. These churches had various beginnings, various histories, they differed according to the character of the persons in them; but all were alike in their desire to adhere to the pattern of primitive Christianity found in the New Testament; therefore they refused infant baptism, which the Reformers could not do, and they refused all worldly aid, without which it seemed to the great professing Churches impossible to maintain themselves. These things were only parts of a whole, which consisted in accepting the Scriptures as the sufficient, revealed will of God for their guidance and in putting their trust in Him to enable them to act upon them. Taking this path they were subject to special temptations, and wherever they yielded to fleshly desires, political aims or covetousness, their fall was great, but by far the greater part were enabled to bear a good testimony to the faithfulness of God. Their own description of the Christian Church is: "the assembly of all believers, who are gathered by the Holy Spirit, separated from the world by the pure teaching of Christ, united by Divine love, bringing to the Lord, from the heart, spiritual offerings. Whoever will be introduced into this Church", they said, "and become a member of the Household of God, must live and walk in God; whoever is outside this Church is out-

* Fontes Rerum Austriacarum. Oesterreichische Geschichts-Quellen. Abth. 2 Bd. 43. "Die Geschichts-Bücher der Wiedertäufer in Oesterreich-Ungarn, u. s. w. in der Zeit von 1526 bis 1785" Gesammelt, Erläutert und Ergänzt durch Dr. Josef Beck.

side Christ. " Their rejection of infant baptism often raised the question as to children who die early, and of them they said, they are made partakers of eternal life for Christ's sake.

In the Chronicles of the Anabaptists in Austria-Hungary, one of them writes: "The foundations of the Christian faith were laid by the Apostles here and there in different countries, but through tyranny and false teaching, suffered many a blow and hindrance, the Church being often so diminished that it could scarcely be seen whether a Church existed at all. As Elias said, the altars were broken down, the prophets slain, and he remained alone; but God did not let His Church disappear altogether. Otherwise this article of the Christian faith would have been proved false: 'I believe there is one Christian Church, one fellowship of the saints.' If she could not be pointed out with the finger, if at times scarcely two or three could be found, yet the Lord, according to His promise, has been with them, and because they remained true to His Word, has never forsaken them, but has increased and added to them, but when they became careless, forgetful of Christ's goodness, God withdrew from them the gifts with which He had endowed them and awakened true men in other places, giving gifts to them, with which they again built up a church to the Lord. So the kingdom of Christ, from the Apostles' time until now, has wandered from one nation to another, until it has come to us. "

"In other lands", he continues, "a good beginning was made and sometimes a good end, when the witnesses laid down their lives, but the tyranny of the Romish Church blotted out almost everything. Only the Pickards and Waldenses kept something of the truth. In the beginning of the reign of Charles V the Lord sent His light again. Luther and Zwingli destroyed as with thunderbolts the Babylonian evil, but they set up nothing better, for when they came to power they trusted more in man than in God. And therefore, though they had made a good beginning, the light of truth was darkened. It was as though one had patched a hole in the old boiler and it was only made worse. So they have brought up a people bold to sin. Many joined these two, Luther and

Zwingli, holding their teaching to be true, and some gave their lives for the truth, and without any doubt are saved, for they fought a good fight. " Then he describes the conflicts with Zwingli in Zürich on the subject of baptism, and how Zwingli, though he had formerly testified that infant baptism cannot be proved by any clear word of God from the Holy Scriptures, yet afterwards taught from the pulpit that the baptism of adults and believers is wrong and should not be endured; and how it was enacted that whoever in Zürich and the district should be baptized should be drowned in water. He shows how this persecution led to the scattering of many of Christ's servants and how some came to Austria, preaching the Word.

The spread of the churches in Austria and the surrounding States was marvellous; the accounts of the numbers put to death and of their sufferings are terrible, yet there never failed to be men willing to take up the dangerous work of evangelists and elders. Of some it is recorded, "they went full of joy to their death. While some were being drowned and put to death, the others who were waiting their turn, sang and waited with joy the death which was theirs when the·executioner took them in hand. They were firm in the truth which they knew and fortified in the faith which they had from God. " Such steadfastness constantly aroused astonishment, and inquiry as to the source of their strength. Many were won by it to the faith, but by the religious leaders, both of the Roman Catholic and Reformed Churches, it was generally attributed to Satan. The believers themselves said: "They have drunk of the water that flows from the Sanctuary of God, from the well of Life, and from this have obtained a heart that cannot be comprehended by human mind or understanding. They have found that God helped them to bear the cross and they have overcome the bitterness of death. The fire of God burned in them. Their tabernacle was not here on the earth but was pitched in Eternity, and they had foundation and certainty for their faith. Their faith blossomed as a lily, their faithfulness as a rose, their piety and uprightness as flowers of God's planting. The Angel of the Lord had swung his spear before them, so that the helmet of Salvation, the golden shield of David, could not be wrested from them. They have heard the horn blown in Sion and have understood it—and on that account they have cast down all pain and martyrdom and not feared. Their holy temper counted the things valued in the world as a shadow, knowing greater things. They were trained by God, so that they knew nothing, sought nothing, willed nothing, loved nothing, but the eternal, heavenly Good only. Therefore they had more patience in their sufferings than their enemies in inflicting them. "

The King, Ferdinand I, brother of Charles V of Spain, was a fanatical persecutor of the brethren.* Many of the authorities were unwilling instruments of his cruelty and would have spared the harmless, God-fearing people, but Ferdinand sent out an incessant stream of edicts and instructions exhorting them to greater ferocity and threatening them on account of their laxity. So we find magistrates in the Tyrol excusing the mildness of which their savage lord accused them, and writing to him— "for two years there has seldom been a day that Anabaptist matters have not come before our court, and more than 700 men and women in the Duchy of Tyrol, in different places, have been condemned to death, others have been banished from the country, and still more have fled, in misery, leaving their goods behind them and sometimes even forsaking their children. . . . We cannot conceal from your Majesty the folly generally found in these people, for they are not only not terrified by the punishment of others, but they go to the prisoners and acknowledge them as their brothers and sisters, and when on this account the magistrates accuse them, they acknowledge it willingly, without having to be put to the torture. They will listen to no instruction and it is seldom that one allows himself to be converted from his unbelief, for the most part they only wish that they may soon die. . . . we trust that your Royal Majesty will graciously understand from this our faithful report that we have not in any way been lacking in industry. "

*Archiv für Oesterreichische Geschichte. 78 Bd. "Der Anabaptismus in Tirol u.s.w. " Aus dem Nachlasse des Hofrates Joseph R. von Beck. Herausgegeben von Joh. Loserth.

After Ferdinand became King of Bohemia also, the refuge which that country and Moravia had provided for so many of the brethren was cut off and there was now no way of escape for them. Increasing rewards were offered to those who would betray an "Anabaptist" into the hands of the Government. The goods of those executed were taken and used in part to cover the expense of persecution. Women about to give birth to children were ordered back to prison until after the birth of the child and then executed. A magistrate in Sillian, one Jörg Scharlinger, was so much troubled at being obliged to have sentence of death executed on two boys, of 16 and 17 years, that he ventured to delay while he made further inquiries, and it was agreed that in such cases the accused were to be educated by Roman Catholics, the expense to be paid out of the confiscated goods of "Anabaptists", until the age of 18, when if they did not abjure they were then to be executed. Imagine a youth who loved the Lord awaiting his eighteenth birthday under such conditions!

Things grew worse and worse but Jakob Huter never ceased to hold meetings, in woods or in isolated houses, and the brethren and sisters as constantly risked their lives by receiving him. On one occasion he and a company of forty who had met for the breaking of bread in a house in St. Georgen were surprised by a party of soldiers and seven of them made prisoners. The rest escaped for that time and Huter among them, but at last he was taken, betrayed for reward. The house in which he was concealed was surrounded by soldiers in the night, and he and his wife and a girl and their elderly hostess were secured. With a gag in his mouth "so that he might not speak the truth" he was carried to Innsbruck, where there was rejoicing at his capture, for the king had been giving the authorities no rest, insisting that Huter must be found. As soon as he received the news he sent word that the prisoner must die, whether he recanted or not. Huter was not the man to recant; indeed he used the most violent language in denouncing King, Pope, and priests and all their ways. A request of the authorities that he might be privately beheaded in order to avoid the risk of a tumult among the sympathizing people was refused by Ferdinand, who insisted that he must be publicly burnt. He was therefore burnt in Innsbruck (1536).

His dangerous place as an acknowledged leader among the assemblies of the brethren was filled by Hans Mändl, a man of gentler spirit but equal courage, who had won the confidence and affection of all by his grace and gifts and unselfish devotion. In the Tyrol he baptized over 400 persons. He was repeatedly imprisoned, but the clergy sent to convert him complained of the kindness with which the magistrates treated him, and his frequent escapes from prison seem to indicate friendliness on the part of those in charge of him. Shortly after one of these escapes he addressed a meeting of a thousand brethren and sisters in a wood, but was captured again the same year (1560), This time he was cast into a deep dungeon in a tower in Innsbruck, where also two other brethren were confined. From his dungeon he wrote: "I have been put in the tower, where my dear brother Jörg Liebich has long lain. . . . he lies deep, but there is a little window high up, so that he gets some light when the sun shines. . . . I went as fearlessly to the torture as though it had been none. After they had questioned me three days they put me back in the tower. I hear the worms at times in the walls, the bats fly about me at night, and the mice rustle round, but God makes it all easy to me. He is most truly with me, even the ghosts which He sends at nights to frighten people He makes to be friendly and useful to me. " When his companion, Jörg Meyer, was examined, he was asked what had induced him to be baptized. He answered that before coming to this faith he had heard how one named Jakob Huter had been burnt in Innsbruck. It was said that a gag had been put in his mouth when he was taken to Innsbruck so that he might not make known the truth. Besides that, he had heard how at Klausen Ulrich Müllner had been put to death, a man acceptable to the people and whom they counted faithful, who had this same faith—a third time, he had seen with his own eyes how in Steinach they had burnt a man who had this faith. All this he took to heart most seriously, and considered that it must be a mighty grace of God that could make them so firm in their faith that they could endure to the

end, and this was the reason why he began to enquire
about these people. The three prisoners answered all the
questions put to them quietly and from Scripture; they
said that though now they had no certain dwelling place,
but were persecuted everywhere, yet a time would come
when they would be rewarded a hundredfold. They
affirmed that their faith was no "cursed sect" as was
said of them, and that they had no "ringleaders".
Mändl explained that he had been chosen by the brethren
and the assembly to which he belonged as a teacher and
guide.

Twelve men were taken from Innsbruck and the district as jurors. After having taken the usual oath that
they would give a verdict according to their judgement,
they were required to take another, namely that they
would approve the Emperor's decree as regards the
prisoners, which meant of course condemning them to
death. This they refused to do. The prosecution was
exceedingly angry, but Ferdinand (now become Emperor) did not like to act too harshly against them for
fear of arousing general opposition. The men were therefore argued with and threatened until nine of them yielded,
but three, remaining firm in their refusal, were imprisoned. After a few days' imprisonment these also
yielded and all the jurymen took the required oath,
which settled the verdict before the trial began. Mändl
was condemned to be burnt, the two others to be beheaded. They had written to the brethren just before,
from prison: "We send you word that after Corpus
Christi they will condemn us and we shall pay our vow
to God. We do it with joy and are not sad, for the day is
holy unto the Lord." Among the crowds that came to
witness their death was Leonhard Dax, formerly a priest,
but now one of the brethren, whose fearless greeting of the
prisoners as they passed, cheered them much. They
addressed the crowd, exhorting them to repentance and
bearing testimony to the truth. When their sentence
was read out they reproached the magistrates and the
jury for shedding innocent blood, and these excused
themselves by saying that they acted under compulsion
of the Emperor. . . . "O blind world" exclaimed Mändl
"each man should act according to his own heart and

conscience, but you condemn us according to the Emperor's order!" They preached further to the people, Mändl continuing until he was hoarse. "Do stop, my Hans!" cried the magistrate, but Mändl continued, and said: "What I have taught and testified is the Divine truth." They spoke up to the moment of their death, for no one would hinder them. One of them was so ill that it was feared he might die before he could be executed, so he was beheaded first. Then the other turned to the executioner and cried with triumphant courage: "Here I forsake wife and child, house and farm, body and life for the sake of the faith and the truth", then kneeled down and offered his head to the fatal blow. Hans Mändl was bound to a ladder and cast alive into the flames where the bodies of his fellow-martyrs had already been thrown. There was one witness, Paul Lenz, who so took all this to heart that he shortly after joined the despised disciples, to share with them in the sufferings of Christ.

In some parts, and especially in Moravia, communities were formed where many believers lived together as one large household, under the same guidance and having all things common. This was done, partly to provide places of refuge, in favoured districts, where those driven out of other parts by persecution might find a home; partly also in imitation of the practice of the church at Jerusalem at the beginning. Though such community of goods was a mark of special grace in Jerusalem, when all the believers lived in one place and could all meet in the temple, yet it was not a command laid upon the Church, was impossible when the churches were scattered everywhere, and was not practiced in New Testament times outside of Jerusalem. These communities in Moravia and elsewhere did provide places of refuge for many; much spiritual blessing was experienced in them in their best days, and the excellent work done, in farming and in the practice of various handicrafts, made them wealthy. But serious disadvantages showed themselves in time. The training of children in such a community suffered as compared with training in a Christian family. A certain gloomy moroseness of temper became noticeable. Many of the divisions which weakened the churches had their origin in the communities. When war spread over the districts where they were, their comparative wealth and the concentration in them of considerable accommodation and supplies, attracted the soldiery, and this was one of the causes which led to their abandonment.

In this period events took place in Münster which, though not connected with the Christian congregations, yet did their cause more harm in Germany than anything that had happened before. In such times of excitement it could not but be that unbalanced minds would be liable to rush into extremes. The cruelty with which innocent people were treated on account of their faith aroused wild indignation in many who yet did not share that faith, and the systematic slaughter of the wisest and best, those who were elders and leaders of the churches, removed the very men most capable of checking extravagance and fanaticism and left large opportunity to inferior men to exercise their influence. The sight of cruel persecution and murder caused many to think that the end had come and the Day of Redemption was near, a day too, of vengeance on the oppressors. Men arose pretending to be prophets and to foretell the near approach of the setting up of the Kingdom of Christ.

Münster* was the capital of a Principality governed by a bishop, who was its civil as well as its ecclesiastical ruler. He levied taxes and filled all important positions with members of the clergy. This kept the citizens in a constant state of discontent. Bernard Rothmann, a young and inquiring theologian, travelled, visited Luther, but was more influenced by Capito and Schwenckfeld, whom he met in Strassburg. He was a good preacher, a man of strong sympathy for all that were oppressed, and personally of ascetic habits. When he came to Münster his preaching drew crowds of hearers,

---

* "History of the Reformation" T. M. Lindsay, M.A., D.D., Edinburgh, 1907.
"Geschichte der Wiedertäufer und ihres Reichs zu Münster" Dr. Ludwig Keller, 1880.

and caused such excitement that many of the citizens
took part in an attack on the images in the church of
St. Maurice, which they destroyed. To quell the rising
disorder the bishop made use of his military force, but
Philip, Landgraf of Hessen, intervened, and as a result
Münster was declared an evangelical city and was en-
rolled in the Smalcald League of Protestant Principalities. This change attracted crowds of persecuted
people from the surrounding Catholic countries to
Münster, which they could now look upon as a place of
refuge. They were of all kinds, some of them saints,
persecuted for Christ's sake, whom it was an honour to
receive, others disorderly or fanatical persons whose
presence endangered the peace of the city. Most arrived
in a destitute state and were received, under Rothmann's
teaching and example, with the utmost kindness and
liberality. One of the immigrants convinced Rothmann
that infant baptism was contrary to Scripture, so that,
as a matter of conscience, he had to refuse to practise it.
On this account the magistrates of the city removed him
from the office of preacher, but his popularity with the
citizens was such that they refused to accept his dis-
missal, and a public disputation on the subject of baptism
was held in which it was judged that Rothmann had
proved his case. An Anabaptist preacher, one of the
strangers who had come in, by the violence of his talk,
excited riots, so that the magistrates had him arrested,
but the guilds rescued him and the conflict reached such
a pitch that the magistrates were deposed from office and
an Anabaptist Council was elected in their place.

Meanwhile the bishop had been collecting troops, and
now invested the city and cut off supplies, which was
the more serious on account of the large number of
destitute strangers who were being fed. Among the
immigrants were two Dutchmen, who in turn came to
exercise paramount influence in Münster, Jan Matthys
and Jan Bockelson, the latter a tailor, usually known as
John of Leyden. Matthys, a tall, powerful man of
commanding appearance, able to sway the crowd by his
eloquence, gave himself out as a prophet, and was
believed in. He was one of those fanatics who are
capable of going to any extreme, and are the more

dangerous because of their sincerity. He obtained absolute control of the Council, and his view as to separation from the world led to an ordinance that no unbaptized person might be tolerated in the city; within a few days all such must be baptized, or leave Münster, or die. Many were baptized, but many left rather than yield. It was wicked and fanatical, but not so wicked nor so fanatical as the action of those Churches and States which for centuries, throughout the greater part of Europe. had condemned to cruel deaths those who did not believe in infant baptism. The city being now purged of "unbelievers", changes took place rapidly, community of goods was introduced, hastened by the necessities of the siege; the keeping of Sunday was abolished, as being a legal institution, all days being considered alike; the Lord's Supper was publicly celebrated at times, with preaching. Matthys had control of the distribution of food and other necessaries, with seven deacons whom he had appointed to help him, and this gave rise to another conflict. A shoemaker named Hubert Rüscher put himself at the head of a body of the original citizens to protest against the foreigners' having taken to themselves the administration of the city, to express their indignation on this account and their fears of what it might lead to if not checked. A popular gathering was held in the Cathedral square where Matthys at once condemned Rüscher to death, and Bockelson, claiming a revelation that he should execute the sentence, wounded the shoemaker severely with his halberd. Three men had the temerity to protest against this injustice, but were themselves imprisoned and hardly escaped with their lives. A few days later the wounded man was brought up again and his execution completed by Matthys, and so the ascendancy of the Council was maintained. All this time fighting was going on with the bishop's troops, and provisions in the city were becoming scarcer. One evening Jan Matthys was sitting at supper, with others, in a friend's house, when it was noticed that he had fallen into deep thought. After a time he rose and said: "Loved Father, not my will but Thine be done", then he kissed his friends and left, with his wife. The next day he left the city, with twenty companions, marched to the outposts of the besieging force and attacked them.

Numbers of the enemy came up and there was furious fighting. One by one the little force fell, overwhelmed, among the last being Jan Matthys, fighting desperately to the end.

There was consternation in Münster, but Jan Bockelson soon took the authority into his own hands, and, pretending to a revelation that the Council should be abolished, as being a mere human institution, did away with it and ruled supreme, appointing twelve "elders" to be associated with him. He combined the power of an orator with practical gifts for organization. New laws were introduced to suit the "New Israel" and the people readily believed that they were the special objects of the love and grace of God and were the true Apostolic Church, and that what they were doing in Münster was the pattern which would in due time be reproduced in the whole world, over which they would rule. The number of men in Münster was small, the number of women was many times more, and there were a great many children. In July 1534, Bockelson called Rothmann and the other preachers and the twelve elders to the Town Hall, and astonished them all by proposing the introduction of polygamy. This was an unheard of suggestion in such a place, for the people were for the most part religious and accustomed to a life of self-denial, and the moral conditions of the city were unusually good. Only a few weeks earlier a tract had been published in the town which treated of marriage among other subjects, and shewed it to be the sacred and indissoluble union of one man with one woman. Bockelson's proposal was resented and refused by the preachers and elders, but he was not to be deflected from his purpose, and for eight days he argued and insisted with all his eloquence and influence. He made use of the failures of some good men in Old Testament days to pretend that Scripture sanctions polygamy. On the same reasoning he might have argued in favour of any sin. His chief argument was that of necessity, because of the great preponderance of women over men in Münster, and at last he gained his point, and for five days the preachers preached Polygamy, in the Cathedral square, to all the people. At the end of this time Bernard Rothmann

promulgated a law that all younger women were to be
married, and the older ones attached to the household of
some man for protection. Bockelson (which may possibly
help to explain his eagerness for the new law) immediately
married Divara, the widow of Jan Matthys, a woman
distinguished for her beauty and attainments. The
opposition, however, was so strong as to lead to civil
war within the besieged city. A master-smith, Heinrich
Möllenbecker, led the revolting party; they captured
the Town Hall and made prisoners of some of the preachers and threatened to open the gates of the city to the
besiegers unless the former government of Münster were
restored. It seemed not unlikely that Bockelson's
government would fall, but the preachers stood by him,
and most of the women supporting him, the opposition
was outnumbered, the Town Hall stormed, and all
resistance quenched. The effects of the new law were
altogether harmful, and before the end of the year it was
abolished.

In spite of all these internal disorders the defence of
the city was carried on with energy and important
successes were obtained in engagements with the enemy.
There was still hope that help might come from outside.
A further stage was reached when Bockelson was proclaimed king. He had his prophet, formerly a goldsmith,
who, in the market place proclaimed John of Leyden as
king of the whole earth, and made known the kingdom
of the New Zion. The coronation took place in great
state in the market place; gold, taken from the people,
was used for crowns and other royal emblems. From
among his many wives Divara was chosen as queen.
The provision for the king and his bodyguard and Court
and for the attendants of the queen was sumptuous and
complete in every detail, but the people, suffering the
extremities of the siege, could hardly be comforted by
promises of the triumph of the kingdom, immediately to
take place. Yet they continued steadfast, and the city
could not be taken until at last by treachery it was
opened to the bishop's troops. Then began the slaughter
of its inhabitants, of whom none were spared. A band
of 300 defending themselves desperately in the market
place were promised a safe conduct to leave the city if

they would lay down their arms. They accepted these terms, the promise was not kept, and they perished with the rest. A court was established for the trial of such Anabaptists as had not been killed. Divara was offered her life if she would recant, but she chose rather to die. Jan of Leyden and other leaders were publicly tortured and executed in the place where he had been crowned, and their bodies were exposed in iron cages on a tower of St. Lambert's church (1535).

Advantage was taken of these events to apply the hated name of Anabaptist to all who dissented from the three great Church systems and, by pretending that the congregations of pious, quiet and long-suffering Christians were of the same mind as those who set up the kingdom and practiced polygamy in Münster, to justify their being treated as dangerous and subversive sects. The control of literature for a long period enabled the victorious party to confound entirely different sets of people and so to mislead succeeding generations. Although Luther and Melanchthon condoned polygamy in some cases, no one tries to prove by this that Lutheranism as a whole is a system which enjoins it, yet the one would not be more unreasonable than the other.

Many churches and Christians have been so unremittingly and violently accused of enormities of wickedness and error that the calumny has come to be generally believed and is usually accepted without question. This should not be a matter for surprise, for the Lord Himself when He announced His coming shame, suffering, death and resurrection, immediately added that His disciples must follow Him. He was misrepresented and falsely accused; a robber was preferred to Him; rulers and mob cried wildly for His crucifixion. His death was in the company of malefactors and His resurrection was not believed in by the world, hardly by His own disciples. What wonder, then, that those who followed Him endured the same. Caiaphas and Pilate, the religious and the civil powers, joined to condemn them to spitting, scourging and cruel death; the multitude, learned and ignorant, cried out against them; they were crucified between two malefactors, False Doctrine and Evil Life, with whom they had no connection but that of being nailed in their midst. Their own books were burnt, and doctrines were invented for them, suited to secure their condemnation. Though they were of godly and kindly life they were described as guilty of conduct which existed only in the vile imagination of their accusers, that the cruelty of their murderers might be condoned. Called Paulicians, Albigenses, Waldenses, Lollards, Anabaptists, and many other names the very mention of which carried to the mind the meaning heretic, schismatic, turner of the world upside down, they went before the same Judge who stood to receive Stephen stoned by the doctors of his day; and their teachings of tolerance, love, and compassion for the oppressed have become the heritage of multitudes to whom their very names are unknown.

Menno Simon, who lived through these times (1492-1559) and was well qualified to speak, being one of the principal teachers among those who practiced the baptism of believers, wrote: "No one can truly charge me with agreeing with the Münster teaching; on the contrary, for seventeen years, until the present day, I have opposed and striven against it, privately and publicly, by voice and pen. Those who, like the Münster people, refuse the cross of Christ, despise the Lord's Word, and practice earthly lusts under the pretence of right doing, we never will acknowledge as our brethren and sisters." "Do our accusers mean to say that because we are outwardly baptized with the same kind of baptism as they, that therefore we must be reckoned as being of the same body and fellowship; then we answer: If outward baptism can do so much, then they themselves may consider what sort of fellowship theirs is, since it is clear and evident that adulterers and murderers and such like have received the same baptism as they!"

After the events at Münster, the congregations of believers, falsely accused of complicity in those fanatical excesses, were persecuted with greater violence than ever, and all expectation that they might gain liberty of conscience and of worship, and become a power for the general good of the German peoples, was extinguished. The scattered and harrassed remnants were visited and sustained, in the face of the greatest dangers, by Menno Simon, after whom some of the reorganized companies, though not of their own choice, came to be called Mennonites.

In his autobiography,* written after he had been for eighteen years engaged in this work, he relates how at the age of 24 he became a priest (Roman Catholic) in the village of Pingjum (in Friesland, North Holland). "As to the Scriptures", he says, "I had never in my life touched them, for I feared that if I read them I might be misled. . . . A year later the thought came to me whenever I had to do with bread and wine in the Mass, that perhaps it was not the Lord's flesh and blood. . . . at first I supposed such thoughts came from the Devil who would lead me astray from my faith. I often confessed this and prayed; however I could not get rid of such thoughts." He passed his time, with other priests, in drinking and various useless pastimes, and whenever the Scriptures were referred to he could do nothing but make fun of them. "At last" he writes, "I decided to read the New Testament once through diligently. I had not gone far with it before I became aware that we had been deceived. . . . Through the Lord's grace I advanced from day to day in the knowledge of the Scriptures, and some called me an Evangelical Preacher, although wrongly. Everyone sought after and praised me, for the world loved me and I the world. Yet it was said generally that I preached God's Word and was a fine man.

"Afterwards, though I had never in my life heard of brethren, it happened that a god-fearing, pious hero, Sicke Snyder by name, was beheaded in Leeuwarden, because he had renewed his baptism. That sounded extraordinary in my ears that another baptism should be spoken of. I examined the Scripture diligently and thought the matter over earnestly, but I could find no news there of infant baptism. When I recognized this I spoke of it with my pastor, and after much conversation, brought him so far that he had to acknowledge that infant baptism had no foundation in the Scripture." Menno then consulted books and asked counsel of Luther

---

*"Geschichte der Alt-Evangelischen Mennoniten Brüderschaft in Russland" P. M. Friesen.

and from Bucer and others.   Each gave him a different reason for baptizing infants, but none of these corresponded with the Scripture.

At this time he was transferred to his native village, Witmarsum (also in Friesland), where he continued reading the Bible and was successful and admired, but continued to live a careless, self-indulgent life.   "See my reader" he continues, "I obtained my knowledge both of baptism and the Supper, by God's great grace, through enlightening of the Holy Spirit by means of much reading of Scripture and meditation on it, and not through the instrumentality of misleading sects, as I am blamed for doing.   Yet if any men have in any way been at all helpful to my progress I will for ever thank the Lord for it.   When I had been about a year in the new place it happened that some brought baptism forward. I do not know whence those came who began it, where they belonged to, or what they were, and I do not now know, I did not even see them.   Then the Münster sect broke out, through which many pious hearts, also from among us, were deceived.   My soul was in great distress, for I noticed that they were zealous and yet in doctrine were in error.   With my little gift, through preaching and exhortation I opposed the error, as well as I could. . . All my exhortations effected nothing, because I myself was doing what I knew was not right.   Yet the report was spread abroad that I was great at stopping the mouths of these people and all thought highly of me.   So I saw that I was the champion of the unrepentant who all referred to me.   This caused me no little anguish of heart, and I sighed on this account to the Lord and prayed : Lord help me that I may not load myself with other people's sins !   My soul was troubled and I thought of the end how that if I gained the whole world and should live a thousand years, and then at last must bear God's heavy hand and wrath, what should I then have gained ?

"After this these poor misled sheep, having no true shepherds, after many cruel edicts, after much slaughter and murder, gathered together in a place called Oude Kloster, and, alas ! following the godless Münster teaching, against the Spirit, Word, and example of Christ, drew the sword in their own defence which the Lord had commanded Peter to put into the sheath. When this took place the blood of these people, although they were misled, fell so heavy on my heart that I could not bear it nor find any rest in my soul. I considered my unclean, fleshly life, my hypocritical teaching and idolatry, which I exhibited daily, though without any liking for it, and striving against my own soul. I had seen with my own eyes how these zealots, though not in the leading of wholesome doctrine, willingly yielded children, goods and blood for their conviction and faith, and I was one of those who had helped to show some of their number the evils of Popery; nevertheless I had continued in my gross living and known evil and that for no other reason than that I liked the comforts of the flesh and wished to avoid the cross of Christ. These thoughts gnawed at my heart to such an extent that I could bear it no longer. I thought to myself: Wretched man that I am, what shall I do? If I continue in this way, and, with the knowledge that has been given me, do not yield myself wholly to my Lord's Word, do not condemn with the Word of the Lord the unrepentant fleshly life and hypocrisy of the theologians, as well as their corrupted baptism, Supper, and false Divine Services, as far as my small gift enables me; if, because of fear of my flesh, I do not open up the real basis of truth, do not, as far as I can, direct the innocent wandering lambs, who would so willingly do right if they only knew how, to the true pasture of Christ, how will not this blood shed, although it is that of erring ones, speak against me in the judgement of the almighty and great God, and pronounce judgement upon my poor soul! My heart trembled in my body. I prayed to my God, with sighs and tears that He would grant the gift of His grace to me a troubled sinner, create in me a clean heart, through the efficacy of the blood of Christ forgive my unclean walk and vain gross life, and give to me wisdom, spirit, courage, and manly heroism so that I might preach genuinely His worshipful high Name and His holy Word and bring to light His truth unto His praise.

"Now I began, in the Name of the Lord to teach publicly from the pulpit the true word of repentance, to direct the people to the narrow way, to condemn all sins and godless ways, as well as all idolatry and false Divine worship, and to testify openly what baptism and the Lord's Supper are according to the mind and principle of Christ, as far as I had, up to that time, received grace from my God.   I also warned everyone against the Münster wickedness, its king, polygamy, kingdom and sword; this I did earnestly and faithfully, until, after nine months, the Lord reached out to me His Fatherly Spirit, His help and mighty hand, so that, all at once, without compulsion, I was able to let go my honour, my good name and reputation, which I had among men, as well as all my antichristian wickedness and my coarse presumptuous life.   Now I placed myself willingly in utter poverty and misery, under the heavy cross of my Lord Christ, feared God in my weakness, sought God-fearing people, of whom I found some, though not many, in real zeal and doctrine; I disputed with those that were turned aside, won some of them through the help and power of God and led them, by God's Word, to the Lord Christ.   Those that were hard and obstinate I committed to the Lord.   See, my reader, thus the merciful Lord through the free gift of His great grace to me a wretched sinner, first stirred in my heart, gave me a new mind, humbled me in His fear, brought me to some measure of knowledge of myself, led me from the ways of death to the narrow way of life and called me in pure mercy into the fellowship of the saints.   To Him be praise for ever! Amen.

"About a year later, as I was quietly reading and writing, searching in the Word of the Lord, it came to pass that six, seven or eight persons came to me, who were of one heart and of one soul; in their faith and life, as far as one could judge, blameless; separated from the world according to the testimony of the Scripture, under the cross, holding in horror not only the Münster, but also all the evils and sects worthy of condemnation in all the world. These besought me with many entreaties, in the name of those who feared God, who walked in one spirit and mind with me and with them, that I might take to heart the heavy sorrow and crying need of the distressed souls, for the hunger is great, the faithful householders very few, and that I might put to usury the

pound that I had undeservedly received from the Lord. . .
When I heard this, my heart was deeply troubled, anguish
and fear encircled me; on the one side I saw the littleness
of my gift, my lack of learning, my weak nature, the
fearfulness of my flesh, the measureless wickedness,
contrariety and tyranny of this world, the great, mighty
sects, the craftiness of many spirits, and the heavy cross
which were I to begin, would press no little upon me; on
the other side, however, I saw the pitiable hunger, the lack
and the need of the God-fearing pious children, for I
saw clearly enough, they were as simple, forsaken sheep
that have no shepherd. At last, after much entreaty, I
placed myself at the disposal of the Lord and His church,
on condition that they would for a time, with me, fer-
vently call on the Lord, that if it should be His gracious
will that I could and should serve to His praise, that His
Fatherly goodness might give me such a heart and temper
that I could testify, with Paul: Woe is me if I preach not
the Gospel; if otherwise, that He would so order it that
the matter should be prevented. . . . See, dear reader,
that I have not been called to this service by the Münster
people nor by any other seditious sect, as is calumni-
ously said of me, but, unworthy as I am, by such a
people . . . who were willing to follow Christ and His
Word, who, in the fear of their God lived a contrite life,
in love served their neighbours, patiently carried the
cross, sought the salvation and good of all men, loved
righteousness and truth, and loathed unrighteousness and
wickedness. These are certainly living and powerful
witnesses that they were not such a perverse sect as they
are accused of being, but true Christians, although
unknown to the world, if it is at all to be believed that
the Word of Christ is true and His spotless, holy example
is infallible and right.

"Thus I, a miserable, great sinner have been enlightened by the Lord, converted, have fled from Bablyon
and entered Jerusalem and finally have come to this
difficult and high service. As the persons named above
did not cease their request, and also my own conscience
impelled me . . . because I saw the great hunger and need
. . . I surrendered myself to the Lord with body and soul,
committed myself into His gracious hand, and began at

that time (1537) to teach and to baptize according to His holy Word, with my little gift to work in the Lord's field, to build His holy city and temple, to bring the fallen stones back to their place.   And the great and mighty God has so acknowledged, in many cities and countries, the word of true repentance, the word of His grace and power, together with the wholesome use of His holy sacraments, through our small service, our teaching and unlearned writings, in fellowship with the true service, the work and help of our faithful brethren; He has made the appearance of His Church to be so glorious, and gifted her with such invincible power, that not only have many proud, haughty hearts become humble, not only unclean ones pure, drunkards sober, the covetous generous, the cruel kindly, the godless God-fearing; but, for the glorious testimony that they bear they have faithfully given goods and blood, body and life, as one may daily see to the present day.   These surely could not be the fruits and signs of a false doctrine, with which God does not work; it could not exist so long under such heavy cross and misery, if it were not the Word and power of the Almighty.   Further, they are armed with such great grace and wisdom, as Christ promised to all His own, they are so gifted of God in their temptations that all the learned of this world and the most celebrated theologians, as well as all the blood-guilty tyrants, who (may God have mercy on them!) boast that they also are Christians, must stand there ashamed and overcome by these invincible heroes and pious witnesses of Christ; so that they have no other weapon, can find no other means but exile, seizing, torture, burning and murder, as has been the habit and custom of the Old Serpent from the beginning, as in many places in our Netherlands, is, alas! daily to be seen.

"See, this is our call and doctrine, these are the fruits of our service, on account of which we are so terribly blasphemed and persecuted with such enmity. Whether all prophets, apostles and faithful servants of God have not produced the same fruits through their service we will willingly leave to the judgement of all good people . . . if the evil world would listen to our teaching, which is not ours but that of our Lord Jesus Christ, and follow it in the fear of God, there is no doubt that a better and more Christian world would appear than now, alas! it is. I thank my God, who has given me the grace, that, even if it should be with my own blood, I desire that the whole world might be snatched out of its godless evil ways and won for Christ.

" . . . I hope also, through the Lord's help, that no one in the whole world may be able truthfully to accuse me of covetousness or of luxurious living. Gold and riches have I none, do not even desire them, although there are some who, out of a dishonest heart, say that I eat more roast than they do mince, and drink more wine than they do beer. . . . He who . . . has bought me . . . and called me to His service, knows me and knows that I seek neither money nor goods, neither pleasure nor comfort on earth, but only my Lord's praise, my own salvation, and that of many. On which account I have had to suffer, with my delicate wife and little child, such excessive fear, pressure, sorrow, misery, and persecution, now these eighteen years, that I have to live in poverty and in constant fear and danger of our lives. Yes, when the preachers lie on soft beds and pillows, we must generally creep secretly into hidden corners. When they openly enjoy themselves at weddings, etc., with pipes, drums, and flutes, we must look round every time a dog barks for fear those should be there who would seize us. Whereas they are greeted by everyone as Doctor or Master, we must let ourselves be called Anabaptists, Corner-Preachers, Deceivers, and Heretics, and are greeted in the Devil's name. Finally, instead of being rewarded, as they are, for their service, with high salaries and good days, our reward and share from them is fire, sword, and death.

"See, my true reader, in such anxiety and poverty, sorrow and danger of death, I, wretched man, have carried out unceasingly my Lord's service to this hour, and hope to continue it further through His grace, to His praise, as long as I wander in this world. What now I and my true fellow-workers have sought in this difficult and dangerous service may easily be measured by all well-wishers, by the work itself and its fruits, but I will once more beg the sincere reader, for Jesus' sake, to receive in love this confession, wrung from me, of my enlightening, conversion and call, and apply it for the best. I have done it out of great need in order that the God-fearing reader may know how things took place, for I have been everywhere slandered by the preachers and blamed contrary to the truth, as though it were by a revolutionary sect that I was called and ordained to this office. He who fears God, let him read and judge!"

Menno Simon* devoted himself to visiting, gathering together again and building up the churches of believers scattered by persecution. This he did in the Netherlands, until (1543) he was declared an outlaw, a price set on his head, any who should shelter him condemned to death, and pardon promised to criminals who should deliver him into the hands of the executioner. Obliged thus to leave the Low Countries, after many wanderings and dangers, he found a refuge in Fresenburg, Holstein, where Count Alefeld was able to protect him, and not him only, but large numbers of the persecuted brethren. This nobleman, affected by the crying injustice from which these innocent people suffered, received them with the utmost kindness, and with him they found not only a dwelling place and occupation, but also liberty of worship, so that a numerous church gathered in the village of Wüstenfelde, and others in the surrounding district. In Fresenburg Menno was supplied with means for printing, and was able freely to publish his writings, which were widely circulated, and, coming into the hands of those in authority in different States, enlightened them as to the true character of the teachings which they, without understanding them, were so ruthlessly endeavouring to suppress. This had its effect in lessening the persecution and bringing about a measure of liberty of worship. Menno died peacefully in Fresenburg (1559).

New industries were established in Holstein by the immigrants, which flourished and brought prosperity to the country until they were swept away by the Thirty Years' War.

* "Fundamente der Christlichen Lehre u. s. w. " Joh. Deknatel.

A small book published by Pilgram Marbeck in 1542 throws valuable light on the teaching and practices of the brethren.* They doubtless differed among themselves on some points, but such a book as this shows the honest, genuine endeavour there was on their part to understand and carry out the Scriptures in a simple, straightforward way. Although this writer expresses an extreme view of the importance attaching to outward observances, yet there is an entire absence in the book of any of the evil teachings so commonly attributed to them. In his long title the writer says that the book is intended to bring help and comfort to all true, believing, pious, and good-hearted men, by showing them what the Holy Scriptures teach as to Baptism, the Lord's Supper, etc.

Referring his readers to many passages of Scripture in support of what he says, the author concludes: "Therefore as we have before made known our thought, understanding, opinion and faith with regard to both baptism and the supper, we will now close with a further general account of the use of both, and especially as to why and for what purpose they have been outwardly appointed. As Christ Jesus desires to be acknowledged, not only in His assembly, but also through it, so He will have His holy name acknowledged and praised by His own before the world. Therefore Christ, alongside of the outward preaching of His Gospel, has also commanded and instituted these two, namely, outward baptism and the supper to carry on and preserve the outward, pure, holy assembly. And if the matter be seen in its true light, we must say that three things are necessary to the economy of a Christian assembly, namely, true preaching of the Gospel, true baptism, and a true keeping of the Lord's Supper. Where these are not carried on, or where one of them is lacking, it is not possible for a genuine, pure Christian assembly to stand and maintain an outward testimony.

* Vermanung - auch gantz klarer, gründtlicher uñ unwidersprechlicher bericht, zů warer Christlicher, ewigbestendiger pundtssuereynigung allen waren glaubigen frummen, und gůtthertzigen menschen zů hilff und trost, mit grund heyliger schrifft, durch bewerung warer Tauff und Abentmals Christi sampt mitlauffung und erklärung jrer gegensachen und Argumenten, wider alle vermeynte Christliche Pündtnus, so sich bissher uñ noch, onder dem nammen Christi zůtragend.

" . . . in order that the outward assembly of God may be gathered, begun and upheld there must be the preaching of the true and wholesome Gospel. That is the living fishing-net which must be cast out among all men, for all men swim in the morass of this world, are like wild beasts and by nature children of wrath. Those that are caught in this net or by this line, that is, with the Word of the Gospel, when they hear it and with firm faith cling to it, are brought out of darkness into light and have power to be changed from condemned children of wrath into children of God. Of these, as Peter says, the temple of God and assembly of Christ is being built up, as with living stones. For the Christian church is an assembly of those who are true believers and children of God, who praise and publish the Name of God. None have a place in it except believers, for we see that by nature all men are without understanding in Divine things, and it is only by the Word that they are brought to a right faith in, and understanding of, Christ; and the Scripture shows us no other way. Therefore this is the first beginning, by which all men must be gathered and through which they must be brought to the knowledge of God and to His Holy Church (as far as we are able to judge) by the preaching and hearing of the Word of God, which is the cause from which faith comes, and then they are counted as children of God, and then they may be reckoned as members of the Holy Church. . . .

"The next thing for the building of the Church is holy baptism, which is the entrance and door into the holy church, so that it is in accordance with the ordinance of God that no one should be allowed to enter the church except through baptism. Therefore any one who is received into the holy church, that is, into the assembly of those who believe in Christ, must have died to the Devil, the world, with its following, grandeur and pomp, also to the pride of all fleshly desires, and must have refused and denied them. Then he must confess with his mouth that wholesome faith which he has believed in his heart. When this has been done he must be baptized in the Name of God, or into Jesus Christ, that is baptized on the ground that through true repentance and faith he is cleansed from sins in order that he may walk in unstained, obedient conduct in God and in Christ. . . . This is therefore the use of baptism, that by it believers might be outwardly joined to and accepted by a holy church. . . .

The general use of the Supper is twofold. First, that the holy Christian assembly shall be held together by it, and preserved in unity of faith and Christian love. Secondly, that all sinful wickedness, and all that does not belong to the holy, pure church of Christ, but causes offences, may be cut off and excluded. "

The writer of this book, Pilgram Marbeck, was an eminent engineer. A native of Tyrol, he executed important works in the lower Inn valley, and marks of distinction given him by the Government showed its appreciation of his services. It is not known exactly when he became attached to the brethren, but in 1528 his confession of faith caused the loss of his dignities. At this time he wrote of himself: "Brought up by godly parents in Popery, I left this and became a preacher of the Wittenberg Gospel. Finding that in the places where God's Word was preached in the Lutheran way there was also a fleshly liberty, I was brought into doubt and could find no rest among the Lutherans. Then I accepted baptism as a sign of the obedience of faith, looking only to the Word and command of God. " He had to leave all he had and go abroad with his wife and child, and his property was then confiscated, but his ability enabled him to support his family wherever he was. In Strassburg he enriched the city by constructing the waterway by which the timber of the Black Forest was brought to it. His spotless character and spiritual zeal won him great favour, for the brethren were numerous and the Reformers, Bucer and Capito, were attracted by Pilgram Marbeck's sincerity and his spiritual and mental gifts. His fearless preaching of the baptism of believers, however, soon stirred up adversaries, Bucer turned against him, and he was imprisoned. Capito was not afraid to visit him in prison, but long discussions ended in the City Council's declaring that it did not hold the baptism of infants to be unchristian, and Pilgram Marbeck was given three or four weeks to realize his property, and left the city in 1532.

Sectarianism is limitation. Some truth taught in Scripture, some part of the Divine revelation, is apprehended, and the heart responds to it and accepts it. As it is dwelt upon, expounded, defended, its power and beauty increasingly influence those affected by it. Another side of truth, another view of revelation, also contained in Scripture, seems to weaken, even to contradict the truth that has been found to be so effectual, and in jealous fear for the doctrine accepted and taught the balancing truth is minimized, explained away, even denied. So on a portion of revelation, on a part of the Word, a sect is founded, good and useful because it preaches and practises Divine truth, but limited and unbalanced because it does not see all truth, nor frankly accept the whole of Scripture. Its members are not only deprived of the full use of all Scripture, but are cut off from the fellowship of many saints, who are less limited than they, or limited in another direction. There is reason to regret the divisions of the Lord's people, for their underlying, essential unity is obscured by these outward and apparent divisions; yet liberty in the churches to emphasize what they have learned and experienced is of the greatest value, and even the sectarian conflicts between churches zealous for different aspects of truth, have led to much searching of Scripture and discovery of its treasures. When this goes on in such a way as to endanger love, the loss is great; nevertheless, worse than sectarian strife is uniformity maintained at the cost of liberty, or reunion made possible by indifference.

An edict of Duke Johann of Cleve, Jülich, Berg, and Mark, runs as follows:* "Although it is known what is to be done with the Anabaptists . . . yet we will, in conjunction with the Archbishop of Cologne, announce it by this edict, so that no one may be excused through lack of knowledge. Hereafter all who baptize again and are baptized again, as well as all who hold or teach that infant baptism is without value, shall be brought from life to death, and punished. . . . In the same way

* "Geschichte des Christlichen Lebens in der rheinisch-westphälischen evangelischen Kirche" Max Goebel.

all who hold or teach that in the most highly esteemed
sacrament of the altar the true body and the blood of
our Lord Jesus Christ are not actually present, but
only figuratively . . . shall not be endured, but shall
be banished from our Principalities, so that if after three
days they are there they shall be punished in body and
life . . . and so treated as is announced with respect to
the Anabaptists. " Records are preserved of the burning,
drowning, and beheading that followed.

In Cologne the assembly held its secret meetings in a
house on the wall, which had two entrances, so as better
to escape discovery and arrest.   In 1556 Thomas Drucker
von Imbroek, a very pious and gifted teacher, though
only twenty-five years of age, was taken from one tower
to another, repeatedly tortured, but in vain, and finally
beheaded. Some of his beautiful letters and hymns,
written in prison, and his confession of faith, came
among the believers, were printed and circulated, and
did much to spread the truth.   His wife wrote to him
in prison (in verse): "Dear Friend, keep to the pure
truth, do not let yourself be terrified away from it,
you know what you have vowed, let the cross be acceptable to you, Christ Himself went this way, and all the
Apostles. " The church in Cologne was not discouraged
by the death of Drucker.   In 1561 three more brethren
were drowned, and the following year two taken prisoner,
one of whom was drowned, and the other at the moment
of death reprieved and banished.   The meetings
continued until 1566, when, one of the members betray-
ing them, the house was surrounded and all were taken.
Their names were noted and they were distributed to
different prisons. Matthias Zerfass, of his own accord,
acknowledged that he was a teacher among them, and
remained firm and patient under torture, and was then
beheaded. He wrote from prison: "The chief object
of our torture has been that we should say how many of
us were teachers, and reveal their names and addresses.
. . . I was to acknowledge the authorities as Christian
and that infant baptism is right; I pressed my lips together, yielded myself to God, suffered patiently, and
thought of the Lord's word when He said, 'Greater love
hath no man than this, that a man lay down his life for

his friends.   Ye are My friends, if ye do whatsoever I command you.'   It looks as though I have still much to suffer, but the Lord alone has it in His hand, and I can pray for nothing except that His will be done. "

An instruction was issued as follows: "In order to arrest the leaders, teachers, bush-preachers, and corner-preachers of the sectaries . . . officials shall send spies into the hedges, fens, and moors, especially at the approach of the more important festivals, and when there is full and continued moonlight, in order to discover their secret meeting-places. "

Yet in 1534 the Bishop of Münster, in writing to the Pope, bore testimony to the excellent lives of the Anabaptists.

Hermann V, Archbishop of Cologne (1472-1552) saw the need of reform in the Roman Catholic Church and made a serious attempt to bring it about.   He was Count of Wied and Runkel, and an Elector of the Empire, was made Dean of Cologne at the age of fifteen, and later Archbishop.   He was a good and liberal man, beloved by his tenantry, though more interested in hunting than in church matters, and no student of theology or Latin.   He opposed Luther and had his works burnt, and his spiritual court condemned two of the Cologne martyrs.   Yet he saw the ignorance and superstition of the people, the neglect of discipline, the churches confided to ignorant clergy, and the income absorbed by absentees.   He saw also the desecration of the Lord's Supper, and the vanity of all efforts to bring the corrupt members of the clergy back to the canonical rules.   In consultation with the best men in the highest offices of the Church he tried to bring about a Catholic Reform after the ideas of Erasmus. When this failed he attempted an evangelical reform of the Church with the help of Bucer and Melanchthon, but the opposition of the clergy, the University and the city of Cologne, organized by the Jesuit Canisius, frustrated his efforts.   Finding no support, he resigned his office as archbishop and retired to his estate.

One who remained apart from the Roman Catholic Church, as well as from the Lutheran and the Reformed, and yet did not attach himself to those called Anabaptists, was the Silesian nobleman, Kaspar von Schwenckfeld (1489-1561), who exercised an important influence in his own country and beyond.* Occupied in matters of business in connection with one or another of the smaller German courts, he did not trouble himself much about the Scriptures, until, when he was thirty years of age, he was awakened out of his indifference by Martin Luther's "wonderful trumpet of God", yielded himself to the "clear light of God's gracious visitation", and became "the soul" of the reformation in Silesia. It was not long before he found himself obliged to criticize some points in Luther's teaching, in the first instance that regarding the Lord's Supper. On this account he was attacked with virulence by Luther, who used his authority to get him treated as an outsider and a heretic. Schwenckfeld, however, never ceased to acknowledge his great debt to Luther in spiritual things, and after suffering for many years from the attacks of Luther and the Lutheran preachers, he gave this counsel to those who sympathized with him, "Let us faithfully pray to God for them, for the time must come at last when they, with all of us, must together acknowledge our ignorance in the presence of the one Master, Christ."

The study of the Scriptures became his great delight. He reckoned that if he read four chapters a day he would read the Bible through once a year, and at first made this a rule, though afterwards he left it to the Holy Spirit to direct his reading and did not bind himself to a certain number of chapters daily. "Christ", he said, is the "summary of the whole Bible" and "the principal object of the whole of Holy Scripture is that we may fully know the Lord Christ." Faith in the accuracy and inspiration of the whole Bible was to him not a holding on to an old and doubtful dogma but a new discovery of illimitable possibilities; not ancient superstition but modern progress. He described his reading of Scripture as "a brooding over, seeking, boring into; indeed a reading and re-reading of all, chewing, meditating, turning over and thoroughly thinking out everything." "For there, undiluted treasure is re-

* "Schwenckfeld, Luther und der Gedanke einer Apostolischen Reformation" Karl Ecke.

vealed to the believer, pure pearls, gold and precious stones." As a "safe rule" for the expositor, he says, "where disputed passages occur, the whole context must be taken into account, Scripture brought to bear on Scripture, single passages brought to the whole, compared with one another and the application found, not only by the outward appearance of a single passage, but according to the sense of the whole of Scripture." He studied Hebrew and Greek and in his work made use not only of Luther's translation but also of "the old Bible" (used by the Anabaptists) and the Vulgate. He found the key to much that is contained in the Old Testament in the typical use made of it in the New. He determined to yield himself to the guidance of the Scriptures in doctrine and in practice, and, "if we do not understand everything" he said, "do not let us blame the Scriptures for it, but rather our own ignorance."

Eight years after his first "visitation" he had a further experience which seemed to him to affect his life even more. Up to this time he had been zealous in proclaiming the Scriptures and Lutheranism; but now what he had intellectually believed turned to an entire persuasion of the heart. He was made aware of his heavenly calling, received an overwhelming assurance of salvation, yielded himself to God as a "living sacrifice." A deep sense of sin and appreciation of the sufficiency of the redemption wrought for us in Christ, by His death and resurrection, captured his will, transformed his mind and brought him to that obedience in which he found liberty to do the will of God.

He also made the discovery that the Scriptures not only give sure guidance as to personal justification and sanctification, but that they also contain definite instruction with regard to the Church. "If we would reform the Church", he said, "we must make use of the Holy Scriptures and especially of the Acts, where it is clearly to be found how things were in the beginning, what is right and what is wrong, what is praiseworthy and acceptable to God and to the Lord Christ." He saw that the Church in the time of the Apostles and their immediate successors, was a glorious gathering, not only in one place but in many. He asks where such assemblies are to be found to-day, for, he says, "the Scripture knows no others than those which acknowledge Christ as their Head and willingly yield themselves to be ruled by the Holy Spirit, who adorns them with spiritual gifts and knowledge." Jesus Himself directs through the spiritual gifts which He dispenses, not only to the whole Church, but also to the separate assemblies. In these assemblies spiritual gifts are manifested for the common good; the same Spirit divides the gifts, but they are manifested in each one of the members. The Spirit has untrammelled liberty. If one, led by the Spirit, rises, the one already speaking must cease. The churches are not perfect, it is always possible that hypocrites may creep in unobserved, but when detected they must be excluded. Schwenckfeld could not therefore recognize the Reformed religion as a Church, because the great mass of the baptized Christians were without the Spirit of Christ and took the Sacrament without the grace of God. He was willing to receive the help of missionary organizations, if they did not pretend to take the place of churches of Jesus Christ. A National Church is one, he said, that has gone back to the stage reached in the Old Testament.

"It is clear and evident" he says further, "that all Christians are called and sent to praise their Lord and Saviour Jesus Christ, to publish His virtues who has called them from darkness to His wonderful light, and to confess His Name before men." Any restriction of the universal priesthood of all believers is a limitation of the Holy Spirit. "If in the time of Paul they had acted thus, and only those appointed by the magistrate had been allowed to preach, how far would the Christian faith have reached? How would the Gospel have reached to our times?" Some are chosen from among the believers to special service, and are fitted for and separated to their office, not by study, election, or ordination, but by the thrust, revelation and manifestation of the Spirit, "that Christ is with them being shown in grace, power, life and blessing." Since their "calling and sending is solely from God, in the grace of Christ, they act with power and with great assurance in the Holy Spirit, souls are born again, hearts are renewed, the kingdom of Christ is built up." "The believers can never be tired of such apostolic, spiritual preachers, nor hear them enough, for they find with them the power of God and food for their souls; it is of such that the Lord

Christ said, 'Verily, verily, I say unto you, he that receiveth whomsoever I send receiveth Me' (John 13. 20). No unconverted person or one of unholy conduct can be a right minister for the increase of the church, even though he might be Doctor and Professor, know the Bible off by heart, and be a great orator. " When "some say that the person and the office are separate, so that even if a bishop, priest or preacher should be an evil man, yet he can occupy a good office, the office of a teacher of the New Testament, and can be a servant of the Holy Spirit, this is against all Scripture and against the ordinance of Christ. " "What sort of ministry is that, where the teacher is himself untaught in his heart . . . and does not believe what he teaches, that is, does not himself do or act what he says, whereas, in the right ministry of the New Covenant, according to the instruction of all Apostolic Scriptures and the example of the Lord Christ Himself, these two must always go together. "

As to baptism, Schwenckfeld taught that it does not save, and that salvation can be had without it; but at the same time he saw its importance and that only those who confess themselves as believers should be baptized, and that as children in the cradle are not capable of faith they are not suitable subjects for baptism.

Yet he did not attach himself to those called Anabaptists. Though he describes them as a God-fearing people, separate from the great mass of those who were indifferent to religion, distinguished by their upright conduct and deep religious earnestness, yet he accuses them of legalism and ignorance, and, in common with so many others, confounds together, as though they were one, the godly, long-suffering brethren, with all the fanatical elements concerned in the Peasants' War, the Münster extravagances and other outbreaks. He claims to have known "the first Baptists" and then describes Müntzer, executed for sedition in the Peasants' War; speaks of men of the type of Balthazar Hubmeyer as being disciples of Hans Hut, although the former was a strenuous opponent of the extreme and unbalanced teachings of Hut; relates a rumour that Hut had committed suicide in prison, though he adds that some say this was unintentional, and he attaches the name "Hutist Baptists" generally to those called by most people "Ana-

baptists". He recounts various detrimental anecdotes
that had been communicated to him by letter, and one that
he himself heard from a person who had left one of the
"Hutist" assemblies, but of whose Christianity he expresses
a poor opinion. He says they had little well-grounded
knowledge as to sin, salvation through the grace of God and
assurance of salvation, and especially that they had not
grasped the ideal of the true Apostolic Church. "They
persuade themselves", he said, "that . . . as soon as they
are received outwardly . . . into their own self-gathered
assemblies, they are the holy people of God, a people that
He has chosen out from among all others, a pure, un-
blemished church, . . . although the gifts of the Holy
Spirit, the ornament and beauty of Christian assemblies
and churches, as described in the Holy Scriptures, are very
little in evidence among them. " An outward orthodoxy
is to them the mark of the true Church of Christ. Therefore
an unbiblical spirit of judging, and spiritual pride, are
characteristic of them. "They are so well pleased with
themselves in all that they do, that all others, who are not
of their way of thinking, that is, who have not accepted
their baptism and will not join their assemblies, are condemned by them, separated from the fellowship of the
saints of God, as they regard it, and considered as under
Satan's power. Even if they were as full of faith as Stephen,
filled with the Spirit and godly wisdom, that counts for
nothing among the Baptists, so fast are they fixed, especially the leaders, in frivolous judgements, in self-love and in
spiritual pride. " They are always breaking bread in their
assemblies, and this, and water baptism, take the place
of that which is inward and more important. "If you were
to see one of their companies you would take them for the
people of God, for there is no doubt as to the piety of their
outward conduct. " He points out, however, that the
Pharisee in the parable had a more pious outward appearance than the Publican. "Not, " he adds, "that we wish
to blame outward piety, either in Baptists or monks, "
but "more is required than just, 'Come here and be baptized.' " He complains also that tyranny was exercised
over the consciences of the members, that there was legality
as regards habits, dress and other outward things, and he
opposed their views as to oaths, war and participation in

civil government. From all which it may safely be gathered that among these people, as among any considerable body of men, even of Christians, there were failures, weaknesses and errors to be found, and that the narrowness and legality complained of were limitations to which some of those called "Anabaptists" were always liable, and against which the better men among them were constantly protesting. Schwenckfeld disapproved of the cruel persecutions to which they were subjected. "I would gladly spare the God-fearing, simple people that are among them" he says, and reminds his hearers that there were true Christians among them, who, in spite of lack of knowledge, had life from God; he points to their joy under suffering, advises that if, as was so often said, they were seditious, the civil government should be left to deal with them, adding that he found them to be peaceful people, without seditious plans.

Through Schwenckfeld's diligent activities, circles of believers were gathered throughout Silesia, beginning in and around Liegnitz. They were a pattern of godliness to those about them. In view of the great misuse of the Lord's Supper, Schwenckfeld discontinued it for the time being, and the influence of his teaching as to the worthy and unworthy taking of it had such an effect that the Lutheran clergy in Liegnitz began (1526) to follow his example. This led many to accuse Schwenckfeld of disparaging the Lord's Supper, though it was the opposite feeling that had influenced him. His great desire was to realize the unity of the Church. "Oh would to God" he wrote, "we were truly the body of Christ, united in the bonds of love . . . but alas there is as yet no sign of anything that could be compared with the first church, where the believers were of one heart and of one mind. " "We will, however, stand fast in the liberty with which Christ has made us free, and not enter into any human sect, nor turn away from the universal Christian Church; we will not be bound by any yoke of bondage but only cling to the one Divine sect of Jesus Christ".. . . "My desire and the wish of my heart is that I might help everyone to the truth and unity of Christ and His Holy Spirit and not that I should be a cause of sectarianism, division or falling away from Christ. . . . As there are now four that are called churches, the Papal, Lutheran,

Zwinglian, and Baptist or Pickard, and each condemns the other, as is to be seen, that Luther condemns the Zwinglian Church and the fanatics, one cannot help asking whether all of them are, or which of them is, the true assembly of the Church of Christ, where one ought to be found and where one may be blessed. . . . We will answer the question in the words of Peter . . . 'Of a truth I perceive that God is no respecter of persons: but in every nation he that feareth Him, and worketh righteousness, is accepted with Him' (Acts 10. 34, 35). . . . So the more these churches condemn one another, so much the more will those who fear God and live uprightly and christianly, be, in the sight of God, unexcluded and uncondemned. . . . Although I have so far fully joined myself to no church . . . yet I have not despised any church, persons, leaders or teachers, I desire to serve every one in God, to be the friend and brother of each who has a zeal for God and loves Christ from the heart. . . . Therefore I pray God to lead me aright in all things, to enable me, according to the Apostolic rule, rightly to recognize all spirits, especially the Spirit of Jesus Christ; to teach me to prove all things and to distinguish, and to accept and hold what is good, so that in this present state of divisions and separations, I may attain, with a clear, sure conscience in Christ, to truth and unity."... "My liberty does not suit all, . . . some call me an eccentric . . . and many look upon me with suspicion, . . . but God knows my heart. . . . I am . . . no sectarian, and with God's help, will not be a disturber of peace." . . . "Rather than destroy anything good, I would die. And therefore I have not fully attached myself to any party, sect, or church, so that I might, in the will of God, through His grace, apart from party serve all parties."

The teachings of Schwenckfeld and the growth of the circles he established drew upon him the attention of King Ferdinand, who regarded him as a despiser of the Lord's Supper, and he was obliged (1529) to leave his native land, where he had always enjoyed a high position and great consideration. For the remaining thirty years of his life he was a wanderer, persecuted by the Lutheran Church, which formally declared him a heretic, but his exile led to a further spread of the groups which received his teaching, especially in South Germany, where some of the rulers protected him.   Under Schwenckfeld's teaching these groups did not consider themselves as churches, such a position would, they thought, imply separation from believers in the existing parties, all of whom they wished to serve.   They left baptism and the breaking of bread in abeyance until better times should come, and, in the meantime, they prayed and looked for a new outpouring of the Holy Spirit before the Lord's coming, which would unite His Church.   Their part was, by Bible readings, visiting, and every means of testimony accorded to them, to prepare saints for that time, as well as, by preaching the Gospel, to gather in from among the unconverted as many as possible to be sharers in the blessings to be revealed.

Their abstention from any church testimony, merely because of the difficulties connected with it, made them a source of weakness rather than of strength to those brethren who were continuing in faith to carry out, as had been done by some from Apostolic times, the teaching of Scripture as regards the churches.   Those principles, when rightly carried out, did not establish a sect or divide them from Christians who did not meet with them, but afforded the one ground on which it was possible for all believers to enjoy fellowship with each other, the ground of their common fellowship with Christ.

Pilgram Marbeck, in conjunction with others, wrote a reply to Schwenckfeld's strictures on the believers who gathered as churches and practised baptism and the breaking of bread.   Schwenckfeld had expressed his disapproval in a work entitled, "Of the New Pamphlet of the Baptist Brethren published in the year 1542." Marbeck's reply had a long title (eighty-three words) and took the form of quoting Schwenckfeld and giving 100 answers.   In it he and the brethren with him say: "It is not true that we refuse to count as Christians those who disagree with our baptism and reckon them as misguided spirits and deniers of Christ.   It is not ours either to judge or condemn him who is not baptized according to the command of Christ."

CHAPTER X

France and Switzerland

1500-1800

Le Fèvre—Group of believers in Paris—Meaux—Farel's preaching—
Metz—Images destroyed—Executions—Increased persecution in France—
Farel in French Switzerland—In Neuchâtel—The Vaudois and the
Reformers meet—Visit of Farel and Saunier to the valleys—Progress in
Neuchâtel—Breaking of bread in the South of France—Jean Calvin—
Breaking of bread in Poitiers—Evangelists sent out—Froment in Geneva
—Breaking of bread outside Geneva—Calvin in Geneva—Socinianism—
Servetus—Influence of Calvinism—The Placards—Sturm to Melanchthon
—Organization of churches in France—The Huguenots—Massacre of St.
Bartholomew—Edict of Nantes—The Dragonnades—Revocation of the
Edict of Nantes—Flight from France—Prophets of the Cevennes—War
of the Camisards—Churches of the Desert reorganized—Jacques Roger—
Antoine Court.

AT the end of the fifteenth and beginning of the
sixteenth century there was in Paris a little,
middle-aged man of quick and lively manner, who
very devoutly observed all the requirements of the
Roman Catholic Church.* This was Jacques Le Fèvre,
the most learned and popular Doctor of Divinity
at the University. Born about 1455 at the small town of
Étaples in Picardy, he studied later in Paris and in Italy,
and his ability and industry were such that when, in the
year 1492, he became Professor in the Paris University he
quickly took a foremost place among his colleagues. The
Revival of Learning had drawn to Paris eager students
from all countries. Le Fèvre encouraged the study of
languages, and finding that neither the classics nor the
scholasticism that had so long dominated theology satisfied the soul, he took his students to the Bible, which he
expounded with such understanding and fervour that large
numbers were attracted both to him and to it, while his
kind and attractive ways made him to be not only the
teacher but also the trusted friend of his scholars.

When Le Fèvre had been lecturing seventeen years at the
Sorbonne and had become widely known through his writings,

* "History of the Reformation of the Sixteenth Century" J. H. Merle
D'Aubigné D.D. trans. H. White, B.A.

a much younger man, Guillaume Farel, then twenty years of age, came to Paris from his mountain home in Dauphiny, between Gap and Grenoble. In the pleasant manor house where the Farel family had long been established, he had left his parents, three brothers and one sister, all like himself brought up in the Church of Rome and its observances. Farel was distressed when he saw the wild and sinful lives of so many in Paris, but as he worshipped in the churches he was struck by the unusual devotion of Le Fèvre. The two became acquainted, the young student was charmed by the kindness and interest of the renowned professor, and the foundations of a lifelong friendship between them were laid. They read the Bible together. Le Fèvre had put much labour into a book he was writing, "Lives of the Saints", arranged in the order in which they occur in the calendar. He had already published an instalment covering the first two months, but the contrast between the absurdities contained in many of these "Lives" and the power and truth of the Scriptures so impressed him that he abandoned the "Lives" for the study of Scripture, taking up especially the Epistles of Paul, upon which he wrote and published commentaries.

He taught plainly: "It is God alone, who by His grace, through faith, justifies unto everlasting life." Such doctrine, preached in Paris before Zwingli proclaimed it in Zürich or Luther in Germany, aroused the most lively discussion. Though it was the old, the original Gospel, preached by the Lord and by His Apostles, yet it had been so long replaced by the teaching that salvation is by the sacraments of the Church of Rome that it appeared new to the hearers. Farel, who had passed through deep exercise of soul, was one of many who at that time laid hold of salvation by faith in the Son of God and the sufficiency of His atoning work. He said: "Le Fèvre extricated me from the false opinion of human merits, and taught me that everything comes from grace; which I believed as soon as it was spoken."

Even at the Court of King Francis I there were those who received the Gospel, among them Briçonnet the Bishop of Meaux, and Margaret of Valois, Duchess of Alençon, the king's sister, to whom he was greatly attached; who, already celebrated for her wit and beauty, became equally famous for her fervent faith and good works. Another adherent was Louis de Berquin, of Artois, known as the most learned among the nobility, careful for the poor, devout in the observances of the Church. His attention was drawn to the Bible by the very violence of the attacks upon it. Reading it for himself, he was converted and joined the little group of believers, which included Arnaud and Gérard Roussel, natives, like Le Fèvre, of Picardy. Berquin at once began to spread literature over France, writing and translating both books and tracts drawing attention to the teachings of Scripture. Such activities aroused opposition, which, under the leadership of the chancellor Duprat, and Noël Beda, an official of the University, became so violent that the more prominent witnesses for the Gospel had to leave Paris, and in 1521 several of them, including Le Fèvre and Farel, took refuge in Meaux, at the invitation of the bishop, who vigorously undertook the reformation of his diocese.

In Meaux, Le Fèvre published his translation into French of the New Testament and the Psalms. The Scriptures became the great theme of conversation, in the town of Meaux among its busy wool-workers and wool merchants, and also in the surrounding villages among the farmers and labourers on the land. Farel preached everywhere, both in the churches and the open air.* "What" said he, "are those treasures of the goodness of God which are given to us in the death of Jesus Christ? Firstly, if we diligently consider what the death of Jesus was, we there shall see in truth how all the treasures of the goodness and the grace of God our Father are magnified and glorified and exalted in that act of mercy and love. Is not that sight an invitation to wretched sinners to come to Him who has so loved them that He did not spare His only Son, but delivered Him up for us all? Does it not assure us that sinners are welcome to the Son of God, who so loved them that He gave His life, His body, and His blood, to be a perfect sacrifice, a complete ransom for all who believe in Him! . . . He who is the Son of God, the power and the wisdom of God, He who is God Himself, so humbled Himself as to die for us, He the holy and the righteous One, for the ungodly and for sinners, offering Himself up that we might be made pure

* "Life of William Farel" Frances Bevan.

and clean. And it is the will of the Father, that those whom He thus saves by the precious gift of His Son, should be certain of their salvation and life, and should know that they are completely washed and cleansed from all their sins. . . . He gives the precious gift of His Son to the wretched prisoner of the Devil, of sin, of hell and of damnation. . . . The gracious God, the Father of mercy, takes such an one as this to make him His child. . . . He makes him a new creature; He gives him the earnest of the Spirit, by whom he lives, who unites him to Christ, making him a member of His body. . . . Let us not, therefore, shrink from laying down this mortal life, for the honour of our Father, for a witness to the holy Gospel. . . . And oh! how bright, how blessed, how triumphant, how joyous and how happy is the day that is coming. Then the Lord and Saviour, in His own body—that body in which He suffered so much for us, in which He was spat upon, beaten, scourged and tortured, so that His face was marred more than any man—in that body He shall come; calling to all His own who have been partakers of His Spirit, in whom by the Spirit He has dwelt; calling them up to the glory, showing Himself to them in the body of His glory; raising them up in their bodies alive with immortal life, made like to Jesus, to reign for ever with Him in joy. For that blessed day the whole creation groans; that day of the triumphant coming of our Saviour and Redeemer, when all enemies shall be put under His feet, and His elect people shall ascend to meet Him in the air. "

Meaux was at this time a centre of spiritual life and Bishop Briçonnet provided for the distribution of copies of the Scriptures in all the diocese. Among many who were converted were two wool-carders, Pierre and Jean Leclerc, with their mother; also Jacques Pavanne, a student on a visit to the bishop, and a man called the Hermit of Livry, a seeker after God, who lived in a hut in what was then the forest of Livry near Paris, supporting himself by begging. He met someone from Meaux who brought him the Bible. Reading this, he found salvation, and his hut soon became the meeting place of such as desired instruction in the Word.

The Franciscans in Meaux quickly complained to the Church and the University in Paris about what was going on in their town, and Beda and his colleagues took prompt measures to crush out the growing testimony of the Gospel. Berquin was seized in his country château, bravely confessed his faith, and was on the point of being executed, when the king intervened and saved him, as he did also Le Fèvre, who was allowed to remain in Meaux, with restricted liberty. Threatened with the loss of everything and with a cruel death, the bishop had yielded and consented to the reintroduction of the Roman system in his diocese. Farel, troubled that his friends in Meaux did not go far enough in following out the Scriptures, had already left, seeking, after a brief visit to Paris, his country home near Gap.

The believers in Meaux and in the district had, from the first, understood that the gifts of the Spirit were not confined to a particular class but were given through all the members of the body of Christ, so, when sudden, severe persecution removed or silenced their more prominent leaders they were not crushed but held frequent secret meetings as they found opportunity, in which brethren ministered the Word according to their ability. Able and zealous in this service was the wool-carder, Jean Leclerc, who also, not content with this and with visiting from house to house, wrote and posted on the cathedral doors some placards condemning the Church of Rome, thus drawing punishment on himself. For three successive days he was whipped through the streets and then branded on the forehead with a red-hot iron as a heretic. "Glory to Jesus Christ and to His witnesses!" cried a voice from the crowd. It was that of his mother. The bishop had to see these things and consent.

Leclerc, with the seared face, removed to Metz, where he earned his living as a wool-carder and diligently explained the Scriptures to all he came in contact with. A learned man, Agrippa of Nettesheim, who had come to live in Metz, was now one of its most prominent citizens. Reading the works of Luther he was attracted to the Scriptures, and, enlightened by these, began to testify to others of the truth he had received. Thus both among the work-people and those in high positions great interest was awakened in the Gospel. Jean Chaistellain, an Augustinian friar who had come to the knowledge of Christ in the

Netherlands, came at this time to Metz, and his eloquent and sympathetic preaching affected many. Another helper who joined this growing church was François Lambert. Brought up by the Franciscans in Avignon, he had been repelled even as a child by the evil he saw around him. He felt an inward power urging him to read the Scriptures, and, finding Christ revealed there, he believed and preached Him. His preaching journeys from the monastery, effective among his country hearers, aroused the derisive hostility of his fellow-monks. Luther's writings helped him much, and, using an opportunity to get away from his convent, he travelled to Wittenberg where he greatly pleased the famous reformer. There he met with printers from Hamburg, arranged for the printing of French tracts and Scriptures and organized their conveyance into various parts of France. Then he married, two years before Luther—the first of the French priests or monks to take this step. Willing to share with him the dangers of returning to France, his wife accompanied him to Metz (1524). They were soon driven out again, but others were continually added—a well-known knight, D'Esch; a young man, Pierre Toussaint, who had been expected to take a high place in the Roman Catholic Church, and many others.

A great festival was at hand, on the occasion of which the people of Metz were in the habit of making a pilgrimage some miles out from the city to a chapel celebrated for its images of the Virgin and the saints. His mind filled with Old Testament denunciations of idolatry, Leclerc, informing nobody of his intention, crept out of Metz the night before the pilgrimage and destroyed the images in the chapel. When, the next day, the worshippers arrived and found the shattered fragments of their images strewn over the chapel floor, they were filled with fury. Leclerc made no secret of what he had done. He exhorted the people to worship God only and declared that Jesus Christ, who is God manifest in the flesh, is alone to be adored. Condemned to the flames, he was first subjected to abominable tortures. As member after member of his body was destroyed, he continued, as long as he could speak, solemnly to recite in a loud voice the words of the hundred and fifteenth Psalm: "Their idols are silver and gold, the work of men's hands. They have mouths, but they speak not: eyes have they, but they see not: they have ears, but they hear not: noses have they, but they smell not: they have hands, but they handle not: feet have they, but they walk not: neither speak they through their throat. They that make them are like unto them; so is every one that trusteth in them. O Israel trust thou in the Lord: He is their help and their shield. " The first to die in this persecution, he was quickly followed by Friar Chaistellain, who was degraded and burnt. D'Esch, Toussaint, and others had to fly for their lives, yet the believers continued to increase in Metz, as also throughout Lorraine. At Nancy a preacher of the Gospel named Schuch was burnt by order of the Duke, Anthony the Good. When he heard his sentence, Schuch simply said: "I was glad when they said unto me, 'Let us go into the house of the Lord.' "

In 1525 the King of France, Francis I, was defeated and made prisoner by the Emperor Charles V, at the battle of Pavia. Advantage was taken of this to press for the extirpation of dissent in France. The restraining influence of Margaret, the king's sister, was neutralized, the regent was easily induced to help, and Church, Parliament, and Sorbonne united in the attack. Parliament presented to the regent an address, in which it was asserted that the neglect of the king to bring heretics to the scaffold was the real cause of the disaster that had overtaken the throne and the nation. With the approval of the Pope, a commission was appointed, consisting of four men, determined enemies of Reform, before whom the ecclesiastical authorities were to bring all persons affected with the taint of Lutheran doctrine, that they might be handed over to the secular power and burnt. A beginning was made with Briçonnet, Bishop of Meaux, as the most exalted offender, and one whose fall would make the deepest impression. True, on a former occasion he had submitted to all that had been required of him, but he had since given abundant evidence that he had acted only under compulsion, and that his inward adherence to the Gospel was unchanged. Seeing that it would better serve their cause to bring him to recant than to put him to death, every imaginable effort was made by the commission to effect this; until at last the bishop, of whose inward faith there is no doubt, yielded an outward submission to Rome and went through all the ceremonies of repentance and reconciliation prescribed. The next to be attacked was Le Fèvre, but he, receiving timely warning, escaped to Strassburg, where Capito received him into his home and, with Bucer, gave him a hearty welcome, where also he found Farel and Gérard Roussel and enjoyed a wider fellowship of the Lord's people than he had ever known before. Among those who suffered imprisonment and death at this time in France was the Hermit of Livry. From the time of his finding peace himself, through believing, he had devoted himself to visiting in all the district, receiving such as came to his hut, and explaining to all from the Scriptures the way of salvation. He was brought with great pomp to the open space before the cathedral of Notre Dame in Paris, an immense multitude was gathered together by the tolling of the great bell, and there he was burnt before all, enduring his martyrdom with quiet fortitude of faith. Louis de Berquin had already been seized, imprisoned and condemned to death, but on the return of the king (1525), he was liberated, and (largely through the influence of the Duchess Margaret) the exiled preachers in Germany and Switzerland were invited to come back to France—excepting Farel, whose teaching, going beyond that of the others, was less acceptable to those who still hoped for some compromise with Rome.

During Farel's stay in his own country, Dauphiny, his three brothers became decided followers of Christ, also a young knight, Anemond de Coct, and many others. Farel preached constantly in the open air and in any buildings available. Many were surprised, even offended, that he, a layman and unordained, should preach. He was, however, an ideal preacher, learned, bold, eloquent, intensely convinced of the truth and importance of what he preached, intimately acquainted with the Scriptures and filled with a sense of his responsibility toward God and with compassionate love toward men. His appearance was striking and impressive; he was of medium height and thin, with a long red beard and flashing eyes and a deep, powerful voice, and his manner, at once serious and vivacious, instantly commanded attention, which his popular and convincing speech maintained. Driven out of Gap and pursued in his hiding-places in the country he knew so well, he at last made his way by remote paths across the frontier and reached Basle. There he was received into the house of Œcolampadius, the two men becoming warmly attached to each other, but he would not even visit Erasmus, whom he considered to be unfaithful and half-hearted in his testimony, and Erasmus therefore became his opponent. An opportunity was given to Farel, with Œcolampadius, to hold a public discussion in Basle, in which they maintained with success the Sufficiency of the Word of God. Farel's fervour and ability charmed most of his hearers, but when after a short visit to Zwingli in Zürich he returned to Basle, he found that hostile influences had procured his expulsion from the city. It was then that he went to Strassburg, was received into Capito's hospitable home and met Le Fèvre and the other exiles from France.

It was in French Switzerland that Farel's greatest work was done. Through his long-continued and ardent labours that beautiful country so long in spiritual darkness was transformed; and the greater part of it became, and has continued to be, a centre of enlightened, evangelical Christianity. Among many instances of the effect of Farel's preaching the story of Neuchâtel is one of the most striking. There seemed to be no opening there, but the curate of the neighbouring village of Serrières allowed him to preach in his churchyard. Accounts of this soon reached Neuchâtel and before long he was preaching in the market-place there. The effect was extraordinary. Large numbers received the message, others were stirred to violent opposition; the whole city and surrounding country were in a ferment. After a few months' enforced absence the preacher was back again, with some companions, and the work not only laid hold increasingly of the town but spread to Valangin, throughout the Val de Ruz, through the villages along the shore of the Lake, to Granson and up to Orbe. At Valangin he and Antoine Froment narrowly escaped being drowned by the angry people in the River Seyon, were beaten in the chapel of the castle so that their blood stained its walls, and were eventually thrust into the prison, from which, however, they were rescued by the men of Neuchâtel. In October, 1530, less than a year after the first preaching in the churchyard of

Serrières, Neuchâtel took a general vote of its inhabitants, and by the narrow majority of 18 abolished Roman Catholicism and adopted the reformed religion, but gave liberty of conscience to all.

The Waldenses, or Vaudois,* in their remote Alpine valleys, as well as in other places where they were settled, in Calabria and Apulia, in Provence, Dauphiny and Lorraine, received reports of the Reformation; while, on the other hand, the neighbouring countries where the Reformation was spreading also heard that in distant parts of the Alps and elsewhere people had been found who had always held those truths which they themselves were now contending for. The name of *Barbe* was given by the Vaudois to their elders, and one of these, Martin Gonin, of Angrogne, was so much moved by the reports that he had heard that he determined to undertake the journey to Switzerland and Germany to see some of the Reformers. This he did (1526), returning with such news as he had gathered. as well as some of the Reformers' books. The information he brought excited the greatest interest in the valleys, and at a meeting held (1530) at Merandol the brethren decided to send two of their *Barbes*, Georges Morel and Pierre Masson, to try to establish connections.

These came to Basle and, finding the house of Œcolampadius, introduced themselves to him. Others were called in and these simple, godly mountaineers explained their faith and their origin in Apostolic times. "I thank God," said Œcolampadius, "that He has called you to so great light." In conversation points of difference were discovered and discussed. In answer to questions the Barbes said: "All our ministers live in celibacy, and work at some honest trade." "Marriage, however", said Œcolampadius, "is a state very becoming to all believers, and particularly to those who ought to be in all things ensamples to the flock. We also think that pastors ought not to devote to manual labour, as yours do, the time they could better employ in the study of Scripture. The minister has many things to learn; God does not teach us miraculously and without labour; we must take pains in order to

*"The Reformation in Europe in the Time of Calvin"   J. H. Merle D'Aubigné D.D.

know." When the Barbes admitted that under stress of
persecution they had sometimes had their children baptized
by Romish priests, and even attended mass, the Reformers
were surprised, and Œcolampadius said: "What! has not
Christ, the holy victim, fully satisfied the everlasting
justice for us? Is there any need to offer other sacrifices
after that of Golgotha? By saying 'Amen' to the priests'
mass you deny the grace of Jesus Christ." Speaking of
man's condition since the Fall, the Barbes said: "We
believe that all men have some natural virtue, just as
herbs, plants, and stones have." "We believe", said the
Reformers, "that those who obey the commandments of
God do so, not because they have more strength than others,
but because of the great power of the Spirit of God which
renews their will." "Ah", said the Barbes, "nothing
troubles us weak people so much as what we have heard
of Luther's teaching relative to free will and predestina-
tion. . . . Our ignorance is the cause of our doubts: pray
instruct us." These divergences did not estrange them;
Œcolampadius said: "We must enlighten these Christians,
but above all things we must love them." "Christ", said
the Reformers to the Vaudois, "is in you as He is in us,
and we love you as brethren."

Morel and Masson then continued their journey to
Strassburg. On their homeward way they visited Dijon
where their conversation attracted the attention of someone
who reported them as being dangerous persons, and they
were imprisoned. Morel succeeded in escaping with the
documents they had in their charge, but Masson was
executed. The report which Morel brought of their con-
versations with the Reformers excited much discussion,
and it was decided to call a general conference of the
churches and invite representatives of the Reformers to be
present so that they might examine these questions together. Martin Gonin and a Barbe from Calabria, named
Georges, were chosen to go to Switzerland with the invitation. In Granson, in the summer of 1532, they found
Farel and other preachers conferring as to the further spread
of the Gospel in French Switzerland. Here they related
the differences which had arisen among them with regard
to some points in the teaching and practice of the Reformers
and brought the request that some might return with them,

so that unity of judgment might be reached and they might take steps for unitedly preaching the Gospel in the world. Farel responded readily to the invitation, and Saunier and another joined him.

After a dangerous journey they reached Angrogne, the home of Martin Gonin, and saw and visited some of the Waldensian hamlets scattered on the mountain slopes. The hamlet of Chanforans was chosen as meeting-place, and, as there was no building that would hold the people, the Conference was held in the open air, rough benches being arranged as seats. The Reformation was a movement outside the sphere of the Waldenses and unconnected with them, but they had retained their old and widespread connections with the numerous brethren and churches that had existed before the Reformation. These churches, though sympathetically interested in the Reformation, had by no means been absorbed into it. So there were present at this gathering elders of churches in Italy, reaching even to the extreme south; from many parts of France, from the German lands and especially from Bohemia. Among the numerous peasants and labourers were also some Italian noblemen, as the lords of Rive Noble, Mirandola and Solaro. Under the shade of chestnut trees and surrounded by the mountain wall of the Alps the meetings were opened "in the Name of God" on the 12th of September, 1532. The thoughts of the Reformers were ably expressed by Farel and Saunier, while two Barbes, Daniel of Valence and Jean of Molines, were the chief spokesmen in favour of retaining the practices current among the Vaudois in the valleys. On the points where these brethren of the mountains had yielded to pressure of persecution from the Romish Church and consented to observe certain feasts, fasts and other rites, to attend the Catholic services occasionally, and even submit outwardly to some of the ministrations of the priests, Farel was able to show that they had departed from their own more ancient custom, and he strongly urged entire separation from Rome. The Reformers maintained that everything in the Church of Rome which was not commanded in Scripture was to be rejected; the Waldenses were content to say that they rejected all connected with Rome which was forbidden in the Scriptures. Many matters of practice were considered, but the question which excited the greatest discussion was one of doctrine.   Farel taught that "God has elected before the foundation of the world all those who have been or will be saved.   It is impossible for those who have been ordained to salvation not to be saved.   Whosoever upholds free-will, absolutly denies the grace of God. " Jean of Molines and Daniel of Valence laid stress both on the capacity of man and also his responsibility to receive the grace of God.   In this they were supported by the nobles present and by many others, who urged that the changes advocated were not necessary and also that they would imply a condemnation of those who had so long and so faithfully guided these churches.   Farel's eloquence and sympathetic earnestness strongly commended his arguments to his hearers and the majority accepted his teaching. A confession of faith was drawn up in accordance with this, which was signed by most present, though declined by some.

The Reformers were shown the manuscript Bibles in use among the churches and the old documents they possessed ; the "Noble Lesson", the "Catechism", the "Antichrist", and others, and saw not only the interest and value of these books but also the need there was of printed French Bibles such as could be freely circulated among the people.   This led to the translation of the Bible into French by Olivetan, a faithful worker among the Reformers from the old days in Paris.   The brethren of the valleys subscribed to the utmost of their ability to the cost of the undertaking and the Bible was published in 1535.   Farel and Saunier mounted their horses and rode back from their eventful visit to continue the work in French Switzerland, having Geneva especially in view.   Jean of Molines and Daniel of Valence went to Bohemia, and after conference among the churches there, the brethren in Bohemia wrote to those in the valleys begging them not to adopt any of the important changes of doctrine and practice recommended by the foreign brethren without the most careful consideration.

When, in the Autumn of 1530, the inhabitants of Neuchâtel destroyed the images in the great church and, by a popular vote established the Reformed religion, it was not clearly seen that though an oppressive tyranny had been broken by the bringing in of liberating truth, and a civil reform of the utmost value had been obtained, yet the churches of God do not properly receive their guidance or authority from a Democratic vote any more than they do from Papal power. This they have from the Lord Himself. Christ is the centre and gathering power of His people. Their fellowship with each other springs from their common fellowship with Him and while this gives them authority to exercise discipline among themselves, they are neither to seek to rule in the world nor are they to be ruled by it. In order to emphasize the distinction between the Church and the world Farel set up tables (in place of the altar that had been cast down in the church at Neuchâtel) where believers might keep the Lord's Supper. Here, taught Farel, believers could worship Christ in Spirit and in truth, purged from everything which He has not ordained; here Jesus only could be seen among them and what He had commanded. The following year, after Farel had preached to a large congregation in the church at Orbe, eight believers there remembered the Lord in the breaking of bread.

In 1533 some believers in the south of France were strongly impressed with the need of coming often together for the reading of Scripture. At that time Margaret, Queen of Navarre, came from Paris to her husband's territories. With her were Le Fèvre and Roussel. They used to attend the Catholic church in Pau and afterwards hold meetings in the castle, where an address was given on the Scriptures, to which many of the country people came. Some of these expressed the desire to partake of the Lord's Supper, in spite of fears as to the danger of doing this. A large hall was found, however, under the terrace of the castle— a meeting place which could be reached without too much risk of attracting attention. Here, at the appointed time, a table was brought, with bread and wine, and all took part in the Supper, without any formality, the Queen and those of the humblest station apprehending their equality in the presence of the Lord. The Word was read and applied, a collection was made for the poor, and the people dispersed. About the same time Jean Calvin, a young man who had been obliged to leave Paris on account of his teaching, was in Poitiers, where he came in contact with many believers and inquirers, all deeply interested in the Scriptures. Luther and Zwingli and their doctrines were discussed and there was the freest criticism of the Roman Catholic Church. As it began to be dangerous to attend these meetings, the Christians took to coming together in a wild district outside the town where there were caves, known as the caves of St. Benedict. There, in a large cavern, they were able to consider the Scriptures without interruption and a frequent topic was the unscripturalness of the Mass. This led to a desire to remember the Lord's death in the way He had appointed, so they met together there and with prayer and the reading of the Word, took the bread and wine among themselves, while any who felt that the Holy Spirit had given a word of exhortation or exposition spoke with liberty.

Next they became concerned about the people living in the district round them and their need of the Gospel, and in one of their meetings three of the brethren offered to travel as evangelists. They were known to have the necessary gifts of the Spirit for such a work, so they were commended to the Lord, a collection was made for the expenses of their journey and they were sent forth. Their labours were very fruitful. One, Babinot, a learned and gentle-spirited man, went first to Toulouse. He had a special power of attracting students and teachers, of whom he won not a few for Christ, and their influence with young people was most valuable in spreading the Gospel. They gave Babinot the name "Good-man" because of his excellent character. He was diligent in finding out and visiting little companies of the Lord's people who met for prayer and to break bread together. Another of the evangelists, Véron, a man of great activity, spent twenty years travelling on foot through whole provinces of France. He so diligently sought the lost sheep and so exalted the Good Shepherd that he was called the "Gatherer". When he came into a place he used to ask who were the most worthy persons there and try to win them to the faith. He also took a special interest in the young people, many of whom became through him steadfast disciples of Christ and proved their ability to suffer for Him. The third of the evangelists, Jean Vernou, worked first in Poitiers and became well known throughout all that part of France for his influence in the colleges. He was eventually taken in Savoie and burnt at Chambéry for his confession of Christ.

The saving power of the Gospel began to be abundantly manifested in Geneva from the time when Antoine Froment, with much trepidation, opened a school there (1532). His Bible stories to the children and his useful knowledge of medicine soon drew large numbers to him. Some distinguished women, belonging to the first families in the city, were converted, then tradesmen and people of all classes. The believers soon began to meet in different houses for the study of the Scriptures and for prayer. These assemblies increased rapidly as more were converted. There was liberty of ministry in their meetings; one or another would read the Word, and such as were able would expound it, or lead the company in prayer. Collections were made, too, for the relief of the poor. If a gifted stranger passed through he would speak in one of the larger houses and all who could get in would crowd to hear his ministry. These assemblies soon had the desire to break bread in remembrance of the Lord; in order to avoid disturbance the believers gathered in a walled garden belonging to one of them, at Pré l'Evêque, just outside the city walls. All these things took place in the face of constant opposition, which became more violent when the believers, as churches, met around the Lord's table. There was dangerous rioting, Froment and others being driven out of the city; yet the meetings continued. On a later occasion about eighty men and a number of women met at Pré l'Evêque. This time one of the brethren washed the feet of the others before they took the Lord's Supper, which increased the popular anger against them. It was amid such disturbed conditions that Olivetan worked at his translation of the Bible. In order to give the sense better he translated into French such words as had formerly been left in a Greek form. Thus for "apostle" he put "messenger"; for "bishop", "overseer"; for "priest", "elder", these renderings being actual translations of the meaning of the Greek words and not mere transliterations. He said that as he did not find in the Bible such words as pope, cardinal, archbishop, archdeacon, abbot, prior, monk, he had no ocasion to change them.

Although, through a series of stirring events, Geneva like Neuchâtel had been delivered from the domination of Rome, it was not long before forms of Government were introduced considerably affecting the churches—though likewise not to be found in the Scriptures. Olivetan had been one of the first to lead his relative Calvin to the study of the Bible. The extraordinary ability of Calvin gave him from his early youth great influence wherever he went. The publication (1536) of his book, *"The Institutes of the Christian Religion"* in Basle, whither he had been obliged to fly on being driven out of France, caused him to be recognized as the foremost theologian of his day. The same year while on his way to Strassburg, Calvin was compelled on account of war to make his way through Geneva, where he stayed at an inn with the intention of continuing his journey the next morning. Farel heard of his arrival, called on him, and showed him what a marvellous work had been done and was still going on in Geneva and the country round; what conflicts there were, what need of helpers, he and those with him being overwhelmed by calls on every side, and commanded Calvin to remain and take up the work with them. To this he demurred, pleading his inability, his need of quiet for study, his character—unsuited to such activities as would be required of him. Farel adjured him not to allow his love of study, or any other form of self-pleasing to stand in the way of obedience to the call of God. Overcome by Farel's vehemence and convinced by his appeal, Calvin consented to stay and with the exception of a period of three years' banishment he spent the remainder of his life in Geneva, with which city his name will be for ever connected. Through much conflict he imposed on the city his ideal of a State and Church organized largely on the Old Testament pattern. The City Council had absolute power in matters religious as well as civil, and it became the instrument of Calvin's will. The citizens were required to sign a confession of faith or to leave the city. Strict rules were enforced regulating the morals and habits of the people. The churches that had begun to grow up in obedience to New Testament teaching almost disappeared in the general organization, for Papal rule was replaced by that of the Reformer and liberty of conscience was still witheld.

One form of prevalent error which Calvin hoped to suppress by his strict rule was Unitarian in character. It was of ancient origin, resembling Arianism in some respects, but at this time began to be described as Socinianism on

account of the association with it of Lelio (1525-62) and
Faustus (1539-1604) Sozini, uncle and nephew, natives of
Siena in Italy.   The latter lived much in Poland, since
there as in Transylvania, Unitarian teaching was permitted
and was wide-spread.   He united the divided sections
of Unitarians in Poland; they were called "Polish
Brethren" and the "Racovian" Catechism expressed their
views.   Socinianism spread from them as a centre.   It
early affected some in the Protestant churches, and later
gained a commanding influence, especially over the Protestant clergy.   Consisting to a large extent of criticism
of existing theology, upon this criticism it based its appeal,
which was more to the intellect than to the heart or understanding.

A Spanish physician, Servetus, holding and teaching
doctrines allied to these, reached Geneva on a journey,
and, as he travelled through, came into conflict with Calvin
and the Council, and refusing to renounce his error, was
burnt (1553).   This was but a logical outcome of the
system that had been established.

Geneva under Calvin's rule became famous, and afforded
a refuge for numbers of persecuted dissenters from different
lands, many coming from England and Scotland.   These
were strongly influenced by Calvin's genius and carried his
teachings far afield, so that Calvinism became a potent
influence in the world, and its severe training has certainly
moulded some of the finest characters.   Farel submitted
to Calvin's dominance but refused all entreaties to settle
in Geneva or to accept any position to which honour and
emolument were attached.   He made Neuchâtel his centre,
and married, but continued his hard life as a travelling
preacher until he passed peacefully away at about seventy-
six years of age.

Meanwhile in France, the growth of Christian churches
and the preaching of the Gospel, which had continued in
spite of great pressure of persecution, in 1534 received a
serious check.   Some of the believers in Paris, impatient
at the slow progress made in France as compared with the
large measure of liberty that had been gained in Switzerland, sent one of their number named Feret, to consult
with brethren there as to whether they should take some

bolder course to obtain liberty for the Word. As a result of this a violent attack on the mass was composed among the Reformers in Switzerland, printed in the form of placards and tracts, and sent to Paris. There was a difference of opinion among the believers there as to whether the placards should be posted and the tracts distributed or not. Couralt, who spoke for the "men of judgement", said: "Let us beware of posting up these placards; we shall only inflame the rage of our adversaries thereby, and increase the dispersion of believers." Others said: "If we look timidly from one side to the other to see how far we can go without exposing our lives, we shall forsake Jesus Christ." The counsels of the more aggressive prevailed, the matter was carefully organized, and in one October night the placards were posted all over France, one even being fastened on to the door of the room in which the king was sleeping in his castle at Blois. It was a long statement, headed: "Truthful Articles Concerning the horrible, great, and unbearable abuses of the Popish Mass, Invented directly Against the holy Supper of our Lord, The only Mediator and only Saviour, Jesus Christ." When, the next morning, the placards were read, the effect was tremendous. The King was won from his indecision to adopt the policy of exterminating the Reform party. On the first day Parliament proclaimed a reward for all who should make known those who had posted the placards and ordered that those who concealed them should be burnt. Arrests began at once to be made among those who were suspected of having attended the meetings, or however moderately, of favouring reform, including those who had opposed the posting of the placards. General terror prevailed. Many left everything and fled abroad. All over France the fires received their living victims, especially in Paris. There was a procession (1535) through the streets of Paris of all the most holy relics that could be brought together. The King and his family and court, great numbers of ecclesiastics and of the nobility and an immense concourse of people were gathered. The host was carried through the streets, and Mass was celebrated at Notre Dame. Then the King and a great multitude witnessed, first in the Rue St. Honoré and then at the Halles, the burning, with apparatus designed to prolong their sufferings, of some of the best citizens of Paris, who, without exception, testified to the end their faith in Jesus Christ, with a courage that compelled the admiration of their tormentors.

The learned and moderate Sturm, Professor at the Royal College in Paris, wrote to Melanchthon: "We were in the best, the finest position, thanks to wise men; and now behold us, through the advice of unskilful men, fallen into the greatest calamity and supreme misery. I wrote you last year that everything was going on well, and what hopes we entertained from the king's equity. We congratulated one another; but, alas! extravagant men have deprived us of those propitious times. One night in the month of October, in a few moments, all over France, and in every corner, they posted with their own hands a placard concerning the ecclesiastical orders, the mass, and the eucharist . . . they carried their audacity so far as to fasten one even on the door of the king's apartments, wishing by this means, as it would seem, to cause certain and atrocious dangers. Since that rash act, everything has been changed; the people are troubled, the thoughts of many are filled with alarm, the magistrates are irritated, the king is excited, and frightful trials are going on. It must be acknowledged that these imprudent men, if they were not the cause, were at least the occasion of this. Only, if it were possible for the judges to preserve a just mean! Some, having been seized, have already undergone their punishment; others promptly providing for their safety, have fled; innocent people have suffered the chastisement of the guilty. Informers show themselves publicly; any one may be both accuser and witness. These are not idle rumours that I write to you, Melanchthon; be assured that I do not tell you all, and that in what I write I do not employ the strong terms that the terrible state of our affairs would require. Already eighteen disciples of the Gospel have been burnt, and the same danger still threatens a still greater number. Every day the danger spreads wider and wider. There is not a good man who does not fear the calumnies of informers, and is not consumed with grief at the sight of these horrible doings. Our adversaries reign, and with all the more authority, that they appear to be fighting in a just cause, and to quell sedition. In the midst of these great and numerous evils there is only one hope left—that the people are beginning to be disgusted with such cruel persecutions, and that the king blushes at last for having thirsted for the blood of these unfortunate men. The persecutors are instigated by violent hatred and not by justice. If the king could but know what kind of spirit animates these bloodthirsty men, he would no doubt take better advice. And yet we do not despair. God reigns, He will scatter all these tempests, He will show us the port where we can take refuge, He will give good men an asylum where they will dare speak their thought freely."

Companies of believers met in many parts of France for reading the Scriptures and for worship, without any special organization.* In one of these, however, in Paris, the birth of a child, causing its father much concern as to how it should be baptized, eventually led to the evolution of a complete system. His conscience did not allow him to take it to the Roman Catholic church, and it was not possible for him to take it abroad for baptism. The congregation met and prayed about the matter and decided to form a church themselves. They chose Jean de Maçon to be their minister, and appointed also elders and deacons and took the ground of an organized church, of which the ministers were authorized to baptize and to undertake such functions as they considered pertained to ordained persons. From the time when this was done (1555) many of the assemblies of believers throughout France acted in the same way, and the numbers of churches that adopted this Presbyterian order increased rapidly. A large proportion of them were supplied with pastors from Geneva. The Reformed churches in Holland and in Scotland were affected by the example of this movement in France even more than they were by the example of Geneva. Calvin favoured the guidance of each congregation by its minister, or ministers, and elders, but the French churches soon introduced the plan of holding Synods of ministers and elders representing, and having authority over, a group of churches. These local gatherings took later to sending delegates who formed a larger, Provincial Synod, and in 1559 the first National Synod

*"A History of the Reformation" Thomas M. Lindsay M.A., D.D.

of French churches was held in Paris. On this occasion a Confession of Faith was agreed upon which every minister was required to sign, and a Book of Discipline was drawn up regulating the order and discipline of the churches, each minister undertaking to submit himself to it.

The adherents of these churches were often called "Gospellers" or "Those of the Religion" but eventually the name "Huguenot"† was more generally applied to them. It is not known with any certainty from what source the name is derived. The South-East of France, which for centuries had been so ready to receive the Gospel, and where the truth had only been suppressed by repeated and relentless massacre, now again showed the old invincible desire for the Word, and in parts became predominantly Huguenot. In other parts of the country the Huguenots were usually a small minority of the people. A state of tension existed between the two religious parties, although liberty of worship was guaranteed to the Huguenot minority by royal decree, and there was hope that reform and tolerance might bring peace. The States-General, or Parliament, was favourable, so was the Queen-Mother Catherine de Medici, who wrote to the Pope: "The number of those who have separated themselves from the Roman Church is so great that they can no longer be restrained by severity of law or force of arms. They have become so powerful by reason of the nobles and magistrates who have joined the party, they are so firmly united, and daily acquire such strength that they are becoming more and more formidable in all parts of the kingdom. In the meantime, by the grace of God, there are amongst them neither Anabaptists nor libertines, nor any partizans of odious opinions." She goes on to argue the possibility of communion with them, and suggests matters that might with advantage be reformed in the Roman communion. The Pope, however, was opposed, and both parties armed in preparation for what might come. Admiral Coligny, as leader of the Huguenot party, could say: "We have two thousand and fifty churches, and four hundred thousand men able to bear arms, without taking into account our secret adherents."

† "The Huguenots their Settlements Churches and Industries in England and Ireland" Samuel Smiles.

The Duke of Guise, leader of the Catholic party, shattered all hopes of compromise by attacking a large congregation of unarmed worshippers in a barn, where he and his soldiers surrounded them, slaughtering the helpless victims at their will.   Civil war followed and devastated the country, but after years of exhausting struggle a truce was made and a marriage was arranged between Henry of Béarn, King of Navarre, now leader of the Huguenot cause, and Marguerite, daughter of Catherine de Medici and sister of the King of France.   The marriage was celebrated in Paris (1572) with great festivities, and as it was looked upon by the Huguenots as bringing peace to the contending parties, great numbers of them, including their chief leaders, crowded into the city to see or take part in the celebrations.

Less than a week after the wedding in Notre Dame, at a given signal and according to a prearranged plan, the Catholic leaders with their troops fell upon the unsuspecting Huguenots, and the massacre of Saint Bartholomew took place.   There was no escape.   Huguenot houses had been marked beforehand; men, women, and children were slain without mercy, Admiral Coligny being among the first to be killed; by the end of four days Paris and the Seine were filled with mutilated corpses, in place of the vigorous men and women and groups of happy children who had thronged the streets a week before.   Throughout France similar deeds were done.   After the first surprise the remaining Huguenots, under Henry of Navarre and the Prince of Condé, organized resistance, and there began the wars of the League, which kept France in misery for more than twenty years longer.

In 1594 Henry of Navarre succeeded to the throne of France as Henry IV.   He was a brave and capable ruler, but not a religious man, and he led the Huguenots more as a political than a religious party.   His position was difficult as Protestant ruler of a country chiefly Roman Catholic, whose kings had always belonged to that Church. He met the problem by becoming a Roman Catholic himself, in order to secure his throne, then using his position to legislate in favour of the Huguenots.   In this way a Roman Catholic dynasty was again fastened upon France, but (1598) the king issued the Edict of Nantes by which liberty of conscience and of worship was given to the Huguenots.

The Catholic League did not submit to him, but he defeated and suppressed it, and he expelled the Jesuits. The Huguenots were a State within the State, had their own cities and districts in some parts, and their rights everywhere. Twelve years after the Edict of Nantes the king was assassinated, and trouble soon began again for the Huguenots; there were massacres which stirred them to armed resistance but Cardinal Richelieu directed the war against them with such vigour that they were repeatedly defeated. Their great fortress, la Rochelle, was captured, and as an armed body and a political power they ceased to exist. Richelieu, however, gave them a measure of liberty so that they were reconciled to the Government, and, devoting themselves with their characteristic energy to agriculture, industry and trade, they became wealthy and influential and a source of much prosperity to France.

When Louis XIV, on the death of Mazarin, himself assumed the government of France, he immediately began to take repressive measures against the Huguenots. Under Jesuit influence every means was used to compel them to join the Church of Rome. Those who resisted were subjected to increasing persecution. They bore it with patience, but their affliction only became more acute. Their children were taken from them to be brought up in convents as Catholics; there were massacres; their meetings were prohibited. Rough soldiers were quartered in their homes, and left to behave as they pleased—the infamous system of the "Dragonnades". When the people fled they were hunted in the woods and other places of refuge, brought back to their homes, and forced to entertain the brutal dragoons who, by every kind of torture and outrage, compelled their "conversion" or hounded them to death.

In 1685 the Revocation of the Edict of Nantes was published and the last hope of the Huguenots was taken away. All their pastors were ordered to leave the country within a fortnight. In a few weeks eight hundred Huguenot meeting-places were destroyed. It was ordered that children were to be baptized and brought up in the Church of Rome; employment was made impossible to those who would not be converted; and any who attempted to leave the country were to be sent to the galleys for life, if men, or imprisoned for life if women. In spite of all difficulties of uprooting themselves, leaving their property, travelling secretly by hidden ways with little children and the aged and the sick, and in spite of the desperate dangers of crossing the closely guarded frontiers, there took place such an exodus of the very best of the French nation as permanently impoverished it, while those countries which received the exiles, Switzerland, Holland, Brandenburg, Britain and others were enriched by the coming among them of these multitudes of capable people, of strong Calvinistic character, who brought with them their ability in manufacture and trade, and took a leading place in political and military and naval life, as well as in the arts and sciences.

Although such large numbers left France on the Revocation of the Edict of Nantes, yet still greater numbers could not or would not go, and these still continued to suffer the iniquities of the Dragonnades. They were most numerous in Dauphiny and in Languedoc, so that there the persecution was the more intense. In these times of extremity a strange spiritual excitement and exaltation spread among them. Pierre Jurieu (1686) wrote an exposition of the Apocalypse in which he taught that the prediction of the fall of Babylon referred to the Roman Church and would be fulfilled in the year 1689. One of his disciples, Du Serre, taught his master's prophetic views to children in Dauphiny, and these, brought up among the horrors of the Dragonnades, now went about in bands as "little prophets", from village to village, quoting terrible judgements from the book of the Revelation and announcing their speedy fulfilment. The most famous of these was a girl known as "la belle Isabeau". Thousands of those who had been forced into the Roman Church were in this way brought back and refused to go to Mass. In Languedoc more than three hundred such child prophets were imprisoned in one place.

In the Cevennes mountains men and women fell into ecstasies, during which they spoke in the pure French of the Bible, whereas otherwise they could only speak their own dialect, and they inspired their hearers with heroic courage. In spite of their sufferings these people remained loyal to the king. In 1683 a representative body of the pastors and nobles and chief men among them met together and sent to Louis XIV a declaration of their loyalty. Yet at that very time the Pope was insisting on their extermination, calling them the "execrable race of the ancient Albigenses."

The Abbé du Chayla, however, who introduced a special instrument of torture, practiced such cruelties on the Dissenters in the Cevennes that at last they rose, killed him, and organized military resistance to the Dragonnades. Among their leaders was Jean Cavalier, a baker's boy, who, at the age of seventeen, led the Camisards, so called from the white shirts which were their uniform, with such astonishing ability that for three years (1703-5) he fought and defeated the ablest marshals of France, though his little force never exceeded 3,000 men and his adversaries brought as many as 60,000 against him. He was able to conclude an honourable peace, but some of his followers, continuing the war, were exterminated.

The Camisard War was exceptional; in other parts the Huguenots suffered without resistance the dreadful miseries laid upon them. Many were hanged or burnt; many women were imprisoned, especially in Grenoble and in Valence. One woman, Louise Moulin of Beaufort, was condemned (1687) to be hanged at the door of her house for the crime of having attended meetings. She begged and obtained the favour of being allowed at the last to nourish her infant once more, after which she died with quiet courage. Under such conditions the "Churches of the Desert" as they were called, or "Churches under the Cross" continued their testimony. One of the exiles from Dauphiny at the time of the Revocation of the Edict of Nantes, Jacques Roger* (1675-1745), stirred by the sufferings of his brethren in his native land, and contrasting the sorrows of their condition with the safety and ease in which he lived abroad, determined to return to France, share in the tribulation there and give such help as he could. Arriving in France, he found the faithful remnant persisting in spite of all the power and rage of the adversaries. He saw, too, that the work of the "Prophets" both men and women, had degene-

*"Un Martyr du Désert Jacques Roger" Daniel Benoit.

rated in some districts into fanaticism and disorder. He thought it necessary to replace the pastors who had fled, and re-establish the system of Synods that had broken down. He was joined by others and, as he travelled, soon met Antoine Court, then a young man of twenty, already highly spoken of, who was to develop into the most prominent of all who laboured for the "Churches of the Desert". Court proved to be a man of sound judgement and quick intelligence, and as a preacher and courageous traveller and indefatigable worker and organizer he led the way in the re-establishment of the Church organization with its Provincial and even National Synods. A training school for pastors and preachers was carried on in Lausanne under his superintendence. It was a martyrs' school, for a large proportion of the men who went from it to the work in France were hanged, some of them quite young; Jacques Roger himself was hanged at Grenoble when seventy years of age. The lives of these men were made up of a constant succession of hairbreadth escapes as they traversed the mountains and forests, visited the village churches and ministered the Word. The "Churches of the Desert" instead of being exterminated, grew steadily until (1787) an Act of Toleration, of Louis XVI, brought relief, and in 1793 the Revolution burst over France, and gave them liberty of conscience.

CHAPTER XI

English Nonconformists

1525-1689

Tyndale—Reading of Scripture forbidden—Church of England established—Persecution in the reign of Mary—Baptist and Independent churches—Robert Browne—Barrowe, Greenwood, Penry—Dissenters persecuted in Elizabeth's reign—Privye church in London—Hooker's Ecclesiastical Polity—Church of English exiles in Amsterdam—Arminius—Emigration of brethren from England to Holland—John Robinson—The Pilgrim Fathers sail to America—Different kinds of churches in England and Scotland—Authorized Version of the Bible published—Civil war—Cromwell's New Model army—Religious liberty—Missions—George Fox—Character of Friends' movement—Acts against Nonconformists—Literature—John Bunyan.

THE Lollard movement was outwardly suppressed, but there were always remains of it, and from time to time persons were punished for meeting together to read the Scriptures. The New Learning and the Reformation quickened interest in the Word, and it was a fresh translation of the Bible which was the most powerful means of bringing widespread revival among the people. William Tyndale,* who had studied at Oxford and Cambridge, and had been greatly affected by the teachings of Luther, was in the habit of discussing with the clergy who came to the house where he was a tutor, and showing them how widely they erred from the teachings of Scripture. This raised persecution which obliged him to leave the country, but he had seen that the great need of the people was to become acquainted with the Bible, and he promised that "if God spared his life, ere many years he would cause the boys that drove the plough to know more of the Scriptures" than the divines who kept it from them! Living as an exile on the Continent, and "being inflamed with a tender care and zeal of his country, he studied how by all means possible to bring his countrymen to the same taste and understanding of God's holy word and verity, which the Lord had endued him withal." The first edition of his translation of the New Testament was published in 1525, and was followed by a second, printed the next year in Cologne. Afterwards

---

* "Memoir of William Tyndale" George Offor.

came the Pentateuch and other parts of the Old Testament, translated in Antwerp and Hamburg, as well as frequent editions of the New. The difficulties and dangers involved in getting such volumes into England were almost as great as those which lay in the way of their distribution. The clergy opposed the new translation with all their might. Sir Thomas More was one who wrote violently against it. Although more than any other translation it influenced the Authorized Version, which is indeed to a great extent founded upon it, it was at first declared to be full of errors. Great exception was taken to its using the word "congregation" for "church"; and More said it was so full of errors that "to tell all would be to rehearse the whole book", "to search for one fault would be like studying where to find water in the sea. "

The Testaments were smuggled into England, and an association calling themselves "Christian Brethren" carried them through the country. Everywhere bought and read with avidity, they soon came into the Universities, where societies were formed for meeting to read them. The Bishop of London very early issued an injunction prohibiting them, saying: "Wherefore we, understanding by the report of divers credible persons, and also by the evident appearance of the matter, that many children of iniquity . . . blinded through extreme wickedness, wandering from the way of truth and the Catholic faith, craftily have translated the New Testament into our English tongue. . . . Of the which translation there are many books imprinted, some with glosses and some without, containing in the English tongue that pestiferous and most pernicious poison dispersed throughout all our diocese of London in great number, which . . . without doubt will contaminate and infect the flock committed unto us, with most deadly poison and heresy . . . we . . . command that within thirty days . . . under pain of excommunication and incurring the suspicion of heresy, they do bring in and really deliver to our Vicar-General all and singular such books as contain the translation of the New Testament in the English tongue. " He affirmed that there were more than two thousand heresies in this translation. Knowing a merchant named Packington who was connected with the distribution, he hoped to destroy the books through him, and it is related: "The bishop, thinking that he had God by the toe, when indeed he had (as after he thought) the Devil by the fist, said, 'Gentle maister Packington, do your diligence to get them, and with all my heart I will pay for them, whatever they cost you, for the books are erroneous and naughty, and I intend surely to destroy them all, and to burn them at St. Paul's Cross.'" This bargain was carried out and money thus provided for the printing of a much larger number of Testaments. A prisoner accused of heresy, when asked how Tyndale and his friends were supported, said: "It is the Bishop of London that hath holpen us, for he hath bestowed among us a great deal of money in New Testaments to burn them, and that hath been, and yet is, our only succour and comfort." Diligent inquisition was made for the prohibited books, and large numbers of people were fined or imprisoned or put to death for possessing them. It is recorded that "Divers persons that were detected to use reading of the New Testament, set forth by Tyndale, were punished . . . but still the number of them daily increased."

By the help of a spy sent from England Tyndale was eventually taken, and at Vilvoord in Belgium, condemned, strangled, and his body burnt (1536). But his work was done, he had taken his valiant part with all those who by translating and distributing the Bible, by practising and teaching the truths it reveals, have helped to bring to men the knowledge of God and show them the Way of Life.

Great changes were going on in England at this time. In 1531 King Henry VIII was acknowledged as the Supreme Head of the Church of England, the Church of England thus taking the place of the Church of Rome, and the King that of the Pope. The conflict between the Pope and the King was that between Church and State on the one hand and State and Church on the other, between the Papist and the Erastian views. The plan of bringing about Reform by making the civil power superior to the ecclesiastical (Erastianism) had already been introduced in the churches of Brandenburg and of Saxony. Cranmer held that this was the best course, and Henry VIII adopted it as his policy in England.

In the year of Tyndale's death, his translation of the

Bible, revised and edited at the King's command by Miles Coverdale, was taken under the Royal patronage, ordered to be accepted as the foundation of national faith and placed in the churches throughout the country. This favour was, however, soon withdrawn. In 1543 a measure entitled, "An act for the advancement of true religion, and for the abolishment of the contrary" enacted that "All manner of books of the Old and New Testament in English, being of the crafty, false, and untrue translation of Tyndale, shall be clearly and utterly abolished, extinguished, and forbidden to be kept or used." The punishments for disobedience were very severe, amounting in some cases to imprisonment for life. Other books might be read, but the reading of the Scriptures was confined to judges, noblemen, captains and justices, who might read the Bible to their families. "Merchants may read it in private to themselves; but no women, or artificers, prentyses, journeyman, serving man of the degree of yeoman or under, no husbandman, nor labourers, shall read within this realm the Bible or New Testament in English to himself, or to any other, privately or openly." Noble women or gentlewomen might read it to themselves. The King declared that by laws dreadful and penal he would purge and cleanse his realm of all such books. But whether permitted or forbidden, the people could not now be prevented from reading the Scriptures. When they were read aloud in the churches crowds came to hear; when they were forbidden all risks were run to obtain them. A labourer wrote in his Testament: "On the invention of things, at Oxforde the yere 1546 browt down to Seynbury by John Darbye, price 14d. When I kepe Mr. Letymers shype I bout thys boke, when the Testament was abergatyn, that shepherdys might not red hit: I pray God amende that blyndnes. Wryt by Robert Wyllyams, keppynge shepe vppon Seynbury Hill." As the people were taught by Moses and the Prophets, by the Histories and the Psalms, especially as, in the Gospels, they learned to know Jesus Christ, and from the Epistles traced the consequences of His atoning work, the whole character of the nation was changed, for, in any nation, the extent to which righteousness and compassion prevail is a measure of the extent to which this Book has affected the hearts and minds of the people.

During the six years of the reign of Edward VI those in power developed the Church of England on more definitely Protestant lines than formerly, but in the following six years of the reign of Queen Mary this policy was reversed, and England returned to her allegiance to the Pope, receiving absolution for her heresy and schism. Where, however, the Government was pliant, the people were adamant. No efforts could induce them to submit to practices which were clearly contrary to the Word of God. Hundreds of people, not only those in high positions, but also from among the humblest, both men and women, were publicly burned to death in the towns and villages of England. The sufferings of these martyrs were more effective in breaking the power of Rome than the policies of rulers or the arguments of divines. Those fires still burn in the memory of the people of England, beacon lights, warning them against any return to a system that could bear such fruits.

There was a church in London, founded on the ground of Scripture, in the reign of Edward VI, composed of French, Dutch, and Italian Christians. There were also English churches of this character considerably earlier, stretching back indeed to Lollard times, for the Bishop of London in 1523 wrote that the great band of Wycliffite heretics were nothing new. There are records of "Congregations" in England in 1555 and Baptist churches are known to have existed in the reign of Queen Elizabeth, before 1589. Both those called Independents or Congregationalists and those called Baptists were independent churches of believers, differing in this that the Baptists practised the baptism of believers only, while the Independents baptized infants one* of whose parents (or whose guardian) was a believer.

Robert Browne was so active in proclaiming the independence of each believing congregation that, following the old habit of giving some sectarian name to those outside of the State Church, such companies were often called "Brownists". Sir Walter Raleigh stated in Parliament that there were thousands of Brownists at that time. Browne's writings, as for instance his book entitled, "A Booke which sheweth the Life and Manners of all true

* "A History of the Free Churches of England" Herbert S. Skeats.

Christians, and howe unlike they are unto Turkes and Papistes and Heathen folke", and another, "A Treatise of Reformation without Tarrying for Anie", exercised a great influence.* For circulating them, two men were hanged in Bury St. Edmunds, in 1583, and as many of the books as could be found were burned. Browne himself, hunted, imprisoned, persecuted, at last broke down in mind and body, and allowed himself to be forced back into the Established Church.

All forms of Dissent were relentlessly persecuted, Puritans, Presbyterians, and especially Baptists and Independents. The gaols were crowded with them, and as these were foul beyond description, unknown numbers died of the diseases, misery, and ill-treatment which then accompanied imprisonment.

The most distinguished men among the Independents were Barrowe, Greenwood and Penry. The two former had shown unanswerably that the only upright and straightforward course for those who did not believe in the Scripturalness of the Established Church was to separate from it, that it was dishonourable for a man to give assent to what he did not believe, or believed only in part, and especially for him to accept position and payment to disseminate it. After years in prison they were both hanged. Penry was so much moved by the miserable condition of the people in Wales that he not only preached and laboured among them indefatigably himself, but tried to incite others to do the same, thus disturbing the neglectful, notoriously evil-living clergy of that country and arousing their envious hatred. He was a man who possessed in an unusual degree the gifts and graces of a minister of Christ; he was of godly life, full of love and compassion for souls, learned, sympathetic, of strong family affections, and devoted in the service of the Gospel. His work was effectual in the conversion of sinners and building up of those who believed, chiefly in Wales, but also largely in Scotland and England. He too, was taken, in London, and hanged, soon after his two fellow-workers in the Gospel.

These men were connected with a church known as the "Privye Churche in London". Its foundation principle was the saying of the Lord: "where two or three are gathered

* "A Popular History of the Free Churches" C. Silvester Horne.

together in My name, there am I in the midst of them"
(Matt. 18. 20). It had no fixed place of meeting, gatherings being held in private houses or in the open fields.
One of its meetings was broken up in 1567, and fourteen or
fifteen of its leading members imprisoned. In 1592 fifty-
six of them were seized in a meeting where they were
worshipping God. Large numbers of them from many
parts lay year after year in utmost misery, in dungeons and
in chains. In six years seventeen died in gaol, and, later,
twenty-four in one year.

During this period a defence of the Church of England
was written, the "*Ecclesiastical Polity*" of Richard Hooker*
a work which was, and still is, greatly admired. In it
Hooker controverted those who maintained that the
Church of England required further reformation, and
laboured to prove that Scripture alone was not sufficient
for the guidance of the Church; that there were many
rites and customs practised by the Apostles which were
not written but are known to be apostolical; that many of
God's laws are changeable; that there are many actions
performed in daily life about which Scripture gives no
instruction and that Scripture is not needed to guide in
every action, but action is to be framed by the law of
reason; that faith may be founded on other things beside
Scripture, for man's authority has great weight; and that
what is narrated in Scripture is not necessarily to be regarded as commanded. The authority of Scripture having
thus been carefully limited and minimized, some practices
and doctrines contrary to it are taken for granted as right,
as, for instance, infant baptism and the necessity of the
sacraments for salvation. He says, we are blamed "that
in many things we have departed from the ancient simplicity of Christ and His Apostles; we have embraced more
outward stateliness, we have those orders in the exercise
of religion which they who best pleased God and served
Him most devoutly never had. For it is out of doubt that
the first state of things was best, that in the prime of
Christian religion faith was soundest, the Scriptures of
God were then best understood by all men, all parts of
godliness did then most abound, and therefore it must

* "Laws of Ecclesiastical Polity" Richard Hooker.

needs follow, that customs, laws, and ordinances devised since are not so good for the Church of Christ; but the best way is, to cut off later inventions, and to reduce things unto the ancient state wherein at the first they were." To this he replies that those who take such a position "must needs confess it a very uncertain thing, what the orders of the Church were in the Apostles' times, seeing the Scriptures do not mention them all, and other records thereof besides they utterly reject. So in tying the Church to the orders of the Apostles' time, they tie it to a marvellous uncertain rule; unless they require the observation of no orders but only those that are known to be apostolical by the Apostles' own writings. . ." "It is not, I am right sure" he writes "their meaning, that we should now assemble our people to serve God in close and secret meetings; or that common brooks or rivers should be used for places of baptism; or that the eucharist should be ministered after meat; or that the custom of church-feasting should be renewed; or that all kind of standing provision for the ministry should be utterly taken away, and their estate made again dependent upon the voluntary devotion of men. In these things they easily perceive how unfit that were for the present, which was for the first age convenient enough. The faith, zeal, and godliness of former times is worthily had in honour; but doth this prove that the orders of the Church of Christ must be still the self-same with theirs, that nothing may be which was not then, or that nothing which then was may lawfully since have ceased? They who recall the Church unto that which was at the first, must necessarily set bounds and limits unto their speeches." Thus, diminishing the authority of Scripture and pointing out that if his opponents were consistent they would go further than they had done in their professed return to the Scriptures, he laid a foundation on which he built up the conclusion that the Church of England did not need further reformation, being more consonant with Scripture and good sense than any other, working his way through its various beliefs and practices and reaching the summit of the structure when he argued that the acknowledgment of King Henry VIII and of each of his successors in turn as Supreme Head of the Church is in true accord with the teachings of Scripture. As to this

Church, he says: "We hold that . . . there is not any man of the Church of England but the same man is also a member of the commonwealth, nor any member of the commonwealth which is not also of the Church of England." Though so positive in his teachings and deductions it is noticeable and commendable that there is in the language of Hooker a restraint and dignity in striking contrast to the violence and abusiveness of speech which all parties allowed themselves in his day.

Before the close of her reign, Elizabeth ceased to imprison those who refused conformity to the Church of England and banished them instead. This drove many called Brownists and Anabaptists to seek refuge in Holland. They formed a church in Amsterdam, which under the guidance of Francis Johnson and Henry Ainsworth published in 1596 "A Confession of Faith of certain English people living in the Low Countries, exiled."

Holland was a centre of spiritual activities of the greatest importance. Among the many eminent teachers there, none exercised a more far-reaching influence than Jacobus Arminius (1560-1609).* Although his name is associated with much religious strife, Arminianism being contrasted with Calvinism, he was not himself a party man or extreme in his views. Since the days when Augustine and Pelagius had striven, the former to maintain the elective sovereignty of God and the latter to expound man's free will and responsibility, these vital questions of the relations between God and man had not ceased to exercise minds and hearts. Calvin, and still more some of his followers, while showing powerfully what is taught in Scripture regarding the sovereignty and election of God, minimized those balancing truths which are also contained in the Scriptures. Thus their logic, setting out from part of revealed truth rather than the whole, led them to conclusions according to which man is the subject of absolute decrees which he has no power to affect. The manifest extravagance of such teaching naturally led to reaction, which, in its turn, tended to become extreme. Brought up under the influence of Calvin's teaching, Arminius—acknowledged

* "Encyclopaedia of Religion and Ethics" Edited by James Hastings. Article, Arminianism.

by all as a man of spotless character, in ability and learning unexcelled—was chosen to write in defence of Calvinism of the less extreme kind, which was felt to be endangered by the attacks made upon it. Studying the subject, however, he came to see that much that he had held was indefensible, that it made God the author of sin, set limits to His saving grace, left the majority of mankind without hope or possibility of salvation. He saw from the Scriptures that the atoning work of Christ was for all, and that man's freedom of choice is a part of the Divine decree. Coming back to the original teaching of Scripture and faith of the Church, he avoided the extremes into which both parties to the long controversy had fallen. His statement of what he had come to believe involved him personally in conflicts which so affected his spirit as to shorten his life. His teaching took a vivid and evangelical form later, in the Methodist revival.

When James I came to the throne, efforts to compel uniformity of religion, which had slackened at the end of Elizabeth's reign, were renewed, and emigration, though checked by the authorities, continued. At this time a congregation of believers met in Gainsborough, of which John Smyth was a leader. From this another church was formed, of members who had been in the habit of coming some ten or twelve miles on Sundays to the meetings in Gainsborough. This fresh meeting-place was in Scrooby Manor House, and the believers there were joined by John Robinson, driven by persecution from his congregation in Norwich. They were not long left in peace, their houses were watched and their means of earning a living were taken from them, or they were imprisoned. Some having vainly tried to escape to Holland, they eventually decided, as a church, to emigrate together (1607). Their journey was interrupted by repeated arrests, imprisonments, and painful separations, so that at last they arrived in little groups, destitute but undaunted, and, rejoining each other, were received by the churches in Amsterdam and elsewhere.

The church in Amsterdam soon began to suffer from differences of view. The Dutch Mennonites were in favour of the baptism of believers and so were John Smyth and

Thomas Helwys. Most of the members, however, disagreed with this; there was much dissension; Smyth and Helwys with about forty others were excluded from fellowship and formed themselves into a separate church. The Baptists also held that the civil power had no right to interfere in matters of religion or to compel any form of doctrine, and affirmed that it should confine itself to political matters and to the maintenance of order; the others believed that it was the duty of the State to exercise a certain control in matters of doctrine and of church order, and, while they protested against the measures of compulsion used against themselves, would not have been willing to allow full liberty to others who differed from them. Those who were with Smyth did not think it in accordance with the Lord's teaching for a Christian to bear arms, nor to serve as a magistrate or ruler. Johnson and Ainsworth inclined increasingly to a Presbyterian form of church Government, with which John Robinson did not agree. In order to avoid further disputing, Robinson and others removed from Amsterdam to Leyden and founded a church there. This church continued in unity and peace, the ministry of John Robinson being distinguished by its power and breadth. These churches not only provided a home for persecuted saints and maintained a testimony to the truth, but came to exercise a far-reaching influence. When it became possible for some of their members to return to England, they greatly strengthened the believers there. Helwys with others formed a Baptist Church in London about 1612. A few years later Henry Jacob, an associate of Robinson, came and took part in the founding of an Independent church in London, from which a church of "Particular", or Calvinistic, Baptists, went out afterwards. But there were others whose course was shaped to wider issues. The thought of establishing churches in the New World, where there would be liberty of conscience, of worship, and of testimony, came to affect these exiles increasingly, and, after much prayer and much negotiation, the "Speedwell" set out on this great adventure. The parting was hard both for those going and those remaining. John Robinson in his memorable charge to the departing company at Delft Haven, said: "I charge you before God and His blessed angels, that you follow me no further than you have seen me follow the Lord Jesus Christ. If God reveals anything to you by any other instrument of His, be as ready to receive it as you were to receive any truth by my ministry, for I am verily persuaded the Lord hath more truth yet to break forth out of His holy word. For my part, I cannot sufficiently bewail the condition of those reformed Churches which are come to a period in religion, and will go, at present, no further than the instruments of their reformation. The Lutherans cannot be drawn to go beyond what Luther saw; whatever part of His will our God has revealed to Calvin, they will rather die than embrace it; and the Calvinists, you see, stick fast where they were left by that great man of God, who yet saw not all things. This is a misery much to be lamented, for though they were burning and shining lights in their times, yet they penetrated not into the whole counsel of God; but were they now living, would be as willing to embrace further light as that which they first received, for it is not possible the Christian world should come so lately out of such thick anti-christian darkness and that perfection of knowledge should break forth at once." The "Speedwell" was joined by the "Mayflower" with a party from England that were to go with them, and the two ships set out together from England, but the "Speedwell" springing a leak, they had to return. All were crowded into the "Mayflower", and the little vessel set sail from Plymouth (1620). A tremendous storm almost turned them back, but, being determined to continue, they struggled on, and after nine weeks' sailing they landed, 102 of them, at Plymouth Bay in New England, and laid the foundations of a State which, become populous and prosperous beyond others, has never ceased to bear the impress of the character of the men and women who founded it in the fear of God and the love of liberty.

The Church of England, having its origin in the Church of Rome, but separated from it, and modified by the influences of the Lutheran and Swiss Reformers, combined characteristics of all these systems. It made the King its Head and so kept a political character, and, in common with the Reformers, it took over part of the clerical system of the Church of Rome, with its necessary bulwarks of infant baptism and the administration of the Lord's Supper by the clergy. Not at first Episcopalian, by the latter part of Elizabeth's reign it had begun to move Romewards in this respect and in a short time had fully adopted that system of government. The Puritans were that element in the Church of England which consistently strove against what was Romish in it, endeavouring to make it more definitely Protestant, and they suffered much for their efforts to maintain the authority of Scripture as against the decrees of those who ruled. The Presbyterians were more in sympathy with the Continental Reformers than the Church of England was. Presbyterianism became the established religion of Scotland, but in England such divergence from uniformity was not allowed; a Presbyterian Church formed at Wandsworth (1572) was dispersed by the authorities. The Independents maintained the scriptural doctrine of the independence of each congregation of believers and its direct dependence on the Lord. They differed so entirely from the established religion, setting aside the king and the bishops from the places they had taken in the Church, indeed denying their right, unless converted, to be members of the Church at all, that no mercy could be shown them. They were crowded into the prisons, fined, mutilated and executed with unrelenting cruelty. The Baptists were looked upon as even worse, for they not only shared to the full the view of the Independents as to the church, but they denied that the state had any authority at all to interfere in matters of religion, and they also repudiated infant baptism altogether and went back to the primitive practice of baptizing believers only, thus cutting at the root of clerical power. Their spiritual relationships were with the Anabaptists, Waldenses, and others like them, and they naturally shared with them and with the Independents the utmost wrath of those who were determined at all costs to force on the whole nation that form of religion which for the time being was ordained by the State.

There were individual true members of the Church of Christ in all these circles, whether Roman, Anglican or Free Church, and there were also companies of believers corresponding to the churches of God of the New Testament among the despised and persecuted congregations, but their witness was maintained, as often before and since, in the midst of circumstances so confusing as to test faith and love to the utmost.

A great impetus was given to the spread of the Gospel by the publication of the beautiful and powerful translation of the Bible known as the Authorized Version, in 1611. Its language and imagery have become an essential part of English speech, and no book has been so widely read or has exercised such an influence for good.

In spite of persecution the congregations of believers increased; it was stated in the House of Lords (1641) that there were eighty companies of different "sectaries" in and around London, those who ministered in them being spoken of contemptuously as cobblers, tailors, "and such like trash."

A great change in conditions was brought about by the Civil War. During the course of the struggle proposals were considered for the formation of a new National Church. As the bishops were irreconcilably on the side of the king, and it was desirable to have the full support of Scotland, the divines appointed by Parliament to draw up a new form of religion adopted the Scottish Covenant and the Presbyterian form of Church government, which was accepted by Parliament. The Presbyterians insisted that this should be imposed on all the people of England, attaching severe penalties to the refusal to conform. The sects were to be extinguished. The few Independents who took part in these discussions at Westminster protested in vain that liberty should be secured to them; the Baptists, who advocated complete religious toleration, were not even consulted. During the war, however, Cromwell's "New Model" army had grown up and become the indispensable means of victory. It was composed of religious men, a large proportion of them "sectaries". Men of various creeds had fought side by side for the same cause; Episcopalians, Puritans, Presbyterians, Independents, Baptists had joined in worship and in war and had learned respect for each other in the stern struggle they had shared. They were not disposed to see the liberty of conscience for which they had fought and suffered cast away by narrow-minded legislators, and by a rapid, striking turn of events, both the Assembly that had drawn up the Westminster Confession and the Houses of Parliament were dissolved; the Commonwealth was established, and with it came such liberty of conscience and of worship, such freedom to speak and publish what was believed as had never before been known.

The Council of State declared (1653) that none should be compelled to conform to the public religion, by penalties or otherwise, that "such as profess faith in God by Jesus Christ, though differing in judgment trom the doctrine, worship or discipline publicly held forth, shall not be restrained from, but shall be protected in, the profession of their faith and exercise of their religion, so as they abuse not this liberty to the civil injury of others, and to the actual disturbance of the public peace." Popery and Prelacy were not included in this liberty. "Triers" were appointed to examine the occupants of the Church livings. Those who were found to be of wicked life or ignorant, and they were numerous, were dismissed, and the pulpits were filled by men who were judged capable of instructing the people. These were mostly Presbyterians and Independents; a few were Baptists. The removal of restraints allowed suppressed gifts to appear, and a host of able preachers and writers was both a response and a stimulus to quickened spiritual life. There was a great increase of Gospel preaching, and not a few of the churches formed as a result of it were of an unsectarian character. A conscience was awakened as to the needs of the heathen, and Parliament constituted a corporation for the Propagation of the Gospel in New England, declaring "that the Commons of England assembled in Parliament, having received intelligence that the heathens of New England were beginning to call on the name of the Lord, felt bound to assist in such a work." The interest which led to this had been awakened by John Eliot, who, driven from England by persecution, crossed to Boston, and, coming among Indians, learned their language, into which he translated the Bible and other books, and preached the Gospel among them, bringing about their spiritual and social uplifting.

At Drayton-in-the-Clay in Leicestershire, Christopher Fox and Mary his wife, godly people, had a son (born 1624)

named George,* who, as a child, "had a gravity and
stayedness of mind and spirit, not usual in children," so
that, he says, "when I saw old men behave lightly and
wantonly towards each other, I had a dislike thereof raised
in my heart, and said within myself, 'If ever I come to be
a man, surely I shall not do so.'" When only eleven years
old he saw that his words should be few and that his "Yea"
and "Nay" should be sufficient asseveration; also that he
should eat and drink, not wantonly, but for health, "using
the creatures in their service, as servants in their places,
to the glory of Him that created them." After a time in
a business situation, at the age of nineteen he felt a command
of God to leave home, and for the next four years travelled,
returning home occasionally. During this time he was in
great spiritual conflict and distress, prayed and fasted and
spent much time in long solitary walks. He also spoke
with many, but was troubled as he found that professors
of religion did not possess what they professed. At festivals, such as Christmas, instead of joining in festivities,
he would go from house to house visiting poor widows and
giving them money, of which he had enough for himself and
for the help of others. On his walks he had what he called
"openings" from the Lord. One day, approaching Coventry,
he was thinking of how it is said that all Christians are
believers, whether Protestants or Papists. "But," he considered, "a believer is one that is born again, has passed
from death unto life, otherwise he is no believer"; so he
saw that many who call themselves Christians or believers
are not so. Another time, one first-day morning, crossing
a field, the Lord opened to him "that being bred at Oxford
or Cambridge was not enough to fit and qualify men to be
ministers of Christ". He was impressed by the Scripture:
"ye need not that any man teach you: but . . . the . . .
anointing teacheth you of all things" (1 John 2. 27), and
used this to justify his not going to church, but rather
taking his Bible into the orchards and fields. Again it
was opened to him: "God, who made the world, did not
dwell in temples made with hands." This surprised him,
because it was usual to speak of the churches as "temples of
God", "dreadful places", "holy ground", but now he saw
that God's people are His temple and that He dwells in

* "Journal of George Fox"

them. At the end of this time, finally leaving his home and relations, he led a wandering life, taking a room in some town, staying a few weeks, and then going on. He had given up seeking help from the clergy and turned to the Dissenters, but neither could these speak to his condition. Then he says: "When all my hopes in them and in all men, were gone, so that I had nothing outwardly to help me nor could I tell what to do; then, Oh! then I heard a voice which said, 'There is one, even Christ Jesus, that can speak to thy condition'; and when I heard it, my heart did leap for joy." Then he entered into peace, enjoyed fellowship with Christ, saw that he had all things in Him who had done all, and in whom he believed. He could not sufficiently praise God for His mercy. He was aware of the Lord's command to go abroad into the world, to turn people from darkness to the light, and, he says, "I saw that Christ died for all men, and was a propitiation for all; and enlightened all men and women with His divine and saving life; and that none could be a true believer but who believed in it . . ." and adds: "These things I did not see by the help of man nor by the letter, though they are written in the letter, but I saw them in the light of the Lord Jesus Christ, and by His immediate Spirit and power, as did the holy men of God, by whom the Holy Scriptures were written. Yet I had no slight esteem of the Holy Scriptures, but they were very precious to me, for I was in that Spirit by which they were given forth: and what the Lord opened in me, I afterwards found was agreeable to them." Many began to come together to hear him and some were convinced, meetings of "the Friends" being begun in place after place.

Refusal to bear arms or take part in war was a principle with Fox; he set aside all use of force and taught that all things were to be borne and all forgiven, that no oath might be taken, and that all payment of tithes was to be refused. The manner of carrying out these principles and this mission was entirely fearless, and reckless of all consequences. An example of this is given in his Journal— "I went", he writes, "to another steeple-house about three miles off, where preached a great high-priest, called a doctor. . . . I went into the steeple-house and stayed till the priest had done. The words which he took for his text were these, 'Ho, every one that thirsteth, come ye to the waters; and he that hath no money, come ye, buy and eat, yea come, buy wine and milk without money and without price.' Then was I moved of the Lord God to say unto him, 'Come down, thou deceiver; dost thou bid people come and take of the water of life freely, and yet thou takest three hundred pounds a-year of them, for preaching the Scriptures to them. Mayest thou not blush for shame? Did the prophet Isaiah and Christ do so, who spoke the words, and gave them forth freely? Did not Christ say to His ministers, whom He sent to preach, "Freely ye have received, freely give?"' The priest, like a man amazed, hastened away. After he had left his flock, I had as much time as I could desire to speak to the people; and I directed them from the darkness to the light, and to the grace of God, that would teach them, and bring them salvation; to the Spirit of God in their inward parts, which would be a free teacher unto them. " A conflict was joined which spread all over the country and far abroad. The methods of the Friends broke down all the Government's purpose of toleration, and local excitement and anger showed itself in utmost violence. The Friends, now derisively called Quakers, were beaten, fined, shut up in loathsome and disgusting prisons and subjected to every possible indignity. Fox himself was repeatedly imprisoned, beaten and ill-treated, and, as their numbers increased, there were seldom less than a thousand Friends in prison at a time. Yet they never quailed, did not attempt to avoid persecution, seemed rather to court it, and, in spite of all, the Society increased, its meetings spread all over the country, and from them preachers went out, both men and women, whom no dangers could hold back; they soon reached out abroad also, westward to the West Indies and the New England settlements, eastward into Holland and Germany.

In the reign of James II circumstances brought liberty for the Friends, among others, and the Society became free to develop those labours for the alleviation of suffering and the removal of injustice which have always so greatly distinguished it.

The power of its testimony lay in the revival of forgotten truth as to the reality of the indwelling of the Holy Spirit.

It did not establish churches in the New Testament sense of the word, since membership of the Society was not based on conversion or the new birth, and the outward ordinances of baptism and the Lord's Supper were not observed. The meetings, however, were occasions when there was liberty for the Spirit to minister through whom He might choose, untrammelled by any human regulations.

At the Restoration there was a return to the old policy of endeavouring to force all into conformity to the Church of England. The Act of Uniformity was passed (1662), which required that every minister in the Church should declare before his congregation his unfeigned assent and consent to everything contained in the Book of Common Prayer and that every minister should obtain episcopal ordination. The result was that two thousand ministers, including naturally the best, refused submission and were ejected from their livings. This greatly strengthened Nonconformity in the country and Act after Act was passed to crush it out. No Nonconformist might hold office in any municipal body, nor might he hold any meeting at which more than five persons were present in addition to the members of his own family, nor might any Government employment be given to him; the ejected ministers were forbidden to go within five miles of any corporate borough or any place where they had formerly ministered. The penalties attached to any contravention of these laws were most severe, yet Baptists and Independents held secret meetings, Quakers continued theirs without concealment, and soon the prisons were again crowded, and fines, pillory, the stocks and noisome gaols were doing their old work. A desperate and unremitting conflict between the Church party and the Dissenters had now been entered upon, or reached a new phase, lasting from this the middle of the 17th far into the 19th century, in the course of which, little by little, in the face of unrelenting hostility, Dissenters obtained the rights of citizens of their native country.

Throughout all these conflicts an extraordinary volume of spiritual and intellectual grace and power was developed, and that in all the different circles. Among a multitude of distinguished men, Baxter, the Presbyterian, is remembered by his "Saints' Everlasting Rest"; John Owens, as being the powerful exponent of the doctrines of the Congregational churches; Isaac Watts, also an Independent, by his hymns, which gave a new expression to worship and praise; and John Bunyan, whose "Pilgrim's Progress" has probably been more read than any book ever written, except the Bible, and who, by his sufferings and labours also, takes rank among the highest.

The church in Bedford, of which he was a member and became an elder and then pastor, has left in its minutes an account of the care exercised,* with frequent prayer and fasting, in the reception of members and the exercise of discipline and also in the visiting and instruction of the believers. Even when it was under stress of persecution and imprisonment, impoverished by fines and driven from one place of meeting to another, the diligence of the elders in fulfilling the testimony and ministry committed to them was unabated. Though a Baptist church, they were emphatic in refusing to make baptism the ground of fellowship, or differences of judgement on the matter a bar to communion. Bunyan desired fellowship with all Christians, and wrote: "I will not let Water Baptism be the rule, the door, the bolt, the bar, the wall of division between the righteous and the righteous," and again: "The Lord deliver me from superstitious and idolatrous thoughts about any of the ordinances of Christ and of God"; further: "Since you would know by what name I would be distinguished from others, I tell you I would be, and hope I am, *a Christian*, and choose, if God should count me worthy, to be called a Christian, a believer, or other such name which is approved by the Holy Ghost."

*"John Bunyan His Life Times and Work" John Brown B.A., D.D.

CHAPTER XII

Labadie, the Pietists, Zinzendorf, Philadelphia

1635-1750

Labadie—Forms a fellowship in the Roman Catholic Church—Joins the
Reformed Church—Goes to Orange—To Geneva—Willem Teelinck—
Gisbert Voet—van Lodensteyn—Labadie goes to Holland—Difference
between Presbyterian and Independent ideals—Reforms in the Middel-
burg church—Conflict with Synods of the Reformed Church—Conflict on
Rationalism—Labadie condemns Synods—He is excluded from the
Reformed Church—A separate church formed in Middelburg—The new
church expelled from Middelburg—It removes to Veere—Then to
Amsterdam—Household church formed—Anna Maria van Schürman—
Difference with Voet—Household troubles—Removal to Herford—Labadie
dies in Altona—Removal of household to Wieuwerd—Household broken
up—Effects of testimony—Spener—Pietists—Franke—Christian David—
Zinzendorf—Herrnhut—Dissensions—Zinzendorf's Statutes accepted—
Revival—Discovery of document in Zittau—Determination to restore the
Bohemian Church—Question of relations with the Lutheran Church—The
negro Anthony—Moravian Missions—The Mission in England—Cennick—
Central control unsuited to expanding work—Philadelphia Societies—
Miguel de Molinos—Madame Guyon—Gottfried Arnold—Wittgenstein—
The Marburg Bible—The Berleburg Bible—Philadelphian Invitation—
Hochmann von Hochenau—Tersteegen—Jung Stilling—Primitive and
Reformed and other churches—Various ways of return to Scripture.

THE line of thought of the mystics in the Roman Catholic
Church affected a young man, Jean de Labadie,[*]
born in Bordeaux in 1610, and educated by the Jesuits
with a view to his becoming a member of their Society.
Dissatisfied with his theological studies he turned to the
New Testament and became deeply impressed by the greatness of the Gospel; saw, too, how corrupt Christendom had
become and that the way of restoration could only be in a
return to the pattern of the first assembly in Jerusalem.
Ordained a priest (1635), he felt that his ordination was not
from the bishop but from the Lord Himself, who had called
him from his mother's womb to reform the Christian Church.

[*] "Geschichte des Christlichen Lebens in der rheinisch-westphälischen
Kirche   Max Goebel.
"Geschichte des Pietismus und der Mystik in der Reformirten
Kirche u.s.w." Heinr. Heppe.
"Geschichte des Pietismus in der reformirten Kirche" Albrecht Ritschl.

He saw that he must leave the Jesuits—with whom he was not yet completely associated. There seemed, however, no possibility of disentangling himself even from the position in which he already was; he had gone too far to turn back; so he committed himself into the hands of God and waited for Him to open the way. Serious and prolonged sickness led to the Jesuits' giving up the idea of his finally becoming one of their number, and he was able to leave Bordeaux and all his old surroundings. His activities in Bordeaux had been so successful that with the consent of the archbishop he accepted a call and began to teach, first in Paris, then in Amiens.

Large numbers were attracted to his lectures. His method was to read a considerable portion of Scripture, several chapters even, and then expound them. People began to give up their rosaries and to occupy themselves with the New Testaments which Labadie circulated widely. He taught that the Gospel is the only rule of faith and piety, and that the manner of life of the primitive Christians is the pattern for all times. With the permission of the bishop a "congregation" or "brotherhood" was formed, consisting of those only who were awakened; they met twice weekly for meditation, and in their own houses they read the Bible. In this circle he made known his earnest desire that, in the will of God, the time might come when the Church would be restored to its original condition, so that it might be possible to read the Word of God there, to preach according to the custom of the original church (1 Cor. 14), and to take the Lord's Supper in both kinds. Persistently persecuted by the Jesuits, Labadie left Picardy and went to Guyenne, his birthplace, accompanied by several members of the brotherhood as a travelling assembly. There he was brought into contact with the teaching of Calvin, which he studied, thinking he might find among the reformed a people who lived for God and acted according to the principles of the Gospel in doctrine, worship, and manner of life. He found that all the most important and decisive convictions he had received had been obtained by him through the study of Scripture, while still in the Roman Catholic Church, and not through the study of Calvin's works. Here he heard of the efforts made in the 16th century by Le Fèvre, Briçonnet, Roussel and others to reform the Church. Continued persecution obliged him to hide among the Carmelites and in the castles of his admirers, where he came among families belonging to the Reformed Church, families by whose life and teaching he was affected and impressed. He had tried to serve and heal the Church of Rome, but came to see that he was in irreconcilable opposition to its clergy. He hoped that if he joined the Reformed Church he might have liberty to confess openly the truths which God had so laid on his heart. Being in general agreement with the teaching of the Reformed Church he entered it in 1650 at Montauban, but did so under the conviction that its discipline was lax and its practice unworthy, and that as his efforts to reform the Roman Catholic Church had been resisted he was called now to bring about reform in the Reformed Church.

In his writings and preaching Labadie showed that the power for outward reform and godly living lies in an inward life of communion with God, and wrote detailed instructions as to prayer and meditation. The constant aim of the Christian, he said, must be conformity of the will to the will of God, union with God. His love to God should be unselfish and unconditional; he would love and glorify God even if God had reckoned him to the lost.

Obliged to leave Montauban, Labadie was passing through Orange, but the presbytery of the church there persuaded him to remain. With the help of the members he set about a thorough reform, so that it might be really a "Reformed" Church, and this was, to a large extent effected. After less than two years the threatenings of Louis XIV making his stay even in the territories of the Prince of Orange dangerous, he accepted an invitation from the French church in London to become its minister. Fearing to pass through France he travelled by way of Switzerland. In Geneva, however, he was restrained from going further, remaining as a preacher in the church there (1659). His preaching was so powerful that the laxity that had followed Calvin's strict rule was immediately checked and there was a return to righteousness which affected the moral condition of the city generally. More special blessing attended the Bible readings which were held in his own house, where a group of young people gathered around him to whom he taught "sound doctrine and holy life" as the "two hands" of the Christian. One of the young men who was helped through these Bible readings was Philip Jakob Spener.

In 1661 Labadie received an invitation to Holland from some who were well known for their earnest Christian testimony. Among them were Voet, van Lodensteyn and Anna Maria van Schürman, who requested him to accept the place of preacher in the church at Middelburg where Teelinck had exercised a ministry of remarkable power and blessing.

Since the freeing of the Netherlands from the yoke of Spain, through the heroic fight led by William of Orange, the Low Countries had been in advance of all their neighbours both in religious liberty and material prosperity, and had become the scene and centre of intense spiritual activities. The University at Franecke was celebrated for the learning and piety of its professors. An originator of much of this life and interest in matters of religion was Willem Teelinck, born in 1579, whose father occupied a prominent position in the administration of the country. Teelinck travelled and studied for seven years in France. Scotland, and England. In London he came into contact with Puritan families, where what he heard and read led him to a change of life. He spent time in prayer, had days of fasting, and determined to give up his legal studies in order to devote himself exclusively to the ministry of the Word. He lived for some time in a family in Bamburgh, where he found such a life of prayer and of good works as he had never before seen or imagined possible. The regular prayer and reading of the Scriptures with exposition in the household; the thanksgiving at meals, conversation at table, singing, attendance at meetings, in all of which the servants and the children were as much interested as the heads of the household, the unfailing kindness, the care of the sick and needy—all this had an influence upon him which affected his whole after life. Returning to Holland, he laboured with great effect in preaching, visiting, and writing. This, with his godly example in personal life and in his household, was the occasion of widespread revival. The last sixteen years of his life were spent in Middelburg, where he died in 1629. He had felt deeply the merely nominal character of reformed Christianity. It seemed to

him that in his own country it was to a great extent as
a body without life, light or warmth, and he devoted
himself entirely to its real reformation. While he trusted
chiefly in spiritual means for this, he still thought that
where fundamental errors could not be suppressed by such
means, the help of the State should be called in.

Gisbert Voet, who continued Teelinck's line of teaching,
took an active part in the theological controversies of his
day, ably defending the Reformed Church against all who
differed from it, and came to be recognized as its most distinguished member. He introduced the practice of holding
conventicles or meetings outside of the regular services of
the church, in which laymen also took part. These conventicles were developed by Jodocus van Lodensteyn, a
disciple of Voet, who had studied also at Franecke. Under
his warm, hearty encouragement the conventicles became
an important part of the religious life of the country.

But to return to Labadie: an invitation from such
people and into such apparently favourable conditions
appealed to him so strongly that, in spite of many
efforts to keep him in Geneva, he removed to Holland.
The journey was dangerous; but a company of eighty
Waldenses was in Geneva, provided with passports,
on their way to the Palatinate (*Pfalz*); three of them were
detained in Geneva through illness, and Labadie and his
friends, Yvon and Dulignon, travelled undetected with the
party, in their place. In Heidelberg they were joined by
Menuret, and there the four vowed themselves to entire
sanctification, to deny the world with its desires, goods,
pleasures and friends; so to follow Jesus Christ, poor,
despised and persecuted, as to grow into His likeness
and carry His cross and shame; to give themselves to
God and to His Gospel, first practicing it themselves that
they might then help others to do so.

Reaching Holland they went first to Utrecht, where they
were invited to the house of Anna Maria van Schürman,
were warmly welcomed by her and Voet and others, and
stayed ten days. During this time Labadie preached with
power and marked effect. Their hostess was captivated by
his teaching, but Voet and van Lodensteyn saw that
Labadie's spirit was very different from what Teelinck's
had been; they wondered whether he and they would be

able to work together, and doubted whether the world could be altogether driven out of the church as Labadie thought it certainly could.

Even at this early stage the difference between the Presbyterian and Independent systems* began to show itself; the former was practised by the Reformed Church, the latter was more prevalent in England, and was the one which Labadie with increasing clearness was coming to approve.   The Independents denied the authority of Synods, looking upon each congregation as directly under Christ and responsible to Him, whereas the Dutch and French Reformed Churches had organized a system of half-yearly Synods, to which each church sent two representatives, who then conveyed the decisions of the Synod to the church.   The Reformed Church attached great importance also to the office and rights of its preachers and to their training for that office, and failures which they observed in the ministry among other bodies, such as the Mennonites, confirmed them in their view.   The Independents did not acknowledge any church office as absolutely necessary and appointed by God, they considered, and so did Labadie, that a church is a congregation of believing people, and this condition of belief the necessary foundation of teaching and testimony.   Teelinck and Voet on the other hand viewed the church as the field in which the power of the Gospel is to become effective and the aim of their work was the conversion of its members, and then the leading of them on in worthy living. Van Lodensteyn would have liked to call the Church not "Reformed" (*Reformata*) but "to be Reformed" (*Reformanda*).   He and Voet long hoped to steer a middle way between the two ideals.   There was a section which thought the Church had fallen so utterly that it was no longer to be found in the world and all that remained was to wait for the coming of Christ.

Soon after reaching Middelburg Labadie found himself deeply disappointed at the low spiritual level to which both the Dutch and French assemblies had sunk.   Church discipline had been neglected and the church was far from

*"Die Vorbereitung des Pietismus in der Reformierten Kirche der Niederlande bis zur Labadistischen Krisis, 1670. " von Wilhelm Goeters, Leipzig.   J. C. Hinrichssche Buchhandlung Utrecht.   A. Oosthock, 1911

Labadie's ideal. He set about reform by means of preaching, catechizing, discipline, and meetings of small groups, but his personal piety and self-denial were more effectual still in influencing the people. He urged upon the members of the Consistorium that with fasting and prayer and absolute separation from all evil they should effectually use the keys of "loosing and binding" that Christ had committed to them, denying self and giving time to meditation and prayer, for only thus would the assembly be changed.

No such preaching as his had been heard in Holland. His habit of extempore prayer, in which he encouraged others also, was new to the church, and he taught the union of the soul with God in an unaccustomed way. Under his guidance the assembly endeavoured to carry out New Testament principles. "Prophecy" was understood among them to be a gift to be exercised by any brother, who, led by the Spirit, might stand up in the meeting, expound the Word and apply it in a way suited to the needs of the church. Labadie wrote a book entitled *"The discernment of a true church according to the Holy Scripture containing thirty remarkable signs by which it may be well known"*. He shows that it is only a company of those who are really born again that can be considered a true church; one where all, through the Holy Spirit, are united in one body and where all members of the assembly are led by the Spirit of Christ.

His teaching won the hearts of great numbers not only in Middelburg but also throughout the Netherlands. At the same time it became increasingly evident that if it were followed it would altogether change the character of the Reformed churches, emphasizing in a way to which those congregations were not accustomed the inner life of communion with God. Such an emphasis, they feared, would endanger the soul's rest in the work of Christ, making more of Christ *in* it than of Christ *for* it, exalting works at the expense of faith, dwelling more on sanctification than on justification. They also saw that the liberty of ministry allowed must affect the guiding power and influence of the ordained ministers of the Church.

Opposition to that which Labadie considered as needful reformation, but which was regarded by most leaders of the Church as a bringing in of strange and disturbing changes,

grew to be definite, organized, and bitter. At a French
Synod held in Amsterdam in 1667 he was required to sign
the Belgian Confession. This he refused to do on the ground
that he now found many unscriptural expressions in it,
though he had formerly signed the identical French Confession at Montauban, Orange and Geneva. This so
strengthened the opposition to him that, at a following
Synod at Leyden, it was decided that if he would not sign
the Belgian Confession at the next Synod, to be held at
Vlissingen, and undertake to conform to the usages of the
Reformed Church, he should be suspended from office.
The people of Middelburg were so indignant at this that
the magistrate was compelled to take action, with the
result that when the Synod met at Vlissingen it was obliged
to have the complaints against Labadie removed from the
minutes of the Leyden Synod.

About this time a book was published by an Amsterdam
doctor, Ludwig Meijer, arguing that natural understanding
should be the ground of all Scripture exegesis. This
rationalistic teaching aroused such opposition among
all in the Netherlands who believed in the inspiration
of the Scriptures that the civil authorities appointed the
learned and well-known Professor Coccejus to write
a refutation. Others also wrote, and among them
Ludwig Wolzogen, preacher of the French Reformed Church
at Utrecht. Wolzogen's book, however, while written
ostensibly to oppose rationalism, diverged so widely from
the accepted teaching of the Church that believers in the
inspiration of the Bible looked upon this book as being
rather an apology for the teaching objected to. Labadie
also wrote, and the church council of the French church
at Middelburg found his book to be so convincing a refutation of the rationalistic teaching that it decided to bring
forward a motion at the next Synod at Vlissingen for a
formal condemnation of Meijer's book. In consequence
of this the Synod appointed the church councils of three
cities, one of which was Middelburg, to prepare a report
on the book for the next Synod, to be held at Naarden
(1668). The reports of the three councils differed considerably, but it was a surprise when a large majority of
the Synod declared Meijer's book to be orthodox and
justified Wolzogen. Labadie left the Synod to consult

with his church council at Middelburg, but in the meantime the Synod proceeded to suspend him from his office provisionally as one who had introduced strange teachings and practices into the church. Further charges were brought against him, namely, that he had taught that the present time is the reign of grace, and that the millennial reign of Christ will not begin until He shall have overcome all enemies and accomplished the object of creation, in spite of the Fall of man, and brought about the restitution of all things to that state in which God created them. If Labadie would not submit he was to be finally removed from office. A commission of the Synod was sent to Middelburg with power to suspend any members of the church council who might resist its decree, but the Middelburg church council refused to accept the decree of the Synod, saying that Labadie was not convicted of falling away from the teaching and order of the church. The council was suspended. It was decided that at the next Synod Labadie should be forbidden to preach.

He was thought the more dangerous because of his extraordinary gifts. He himself never thought of yielding, but continued to preach, and wrote declaring that he could have no fellowship with the Synod, which had fallen altogether into error and evil. He not only found error in the Belgian Confession, but asserted that the Synod rejected the teaching of 1 Corinthians 14. He also condemned the whole system of Synods and Consistoriums, the stereotyped liturgical forms, the reading of Scripture without explanation, the misuse of the Sacraments by accepting those who were not born again as witnesses at baptisms and to partake of the Lord's Supper. He pointed out too that at marriages notoriously ungodly people were made to take Christian vows and promised God's blessing, that the church authorities took Papal powers to themselves, and bound people's consciences with their ordinances. He said that there is no authority in the church but that of the Spirit and the Word of God, *i.e.*, what is contained in the Holy Scriptures, and the inward witness of the Word which corresponds with this. As therefore the Christian conscience is only guided by the authority of the Word of God, it is not rebellion to refuse the ordinances of Synods and other human institutions when they are contrary to this; it is, on the other hand, rather the duty of a Christian assembly to do this in the interests of Christian liberty and to oppose the setting up of a new Popery which would act as though it were above the Word of God.

The much looked for Synod was held at Dordrecht in the year 1669. Labadie and the Middelburg church council with some members of the church waited a week in Dordrecht that they might appeal against the treatment they had received. They were not given a hearing. The Synod confirmed the expulsion of Labadie and all his supporters, "because they had shown themselves disobedient to the laws of the Church and intended to bring about division".

Labadie was assured that he had been called by God to re-establish Apostolic churches. Until he was forty years of age he had laboured for the reform of the Church of Rome, and then for twenty years for that of the Reformed Church. He had thrown his excellent gifts and his whole life into both these attempts with enthusiasm and delight—now both had failed! This brought him to the conclusion that "a reform of the existing church bodies is impossible, and that restoration of the Apostolic church can only be accomplished through separation from them". He at once introduced this principle into the Middelburg church, and some three hundred separated from it and formed a new gathering. Several elders and three pastors took the oversight of this; meetings were held twice daily, and on Sundays three times. The meeting room had nothing in it but benches, not even a pulpit. One bench was a little higher than the others, and on this sat the elders and preachers, all of whom were in the habit of speaking in the meetings. They would not use the name "Reformed", but preferred to be known as "Evangelical". Only those might be members of whom there was reason to believe that they were born again.

Differences between the Reformed Church and this newly formed congregation induced the town authorities to ask the members of the latter to leave Middelburg. No sooner was this known than the town of Ter Veere, an hour distant, invited the exiled church to remove there. The invitation was thankfully accepted, but the chief magistrate of Middelburg soon saw that he had made a mistake, for crowds flocked to Ter Veere to hear Labadie preach, while Middelburg was deserted. Annoyed at the material loss this involved, the Middelburg magistrate persuaded the higher district authorities to order the Veere magistrate to expel Labadie and Yvon on the ground that they had caused division in the church and unrest among the people. The Middelburg magistrate armed his men to enforce the decree, but the people of Veere rose as one man to resist forcibly. Civil war was imminent. Then Labadie came forward and said that no blood should flow on his account, he saw the hand of God leading them from Veere, and would go to Amsterdam, with those who wished to accompany him. There was dismay in Veere, but Labadie remained firm, and the citizens had to yield, the magistrate said he only let him go "most unwillingly and on the ground of utmost necessity. "

Labadie and his three friends, with some other sympathizers, moved to Amsterdam, where they were well received and promised protection and religious liberty. The influence of Labadie's work had been such that in Amsterdam there were many thousands who were attached to the new church and abstained from taking the Lord's Supper in the Reformed Church, and it was the same in all the larger churches in the country, while many who did not actually join these companies were greatly influenced by them. This serious danger to their system induced the leaders of the Reformed Church to ask the help of the Government, but under the eminent statesman, Jan de Witt, religious freedom was assured, and no steps could be taken.

Unhappily, however, events in his own mind and in his immediate circle did more to injure Labadie's testimony than any outward attack could have done. He had learned by experience and from the Word, that it is not possible so to reform a town or a church system as to bring it to the condition he aimed at; but he was not content with the formation of churches of the Apostolic pattern—gatherings of persons saved, indeed, and separated from the surrounding world, but many of them weak and failing and needing constant patient care—so he decided to form a Household Church, where the household and the church would be the same and it would be possible, as he supposed, to know each member and lead each into the true following of Christ and union with God. A house was rented in Amsterdam where there was accommodation for about forty and the new household was gathered. Regular meetings were held, and once a week a meal was taken in common. The meetings were attended by many from outside, and when French was spoken it was translated into Dutch. Yvon, Dulignon and Menuret went out on preaching expeditions throughout the Netherlands and surrounding countries.

Anna Maria van Schürman moved to Amsterdam, rented an apartment in the house, and threw in her lot with the new household. She was considered the most accomplished woman of her time. She corresponded in various languages with the most famous literary men in Europe, and her opinion and counsel were sought and valued by those who were themselves experts in the arts and sciences. She had been a devoted Christian from her childhood. In her book, "Eukleria", written in Latin, she relates, "as a child of scarcely four years old I sat with my nurse on the banks of a stream. She repeated to me the words, 'I am not my own but belong to my truest Saviour, Jesus Christ.' I was filled with such an inward sense of love to Christ that in all my following years nothing has ever been able to erase the vivid remembrance of that moment". In justifying her adhesion to the new company she wrote: "As I have now seen for a number of years, with pain, the departure of Christendom from its origins, and its almost entire unlikeness to the same . . . and had lost any hope of its restoration in the usual course of things which is followed by our clergy (most of whom are themselves greatly in need of reformation), who can rightly object that I have, with a happy heart, chosen for my own those teachers fitted by God to bring about a reform of degenerate Christianity?" Her renown caused this step to be everywhere spoken of and she was overwhelmed with letters calling her back to the Reformed Church, but she rejoiced that she had now put aside the old man and chosen that good part that would not be taken away from her. She had formerly sought God's honour, but her own also, now she sought none for herself but only for God. She sold what she had and gave it to Labadie and never seems to have regretted this. In all the many vicissitudes of the family she was an invaluable helper, and in her old age its most trusted counsellor.

Voet saw dangers in this new development and, though he had hitherto been one of Labadie's most important supporters, now became his opponent. He wrote to show that no one should leave the Reformed Church because evil, lukewarmness and weakness were to be found in it, or in order to join a separated, cloister-like union taking the place of the church, and said that a household such as that proposed would give rise to evil surmisings. The publication of this book had an extraordinary effect. An anonymous reply appeared in which Voet was attacked in a violent and unworthy way. It was found that Labadie was the author, and his reputation was seriously injured by it. Many wrote against him, but the increase of these attacks only drew the members of the household more closely together, and they were joined by others, including the Burgomaster of Amsterdam.

Troubles arose in the household however. A member of it, a widow, died, and a false report was circulated that she had been killed, and that her body was to be buried in the garden. A mob surrounded the house, which had to be protected for three days by a military force. Menuret, whom Labadie loved as a son, became mentally afflicted and died in a frenzy of madness. Members of the household questioned whether such a thing could happen in a church that was really of God. It was found that in spite of all their care, one of the household held Socinian views, and that another had Quaker ideas. When they were reproved for these, they published a pamphlet full of calumnies, in revenge. The matter came before the courts and the statements in the pamphlets were proved to be false, but the report gained currency nevertheless that there were members of the family who were dangerous sectaries. So much prejudice was excited against them, that in the interests of peace, the magistrates forbade anyone to attend meetings in Labadie's house except the members of the household. This checked their growing numbers and cut off the hope of development.

To escape these difficulties Anna Maria van Schürman appealed to her old friend Princess Elizabeth, Abbess of

Herford, who invited all who would come to take refuge on her free estate, so Labadie and a party of about fifty sailed from Amsterdam to Bremen, and travelled from there by waggon to Herford (1670). The Lutheran inhabitants of Herford violently resented the coming of the "Quakers", as they called them, and it was only the authority of the Princess that made it possible for them to remain. The hatred and enmity by which they were surrounded isolated the household still more from the world, and they became increasingly occupied with their own religious exercises. The preaching of Labadie at this time so affected his hearers that they felt they had only now attained to an entire yielding of themselves to God, and this led to their introducing community of goods as a means of expressing their giving up of all worldly things and their denial of self and entire union with the members of the body of Christ. At the introduction of this change they were engaged in the breaking of bread in memory of the Lord's death when a strange spiritual ecstasy came over, first some, then all of them; they began to speak with tongues and then stood up and danced and this lasted for about an hour. At somewhat rare intervals similar manifestations were repeated. To most of them these things seemed to show that they were now really of one heart and one soul in the Lord. Others disapproved and withdrew from their fellowship. The hatred of those outside was embittered as such doings were related. Until this time the community had, on the whole, discouraged marriage, but now took another view of this and Labadie, Yvon and Dulignon all married, finding wives who were a help to them in their testimony.

The growing animosity of the people obliged them at last to leave Herford in spite of the protection of the Princess, who never ceased to defend them, and they found a quiet dwellingplace in Altona, where they rented two houses. Here Labadie died peacefully (1674), and here Anna Maria van Schürman wrote her book "Eukleria". War obliged them to leave this retreat and they moved to Castle Waltha, in the little village of Wieuwerd in West Friesland, which had been placed at their disposal. This was their last home. The country people received them gladly and a commission appointed by the Reformed

Church to inquire into their views and ways reported them to be harmless, which led to their being allowed to remain in peace. Here Anna Maria van Schürman died, aged 71; also Dulignon and his wife.

The community increased and large numbers attended the services from the country round. Considerable parties were sent out, one to Surinam and one to New York. They were financed and controlled by the Wieuwerd community, but both parties returned unsuccessful, chiefly because, instead of trying to win the heathen to Christ, they had occupied themselves with endeavouring to gain the Christians there to their party. These expeditions impoverished those left at home, and the practical difficulties of having community of goods compelled them to abandon the system after carrying it on for twenty years.

This change caused great distress, since most of the members were poor, many had not been in the habit of earning a living, and many were unfit to do so, and had depended on those who had means. Yvon explained that when the first church at Jerusalem was scattered, community of goods ceased, and that they themselves also were now called to spread in the world and work as a leaven there. If this had been seen earlier it would have saved them from giving up the Scriptural church order which they practised at first and exchanging it for a community life which narrowed their testimony and hindered it from the wider development of which it had given promise. The household was broken up and scattered. Yvon remained at Castle Waltha, where he died, and twenty-five years later, the castle passing into other hands, the last of the Labadists left

The life of Labadie was one of valiant effort, the source of which lay in inward communion with God, nourished by systematic prayer and instructed by diligent study of the Scriptures. He learned that his great idea of a reformation of the Roman Catholic Church was impossible of attainment. Then he found by large experiment that a city or state cannot, as such, be converted and become a church. He found later that the Reformed Protestant Church was incapable of reformation and of being restored to the New Testament pattern. Then through long conflicts he came to see the true churches of God as they were at the first and always have been. Afterwards, discouraged by much opposition and many disappointments, he sought refuge in a household church, thinking that in its limited circle purity could be maintained, but he missed the track here, for the true churches are not the resting places of perfect people but the nurseries and schools where all are received who confess Christ and where all their weakness and ignorance and imperfection must be borne with and instructed in the patience of unfailing love. In Labadie we see a man whose life held elements of heroic failure and yet of abiding success. First he tried to include too much in the Church; great worldly systems from which the true churches must be separate. Then he included too little, thinking that the churches must contain only those who are perfect. There was a period when he founded true churches of God and the influence of what he then taught and accomplished continued beyond his lifetime. Taking a limited view of the church involved him in the mistakes to which such a course leads—the narrowed communion favoured the extravagances and lack of balance which accompany undue restriction. His experiences remain strikingly valuable, illustrating the excellence of the way of the Word and the danger of turning to the right hand or to the left—of including the world in the churches or of excluding the saints from them.

At the close of the Thirty Years' War in 1648, the Protestant countries, exhausted economically and suffering from the moral degradation of a generation brought up in conditions of violence and disorder, were also in a low and careless spiritual state. The Lutheran, and to a less degree the Reformed, churches were more occupied with a rigid orthodoxy than with a godly manner of life.

Spener,[*] born in Alsace in 1635, became at the age of 35 chief pastor of the Lutheran Church in Frankfurt. Deeply impressed with the crying need for reform in the Church, he held meetings, first in his own house and afterwards in the church, the aim of which was to bring into practice "the old apostolic way of church meetings...as Paul in 1 Corinthians 14 describes it, when those who have gifts

[*] "Geschichte des Pietismus in der reformirten Kirche"   Albrecht Ritschl.

and knowledge should also speak and, without disorder and strife, express their pious thoughts on the matters in hand, and that the others might judge". The believers came together regularly, and an appointed subject was considered and a conversation on it took place. The men and women sat apart and only the men took part. It was understood that other people were not to be judged and that all gossip was excluded. At first edifying books were read and discussed, but later they confined themselves to the reading and general consideration of the New Testament. In many of the private meetings after this there followed questions, confessions or experiences, designed to bring out what was learned. Spener himself did not encourage this but kept to the exposition of the Word. He objected to names, as Pietist, Spenerite and others, as he did not want to found a sect, or that they should become a monkish community, but only that they should come back to the old and universal Christianity. Spener could allow and even support in other churches what he would not do himself. He felt that he had not himself the energy and force of a Reformer, but rather an ability to tolerate differences. He allowed the self-examination and confession that prevailed in some meetings but did not introduce them into his own, and valued the mysticism of some believers while confessing that he had had no experiences of the ecstasies they enjoyed in the revelation of the Bridegroom, nor of the Quietist self-abandonment that they practised. His desire was expressed in his words: "Oh that I knew a single assembly upright in all things, in doctrine, order, and practice, all that would make it what an apostolic Christian assembly should be in doctrine and life!" He did not expect an assembly "without weeds", but one where the preachers carried out their work in the leading of the Holy Spirit and the greater part of the hearers were such as had died to the world and led not only an honest but also a godly life. He said the greater part of professing Christians were not born again and many of the ministers of the Word did not understand as they should the true doctrines on which the steadfastness of the church depends. After a time the members of Spener's church in Frankfurt abstained from the Lord's Supper so that they might not take it with those who took it unworthily.

From Frankfurt Spener was removed to Dresden as Court chaplain, and then to Berlin, where he was diligent in service until his death (1705). The societies, called *Pietist*, which he did so much to found and encourage became a vivifying force; though attacked and ridiculed by official Christianity, they did not separate from the Lutheran Church but formed centres within it which attracted seekers after godliness and bore fruit in many and far-reaching spiritual activities.

One to whom Spener was a help was August Hermann Franke,* who became his chief successor in the Pietist movement. He was born at Lübeck (1663), and studied theology, which, though it had a certain value for him, did not bring peace to his soul. His studies, however, awakened in him an earnest desire to understand in his life and conduct what he had merely apprehended in the mind and memory, and, after some years of anxious seeking he experienced a sudden conversion by which all his unbelief was dissipated and he received an entire assurance of salvation. His insistence on conversion and godliness brought blessing to many, but also made him enemies; he was branded as a Pietist and expelled from Erfurt, where he was minister, at forty-eight hours' notice. The same day an invitation from the Court of Brandenburg led to his being appointed Professor of Greek and Oriental Languages at the University which was being founded at Halle. There he was much affected by the distress of the poor and set up a box into which contributions might be put, which he then distributed. One day a larger sum than before was put in, about 15/. "On taking this sum into my hand", he wrote, "I exclaimed with great liberty of faith: This is a considerable sum, with which something really good must be accomplished; I will begin a school for the poor with it." This was the beginning of the extensive institutions at Halle, which were built up and carried on without appealing for money and without any visible supply, "but solely and simply," he said, "in reliance on the living God in heaven". At Franke's death 134 orphans were being supported in the Home, cared for by 10 women and men; 2200 children and young men were being taught in

*"The Life of Aug. Herm. Franke" H. E. F. Guerike. trans. S. Jackson.

the different schools, mostly without charge, by 175 teachers; hundreds of poor students were fed daily, and there were in operation printing and bookselling, a library, a dispensary, a hospital, and other institutions. As a boy in this school, and, later, sitting at Franke's table and listening to the stories of missionaries, who were often there, Zinzendorf received impressions which were fruitful in his after life.

In 1690, seventy years after the battle of the White Mountain,* and sixty-two years after Comenius had led the last band of exiles from Moravia, Christian David was born, not far from Fulneck. The "hidden seed" which Comenius had prayed might be preserved was still hidden; Christian's parents were Roman Catholics, like their neighbours, and he as a shepherd boy and then a carpenter was very devout, while inwardly concerned as to how he could be assured that God had forgiven his sins. Reading and inquiring he got such contradictory answers to his questions that he was altogether perplexed, left home and wandered away into Germany, seeking truth. After many adventures and constant disappointments he met with Pastor Schäfer in Görlitz, a Pietist, from whom he learned the way of salvation. Full of joy and zeal he returned to Moravia and went about preaching everywhere. The forgotten truths of former times were revived in the hearts of many of his hearers as they listened to his homely discourse. Those, however, who obeyed the Gospel were met at once by crushing persecution. David went back to Schäfer in Görlitz to see whether a place of refuge could be found in Saxony, and through him met with Count Zinzendorf.

From his earliest childhood Zinzendorf had been a lover of Jesus Christ, and his training in Pietist circles had strengthened his devotion. At the time when Christian David met him he was living in his castle of Berthelsdorf, near the Bohemian frontier, where he and his friend, Pastor Johann Andreae Rothe were engaged in serving the Lord among the surrounding people. The two young men, Zinzendorf 22, David ten years older, discussed the need in Moravia, and Zinzendorf invited the persecuted be-

* "History of the Moravian Church"   J. E. Hutton M.A.

lievers there to come and settle on his estates in Saxony. David was quickly back in his own country, where he gathered a few families of believers, who were able to steal away from their homes and whom he led over the mountains into Saxony and to Berthelsdorf. There they were cordially received, but there was no place where they could live. About a mile away, on Zinzendorf's estate, was a low, wooded hill called Hutberg, or the Watch Hill. This they re-named *Herrnhut*, the Lord's Watch, and decided to build a home for themselves there. Christian David, taking an axe, felled the first tree, and, an indefatigable workman and preacher, he guided and encouraged the builders so that in a short time (1722) a house was finished, the beginning of the extensive buildings now forming Herrnhut, and the pattern for many that were to follow in different parts of the world.

One day David, nailing a plank in the castle in Berthelsdorf, his thoughts in Moravia, suddenly left his tools and even his hat, set off, without preparation, and walked the two hundred miles to Kunewald, where there were a number of believers, descendants of families that had belonged to the old Church of the Bohemian Brethren. He brought away a party of these, among them the families Nitschmann, Zeisberger and Toeltschig, afterwards to become well-known in connection with the missionary enterprises of the new Moravian Church. They reached Herrnhut just as Zinzendorf and his friend de Watteville were laying the foundation stone of the first meeting-house to be built there, and they threw in their lot with the company that had preceded them.

After this many came from Bohemia and Moravia, some escaping from prison or leaving hiding places in the forests. As this place of refuge for the oppressed came to be more widely known, others came there, of divers views, some followers of Schwenckfeld, some Pietists, and some who could agree with no one. Bitter disputing took the place of brotherly accord, and the settlement was threatened with disruption. In the meantime Zinzendorf had been converting Berthelsdorf into a model village, where everything was done in accordance with his wishes, and those of his friend Pastor Rothe. The Count believed in organizing an appeal to the imagination. As a boy at Halle his missionary enthusiasm expressed itself in the formation of the "Order of the Mustard Seed", with promises and emblems and motto and ring, which, beginning with five boys of whom he was the Grand Master, grew to be a powerful incentive to devotion in missionary work. In Berthelsdorf he had founded the "League of the Four Brethren", himself, de Watteville, Rothe, and Schäfer, to make known to the world the "Universal Religion of the Saviour and His Family of Disciples, the Heart-Religion, in which the Person of the Saviour is the central point"; in later days his "Warrior Band" became an effectual missionary instrument. Now he intervened in Herrnhut. He recognized the honest intent in these quarrelling partisans, was able to say of one of the most impetuous of them: "Although our dear Christian David was calling me the Beast and Mr. Rothe the False Prophet, we could see his honest heart nevertheless, and knew we could lead him right. It is not a bad maxim, when honest men are going wrong, to put them into office, and they will learn from experience what they will never learn from speculation". He gathered them together, and in a three hours' address, expounded to them the *Statutes, Injunctions and Prohibitions* which he had made out to regulate every particular of their lives. A spiritual revival was given them at this time, power to forgive and be reconciled, and they settled down peaceably to the new order.

About the same time Zinzendorf found in the library of the neighbouring town of Zittau, a copy of the *Order of Discipline* drawn up by the last meeting of the *Bohemian Brethren* just before the battle of the White Mountain, edited by Comenius. From this Zinzendorf saw that the settlers he had received represented the ancient church that had existed so long in Bohemia. He was profoundly touched by the lament of Comenius as he recorded the destruction of its testimony, and he resolved that he and all that he had should be devoted to the preservation of the little company of the Lord's disciples that had taken refuge with him. When this document was communicated to the refugees they were stirred to restore the old church, from members of which many of them were descended.

The question of the relations of the communal society at Herrnhut to the Lutheran Church naturally arose. Zinzendorf, himself a Lutheran, wanted the community to attach itself altogether to the Lutheran Church.   This they were determined not to do.   Eventually the matter was decided by lot, a method much in use among them, and the lot decided against joining the Lutheran Church. Then Zinzendorf, to avoid friction with that, the established Church, had himself ordained as a minister in it, while one of the refugees was consecrated bishop by Daniel Ernst Jablonsky, Court preacher at Berlin, and the only surviving bishop of the old Church of the Bohemian Brethren.   In this way they were acknowledged as a community within the Lutheran Church and so able to administer the sacraments.   In spite of this the forces opposed to them were such that Zinzendorf was banished from the kingdom of Saxony (1736).

Visiting the King of Denmark, Christian VI, he met a negro, Anthony, whom he invited to Herrnhut, and Anthony's description of the condition of the slaves in the West Indies so affected his hearers, that one, Leonard Dober, offered to go and carry the Gospel to them.   The project was confirmed by casting lots and the young man, with another, David Nitschmann, set out.   They were practical men, a carpenter and a potter, had been well educated in the Herrnhut schools, and were able speakers.   They set forth on their journey on foot, with no more baggage than they could carry on their backs and with 18/ between them. This was the beginning of the Moravian Missions, which turned the whole Body into a Missionary Society (1732). Devotion to Christ led many of the missionaries to choose by preference the most difficult and dangerous regions to work in.   Herrnhut became a centre associated with all parts of the world.   In many countries settlements modelled upon it were established.   In its large cemetery are the graves of natives of the most diverse countries, who came from their distant lands to visit the parent settlement.

The work of the Moravians in England began in 1738, when Peter Boehler, on his way as a missionary to South Carolina, spoke in London in a Society founded by James Hutton, a London bookseller.   Hutton and his friends were seekers after salvation, but had not found assurance, and as Boehler, in broken English, but with much ability, expounded the Scriptures to them, "it was", said Hutton, "with indescribable astonishment and joy that we embraced the doctrine of the Saviour, of His merits and sufferings, of justification through faith in Him, and of freedom by it from the dominion of guilt and sin. " This company accepted the Herrnhut rules given them by Boehler, and a preacher from Germany was sent to them, though they still remained members of the Church of England. Four years later Spangenberg came from Germany, and admitted them as a congregation of the Brethren's Church, introducing the rules and officers of the German congregations. At first there was much intercourse between them and Wesley, who was largely influenced by their example in his organization of Societies within the Established Church, class meetings and love feasts. Benjamin Ingham, a clergyman at Ossett, in Yorkshire, was one of those who in these days of revival was active and greatly blessed in his work. Not confining himself to his parish, he travelled over the country from Halifax to Leeds, and founded some fifty little societies for reading and prayer. Seeing a need of more helpers, he invited the Moravians, who, responding immediately, sent twenty-six workers, men and women, into Yorkshire. They set to work methodically. Spangenberg directed operations from Wyke as a centre; Toeltschig, who had come with Christian David from Moravia, was at Holbeck; altogether there were five directing centres arranged, controlling in a short time nearly fifty preaching places, which were carried on with the help of *"National Assistants"* or native helpers. The preachers had all the tumultuous experiences usual at that time, and it was decided to establish a more solid base by building a Herrnhut in England. Count Zinzendorf came over and helped them in securing land at Pudsey between Leeds and Bradford, money was sent from Germany and Fulneck was built, its name chosen to commemorate its connection with Fulneck in Moravia. Here a settlement was established on the Herrnhut model, and others on a smaller scale at Wyke, Mirfield, and Gomersal, where Zinzendorf's rules and regulations were reproduced.

Similar work was done in some other parts of the country; the most successful evangelist being John Cennick, born in England but descended from a Bohemian family that had taken refuge in England at the break-up of the Old Bohemian Brethren's Church. Cennick was at first an active helper of the Wesleys but his leanings to Whitefield's doctrines led them to repudiate him, and eventually he became fully associated with the Moravians. He was an open-air preacher of extraordinary power and a man of a gentle and winning disposition. His short life was wholly devoted to the Lord's service, and in the West of England and Northern Ireland the fruit of his labours was very abundant.

The endeavour to control from Germany this widespread organization proved an increasing hindrance to the work, and even when modified as it was later in England and America, the unsuitability of the settlement system to meet the varied needs of different national characteristics, and of changing circumstances, emphasizes the fact that the wisest plans of even the best of men are not fitted for permanent or universal application, whereas the teaching and example of the New Testament as to the founding and conduct of the churches of God prove suitable to every variety of need.

In the eighteenth century the Philadelphia societies or churches were formed as the result of the meeting of two streams of spiritual experience.

The first owed its origin to the desire of the soul for immediate communion with God, and union with Him.

The second sprang from a sense of the essential unity of all the children of God, and a desire to express this communion of the true Church.

The Roman Catholic Church early introduced its clergy and sacraments between the soul and the Saviour, but while this system kept many at a distance from Him, there were those whose longing for communion with God, as He is revealed in Christ Jesus, and desire for the Heavenly Bridegroom was so strong that they devoted themselves to the attainment of the full knowledge of Him and the experience of union with Him. This they sought in the way of following Jesus, of the imitation of Christ. They thought to attain this by meditation on Him, so that His beauty and blessedness might be increasingly revealed to them, and by an asceticism which should subdue the body and the natural will.

Protestantism accentuated the divisions among the

professing people of God and induced the bitterest strife
and enmity between the numerous parties. There were,
however, those who lamented this and tried to emphasize
the underlying unity in life and love of those who are
separated from the world but joined to Christ and His
members by faith.

Those in the Roman Catholic Church, often called
Mystics or *Quietists*, were long looked upon as patterns of
the Christian life, some of the best known among them
being canonized, but later the influence of the Jesuits and
of Louis XIV of France caused them to be persecuted.
The Spanish priest, Miguel de Molinos (1640-1697), coming
to Rome about 1670, became the greatest spiritual power
there. His book the *"Spiritual Guide"* was used as a rule
of life by large numbers, especially of the aristocracy and
the priesthood. He was the confessor and most trusted
adviser of the Pope Innocent XI, a Pope who was personally opposed to persecution, yet Molinos was eventually
condemned to lifelong imprisonment, and died in the hands
of the Inquisition, though in what manner remains unknown. Madame Guyon (1648-1717) by her life and writings led wide circles to strive after a life of perfect love and
entire acquiescence in the will of God. The gifted and
saintly Archbishop Fénélon accepted and defended her
teaching at the cost of all his popularity and prospects at
court. Louis XIV imprisoned her repeatedly, at last in
the dreaded Bastille, but those stone walls, twelve feet
thick, could not check the influence and spread of her
teaching.

In Protestant circles the writings of Gottfried Arnold
(1666-1714) had a great effect. He studied at Wittenberg
and became Professor of History at Giessen, but withdrew
from the position as he found that the social and ceremonial
duties it involved hindered his inner life of communion
with the Lord. Spener disagreed with this, maintaining
that we must hold on to what we do not approve even if it
endangers our own souls, as long as there is any hope of
helping others. Arnold, however, regarded the Lutheran
Church as Babel and incapable of reformation, and felt
that the way he took of lonely separation was more in
accord with the example of the Apostles. His first book,
"First Love, that is a True Picture of the First Christians

according to their Living Faith and holy Life" was a history
of the Church in Apostolic times and until the time of
Constantine, in which he showed the evils brought in by
the union of Church and State. Being increasingly impressed by the fact that Church history has been written by
representatives of the dominant churches and from a party
point of view, he thought it necessary to present that
important history in an impartial way, and so wrote the
history by which he became so widely known in his own and
succeeding generations, entitled *"Impartial History of
the Churches and Heretics from the Beginning of the New
Testament to the Year of Christ,* 1688". Abandoning the
idea that the Church is bound up with some particular
society or organization, he sought the universal Church,
hidden and scattered throughout the whole world and
among all peoples and churches. Naturally opinions of the
book differed. One theologian wrote that it was the most
harmful book that had been written since the birth of
Christ and another called it the best and most useful book
of its kind after the Holy Scriptures.

Madame Guyon's writings opened to many the view of
the possibility of a life in perfect communion with God.

Arnold's book awakened the hope of separation from the
world and communion with all saints.

About 1700 there was a drawing together of these various
scattered elements into societies or churches, to which the
name of *Philadelphia* (Brotherly love) was given.

The little country of Wittgenstein,* at the southern end
of Westphalia, had a series of good and tolerant rulers, and
this attracted a large population of very varied character.
Fugitives from the Cevennes in France were kindly received,
the more so as the two brothers who ruled respectively the
northern and southern parts of the country had married
(1657) two sisters, daughters of a French nobleman who
had escaped to the Netherlands from the massacre of St.
Bartholomew. Both these families were devoted Christians.
In 1712 the northern part of the country, called Berleburg,
was ruled by a descendant of one of these families, Count
Casimir, who, with his wife and widowed mother, was
the consistent protector of all who were oppressed.

*"Geschichte des Christlichen Lebens in der rheinisch-westphälichen
evangelischen Kirche" Max Goebel.

They were connected with the Philadelphia churches which spread widely at this time. Jane Leade of Norwich and others taught that the messages to the churches in the 2nd and 3rd chapters of the Revelation had a progressive historic meaning. Sardis represented Protestantism, having a name to live and yet being dead. The indifference and apostasy of Laodicea were coming. All awakened souls were called to realize and be joined to faithful Philadelphia. A Philadelphia church was founded in London in 1695, not, they said, to form a new sect, but to preserve in their meetings the spirit of love and the form of the first holy and Catholic Apostolic Church. The members did not necessarily separate from the churches to which they had belonged and did not persuade others to do so, yet they held their regular meetings at the same time as the churches had their services, so that attendance at the latter was made impossible for those who attended the former. At present, they said, the Philadelphia church is weak, and until it is manifested in power it is not to be expected that those things will take place which are looked for, the conversion of the Jews, the bringing in of the Turks and other unbelievers, the recovery of the apostasy, the restitution of all things and the personal appearing of Christ on the earth. Similar meetings were begun in many parts of Germany, Holland, and elsewhere, and Berleburg became the centre of an important revival spreading over all west Germany from the Alps to the sea.

In these circles, in 1712, the Marburg Bible was published with the title, "Mystic and Prophetic Bible, that is the whole of the Holy Scriptures of the Old and New Testaments, newly translated from the original, with explanations of the Principal Types and Prophecies, especially of the Song of Songs of Solomon and the Revelation of Jesus Christ, with their principal Doctrines, etc." Later (1726-1742) a larger work was produced, the Berleburg Bible, in eight volumes, beautifully printed in large type and containing extensive notes, among which some of the teachings of Madame Guyon were included.

The Philadelphia society or church was the outcome of a great variety of different movements and it aimed at setting aside the differences in the churches and uniting all in love and thought the purifying and perfecting of the soul more important than the observance of the outward forms of the "churches".

In order to help one another they set aside a time each morning when, in all the different places where they were, they would join in spirit in waiting on God.

An active member of the society in Berleburg was Dr. Carl, medical attendant to Count Casimir. In 1730 he issued the *"Philadelphian Invitation"*, an appeal to undying souls to turn from the circumference of opinions and passions to the centre, to worship in Spirit and in truth. Those whose ears are opened do not differ (it says) in their sentiments, they have one language, taste and affection. But such central unity is only found in those who leave the fleshly letter and self-made articles and turn continually into themselves in spirit and in truth and taste the theology of the heart as the sweet Word of God. They may be called Roman Catholic, Lutheran, Reformed, etc.—there Tauler, Kempis, Arndt, Neander are all one. The real, abiding part of Christianity is the putting to death of the old man and making alive of the spirit.

This appeal awakened a response in countless hearts, especially in Württemberg and Switzerland. Many who did not join the outward circle of Philadelphia belonged to it in heart. All these sought the Kingdom of God and practised piety, they looked upon Philadelphia as the society to which they belonged inwardly because they believed they saw in it that which is essential to the Kingdom of God, whereas in the churches of the different confessions they saw only outward shells and forms, among which the spirit of the Antichrist was hidden. Zinzendorf tried to organize these societies and attach them to the Moravian Brethren's Unity, but without success.

The preaching of Hochmann von Hochenau at this time was one great means of revival, in the conversion of sinners and founding of Philadelphia churches. His constant journeys, when he was attacked by mobs, imprisoned by the authorities, and yet listened to everywhere by enormous crowds, filled a life of enthusiastic service for the Lord with blessing to countless numbers of his hearers. His only periods of rest were when he retired from time to time to a little hermitage he had in the forests of Wittgenstein, otherwise his love to all men,   especially the Jews, kept him travelling and preaching all over western and northern Germany. The preaching of Hochmann was the means of the conversion of a young student of theology, Hoffman, whose meetings, outside the Established Church, helped towards the conversion of Gerhard Tersteegen, who became later a powerful witness for Christ and has ministered to succeeding generations also by his beautiful hymns. Jung Stilling (1740-1817), whose life and writings exercised a great influence, wrote of these days: "In the whole history of the Church is no time in which the expectation of the Lord's coming was so instant and so universal as in the first half of the century just ended, the revivals at Halle led the way, the restoration of the Brethren's Church through Zinzendorf followed immediately, then the mystic Philadelphia society at Berleburg, the fruit of which is the Berleburg Bible. At the same time two heralds appeared, Friedrich Roch and Hochmann von Hochenau, then Gerhard Tersteegen and many other men. "

Those called Waldenses, or Anabaptists, and others of like character, were not reformers of the Roman Catholic Church, nor, afterwards, of the Lutheran and Reformed Churches. Their origin was earlier and they carried on their primitive Bible teachings and practices from before, and then through the times of the rise and progress of those later-developed communions.

In the same way those called Paulicians, and others spiritually related to them, were not reformers of the Greek Orthodox Church, but preceded it and were later contemporary with it, but always separate from it.

There were, however, other movements which were movements of reform, in connection with both the Catholic and the Protestant churches. Some of these made efforts to influence the existing communion from within, while others formed groups which left, or were expelled from it. Of these latter "the Reformation" came out of the Roman Catholic Church and formed Protestant denominations, which represented varying degrees of reform of Roman Catholicism.

There were also attempts at reform within the Roman Catholic Church, such as those of Francis of Assisi, and of several of the Popes, who made genuine efforts to remove

abuses, but found long established custom and entangle-
ment of financial obligations too strong for them.

Similarly, in the Lutheran and Reformed Churches there
were some who attempted reform from within, as the
Pietists. There were also others who separated from them,
such as those called Labadists.

The Bohemian Brethren were originally of primitive,
Waldensian belief, but when Zinzendorf reorganized them
it was on those Pietist lines which tended to keep them
within the established churches.

The Mystics represent those who, not seeing any possibility of returning to the order of the primitive church,
took refuge in personal sanctification and communion with
God and remained in the ecclesiastical associations in which
they were, and which they valued more or less according
to their individual character. They had spiritual affinities
with what was best in monasticism, and were found in
both the Catholic and Protestant communions. They
endeavoured to form actual churches at the time of the
"Philadelphian Invitation".

Departure from the commands of Christ and from Apostolic doctrine had been very great, and had extended to
every particular of the teachings of Scripture, therefore the
long way back was not found all at once; first one truth was
recovered, then another. As these spiritual revivals
occurred in various surroundings and at different times they
produced a number of churches, differing from each other in
their history, in the measure of their apprehension of
original revelation, and of their return to primitive practice. On this account they incur the reproach of multi-
plying sects, but in reality they are many paths back to
the first unity—that first unity which will be their final
one, for the travellers will reach the goal at last, according
to the Lord's prayer for them: "I in them, and Thou in
Me, that they may be made perfect in One; and that the
world may know that Thou hast sent Me, and hast loved
them, as Thou hast loved Me" (John 17. 23).

CHAPTER XIII

Methodist and Missionary Movements

1638-1820

Condition of England in the 18th century—Revivals in Wales—Temporary schools—Societies formed—The holy club at Oxford—Mrs. Wesley—John and Charles Wesley sail to Georgia—John Wesley returns and meets Peter Boehler—Accepts Christ by faith—Visits Herrnhut—George Whitefield — Preaches to the colliers at Kingswood — John Wesley also begins preaching in the open air—Lay preachers—Strange manifestations—Great revivals—Charles Wesley's hymns—Separation between Moravian and Methodist Societies—Divergence in doctrine of Wesley and Whitefield—Conference—Separation of Methodist Societies from the Church of England—Divisions—General benefit from the movement—Need of missionary work—William Carey—Andrew Fuller—Formation of Missionary Societies—Difference between Mission Stations and churches—The brothers Haldane—James Haldane preaches in Scotland—Opposition of Synods—Large numbers hear the Gospel—A church formed in Edinburgh—Liberty of ministry—Question of baptism—Robert Haldane visits Geneva—Bible Readings on Romans—The Lord's Supper in Geneva—A church formed.

INFIDELITY and indifference to matters of religion and morals prevailed in England in the 18th century, to an extent, and with consequences, that arrested the attention of all careful observers. With the upper classes it was fashionable to be irreligious and immoral, while the lower classes were plunged in the grossest ignorance and sin. The clergy were, with few exceptions, no better than the people, literature was atheistic and impure, drunkenness was considered no disgrace, violence and crime were rampant. The effort to restrain crime and preserve property by savage punishments increased recklessness, the condition of prisons was abominable, the oppression of the poor and helpless was without mercy. There remained a strong undercurrent of religion and faith, but it was hidden by the popular indulgence in sin and mockery of all that was good. The companies of believers were few in number compared with the bulk of the population and a certain langour had crept over many of them which showed that they were in need of reviving.

It was in these circumstances that a spiritual revival was given of extraordinary extent and fruitfulness.* Wales was as dark as England, and suffered the additional disadvantage that many of its clergy were English and out of touch with the people in sentiment and language. There were, however, some Welsh clergymen of the Established Church who were notable exceptions. William Wroth, rector of Llanvaches, suddenly converted, had a message of life which the hungry people crowded to hear, so that his church would not contain them; he preached in the open air and even outside his own parish, and when punished for such doings by the loss of his benefice, he founded an independent church of believers in Llanvachery, in 1638. His influence led Walter Cradock, expelled from his curacy in Cardiff, to travel about and preach the Gospel to the crowds who were eager to hear, and to attach himself to the Congregational churches. Rees Pritchard was another who had the message of salvation, which such numbers gathered to hear that he also preached in the open air. He was summoned before the Ecclesiastical Court for this, but influence was used which enabled him to continue his preaching and still remain in the Church of England. Another clergyman, · Griffith Jones, also a Welshman, early in the eighteenth century prepared his country for the greater work that was to come. As he preached and taught in his parish he saw how great was the disadvantage from which the people suffered in being unable to read the Bible for themselves, so, with the help of friends, he employed teachers to travel from place to place and hold temporary schools. Later, the lack of suitable teachers led him to open a training-school where only persons of religious principles were accepted, most of them being Nonconformists. People of all ages attended his schools, in spite of the opposition of the clergy, glad of an opportunity they had never had before, and a great reformation was wrought in the character and conduct of the nation. At the death of Griffith Jones, twenty years after he began his schools, there had been about three thousand five hundred of them at work and a third of the population of Wales had passed through them.

About the same time a young man, Howel Harris, was

* "A History of the Free Churches of England" Herbert S. Skeats.

refused ordination on the ground that he had begun to preach before receiving it. Undeterred, however, and remaining still a member of the Established Church, he continued his preaching apart from it, in the open air, in houses, and any other available buildings. The Gospel was effectual; large numbers were converted, many lives were changed, and in homes formerly godless family worship was established. Other workers joined Harris, both clergy and laymen, and in order to encourage those affected by the Word societies of religious people were formed. As was to be expected, opposition was excited; riotous mobs, led by the civil authorities and the clergy, subjected the preachers to every kind of indignity and abuse. One of the most gifted of them was Daniel Rowlands, also a clergyman, dismissed from his curacy for preaching outside the bounds of his own parish. To Llangeitho, where he preached, thousands used to come, travelling from all parts of the Principality to hear him, there being a power in his ministry which those who heard him found it impossible to describe. This movement in Wales soon came into touch with a similar movement in England. The whole character of the Welsh people was changed. Nor was this change transitory, for Wales at the present day, instead of being, as formerly, irreligious and spiritually dead, is renowned for the widespread working and depth of its spiritual life.

A little group of students in Oxford began to meet in 1729 for the purpose of helping one another in the common object that was before them, that of saving their souls and living to the glory of God.* Their ways soon brought upon them the ridicule of their fellow-students and of some of the officers of the colleges, for they differed completely in their manner of life from most of the students; they lived according to a careful and ascetic rule, visited prisoners and sick people, and helped the poor. They were styled "the Holy Club" or "the Godly Club", the "Enthusiasts", or "Methodists". Among their founders were John and Charles Wesley, and they were soon joined by George Whitefield.

The mother of the Wesleys was a woman of such unusual character and ability that it is evident that the extra-

*"John Wesley's Journal"

ordinary career and influence of her sons owed much to her and to her early training of them. Her husband was a clergyman, they had a large family and a considerable household. She was not only most careful in the bringing-up of each one of her children, but, during the frequent absences of her husband on duty she felt it right to gather her whole household together at stated times and to read the Scriptures and speak and pray with them. Through the servants present these gatherings were spoken about and others begged to be allowed to come, so that, at times, as many as two hundred crowded in and some had to go away for lack of room. Complaints were made to her husband that she took a part unbecoming in a woman. Replying to him, when he wrote to her on the subject, she said: "As I am a woman, so I am also mistress of a large family; and . . . in your absence, I cannot but look upon every soul you leave under my care, as a talent committed to me under a trust, by the great Lord of all the families, both of heaven and earth. . . . I cannot conceive why any should reflect upon you, because your wife endeavours to draw people to church, and to restrain them from pro-faning the Lord's Day, by reading to them, and other persuasions. For my part, I value no censure on this account. I have long since shook hands with the world; and I heartily wish I had never given them more reason to speak against me. As to its looking particular, I grant it does. And so does almost anything that is serious, or that may any way advance the glory of God, or the salvation of souls. . . . But there is one thing about which I am much dissatisfied; that is, their being present at family prayers. I do not speak of any concern I am under, barely because so many are present. For those who have the honour of speaking to the great and holy God, need not be ashamed to speak before the whole world; but because of my sex. I doubt if it is proper for me to present the prayers of the people of God. Last Sunday I would fain have dismissed them before prayers; but they begged so earnestly to stay, I durst not deny them. "

After their ordination, and still seeking their souls' salvation, John Wesley, his brother Charles, and two others, sailed for Georgia. On board they met a party of Moravians and John Wesley describes the deep impression made on his mind by the meekness and peace and courage they showed under all circumstances. His stay in Georgia, in spite of the practice of severe self-denial and conscientious work, was a failure, and he soon returned to England, in a state of spiritual wretchedness. "I went to America" he cried, "to convert the Indians; but oh! who shall convert me!" On reaching London (1738) he again came into contact with Moravians, and on "A day much to be remembered" met Peter Boehler, just landed from Germany. With him he had much conversation and by him, he says, "in the hand of the great God I was . . . clearly convinced of unbelief; of the want of that faith whereby alone we are saved." Should he then leave off preaching, he asked Boehler: "No", he replied, "preach faith till you have it; and then, because you have it, you will preach faith." So Wesley offered salvation by faith only to all whom he met, but still he could not apprehend that salvation could be immediate. Searching through the Acts of the Apostles to find whether there were any such cases recorded there, he found, to his astonishment, that nearly all were converted in this way. Then he took refuge in the thought that such things might happen in the early days of Christianity, but that times are changed now. He was, however, driven from this refuge by the testimony of many about him to their own experience of immediate salvation on believing. So at last he accepted Christ by faith as his Saviour.

His brother Charles and others were angry with him for saying that he, who had done so much, had never been saved until now, but soon afterwards he records: "My brother had a long and particular conversation with Peter Boehler. And it now pleased God to open his eyes; so that he saw clearly what was the nature of that one true living faith, whereby alone 'through grace we are saved.'"

A society was formed, to consist of little bands of members who should meet weekly to confess their faults to one another and for intercession. As John Wesley preached diligently in many of the London churches "free salvation by faith in the blood of Christ" he was officially informed in one after another that this was the last time he would be allowed to preach there.

He now visited the Moravian settlement at Herrnhut and also Count Zinzendorf, and was much helped in intercourse with those he met. Then he returned to England and began once more to preach and to visit, and going to Bristol he met again his old friend George Whitefield. "*

Whitefield was born at the Bell Inn, Gloucester (1714). Some time after his mother became a widow and was much reduced in circumstances, so that her youngest son's ambition to become a clergyman was only fulfilled with difficulty by the help of friends, who enabled him to get a post as servitor at Pembroke College and so to study. There he passed through an experience of great spiritual anguish as a seeker after salvation. He joined the "holy club" and by fasting and other mortifying of the flesh reduced himself to serious weakness. He then became a student of the Scriptures and records: "I got more true knowledge from reading the Book of God in one month than I could ever have acquired from *all* the writings of men". Having thus learned and experienced justification by faith, he was anxious to preach, and as soon as he was ordained began to do so; with such startling effect that it was commonly reported that his first sermon drove fifteen persons mad. His gift as a preacher was, from the beginning, so remarkable that crowds pressed to hear him. A sermon he preached in Bristol, *"On the Nature and Necessity of our Regeneration or New Birth in Christ Jesus"* was the beginning of the great awakening that followed in Gloucester, Bristol and London. For a short time he was away in Georgia, where he founded an orphanage. Returning to England, he found that his habit of going from house to house where he was invited and expounding the Scriptures, so incensed the clergy against him that almost all the pulpits were closed to him. Some of his friends had suggested to him that as he had been out to America to preach to Indians he might as well preach to the rough, neglected colliers at Kingswood, near Bristol, and he says: "Finding that the pulpits are denied me, and the poor colliers are ready to perish for lack of knowledge, I went to them, and preached on a mount to upwards of two hundred. Blessed be God, that the ice is now broken, and I have now taken the field. . . . I thought it might be doing the service of my Creator, who had a mountain for His pulpit, and the heavens for His sounding-board: and who, when the Gospel was refused by the Jews,

*"George Whitefield A Light Rising in Obscurity" J. R. Andrews.

sent His servants into the highways and hedges." The
next time he preached ten thousand people came together;
his marvellous voice reached them all as he spoke to them
for an hour. He tells how "the first discovery of their being
affected was to see the white gutters made by their tears,
which plentifully fell down their black cheeks as they came
out of their coal-pits. Hundreds and hundreds of them
were soon brought under deep conviction, which, as the
event proved, happily ended in a sound and thorough
conversion."

It was here that Whitefield sent for John Wesley to come
and help in the work. Wesley, who was a devoted church-
man, says: "In the evening I reached Bristol, and met Mr.
Whitefield there. I could scarce reconcile myself at first
to this strange way of preaching in the fields, of which he
set me an example on Sunday; having been all my life (till
very lately) so tenacious of every point relating to decency
and order, that I should have thought the saving of souls
almost a sin, if it had not been done in a church. In the
evening (Mr. Whitefield being gone) I began expounding
our Lord's Sermon on the Mount (one pretty remarkable
precedent of field preaching, though I suppose there were
churches at that time also) to a little Society which was
accustomed to meet once or twice a week in Nicholas
St. At four in the afternoon, I submitted to be more
vile, and proclaimed in the highways the glad tidings of
salvation, speaking from a little eminence in a ground
adjoining to the city to about three thousand people."

In this way the barriers were broken down and unre-
stricted preaching of the Gospel spread over the country.
It was accompanied by a power of the Spirit that nothing
could resist. The crowds that came together to hear num-
bered sometimes tens of thousands. Not only were the
lowest of the people converted to God in vile gaols and
filthy slums, but when the Countess of Huntingdon threw
herself and her influence into the work the aristocracy was
reached and many of its members became disciples of Christ.
The lack of clergy for the work overcame the strong scruples
of John Wesley so that he was obliged to acknowledge that
the Holy Spirit had sent numerous laymen to preach the
Gospel, some of them, as John Nelson, unlettered, but
having that spiritual experience and power which fitted

them to be powerful and effectual witnesses for Christ. In the early days there were strange manifestations in the meetings. Hearers would be smitten to the ground in convulsions, cry out in an agony of repentance or fear, sometimes in wild blasphemies, before they obtained deliverance of body and soul. Most violent opposition assailed the preachers from all sides. Riotous mobs attacked them and those who with them had confessed Christ, doing grievous injury to persons and property, but all this was met by a courage and meekness which the adversaries were not able to withstand.

The journeys of Wesley and Whitefield and others were incessant. Mostly on horseback, in all kinds of weather, they constantly traversed all England and Wales; one of the greatest revivals was through Whitefield's preaching in Scotland; in Ireland, North and South, the results were the same; Whitefield repeatedly visited New England, and the same power was manifested there. It was while preaching there that he died, in 1770. John Wesley, however, continued his indefatigable labours until his 88th year in 1790, feeling, almost to the end, "none of the infirmities of old age". Dying, he gathered his remaining strength, and, lifting up his arms and voice among those who surrounded him, cried out twice: "The best of all is, God is with us".

Charles Wesley,* though not equal to his brother in ability as a preacher, fully shared his labours. His greatest and lasting service to the Church is in the hymns he wrote; they exceed six thousand in number, and many of them are of a poetic beauty and a spiritual value which place them among the best that have ever been written. They contain, in beautiful and arresting form, sound expositions of many of the principal doctrines taught in Scripture, and they express worship and the inward experiences of the spirit in a way which make them continually suited to give utterance to the longings and praises of hearts touched by the Spirit of God. The Wesleys, finding that most people take their theology more from hymns than from Scripture, wrote hymns with the definite purpose of teaching doctrine by them.

*"The Poetical Works of John and Charles Wesley. Reprinted from the Originals, with the last corrections of the authors; together with the Poems of Charles Wesley Not before published Collected and arranged by G. Osborne D.D."

Among the many workers for the Kingdom of God at this time it is not to be wondered at that differences of view developed on various points. Laying hold afresh of neglected truth revealed in the Word of God, some apprehended more fully one aspect of it, some another; while each was inclined to emphasize what he had seen and to suspect danger in the vision of the other. Though the Holy Spirit is given to lead into all truth, yet not all receive this fulness; indeed, the very magnitude and variety of the Divine revelation often leads to partial and differing apprehension of it.

Although so greatly helped by the Moravians at the beginning, Wesley gradually came to differ from them on various points. Their historical connection with the Bohemian Brethren gave them tendencies which he regarded as mystical and quietist, unattractive to his practical, aggressive nature. The gathering in Fetter Lane where both Moravians and Methodists had met together divided in 1702, the Moravians remaining there and the Methodists moving to a place called the "Foundery".

Wesley and Whitefield diverged early in doctrine, Whitefield holding Calvinistic views with regard to election, which Wesley strongly repudiated, and when Whitefield returned from America in 1741 he preached openly against "General Redemption", not refraining from doing this even when preaching at the Foundery and in the presence of Charles Wesley. The sympathies of the Countess of Huntingdon were with Whitefield rather than with Wesley, and the Methodist Societies which spread over England were Wesleyan and Arminian, while those in Wales were Calvinistic as were also those of the "Countess of Huntingdon's Connexion".

These differences did not personally alienate Wesley and Whitefield, and it is noticeable that the preaching of justification by faith whether by the one or the other was equally effectual in the conversion of sinners. The styles of preaching, too, of Wesley and Whitefield were entirely different, but the same truths preached produced the same results. Whitefield's preaching was eloquent, impassioned, so dramatic that people seemed to see the scenes he depicted; he would sometimes break into weeping as he saw the need of the souls before him. Wesley was clear and

logical, his preaching largely expository, yet he captured
the attention of the roughest audiences.

Wesley's determined adherence to the Established
Church prevented him from seeing those principles which
are taught in Scripture regarding the churches of God, and
he never attempted to follow up his Gospel preaching by
forming churches, on the New Testament pattern, of those
who believed. Yet in 1746 he wrote, "On the road I read
over Lord King's account of the Primitive Church. In
spite of the vehement prejudice of my education, I was
ready to believe that this was a fair and impartial draught;
but if so, it would follow that Bishops and Presbyters are
(essentially) of one order; and that originally every Christian congregation was a church independent on all others!"
He organized what seemed to him practical methods of
giving permanence to the work; his "Bands" and
"Societies" did not profess to be companies of believers, but
rather of seekers. Their basis of fellowship was experimental more than doctrinal, the condition of admittance was a
desire to flee from the wrath to come and to be saved. Members were free to attend such places of worship as they preferred and to hold their own opinions on different points,
but they were not allowed to make of them subjects of discussion or contention. In 1740 a member was excluded because he insisted on arguing about election and reprobation.

From time to time Wesley purged the societies of unworthy members, as he saw fit. As long as he lived he
controlled the organization, and the "Conference" which
he established to take control after him was an entirely
clerical body. His efforts to keep the movement within
the Church of England failed, partly because the Established Church disowned and systematically opposed it,
partly because it was not possible for the new life and
energy to be confined in such bonds; the time inevitably
came when formal separation had to take place.

Conference was not able to hold the Wesleyan Methodist
Societies together. Being a clerical body it was, like all
such bodies, jealous of privilege, and its resistance to an
effort to bring in lay representation led to the formation of
the Methodist New Connexion. Later, its attempt to
control open-air preaching and its expulsion of some who
held "camp meetings" without its permission, gave rise

to that very active and devoted body, the Primitive Methodists. In the course of further conflicts and divisions Conference gradually came to accept some of the innovations it had at first resisted.

The formation and remarkable growth of these vigorous denominations was not, however, the only, nor even the principal result of the spiritual awakening of the 18th century. That is found in the powerful influence it exercised on the English-speaking peoples, on the character of the British Empire and of the United States, stirring large numbers of people to devote themselves to removing abuses, to working righteousness, and to delivering the oppressed. It gave an impetus to better legislation, to liberty of conscience, to the abolition of slavery, to prison reform, and to missionary activity. The Established Church also gained greatly by it, becoming the scene of evangelical and other revivals in which the gross evils that had so long prevailed disappeared. The churches, whether Baptist or Congregational, also derived benefit from the general reviving, and their activities were enlarged.

The fact that, after so many centuries, the Lord's command "Go ye into all the world, and preach the Gospel to every creature" remained unfulfilled, and that many millions of men had never had the opportunity of hearing the Gospel, had weighed on the consciences of Christian people at various times, and there had been some who had devoted themselves to reaching out to needy parts of the world. A great revival of this sense of responsibility and of love to Christ and to mankind was brought about through William Carey, * a village shoemaker, who was also pastor of the Particular Baptist church at Moulton, where he with difficulty maintained his family, studied languages and collected information as to the state of the heathen world. In his work-room might be seen a large map, made of sheets of paper pasted together, on which every country in the world was shown and on which he entered all he could ascertain as to the condition of each. This map was his prayer-book and subject of conversation and preaching.

At a meeting of ministers at Northampton, an oppor-

* "The Life of William Carey Shoe-maker and Missionary" George Smith C.I.E., LL.D.

tunity being given for younger brethren to suggest some sub-ject for discussion, Carey proposed: *"whether the command given to the Apostles to teach all nations was not obligatory on all succeeding ministers to the end of the world, seeing that the accompanying promise was of equal extent."* This was set aside as a wholly unsuitable subject, the extreme Calvinism of most in that circle preventing their seeing the necessity of active obedience to this command of Christ.

The sermons of Andrew Fuller helped to overcome this hindrance. Carey published *"An Enquiry into the Obliga-tions of Christians to use Means for the Conversion of the Heathens, in which the Religious State of the Different Nations of the World, the Success of Former Undertakings, and the Practicability of Further Undertakings, are considered by* William Carey". After stating the principles involved and referring to the work already accomplished by some, he deals with a number of difficulties that might be raised against such action. Among these is the "uncivilized and barbarous way of living" of some of the heathen; "this", he argues, "can be no objection to any, except those whose love of ease renders them unwilling to expose themselves to in-convenience for the good of others. It was no objection to the apostles and their successors, who went among the barbarous Germans and Gauls, and still more barbarous Britons! They did not wait for the ancient inhabitants of these countries to be civilized before they could be christian-ized, but went simply with the doctrine of the cross"; they "found that a cordial reception of the gospel produced those happy effects which the longest intercourse with Europeans without it could never accomplish." He suggests that two at least should go together, preferably married men, and that they might be accompanied by some who would soon be able, by agriculture or in such other ways as experience might indicate, to earn sufficient for the needs of all. The necessary qualifications, spiritual and otherwise, are dwelt upon, and he adds: "It might likewise be of importance, if God should bless their labours, for them to encourage any appearance of gifts amongst the people of their charge; if such should be raised up many advantages would be derived from their knowledge of the language and customs of their countrymen; and their change of conduct would give great weight to their ministrations."

The ministers' meeting of 1792 was held in the house of a widow, Mrs. Wallis, in Kettering, and there a Society was formed to forward the spread of the Gospel in other lands. A brief account of its aims was drawn up and signed by twelve persons and a few months later Carey was on his way to India, while Fuller, to the utmost of his ability and zeal, was arousing the Christians of Great Britain to an understanding of the responsibility laid upon them for the spread of the Gospel in the whole world.

Difficulties which appeared to be insuperable were patiently overcome and eventually the success of the enterprise was assured in the blessings it brought both to India and to Britain. It was not until after seven years of work and prayer that the firstfruits among the Indians began to be seen; Krishna Pal, with his family, confessed Christ, and he became an effective preacher of the Gospel as well as a hymn-writer.

The interest thus aroused led to the formation, in 1795, of the London Missionary Society, at first undenominational, but becoming later Congregationalist, while in 1799 the Church Missionary Society was organized. The Wesleyan Methodist Missionary Society enlarged the scope of its activities and others followed.

The devotion and ability directed by these organizations have borne abundant fruit in many parts of the world. Their records contain some of the most inspiring histories in the annals of mankind. Of necessity, however, this manner of carrying Christianity to those outside has brought the divisions and the religious historical developments of Europe among heathen and Mohammedan peoples, so weakening the testimony of the Gospel, and has tended to establish Mission Stations representing and depending on the various Missionary Societies, rather than independent churches, spreading by their own testimony among their own people as was the case with the churches founded in apostolic days.

Two brothers, Robert and James Alexander Haldane, * belonging to a wealthy and well-connected Scottish family, who, as young men, served with distinction in the navy, were converted and became diligent students of the Scriptures.

* "Lives of Robert and James Haldane" by Alexander Haldane.

The younger, James, relates how, after his marriage: "When I first lived in my own house, I began family worship on Sabbath evenings. I was unwilling to have it more frequently, lest I should meet with ridicule from my acquaintance. A conviction of duty at length determined me to begin to have it every morning, but I assembled the family in a back room for some time, lest anyone should come in. I gradually got over this fear of man, and being desirous to instruct those who lived in my family, I began to expound the Scriptures. I found this pleasant and edifying to myself, and it has been one chief means by which the Lord prepared me for speaking in public. . . . I began secretly to desire to be allowed to preach the Gospel, which I considered as the most important as well as honourable employment. I began to ask of God to send me into His vineyard, and to qualify me for the work. This desire continued to increase, although I had not the most distant prospect of its being gratified, and sometimes in prayer my unbelieving heart suggested that it could not be. I had no idea of going to the highways and hedges, and telling sinners of the Saviour. However, I entertained some distant hope that the Lord would direct."

Soon after this he and some others became interested in meetings for preaching the Gospel in a neglected colliery village and, as it was not always possible to get an ordained minister, sometimes laymen would speak. One evening the preacher expected did not come, so James Haldane took his place and preached his first Gospel sermon. This was in 1797, and led on to his undertaking, with others, itinerary Gospel preaching, which in the following years took him all over Scotland, and beyond.

The preachers travelled in a carriage and were well supplied with tracts which they themselves wrote, printed, and distributed. They spoke in churches, when these were lent to them; in schools and other buildings, but chiefly in the open air. Hundreds—sometimes thousands—gathered to hear them; there was much power with their testimony and large numbers were converted. The spiritual needs of the country at that time were great but the idea of laymen's helping was resented by many; though, on the other hand, the strangeness of it often attracted hearers, who were then affected by the earnestness and sincerity of the speakers.

The Synod of the Established Church of Scotland, meeting in Aberdeen, passed acts against "vagrant teachers and Sunday Schools, irreligion and anarchy"; unlicensed preachers and unauthorized Sunday School teachers were forbidden. The General Synod of the Anti-burgers condemned Missionary Societies and warned their members against "attending upon, or giving countenance to, public preaching, by any who are not of our communion" and excommunicated those who disregarded this decree, including one of their most gifted ministers. The Cameronians acted in the same way, and the Relief Synod agreed "that no minister shall give, or allow his pulpit to be given, to any person who has not attended a regular course of philosophy and divinity in some of the Universities of the nation, and who has not been regularly licensed to preach the Gospel". These injunctions were disregarded by many and indeed often served to increase the interest of hearing the Scriptures preached and expounded by men who really believed them.

In justifying himself and his fellow workers James Haldane said: "We would not . . . be understood to mean that every follower of Jesus should leave the occupation by which he provides for his family to become a public preacher. It is an indispensable Christian duty for every man to provide for his family; but we consider every Christian is bound, wherever he has opportunity, to warn sinners to flee from the wrath to come, and to point out Jesus as the way, the truth, and the life. Whether a man declare these important truths to two, or two hundred, he is, in our opinion, a preacher of the Gospel, or one who declares the glad tidings of salvation, which is the precise meaning of the word preach". . . . "We deemed the low state of religion a sufficient call for us to go to the highways and hedges, and endeavour to compel our fellow sinners to lay hold on the hope set before them in the Gospel". The preachers laid great stress on justification by faith in the death and resurrection of Christ, without works. Visiting many places, they found religion at a low ebb everywhere but also a desire to hear the Word. As far north as Orkney, where they preached at the fair at Kirkwall, three to four thousand listened daily, and on Lord's Day some 6000 gathered together to hear.

A hearer, invited to attend a meeting and going out of

curiosity because of the pressing invitation he received, thus describes his impressions: "Captain Haldane arrived on horseback at the place where the people were assembled to hear him. He dismounted, and gave his horse to the charge of another gentleman who stood by. He was then a young man, under thirty years of age, and had on a blue great-coat, braided in front, after the fashion of the times. He also wore powder, and his hair tied behind, as was then usual for gentlemen. I can never forget the impressions which fell on my heart as he, in a distinct, clear, and manly tone, began to address the thoughtless multitude that had been attracted to hear him. His powerful appeals to the conscience, couched in such simple phrase, were so terrifying that I never closed an eye, nor even retired to rest that night. The impression produced by what I heard was never effaced from my mind, for though I did not fully embrace the Gospel for years after, yet I never relapsed again into my former state of carelessness and indifference to eternal things".

This work of conversion, and the reviving of many who were already Christians, awakened questions as to what was the further course they should take in following out the teachings of Scripture. The brothers Haldane as well as a number of those with whom they worked came to be oppressed by the union with manifestly unconverted people in which they found themselves in the Established Church, so they separated from it, and began to meet with those only who gave evidence of being children of God. They formed a church in Edinburgh, which began with some 300 members and grew very rapidly. One of their first acts was to ordain James Haldane as pastor. Robert Haldane provided large meeting places, or "Tabernacles", not only in Edinburgh but also in other centres where churches were gathered. Following the principle that the New Testament contains the teaching and example which it is the duty of the Lord's disciples to observe to-day, these churches began to take the Lord's Supper each first day of the week; they also ceased to make collections of money from the general congregations, but the members of the church contributed what they were able. This came about gradually. Robert Haldane wrote:* "I began with

* "Letters to Mr. Ewing respecting The Tabernacle at Glasgow etc." By Robert Haldane. Edinburgh, 1809.

practising the Lord's Supper monthly. Afterwards I became convinced that on the principles I held, I ought to observe it weekly. . . . I began with a few individuals . . . who erected themselves into a church; and I am now convinced that any set or number of Christians, where there is no church of Christ, may act as we did. . . . I began with being persuaded that churches should not hold fellowship with the world, except in the contribution of their money. I now blush when I think of such an exception".

Little by little they came to understand that the Holy Spirit, if not hindered by human arrangements, will give variety of ministers and ministry, and as they gradually became accustomed to His working freely through whom He would, they found much joy and power in the experience.

For some years James Haldane was troubled by doubts as to infant baptism, but put the question aside, partly because he felt that occupation with it might lead to a diminution of his usefulness. There came a time, however, when conscience obliged him to refuse to baptize infants, and, later, to submit himself to baptism, as did also his brother and others whose study of the Scriptures had led them to the same conclusion. They did not see any ground for separation from their brethren when they decided on this step. They believed and taught that believers should practise forbearance towards one another in the matters in which they differ and earnestly desired that their action should not lead to division in their happy circle. In spite of their efforts to maintain unity, however, division took place. The greater number remained together, some of them baptized, others not, but all united as to the principle of forbearance with one another in such matters; some formed a congregation on the same lines as before but rejecting baptism by immersion and practising the baptism of infants; some went back into the Established Church and others joined other denominations.

This division was a cause of sorrow, and difficulties that arose were accentuated by the fact that so many of the meeting places were the property of Robert Haldane; while efforts to train young men in Bible Schools as evangelists and pastors proved to be a source of much difficulty

and disappointment. The church which remained after
so many had left, though grieving on account of its diminished numbers, continued its testimony, in which it
continued to be blessed.

Robert Haldane, in the midst of his various activities,
had long had a desire to make known the Word of God further
afield, and in 1816 he and his wife crossed to the Continent.
They knew no one there and could form no plan; did not
even know whether their visit would only be for a few
weeks or be much prolonged. In Paris they made a few
acquaintances which led to their going to Bern and Geneva.
They were about to leave the latter city again, finding no
opening there, when what appeared to be a chance meeting
with a young student of divinity led to their remaining
two years. This student was so deeply impressed by the
conversation they had together that he came again next
day bringing another with him. They both proved to
be in utter darkness, without hope of salvation or knowledge of the Scriptures, which they had never studied,
as their studies had been directed rather to the writings of heathen philosophers. Being awakened to see
their ignorance of Scripture and of the way of salvation
they greatly desired instruction and this decided Robert
Haldane to stay.

The burning of Servetus had not prevented the persistence of some of the doctrines he taught and the theological
professors and ministers of the Church of Geneva had fallen
under the influence of Socinian and Arian doctrines, with
deadening consequences to spiritual life.

Taking lodgings in the Place Maurice, where two large
rooms could be thrown into one, Robert Haldane held
regular Bible Readings to which, in spite of being forbidden
by their professors, twenty to thirty students came, who
sat round a long table, with Bibles in different languages,
while Haldane, speaking by interpretation, expounded the
Scriptures and answered questions.

He went through the Epistle to the Romans, explaining
its teaching in detail and comparing it with other Scriptures. It was new to his hearers and they were attracted
by his knowledge of Scripture and entire belief in it. These
readings were the means of abiding spiritual blessing to the

students; many of them proved to be gifted and devoted men and became distinguished and influential in wide circles, so that the fruit of those studies and of that intercourse was far-reaching and of incalculable value. From among them Malan the hymn writer, Merle D'Aubigné the historian, and, later, Adolph Monod, Félix Neff and others carried what they had learned there to the French-speaking world and even further. All this was not allowed to pass without opposition, and though it proved impossible to silence Robert Haldane, those ministers and students who accepted and acted upon what they had learned from the Scriptures through him, were made to suffer for it. Some were deprived of their positions, some driven out of the Church, and some even obliged to leave the country.

Robert Haldane left Geneva without having progressed beyond the doctrines of the Gospel or taught those which concern the Church. Though some knew that he had been baptized, he did not speak of it. Possibly his experience in Scotland had discouraged him. He went into France, to do at Montauban, where pastors were trained for the Protestant Church, a similar work to that which he had done in Geneva, the continuance and carrying forward of which latter was left to others. One of the young ministers in Geneva who had to suffer for following the truth was César Malan.

Malan was one of the company of ten believers who, at this period, took the Lord's Supper together for the first time outside the Established Church. Another of these, Gaussen, describes the meeting, mentioning the names of Pyt, Mejanel, Gonthier and Guers, as being also present. "It reminded us", he says, "of another Supper, that which, in 1536, another disciple of Jesus, M. Jean Guerin, distributed to some pious souls, assembled in the garden of Étienne Dadaz, at Pré l'Evêque, and which was the first communion of the Protestants of Geneva."

The church now formed met later, among other places, in a street near the Cathedral, La Pélisserie, and the Gospel testimony which went out from it was the means of the conversion and gathering in of many. Guers, Pyt, Gonthier and others held meetings also in the same building where Froment had formerly held the school which was the beginning of the Reformation in Geneva. Another student, Du Vivier, preaching in the oratory of Carouge, proclaimed the Divinity of the Lord, the corruption of human nature, and the Atonement. This was pronounced scandalous, and to guard against any further such disorder it was enacted that no student should preach unless his sermon had first been passed by three professors of Divinity.

CHAPTER XIV

The West

1790-1890

Thomas Campbell—A "Declaration and Address"—Alexander Campbell —Church at Brush Run—Baptism—Sermon on the Law—Republican Methodists take the name "Christians"—Baptists take the name "Christians"—Barton Warren Stone—Strange revival scenes—The Springfield Presbytery formed and dissolved—Church at Cane Ridge—The Christian Connection—Separation of Reformers from Baptists—Union of Christian Connection and Reformers—Nature of Conversion—Walter Scott—Baptism for the remission of sins—Testimony of Isaac Errett.

A minister of one of the Seceder branches of the Presbyterian Church, Thomas Campbell, left his home in the North of Ireland, on account of his health, and came to America (1807).* He was well received by the Synod then sitting in Philadelphia and sent to Western Pennsylvania, where his unusual gifts and spiritual character made him acceptable. Some, however, doubted his loyalty to the "Secession Testimony" as he taught that the Scriptures alone provide the true basis of faith and conduct, and deprecated the prevailing party spirit in the churches.

Being sent to visit in a sparsely populated district in the Alleghany Mountains he received at the Lord's Supper believers who, though Presbyterians, did not belong to this particular circle. For this he was censured, and, defending his action as being in accordance with the teachings of Scripture, he was treated in so hostile a spirit as to induce him to withdraw from the Seceder body.

Many Christian people of different denominations continued to attend his ministry, being dissatisfied with the divided state of religion and sympathizing with his teaching that union could only be obtained by a return to the Bible, and that a better understanding of the difference between faith and opinion would lead to a forbearance likely to do much towards checking divisions.

In a house between Mount Pleasant and Washington

* "Memoirs of Alexander Campbell" Richardson. The Standard Press, Cincinnati, Ohio.

a meeting was held (1809) where those present conferred as to the best means of putting these principles into practice. Thomas Campbell spoke of the evil of divisions, showing that they are not inevitable, since God has provided in His Word a standard and guide sufficient for the needs of the churches in all times. It is by building up religious theories and systems outside of the Scriptures that strife and dissension have come in, therefore it is only by a return to the teachings of the Word that true unity can be regained. As a rule for their guidance he proposed that "where the Scriptures speak, we speak; and where the Scriptures are silent, we are silent." A Presbyterian present said, "If we adopt that as a basis, then there is an end of infant baptism," to which Thomas Campbell replied, "If infant baptism be not found in Scripture, we can have nothing to do with it." Another rose and under strong emotion, moved even to tears, exclaimed, "I hope I may never see the day when my heart will renounce that blessed saying of the Scripture, 'Suffer little children to come unto Me, and forbid them not, for of such is the kingdom of heaven.'" A prominent Independent said, "In the portion of Scripture you have quoted there is no reference whatever to infant baptism."

In spite of this immediate evidence of their divergence of view, most of those present joined in forming "The Christian Association of Washington" and appointed Thomas Campbell to prepare a statement of their aims. This, to which they all agreed, took the form of a "Declaration and Address," in which they expressed their persuasion that since no man can be judged for his brother so no man can judge for his brother, each must judge for himself and must give account of himself to God. Each one is bound by the Word of God but not by any human interpretation of it. Tired of party strife they desired to take and recommend such measures as would give rest to the churches. They despaired of finding this in a continuance of party contention or discussion of human opinions; it can only be found in Christ and His unchanging Word. Let us therefore return (they wrote) to the original pattern and take the Word of God alone as our rule. They had no intention of forming a church, but only a society for the promotion of Christian unity and of "a pure evangelical reformation.

by the simple preaching of the gospel, and the administration of its ordinances in exact conformity to its Divine standard.''

When Thomas Campbell came to America he left his family behind to follow somewhat later. His wife was of Huguenot descent, and their son Alexander was preparing for ordination as a minister in the Seceder Presbyterian Church. While staying in Glasgow Alexander Campbell came into contact with the teaching and work of the brothers Haldane. These raised doubts in his mind as to the scripturalness of the control of churches by Synods and led him to accept the Congregational system as being in accordance with apostolic teaching and practice. His attachment, however, to the Seceder Church and his respect for his father's wishes kept him from any outward expression of his thoughts, but inwardly he separated from the Presbyterian system and when the time came for the half-yearly communion of the Seceders, although he passed the required examination and received the token authorizing him to partake of the Lord's Supper with the large number of communicants, he abstained from doing so, feeling that this would indicate approval of a system he could no longer accept.

When the time came for Thomas Campbell's family to cross to America, Alexander took charge of his mother and her younger children; they reached New York and travelled inland by waggon, staying at the large, commodious inns on the way. Thomas Campbell, hearing of their approach rode out from Washington to meet them. They met on the road and, travelling then together, related to each other all that had happened to them during their separation.

Neither Thomas Campbell nor his son knew that the other had left the Seceder body and each was concerned to know how the other would receive the news. When they learned that each separately and by different ways had come to the same conclusion they were strengthened, and filled with thanksgiving for the Lord's manifest leadings. When Alexander saw the "Declaration" which his father had written and heard the principles on which he was acting he found that they expressed the very convictions to which he himself had come and he determined to devote himself to the great cause of bringing about the unity of the Church by a return to the Scriptures.

Fearing that the "Christian Association" might develop into a new party, or become a church, Thomas Campbell decided to try whether the members of the Association would be allowed the privileges of Christian and ministerial communion among the Presybterians. The Synod of Pittsburg was due to meet in October 1810 and Thomas Campbell brought before it an application, at the same time explaining the principles of the Association, and asked whether the Synod would agree to "Christian union upon Christian principles." The suggestion was refused and the activities of the Association were severely condemned. Alexander Campbell made this the occasion of a much fuller explanation and a defence of the objects of the Association. It had become clear to him that to join any party would be contrary to the principle of return to the teachings of Scripture.

In 1811 Alexander Campbell married and joined his father-in-law in farming, in which he was active and successful. Thomas Campbell also left Washington and took a farm near the village of Mount Pleasant. His farm was chiefly managed by his friendly neighbours as his own time was occupied in visiting and preaching, but his son's energies and abilities were so unusual that he could earn sufficient by farming without ceasing his spiritual labours.

The hostility of all the religious bodies to the "Christian Association" gradually convinced its members that they could not have the advantages nor perform the duties of a church unless they themselves took the position of a congregation of believers, a New Testament church. As they were not able to transform the existing churches they hoped that the example of a church outside of all parties and exhibiting the principles of the New Testament would give further effect to the truth of unity by a return to the Scriptures in which they believed.

This church was solemnly formed (1811) at Brush Run. An elder, an evangelist and deacons were chosen. The Lord's Supper was taken on the first day of the week, and this was done each week. There were about thirty members. Rejecting all claims to apostolic succession, they found that in each of the New Testament churches there were several elders (or bishops, or overseers) and deacons (or servants) for the building up of the church, and there were evangelists sent out to preach the truth in the world. The form of ordination was not regarded as conferring authority but as a testimony that those ordained had authority. There was no distinction of clergy and laity. The question of baptism had been shelved. Both Thomas and Alexander Campbell thought that infant baptism had obtained such a position that it might be left. Why should those already in the church go out of it "merely for the purpose of coming in again by the regular and appointed way?" They baptized by immersion those believers who desired it. But the birth of Alexander Campbell's first child brought the question to a practical issue, and now he examined the Scriptures carefully as to this matter. He came to the conclusion that nothing else is taught in the New Testament than the baptism of believers by immersion and that this is a command of the Lord and was the apostolic practice and of such importance that it should not be set aside.

In a deep pool in Buffalo Creek, where already several members of the Brush Run church had been baptized, Alexander Campbell and his wife, his father and mother and sister, and two others were baptized (1812).

This course, while increasing the enmity of most of the religious denominations, gave pleasure to the Baptists, who proposed that the church at Brush Run should be associated with them. The Baptists in the district had formed themselves into an Association of Churches, called "Redstone," and in spite of their principle of independent congregations, their pastors, who controlled the action of the associations, exercised so great an influence that the church at Brush Run feared that its independence might be jeopardized by closer union. Also, the Baptist Association had adopted a Confession of Faith issued in 1747 by a Baptist Association in Philadelphia, which contained theories unacceptable to the Brush Run church. The Baptists themselves, however, were godly people, lovers of the Word and insistent that Alexander Campbell should come among them and minister. The Brush Run church, after consideration, put before the Redstone Association a full account of their position, their "remonstrance against all human creeds as bonds of communion or union among Christian Churches" and expressed willingness to co-operate with them if they were left free to teach and preach whatever they learned from the Holy Scriptures. This proposition was accepted by a majority of the Association. Those, however, who dissented formed a distinct opposition.

This opposition became more manifest when at a meeting of the Association at Cross Creek (1816) Alexander Campbell preached a "Sermon on the Law" in which he showed clearly the differences of the dispensations and that we are no longer under the Law but under Christ, Who is the "end of the law for righteousness to every one that believeth." He showed how many practices in Christendom are derived from the Old Testament, which led up to and is superseded by the New, in which latter we have the Gospel and teaching for our present age. This was so contrary to much of the teaching current among the Baptists that some of their pulpits were closed to Alexander Campbell.

At the beginning of the nineteenth century there were a number of spiritual movements actuated by a desire for deliverance from the theological systems and traditional practices which had so long prevailed, and by the belief that a return to the Scriptures would prove them to contain all that is needed for faith and conduct, both for the individual and for the churches.

One of these movements developed among Methodists. American independence had released them from control from abroad and as they considered the question of church government most of them agreed in establishing an episcopal system. Others argued in favour of the congregational system and desired that their churches should be according to the pattern of the New Testament. These were a minority and unable to carry through what they believed, so separated from the larger number (1793). James O'Kelly and other preachers in North Carolina and Virginia were leaders in the formation of these churches, which at first took the name of "Republican Methodists" but soon abandoned this and decided to take no name but that of "Christians". They acknowledged no head of the Church but Christ, formulated no creed or rules, but accepted the Scriptures alone for their guidance.

Soon after this a similar movement originated among

Baptists. A doctor, Abner Jones, and a Baptist preacher, Elias Smith, founded churches in the Eastern States, where faith and godliness were made the basis of reception and not membership of any particular sect (from 1800). Other preachers from among the Baptists joined them and gifted men were raised up in the new churches who carried the Gospel far afield. All these took the name of "Christians" only and accepted the Scriptures alone as their sufficient guide.

At Cane Ridge, Kentucky, in the last decade of the eighteenth century, the early Presbyterian settlers put up a log building as their Meeting House. In 1801 their minister was Barton Warren Stone* (1772-1844).

Relating his own experience he wrote, "About this time my mind was continually tossed on the waves of speculative divinity, the all-engrossing theme of the religious community at that period . . . I at that time believed, and taught, that mankind were so totally depraved that they could do nothing acceptable to God, till his Spirit, by some physical, almighty and mysterious power, had quickened, enlightened and regenerated the heart, and thus prepared the sinner to believe in Jesus for salvation. I began plainly to see that if God did not perform this regenerating work in all, it must be because he chose to do it for some and not for others, and that this depended on his own sovereign will and pleasure . . . this doctrine is inseparably linked with unconditional election and reprobation. . . . They are virtually one; and this was the reason why I admitted the decrees of election and reprobation, having admitted the doctrine of total depravity. They are inseparable. . . . Often when I was . . . persuading the helpless to repent and believe the gospel, my zeal in a moment would be chilled at the contradiction. How can they believe? How can they repent? How can they do impossibilities? How can they be guilty in not doing them? . . . On a certain evening, when engaged in secret prayer and reading my Bible my mind came unusually filled with comfort and peace. I never recollect of having before experienced such an ardent love and tenderness for all mankind, and such a longing desire for their salvation. . . . for some days and

*"Autobiography of B. W. Stone" (The Cane Ridge Meeting House, James R. Rogers). The Standard Publishing Co., Cincinnati, Ohio.

nights I was almost continually praying for the ruined world . . . I expressed my feelings to a pious person, and rashly remarked, 'So great is my love for sinners that, had I power, I would save them all.' The person appeared to be horror-stricken, and remarked, 'Do you love them more than God does? Why, then, does he not save them? Surely he has almighty power.' I blushed, was confounded and silent, and quickly retired to the silent woods for meditation and prayer. I asked myself, Does God love the world—the whole world? And has he not almighty power to save? If so, all must be saved, for who can resist his power? . . . I was firmly convinced that according to Scripture all were not saved; the conclusion, then, was irresistible that God did not love all, and therefore it followed, of course, that the spirit in me, which loved all the world so vehemently, could not be the Spirit of God, but the spirit of delusion. . . . I prostrated myself before God in prayer, but it was immediately suggested, you are praying in unbelief, and 'whatsoever is not of faith is sin.' You must believe or expect no good from the hand of God. But I can not believe; as soon could I make a world. Then you must be damned, for 'he that believeth not shall be damned.' But will the Lord condemn me to eternal punishment for not doing an impossibility? So I thought . . . blasphemy rose in my heart against such a God, and my tongue was tempted to utter it. Sweat profusely poured from the pores of my body, and the fires of hell gat hold on me . . . in this uncommon state I remained for two or three days. From this state of perplexity I was relieved by the precious word of God. From reading and meditating upon it, I became convinced that God did love the whole world, and that the reason why he did not save all was because of their unbelief; and that the reason why they believed not was not because God did not exert his physical, almighty power in them to make them believe, but because they neglected and received not his testimony given in the Word concerning his Son. 'These are written, that ye might believe that Jesus is the Christ, the Son of God, and that believing ye might have life through his name.' I saw that the requirement to believe in the Son of God was reasonable, because the testimony given was sufficient to produce faith in the sinner, and the invitations and encouragement of the gospel were sufficient, if believed, to lead him to the Saviour, for the promised Spirit, salvation and eternal life. This glimpse of faith, of truth, was the first divine ray of light that ever led my distressed, perplexed mind from the labyrinth of Calvinism and error, in which I had so long been bewildered. It was that which led me into rich pastures of gospel liberty".

At this time Stone went to see for himself something of the revival which he heard was going on in Kentucky and Tennessee. People were struck down and came into great spiritual anguish or joy; all classes were affected. After abundant and careful examination of the circumstances he was convinced that it was an awakening given by God. When he returned home to Cane Ridge and preached, the same things happened. At one meeting some 20,000 people were assembled and the meeting lasted for days. Presbyterian, Methodist and Baptist preachers preached at the same time in different parts of the camp. Party spirit disappeared. About 1000 persons of all kinds experienced these strange manifestations. Good results remained after the great excitement had passed. Slaves were liberated, churches increased in numbers and in zeal.

Several Presbyterian ministers, with Stone, at this time preached the sufficiency of the Gospel to save men, and that the testimony of God was designed and able to produce faith. Stone records, "the people appeared as just awakened from the sleep of ages—they seemed to see for the first time that they were responsible beings, and that the refusal to use the means appointed was a damning sin. "

Party zeal began to revive after a time and the Presbytery of Springfield, Ohio, brought one of these preachers before the Synod at Lexington. This led to the secession of five ministers, who formed the Springfield Presbytery and declared their abandonment of all confessions and creeds and their acceptance of the Scriptures alone as the guide to faith and practice.

Stone gathered his congregation together and told them that he could no longer support any religious system but would work henceforth for the advancement of Christ's kingdom and not for any party. He gave up his salary and worked hard at his little farm, while continuing to preach.

After a year, during which he acted in unison with the Springfield Presbytery, they all came to see that such an organisation was unscriptural, so gave it up. Their reasons are recorded in a document entitled "The last Will and Testament of Springfield Presbytery." They took the name of "Christian", which they believed to have been given by Divine appointment to the disciples at Antioch.

This company, meeting thus at Cane Ridge in 1804, thought that it was the first church that had met on the original Apostolic principles since the great departure from them in the time of Constantine.

Similar churches soon multiplied and each congregation was considered as an independent church. Believers' baptism began to be taught among them and was accepted and became their practice.

The movement spread rapidly through the Western States and coming into touch with the two others in the East and South, combined with them to form the "Christian Connection," all being of one mind to leave the bondage of human creeds, take the Scripture only as their guide and walk in the simplicity of the primitive churches.

These movements, arising independently of each other and only later discovering one another, had much in common with those churches where the Campbells were prominent. The churches of the "Christian Connection" were more active in preaching the Gospel and so increased more rapidly; the others were more occupied with teaching, so made more progress in knowledge.

The unusual ability and tireless activity of Alexander Campbell as editor, author, teacher, preacher, in public disputations, in educational work, in New Testament revision, and in other directions, led to a wide acceptance of his teaching.

The Baptist communities were greatly influenced by it, but those who were not prepared to accept the reform, gradually organized opposition which began to show itself in different places by a separation between the Baptists and the Reformers, and eventually the action of one of the Baptist Associations in excluding several prominent Reform preachers who worked among them, and further, in advising churches to exclude all Reformers from their communion, brought about a general separation (1832).

At the same time congregations and individuals connected with Alexander Campbell, and others associated with the older movement in which Stone was active, becoming acquainted with each other, found that their aims and principles were in most essentials alike. Where they differed they were rather complementary to each other than opposed, so that they began to coalesce. Both thought that a formal union, as between two bodies of believers, would be harmful, but in 1832 the fellowship of all these churches was acknowledged.

There had long been in these circles discussion as to the nature of conversion. It had been generally held that man is incapable of doing anything toward his own salvation, cannot even believe except by an operation of the Holy Spirit. Therefore there was much waiting for some inward spiritual experience which would be evidence of the work of the Holy Spirit in the heart. Then some began to point out that man's will must be exercised, that when he hears the Gospel he is responsible to accept it by faith, and that the responsibility for refusing or neglecting it, with consequent abiding loss, also lies upon him.

Walter Scott, one of the most devoted and successful evangelists working in connection with Thomas and Alexander Campbell, and who, before them, came into close intimacy of service in the Gospel with friends of Barton Warren Stone, was strongly affected by this question. He felt that much preaching is apparently ineffectual because it is not sufficiently impressed on the hearers that they are responsible to accept Christ by faith as their Saviour on the testimony of Scripture and apart from any feelings in themselves which they might consider were evidence of the working of the Holy Spirit. He noticed in the New Testament that those who believed were baptized, they were not afraid to take that definite action. Also he considered Peter's words recorded in Acts 2. 38, "Repent and be baptized every one of you in the name of Jesus Christ for the remission of sins, and ye shall receive the gift of the Holy Ghost": and began to appeal to his hearers to come forward and be baptized "for the remission of sins", adding these words, when he baptized, to those commanded by the Lord in Matt. 28. 19. This came to be a usual practice. Scott described conversion as: (1) faith, (2) repentance, (3) baptism, (4) remission of sins, (5) receiving the Holy Spirit.

The fellowship of so many churches and their occupation with the Scriptures quickened the preaching of the Gospel. Many men of all classes were raised up and fitted for service. They preached Jesus Christ and Him crucified, and their word was effectual. Thousands were converted and added to the churches, which grew and increased with great rapidity. Their opponents liked to call them "Stonettes" or "Campbellites," but they rejected these and all sectarian names. They spoke of themselves as "Christians", "Disciples", "Churches of Christ".

One of their leaders in the second generation, Isaac Errett (1820-1888) describes them thus:—"With us the divinity and Christhood of Jesus is more than a mere item of doctrine—it is the central truth of the Christian system, and in an important sense the creed of Christianity. It is the one fundamental truth which we are jealously careful to guard against all compromise. If men are right about Christ, Christ will bring them right about everything else. We therefore preach Jesus Christ and Him crucified. We demand no other faith, in order to baptism and church membership, than the faith of the heart that Jesus is the Christ, the Son of the living God; nor have we any term or bond of fellowship but faith in the divine Redeemer and obedience to Him. All who trust in the Son of God and obey Him are our brethren, however wrong they may be about anything else; and those who do not trust in the divine Saviour for salvation, and obey His commandments, are not our brethren, however intelligent and excellent they may be in all beside. . . . In judgments merely inferential we reach conclusions as nearly unanimous as we can; and where we fail, exercise forbearance, in the confidence that God will lead us into final agreement. In matters of opinion—that is, in matters touching which the Bible is either silent, or so obscure as not to admit of definite conclusions—we allow the largest liberty, so long as none judges his brother, or insists on forcing his opinions on others, or making them an occasion of strife."

These churches spread widely in Australia, were established in the United Kingdom, and reached many other countries. Tendencies towards the development of a denominational system naturally showed themselves in time. Some came to advocate drawing "missionary" work into dependence on a central organization. The influence of the popular rationalism of the day was felt in some quarters. At times discussions as to the interpretation or application of Scripture issued in divergencies of practice. All these experiences continue to illustrate the importance of the original "restoration testimony" as to the fact that a return to the Scripture is the one way to true unity of the churches and to their power to spread in the world, by giving to it the whole Word of God.

CHAPTER XV

Russia

1788-1914   850-1650   1812-1930   1823-1930   1828-1930

Mennonite and Lutheran emigration to Russia—Privileges change the character of the Mennonite churches—Wüst—Revival—Mennonite Brethren separate from Mennonite Church—Revival of Mennonite Church—Meetings among Russians forbidden—Circulation of Russian Scriptures allowed—Bible translation—Cyril Lucas—Stundists—Various avenues by which the Gospel came into Russia—Great increase of the churches—Political events in Russia lead to increased persecution—Exiles—Instances of exile and of the influence of the New Testament—Decree of the Holy Synod against Stundists—Evangelical Christians and Baptists—General disorder in Russia—Edict of Toleration—Increase of churches—Toleration withdrawn—Revolution—Anarchy—Rise of Bolshevik Government—Efforts to abolish religion—Suffering and increase—Communists persecute believers—J. G. Oncken—A Baptist church formed in Hamburg — Persecution — Tolerance — Bible School — German Baptists in Russia—Gifts from America—Nazarenes—Fröhlich—Revival through his preaching—Excluded from the Church—The Hungarian journeymen meet Fröhlich—Meetings in Budapest—Spread of the Nazarenes—Sufferings through refusal of military service—Fröhlich's teaching.

1788
-1914   THE descendants in Holland of those churches that had been revived by the labours of Menno in the 16th century prospered much when the power of Spain there had been broken under the leadership of the Prince of Orange and its tyranny replaced by an unprecedented liberty of conscience and freedom of worship.   By the 18th century they had become a wealthy body.   In Prussia, however, partly because of their refusal to do military service, they were subject to such disabilities that they became poor and dejected, so that, when an offer came from the Empress Catherine II of Russia, of land in the newly-occupied regions of South Russia, with liberty of worship and freedom from military service, it was welcomed as a God-given deliverance. *

The poorest were the most ready to go, and in 1788 there took place the first exodus of 228 families or some 1500 souls, who were established by the following year in the

---

* "Geschichte der Alt-Evangelischen Mennoniten Brüderschaft in Russland" P. M. Friesen.

Province of Ekaterinoslav, in the Chortitza District, on the river of the same name, which flows into the Dnieper. At first they had a struggle for mere existence, but other parties followed them, including some who were better supplied with means, and diligence soon brought prosperity. The expectation of the Russian Government that these farmers would raise the standard of agriculture and of living generally, was soon fulfilled. As the rich black soil yielded its abundant harvests of grain, orderly villages grew up, their wide straight streets lined with well-built homesteads; and the surrounding Russians and Tartars saw possibilities of wealth from the land of which they had never previously dreamed. Nor were these the only immigrants. Large numbers of Lutherans, chiefly from persecuted Pietist circles in Württemberg, also came to till the land and build villages over the country.

These were the beginnings of a colonization which increased greatly. In course of time the settlements spread over the south of Russia, into the Crimea, especially along the lower reaches of the Volga, to the Caucasus, and then away into Siberia and even to Turkestan and as far as the borders of China. Unabsorbed by the surrounding populations, the colonists kept their own language, religion and customs—compact bodies scattered like islands in the sea of Orthodox Slavs and other peoples of the vast Empire.

The privileges given by the Government quickly changed the character of the Mennonite churches, for in order to share these privileges the children had to become Mennonites, and so they were received into the church, not, as before, on the ground of their confession of faith in Christ and of giving evidence of the new birth, but were baptized and became members when they reached a certain age, or married. Thus the church became a National Church, having both converted and unconverted members. Speedily the moral tone degenerated. Families which, when they came, had been distinguished by their sobriety and piety, sank into open sin of all kinds, so that drunkenness, immorality and covetousness soon prevailed. There was always a godly remnant which protested against these evils and for themselves and their people deeply repented the failure of their testimony.

Their prayers were heard and it was from an unlooked-for quarter that help came. The keeper of an inn in Murrhard, Württemberg, had a son, Eduard Hugo Otto Wüst, whom he sent to study theology. In spite of a sinful life at the University of Tübingen the young man passed the requisite examinations, and, in 1841, entered on his clerical functions in the Württemberg National Church at Neunkirchen and Riedenau. He threw himself into his work with all his natural energy, became intimate with Pietists, Moravians and Methodists, and some three years after ordination experienced a change of heart and was enabled to put away the sinful habits which still clung to him. He received the full joy of the knowledge of the forgiveness of sins and the assurance of being a child of God, while awaiting the dawn of the year 1845. His preaching and Bible readings, both attractive and effectual, not only drew many around him but also aroused the envy and hatred of his fellow clergy. He was being subjected to vexatious and humiliating hindrances in his work, when through Pietist influence he received a call to a "Separatist" church at Neuhoffnung in South Russia. At the age of 28 he preached his first sermon in the church there. He was a big, strong man, with a powerful and pleasant voice and his warm sympathies attracted those with whom he came into contact. In his preaching he showed from the Scriptures what he had in his own heart experienced, the sufficiency of the atoning work of Christ and the assurance of salvation those may have who put their trust in Him. To an already overcrowded church came additional hearers from all the various circles, among them Mennonites. Wüst allowed no difference of denomination to limit his activities, so was soon holding Bible readings in Mennonite houses and preaching in their meeting rooms. A great awakening resulted. Sinners were brought to repentance and numbers of souls found peace through believing; there was a mighty turning from sin to godliness. Opposition soon showed itself. Wüst was forbidden the use of the Mennonite meeting rooms, but this did not check the progress of the revival. Difficulties arose through some who yielded themselves to excited and extravagant expressions of joy, mistaking their feelings for the leadings of the Spirit, but this feature of the movement, which could lead only to folly and sin, was eventually overcome and the good work persisted in spite of both inward and outward attacks. In 1859 Wüst died, being only in his 42nd year. In his lifetime some of the converted Mennonites took the Lord's Supper in his church with members of his own congregation.

After his death, in the same year, a number of Mennonite believers, feeling it to be no longer possible to take the Lord's Supper in their church together with the unbelievers, began to take it from time to time in private houses, with those only who confessed faith in Christ. This aroused great resentment, and although they had wished to avoid divisions, several were obliged to separate from the Mennonite church. Others soon followed and in 1860 a separate congregation of Mennonite brethren was formed.

The old Mennonite Church now acted towards the newly-formed churches of Mennonite Brethren in the same way as the state churches had acted in former times towards their own ancestors; they condemned them and handed them over to the civil authority for punishment, asking that they might be deprived of all their rights as Mennonites, and even threatening some with banishment to Siberia. For years this question was a subject of constant negotiation with the Government, during all which time the "Brethren" suffered severely; at last the Government granted to all Mennonites their original privileges, apart from any question as to their belonging to a particular church.

The meetings of Mennonite Brethren steadily increased, and, with their growth, the gifts of the Holy Spirit were abundantly manifested among them. In their endeavour to follow the New Testament teaching and pattern in their churches they saw that the method of baptizing in the Mennonite Church, by sprinkling, was not that of the Apostles, so they introduced the baptism of believers by immersion. Later some understood that fellowship should be with all saints and not only with Mennonites, and, though they were not all of the same mind in this matter, some of the churches had liberty to receive all whom they believed to belong to Christ. Visits from ministering brethren from abroad, from different bodies, helped in this.

One result of these events was a great change in the Mennonite Church. Although it continued to include believers and unbelievers in its membership, yet the reviving which had brought so many out from it proved effectual among many who remained in its fellowship. The Gospel was preached by its ministers with saving power, the godly life of those who were converted was a constant testimony to those around, so that sin was rebuked and the general tone of society, even among the unconverted, was raised. The bitterness, too, between the "Church" and the "Brethren" gradually softened and the believers in both branches were able to enjoy fellowship in Christ in spite of their divergences of view.

The vast need of the heathen world and the responsibility of taking the Gospel among those who had not heard it began to weigh upon many hearts, with the result that missionaries were sent out to India and other parts. The rapidly increasing wealth of these colonists became a temptation to many of them to be too much occupied with material things, but there were also those who used their wealth in the fear of God and for the advancement of His kingdom. Large numbers of them had emigrated to America, so that, in various ways, their interests stretched out far beyond their first limited circle into distant parts of the world.

Along with the privileges which the Mennonites received from the Russian Government there were also obligations and limitations. In place of military service, their young men were employed a certain number of years in forestry. It was altogether forbidden to them to hold meetings among the Russians or in any way "make propaganda" among members of the Greek Orthodox Church, and this condition, on which their own liberty of meeting was granted, they accepted and observed. There was remarkable spiritual activity and blessing in their villages scattered over the wide Russian steppes. Many Russian workpeople were employed by the Mennonites; some of these were present at the family worship daily held in the homes of the believers and there heard the Word of God. In the daily intercourse of men meeting each other on the farm or at market, and of women coming together in the house or on the fields, the Gospel became the subject of conversation.

850-
1650   The Russians did not know the Scriptures, read in their churches in the ancient Slav tongue no longer understood; as there was no preaching, only the ritual regularly gone

through, and the beautiful singing, they remained, with their priests, in comparative ignorance of the Divine revelation. The Orthodox Church, however, did not oppose the circulation of the Scriptures, but taught the people to regard the Bible as a holy book, the book of God. There was therefore an eager interest on the part of these Russians—a naturally religious people—to hear the unknown contents of the book they revered, and as the wonderful Gospel story reached them it was gladly received in many hearts.

As with many other nations, so among the Slav peoples also, the Bible was the beginning of literature. It was in order to bring the Bible to them that Cyril, in the 9th century, devised the Cyrillic alphabet, combining some Greek with the old Glagolitic characters in order to express the sounds of the Slavonic languages, and translating a great part of the New Testament. His companion, Methodius, laboured to preserve the right to use it when it was threatened by the advocates of Latin. From Moravia, where it originated, this old Slavonic Bible language spread, and became, rather than Greek, the church language of most of the countries of the Greek Orthodox Church. As the various branches of the Slav languages developed, the old language was no longer understood by the people, but in the 11th century the Russian ruler of Kiev, Yaroslav, translated parts of the Bible into the language spoken by his people.

It was the study of the Scriptures which led a shepherd and a deacon in the 14th century to preach at Pskov and afterwards in Novgorod, where crowds gathered to the fair. They showed that the priests of the Orthodox Church did not receive the Holy Spirit at their ordination and that there was no value in the sacraments they administered; that a church is an assembly of true Christians which can choose its own elders; that the members may take the Lord's Supper among themselves and baptize, and that every Christian may preach the Gospel. As usual in Russia, the Scriptures might be read but not acted upon, so their followers were suppressed and scattered.

In 1499 the Archbishop of Novgorod collected various Slavonic translations and published the whole Bible, which was printed in a complete form in Ostrog in 1581.

The Greek Orthodox Church differed from the Roman
Catholic Church in that it had not gone through any
experience comparable to the Reformation, but an attempt
to introduce the principles of the Reformation into it was
made, and that in the highest quarters. Cyril Lucas
(1572-1638), a native of Crete, was known as the most
learned man of his day. He was made successively Patriarch of Alexandria (1602) and Patriarch of Constantinople
(1621). It was he who discovered on Mount Athos a fifth-
century MS. which was then the oldest Greek Bible known.
He sent it from Alexandria to Charles I, King of England,
and it is in the British Museum, known as the Codex
Alexandrinus. While still Patriarch of Alexandria Cyril
began a careful comparison of the doctrines of the Greek,
Roman and Reformed churches with the Scriptures and
decided to leave the Fathers and accept the Scriptures as
his guide. Finding the teaching of the Reformers more in
accordance with the Scriptures than those of the Greek or
Roman churches he published a "Confession" in which he
declared himself in many respects one with the Reformers.
"I can no longer endure", he said, "to hear a man say that
the comments of human tradition are of equal weight with
Holy Scripture". He vigorously denounced the doctrine
of transubstantiation and the worship of images. He
taught that the one true Catholic Church must include all
the faithful in Christ, but, he said, there are visible
churches in different places and at different times; these
are capable of error and the Holy Scriptures are given as
an infallible guide and authority to which we must
always return; so he commended the constant study of
Scripture, which the Holy Spirit will enable those who are
born again to understand as they compare one part of it
with another. Such teachings coming from such a source
excited great discussion, and Cyril Lucas was involved in
strenuous conflict. Five times he was banished and as
often recalled. The Sultan's Grand Vizier trusted and
supported him, but this, while enabling him to keep his
position, injured his testimony, as it was felt to be incon-
gruous that a Christian teacher should depend for support
on a Mohammedan politician. At a Synod of the Greek
Church held in Bethlehem a general confirmation of the
old order in the Orthodox Church was reached, deprecating

reform. But the most effective opposition to this Greek Reformer came from the Latin Church, which through Jesuit intrigues repeatedly hindered his work, and at last by misrepresenting him in his absence to the Sultan Amurath, as this latter was marching on Bagdad, obtained a hasty order for his death and he was strangled with a bowstring in Constantinople and his body cast into the sea. After his death Synod after Synod condemned his doctrines.

1812
-1930

In 1812 the Czar Alexander I encouraged the establishment of the British and Foreign Bible Society in Russia, giving it special privileges, and a large number of branches were opened extending to the remotest parts of the Empire. There was an eager desire to obtain the Scriptures in the various languages spoken in the Empire, especially among those who spoke Russian, and the sales continually increased. The effect of this reading was wonderful, great numbers being turned from ignorance and sin to become diligent and whole-hearted followers of the Lord Jesus Christ. This naturally aroused opposition and the Holy Synod became active in hindering as far as possible the spread of the Scriptures, but until the establishment of the Bolshevik Government there remained many facilities for supplying a longing people with the Word of God.

The meetings of the German colonists were called in their own language *"Stunden"*, and as the Russians began to meet together for reading the Scriptures and prayer, they were called by way of reproach *"Stundists"*—that is, those who forsook their church for the "meeting". They did not themselves use this name but called each other brethren.

Reading the Scriptures was for these Russians an extraordinary revelation and power. They saw that the religious system in which they had been brought up had held them in ignorance of God and of His salvation in Christ. Repentance for their sins, which were many, was complete and unreserved. Their acceptance of Christ as their Saviour and Lord was in fulness of faith and love. Seeing the entire disagreement between the Russian Church and the teachings of Scripture, they left the former and attached themselves to the latter to the full extent of their knowledge.

Baptism was practised in different ways by the German colonists, but at the first none of them baptized by immersion; in the Greek Church baptism was indeed by immersion but was administered to infants. The Russian believers went to the Word and, uninfluenced by the practices that prevailed around them, came straightway to the conviction that the New Testament teaching and pattern was the baptism of believers by immersion, and in their thorough consistency immediately put this into practice, so that it became universal among those who believed. They apprehended, too, that the breaking of bread was the Lord's command and was for believers only, and on this apprehension they also acted. The clerical system of the Orthodox Church disappeared as they understood from the Scriptures the constitution of the Church and the churches, the priesthood of all believers, the indwelling of the Holy Spirit, the gifts and the liberty of ministry He gives for rule in the churches, for edifying the saints, and for spreading the Gospel among all men.

This movement, called *Stundist* by those outside, rapidly became so extensive, each group of converts becoming at once a church and centre from which the testimony radiated further, that it was evident the work of the Spirit wrought among the foreign colonists had been but the introduction and beginning of a far greater work laying hold of the masses of the Russian people. But the liberty of worship granted to the colonists was not accorded to the native citizens of the country, and the Russian churches had from the very beginning to endure persecution, which yet could not check their patient enthusiasm.

Although the Mennonites were so important a means of introducing the Gospel which was to prevail throughout wide areas of Europe and Asia, yet they were not the only agency employed. Bohnekämper,* sent by the Basle Mission to the Caucasus and expelled from that country, took a position as pastor in a German colony near Odessa, where he held Bible readings in Russian for the workpeople who came from many parts to work in the harvest and then carried back to their homes the Word they had received.

Members of the Society of Friends, as Étienne de Grellet, William Allen and others, visited St. Petersburg and had

* "Russland und das Evangelium" Joh. Warns.

intercourse there with the Czar Alexander I, influencing him in favour of the completion of the translation of the Bible into Russian. The Czar related to these Friends how he had never seen a Bible until he was forty years of age, but when at that time he was directed to it he devoured it, discovering there the expression of all his troubles as though he had described them himself; that from it he had received the inward light he possessed and had found it to be the unique source of the knowledge which saves. This experience made him willing to support the suggestions made by the Friends and to give facilities for the introduction and sale of the Scriptures in Russia, which were of incalculable value.

A Scotchman, Melville, known in Russia as Vassilij Ivanovitch, an agent of the British and Foreign Bible Society, devoted sixty years of his life to the circulation of the Scriptures in the Caucasus and South Russia, and not only to the distribution of the books, but also to the application of their contents to the consciences of those who bought them. He remained unmarried and made the spread of the Word of God in those countries his one object, in which he was a leader and example to many devoted colporteurs who followed in his footsteps.

The coming of a New Testament into a district has often been the means of the conversion of souls, the formation of a church and the further spread of the Gospel, before the existence of other brethren carrying out the Scriptures has been discovered. Examples of this have been met with in many places from Northern Siberia to the Southern shores of the Caspian.

From another side came Kascha Jagub, a Nestorian from Persia, who, by the help of the American Mission, came into Russia, developed a great gift for evangelization, especially among the poor, and, under the Russian name of Jakov Deljakovitch, travelled and preached throughout Russia and Siberia for nearly thirty years in the latter part of the 19th century.

Another class was reached by Lord Radstock, who, setting out from England in 1866, visited many lands, making known the Gospel, and came to St. Petersburg. There he held Bible readings in the houses of some of the aristocracy and a mighty work of the Spirit was manifested.

Numbers belonging to the highest circles were converted as they listened to his simple, straightforward expositions of Scripture, enforced by illuminating illustrations. Souls were affected even in the Imperial family and household. These believers carried out the teachings of the Word as consistently as the farmers and workpeople in the South, with whom they were soon in brotherly communion; they were baptized and observed the breaking of bread, and in their palaces the poorest and most ignorant Christians sat side by side with the highest in the land, united by the bond of a common life in Christ.

Among those converted was a wealthy landowner, Colonel Vassilij Alexandrovitch Paschkov. He gave the ball-room of his palace for meetings and himself preached the Gospel everywhere, in prisons and hospitals as well as in meeting-places and houses. He used his great wealth in distributing the Scriptures, publishing tracts and books, helping the poor and in every way furthering the kingdom of God. Paschkov was forbidden to hold meetings in his house (1880). As he continued to do so he was banished, by the influence of the Holy Synod, first from St. Petersburg and later from Russia, and much of his property confiscated.

The German Baptists had spread into Russia from Germany and become numerous in Poland and many other parts, but had liberty only on condition that they confined their ministry to Germans or others not of the Orthodox Church. Their influence, however, led in time to the establishing of congregations of Russian Baptists which also spread with great rapidity. The chief difference between these and the other churches was that the Baptist churches belonged to a definite federation or organization of churches, while the others looked upon each church as an independent congregation in direct dependence on the Lord, the communion between the different churches being maintained by personal intercourse and the visits of ministering brethren. Also, among the Baptists each church had, as far as possible an appointed pastor, while among the others there was liberty of ministry and the elders were chosen among themselves.

So through various avenues the Gospel came into those immense territories, but, once received, it was taken up

by the Russians themselves, and was never a "foreign
mission" or a foreign institution among them.   They
apprehended from the first that the Word of God was for
them, immediately, without the intervention of any
Society or Mission, and that the responsibility of the
ministry of reconciliation was committed to them.   This
responsibility with all its cost and all its suffering they
undertook with a whole-hearted zeal that nothing could
quench.   On this account the Gospel spread, and continues to spread, over those continents in a way altogether
different from what is possible where the work is maintained and controlled by a foreign Missionary Society
The churches in Russia are now to be counted by thousands
and their members by millions.

From their early beginnings these churches had been
subject to irregular persecution but this became more
general and more severe owing to developments in the
political situation.   The autocratic form of government,
with its harsh suppression of individual liberty, led to the
formation of secret societies, the aim of which was to break
the existing tyranny by any means, however ruthless, and
the murders and outrages of these Nihilists terrified the
ruling class into still more drastic measures of repression.
The Czar, Alexander II, was personally desirous of reform
though he did not realize the gravity of the gathering storm
of resentment and indignation   caused by   centuries
of unrestrained oppression.   Yet he was seriously occupied
in bringing in important changes in this direction when,
in 1881, he was blown to pieces by a Nihilist bomb in the
streets of St. Petersburg, and a violent reaction to the most
complete absolutism resulted.   His successors, with their
advisers, set themselves to crush, not only the desperate
revolutionaries, but also every kind of divergence from their
ideal of a Holy Russia with absolute autocratic government in State and Church.   Political dissenters, the non-
Russian elements in the population of the Empire, especially the Jews, the Universities, too, and many others
came under the rod, and it was evident that the churches
of believers outside the Orthodox Church would not be
spared.

In Pobiedonostsef, the head of the Holy Synod, they

found a bitter and consistent adversary. Imprisonment,
fines and exile were their lot, while the priests incited the
people to attack and maltreat them and to destroy their
homes and their goods. Their meetings were forbidden,
and when they were found coming together secretly for
prayer and reading the Scriptures their gatherings were
forcibly broken up and arrest and punishment followed.
Increasing numbers, especially of the elders and leaders
of the churches, were banished to Siberia or the Caucasus.
This proved to be a means of spreading the testimony, for
wherever these exiles went they were witnesses for Christ.
Sometimes the disciples were brought before courts and
formally condemned and sentenced, often they were exiled
by administrative order, and then no accusation or trial
was required. Banishment was an especially cruel punishment. Heavy chains were fastened on the hands and feet
of those condemned, those on the feet being so long that the
prisoner had to lift and carry them in his hands in order to
walk. The hundreds of miles to the places of banishment
were, in the earlier years, covered on foot; later, many
were sent by rail in waggons into which air and light
entered only through a small, closely barred opening.
If means were available, the wives and children of the
exiles might accompany them into exile. All were at the
mercy of the rough and brutal soldiery which drove the
wretched train of criminals, mingled with political and
religious dissenters, adding to their misery with the cruel
knout and anything else caprice suggested. The prisons
on the way were the halting places. There different bands
were collected until the order for the further march was
given, waiting sometimes hours and sometimes months.
These prisons were terribly overcrowded; often at night
there was not room for all to lie upon the floor so that they
had to lie one on top of another. There was no sanitary
accommodation nor any means of washing, while the lice
and other vermin swarming over the prisoners, who were
often covered with sores, added to their wretchedness.
The food was of the worst, nor was there refuge for any
man, woman, or child, from any injustice or outrage
those in charge of them might like to inflict. There were
some humane men among the officials, but they could do
little against the crushing system of which they formed a

part.   In the distant places of their banishment the exiles had to maintain themselves as best they could. They were not allowed to leave the town or village allotted to them, where sometimes they did not understand the language spoken. Large numbers died of the privations and cruel treatment they received on the way and never reached their destination. When banishment was not for life a term of years was set, but frequently, when this had expired and the captive looked for liberty, a further term was added. In countless Russian villages and in all the towns, year after year, the conflict was carried on. On the one side, an ever-increasing number of people, of all classes, who through the Scriptures had found in Christ their Saviour and their Lord and were set on following Him and on making the Word of God their guide in all things; on the other side, all the resources and power of the vast Russian Empire used to make this impossible, to compel these Christians to deny the faith and to return to the dead forms and idolatries from which Christ had set them free. All these powers, Imperial and Orthodox, failed before the indomitable patience and burning zeal of the saints.

At the very time that these persecutions were going on the sale of the New Testament was favoured and there were instances where, through personal influence in the highest quarters, permission was obtained to visit the prisons and distribute the Book, Dr. Baedeker being one who was devoted and untiring in this service; but those who acted on its precepts were treated as criminals and suffered accordingly.

Among countless incidents on record a few may give some faint impression of the whole. In Poland a young man attended meetings where he heard the Gospel preached and was converted to Christ from his careless, sinful life. He could not help telling others of the salvation he had found, and a number of sinners turned to God. He became one of a group of fourteen young men who were exiled to a place beyond Irkutsk in Siberia. Of these, seven died on the way, the remainder were kept three and a half years in prison and then liberated. Six of them died very soon of consumption contracted in prison. The one who was left, having lost all touch with his people in Poland (though he had been married there and had left his wife and baby son behind) and being without means for accomplishing the long journey back, got work as a blacksmith and remained in Siberia. He did not cease to witness for Christ and a church was founded and grew and prospered in the place where he was.

A young woman living with her parents, well-to-do farmers, was converted and was diligent in speaking to her friends and neighbours of the Saviour. She was sentenced to life-long banishment to Siberia. It was made possible for her to take the journey by rail. When the prisoners' wagon in which Maria was known to be, came to the station nearest to her home, a large crowd of relations and sympathizers gathered round. Only a glimpse of her face could be seen as she pressed it to the thick bars of the small opening, but she could better see them. "I love you", she said, "Father, Mother, brothers, sisters, friends, I shall never see you again, but do not think that I regret what I have done; I am glad to suffer for my Saviour's sake, who suffered all things for me". The train moved on, she was not heard of again, but a boy in the crowd went home weeping and soon decided to follow Christ himself. He grew up to be an effectual preacher of the Gospel through whom many were brought to the obedience of faith.

A peasant living in a village some distance north of Omsk where the openings in the great forests of larch and silver-birch give room for cultivation, was called up for military service and took part in the Japanese war. From a comrade he obtained a New Testament, in reading which he became a new man. His former drunken and wicked habits were changed into the sobriety and honesty and peace becoming a Christian. When he returned to his native village the change was noticed, but his friends were less struck by his altered conduct than by what seemed to them to be his loss of religion, since he took no part in the ceremonies of the Orthodox Church nor did he keep the usual ikons or holy pictures in his house. He took to reading his Testament with a neighbour, who also accepted Christ by faith and showed it in his changed life. This alarmed the priest, upon whose advice the second farmer was caught and beaten by his father and brothers until they supposed that he was dead.   His wife, however, dragged him into their hut and nursed him back to life. In the meantime others, hearing the contents of this Testament, followed Christ, and those that believed met on every possible occasion for the reading of the book. They found as they read that it was the practice of the early disciples to baptize those that believed, so they went to the river Irtish which flowed past their village of disorderly scattered huts, and there the ex-soldier began to baptize, and he and others continued this as occasion required. They understood as they read, from the beginning, that they were a church, such as is described in the Scriptures, gifts of the Holy Spirit were evident among them, there were elders, fitted to guide, teachers, evangelists—indeed each was in some way helpful to the whole.   Each first day of the week they met and remembered the Lord's death in the breaking of bread, having found this also as they read.   The priest and his sympathizers took such measures as seemed to them suitable to check the movement.   Windows and doors of the believers' houses were broken, they themselves were beaten, their cattle were driven away, all kinds of injuries were inflicted and were borne with patience and courage and made a constant occasion of prayer.   When about half the inhabitants of the village had been added to the church such violence could not be continued. Then the priest had recourse to asserting that the new religion was only the idea of an ignorant Russian *moujik*, or peasant, that no intelligent people believed such things. One day four strangers drove into this remote village and were surprised when their carriage was surrounded by the people, who drew them out and into their houses, plying them with questions more quickly than they could answer them. Soon the whole village was gathered together and each of these strangers, one after the other, declared that he had been saved by the grace of God through faith in the Lord Jesus Christ, and that his aim now was to act in all things in obedience to the Word of God.   This gave great joy to the brethren in the village, they would not have been turned aside had these visitors spoken otherwise, but it was a confirmation of faith to find that they were brethren, and many who had still hesitated confessed Christ.   A further supply of Scriptures was brought in and as long as these brethren stayed Bible study was the eager occupation of the church almost continually, day and night.

A working man in South Russia was a diligent and faithful helper in the congregation of believers in the place where he lived. On this account he had much to suffer, and one night his hut was surrounded by armed police who broke into it and brutally ill-treated him and his wife and children. He was arrested and taken away. The wife gave birth to a child and died, the child also. There were four children left, the eldest a girl of about 13. They had now only one object in life, and that was to find and rejoin their father. They learned that he had been banished to Vladikavkas in the Caucasus, and determined to follow him there. Slowly they crossed the wide steppes, sometimes helped by the brethren and sometimes begging as they went. On reaching Vladikavkas they found that their father had been forwarded to Tiflis. The believers kept them and refreshed them, and then set them out on the fine mountain road up the valley of the Terek; they saw the great massif of Kasbek and descended the sunny southern slopes of the Caucasus range to Tiflis. Here they were kindly received by the brethren, Russian, Armenian and German, but were told that their father had just been sent further to a remote part, among the Tartars, near the Persian frontier. They could go no further, but, seeing their distress, two brethren undertook to follow the father, carry supplies to him, and assure him that his children would be cared for. They reached the town just after his arrival, only to learn that having at last come to his place of exile, broken in health and heart, he had lain down and died.

In 1893 a decree was published giving regulations arrived at some time before by the Holy Synod, meeting under the presidency of Pobiedonostsef, according to which the children of Stundists were to be taken away from their parents and given over to relatives in the Orthodox Church, failing whom, they were to be put under the charge of the local clergy. The names of the members of this sect were to be made known to the Minister of Communications who was to post up the lists of names in the offices and workshops of the railways, so that they might find no employment there. Any employer having a Stundist in his service would be liable to a heavy fine. Stundists were forbidden either to rent or purchase land. It was forbidden to all "sectaries" to remove from one place to another. They were declared legally incapable of carrying on banking or commerce. Leaving the Orthodox Church was to be punished by the loss of civil rights and with exile, at the least with a year and a half in a Reformatory. Preachers and authors of religious works were to be punished with 8 to 16 months' imprisonment; in case of a repetition of the offence, with 32 to 48 months in a fortress; the third time with exile. Anyone spreading heretical doctrines, or assisting those who did so, was to be punished with banishment to Siberia, Transcaucasia or some other distant part of the Empire.

The Baptists, being an organized body, received at times a measure of toleration not granted to those often called "Evangelical Christians", among whom each congregation was an independent church. These latter, having no earthly head or centre, could not be brought under Government influence or control even to the limited extent possible in the case of the Baptist federation. Increasing pressure was put upon them to organize and to appoint some representative with whom the Government could .eat; some yielded in order to obtain relief; but others refused on the ground that such a course would draw them away from direct dependence on the Lord Jesus Christ and responsibility to Him.

Repressive measures in Russia generally grew, and were answered by further outrages. The Japanese war did not arouse enthusiasm and its failure awakened hopes of successful revolution. Strikes and rioting broke out in many places, and a general strike of railway workers paralyzed communications. Small, insufficient reforms only increased the irritation, and attacks of Tartars on Armenians fomented in the Caucasus, or of Russian mobs on Jews, or of the Baltic peoples on the German-Russians there, led to dreadful massacres while in no way checking revolutionary activities, and soon Russia was in disorder from end to end.

Compelled by events, the unwilling Government yielded large measures of reform and among these an edict of the Czar in 1905 granted liberty of faith and conscience and also freedom of meeting. Pobiedonostsef retired and the

Metropolitan of the Russian Church declared: "True faith is obtained by the grace of God, through instruction, humility and good examples; on this account the use of force is denied to the Church, which does not count it needful to hold erring children fast against their will. Therefore the Orthodox Church has nothing against the rescinding of the law forbidding to separate from the Orthodox Church. "

Large and immediate use was made of the new liberty. Meetings were held everywhere—crowded with hearers who seemed as though they never could hear enough of the Word. Great numbers confessed Christ. The preaching was often punctuated by the responses of the hearers; many would fall on their knees or on their faces; when there was prayer they could not wait for each other, but many would be praying aloud at the same time, and this was intermingled with responses, confession of sins, thanksgiving for salvation. Many hidden companies of believers came to light and it became evident that the number of the Lord's disciples was far larger than had been supposed. Hindrances to the study of the Word being removed, Bible readings and expositions of Scripture increased on all hands. There was the same desire as before to carry out the Word of God in every way, and gifts of the Spirit for the ministry were manifested among the believers, and that from all classes and positions.

This liberty did not last long. As the Government and the Orthodox Church regained power the concessions wrung from them were withdrawn, persecution began again in the accustomed way, and in a short time the believers and the churches were suffering as before. When, in 1914, the war broke out which was to involve so great a part of the world, a number of elder brethren among the "Evangelical Christians" and of Baptist pastors were banished to Siberia and to the shores of the White Sea. In 1917 the Revolution began, before which, in so short a time, the Czar and his Ministers, the Orthodox Church and all the old Russia fell, and a new era made its stormy entrance.

At the beginning of the Russian Revolution religious liberty was proclaimed, but the country, after such long oppression and suffering, added to now by the losses of war, was thrown into further disorder by the struggles of conflicting parties striving for rule. In large districts there was absolute anarchy, armed bands of ruffians subjecting the helpless people to frightful outrage. As the Bolshevik party gained control, the introduction of its principles was accompanied by wholesale murder, robbery and destruction. Famine soon appeared and this vast country, once so rich in food supplies, became a veritable sepulchre. The Bolshevik Government set itself to destroy utterly all religion of every kind, so that the Orthodox Church, once the persecutor, became now the persecuted. The Roman Catholics, too, and the Lutherans, had to suffer in their turn, and the congregations of believers with the rest.

In South Russia bands of brigands sometimes grew to the size of armies; they were attracted by the wealth of the Mennonites, who suffered so terribly from them that many of the men, in spite of their traditions, followed the example of others and joined the companies formed for the protection of the women and children. The experiences of the brethren were as in the early days. As, then, James was killed "with the sword" while Peter was delivered from prison, so, now, some had miraculous deliverances while others were allowed to suffer all that the wickedness of men could inflict upon them. Many thought they were living in the days of the "great tribulation". There was great power with the Gospel; large numbers were converted, including the most desperate sinners, soldiers of the Red Army, so degraded that they had ceased to take pleasure in anything but shedding blood. Suffering saints were greatly sustained; it was often said by those who had passed through every extremity of misery and outrage: "Do not pity us, we have rather reason to pity you, for we have learned things about God that you cannot know".

When the first rage of murder was over, and people began to accommodate themselves as best they could to the new form of tyranny which had replaced the old, the churches of those that believed found themselves face to face with new forms of trial. Greatly increased in numbers, they had at times, and in some places, considerable liberty, and they increased more rapidly than ever before, though always liable to a return of ruthless repression. The anti-

Christian propaganda of the Government called for special gifts and ability on the part of the evangelists and others who had to meet it, and these were abundantly given to them. The unorganized congregations were pressed by promises and threats to join in a "Soviet" or Federation with which the Government could deal in a way that it could not with a multitude of independent churches; many yielded, but many chose to continue in the way they saw to be according to the teaching of the Word and Apostolic example, accepting the deprivations and losses that accompanied it.

Atheism was imposed upon the people by force; violence and cruelty were used to compel them to profess the belief that there is no God. Then the devastating German invasion (1941) and the resistance to it brought about rapid and fundamental changes and developments which had an important part in moderating religious persecution, and an increasing measure of toleration and liberty of conscience was obtained. The vast extent of Russia and the character of many of its inhabitants give special importance to these developments. Multitudes who were illiterate now read; an agricultural people has seen a feverishly rapid introduction of industry; and to give spiritual liberty to such is likely to unleash energies of immense and salutary importance.

1823-
1930   What has passed current for history has been so successful in confounding those godly men who practised the baptism of believers only with the authors of the sinful extravagances of Münster in the 16th century, that when in 1834 some ten men and women living in Hamburg were baptized as believers, by immersion, in accordance with what they believed to be the teaching of Scripture, the prejudice against it was so strong that the baptism had to take place secretly, at night, in order to avoid menacing interruption.

One of those baptized was Johann Gerhard Oncken*, and his inclusion in the company was of unforeseen importance, for he originated Baptist churches, which, after early struggles against bitter prejudices, spread rapidly through Germany and adjacent lands, into South-Eastern Europe and into vast Russia, so that their members came to be counted by hundreds of thousands.

* "Johann Gerhard Oncken. His Life and Work." John Hunt Cook.

Oncken's life covered most of the 19th century; he was born in 1800 and lived until 1884. He was a native of the little Duchy of Varel, ruled by the Bentinck family, a branch of which crossed to England with William of Orange and became famous here. Oncken's father was concerned in one of the patriotic risings against Napoleon and had to escape to England, where he died, never having seen his son Johann Gerhard, who was born just after his father's flight.

The Lutheran church in Varel had come at this time under the influence of Rationalism and the young man grew up without the knowledge of the way of salvation. When he was 14 a Scotsman doing business in Varel liked the lad and asked him whether he had a Bible. "No", said he, "but I have been confirmed". The Scotsman gave him a Bible, and also took him with him to Scotland. There, in a Presbyterian church, he first clearly heard the Gospel, and was impressed. Later, in London, living in a godly family, he was further affected, especially by their family worship and by the preaching in the Congregational church to which they belonged; and at last, listening to a sermon in Great Queen Street Methodist chapel, he found assurance of salvation and a joy in the Lord which led him from the first day to be a witness for Christ and to try to bring others to the Saviour.

In 1823 he returned to Hamburg, appointed as their missionary to Germany by "The Continental Society" founded shortly before in London for evangelical work on the Continent of Europe. He soon showed gifts as a preacher which attracted increasing numbers, and conversions took place as he announced the Gospel in rooms and various places up and down the city. Opposition to what people called "the English religion" involved him in fines and imprisonments, but his activities continued. *
He opened a Sunday School; and, having always been active in distributing the Scriptures, in 1828 he also became agent for the Edinburgh Bible Society, a position he occupied for fifty years, printing and distributing in that time two million Bibles.

* "To the Members of the Sixth Assembly of the German Evangelical Churches held in Berlin 1853. Subject, 'How the Church should act in reference to Separatists and Sectarians viz. Baptists and Methodists'" G. W. Lehmann.

Studying the Scriptures himself, Oncken gradually came to the conviction that the New Testament teaches the baptism by immersion of believers, and as he considered the numbers of converts and of friends with whom he was associated the thought shaped itself in his mind that these should be gathered into churches on the New Testament pattern, by which he understood that none but believers baptized by immersion should be admitted as members. Although several, after studying the Scriptures together, had decided to be baptized they were hindered in carrying out their project by the difficulty of finding anyone to baptize them. Some of their number suggested that they should organize churches in the meantime without baptism and take the Lord's Supper together. Oncken, however, thought this would be a bad beginning and likely to spoil the whole movement from the first. After waiting five years they came into touch with an American Baptist, Professor Sears, who baptized them, and on the following day those baptized formed themselves into a church and chose Oncken as their pastor, whom Sears then ordained.

The civil authorities in Hamburg soon announced their intention not to tolerate this new "sect" in their city, and Oncken and others had to undergo fines and imprisonment. One place where they were imprisoned was the Winserbaum, a prison building washed on two sides by the water, an unhealthy and evil-smelling place.

Capable fellow-workers joined Oncken, among them Julius Köbner, the son of a Jewish Rabbi in Denmark, a hymn writer and preacher, also Gottfried Wilhelm Lehmann, baptized in Berlin with five others, by Oncken, who then organized them as the first Baptist church in that city. The work spread rapidly, accompanied by persecutions, chiefly fines and imprisonment imposed by the authorities, but also at times violence of the people. Gradually the confidence of the authorities was gained and persecution lessened. In 1856 the Hamburg church was given full toleration, and in 1866 all religious denominations were declared to be on an equality in that city.

Oncken and Köbner began to give short courses in Bible study to young men in order to prepare them to become pastors of the churches that were springing up. From this beginning the Hamburg Baptist College developed, giving

a four years' course of training to those about to become
pastors. The growing movement was organized in the
different countries to which it spread, annual conferences of
delegates were held and committees of "managing brethren" appointed to attend to various business. Large
financial help was given from America. Oncken was made
a missionary of the American Baptist Missionary Society,
and so enabled to travel extensively, support being given
to the College and other organizations and to the work
generally. At the same time the converts of different
nationalities took their share in the burdens.

As churches of German Baptists grew up among the large
German population of Russia they came into touch with
older companies of Russian believers who also practised
believers' baptism, and in many instances the German
Baptists succeeded in absorbing these into their organization, so that the numerous Russian churches came to be
divided into two great streams. The original Russian
churches maintained the independence of each congregation,
whereas the Baptists formed a federation affiliated with
churches in Germany and America. The Baptists aimed at
having a pastor over each church, and the administration of
baptism and the Lord's Supper lay chiefly in his hands; the
older Russian churches had elders in every church and
emphasized the priesthood of all believers and liberty of
ministry. The experiences of the different congregations
were affected by these points. The Government favoured
the Baptist system, because it was easier to deal with
pastors locally, and with an organization generally which
had a visible centre and head, than with the brethren
who maintained their independent, congregational
principle, for they were less easily influenced by pressure
from without. On this account the authorities, who often
imposed on the latter the name "Evangelical Christians",
tried in various ways to oblige them to organize and appoint a central Committee and President.

The question, too, of the acceptance of large gifts from
American Baptists was diversely judged. It was evident
that the Russian Baptists were greatly helped in their work
by these gifts, and a proposal was made that they might
be extended to those congregations of brethren who did
not take the name Baptist. The liberal and kindly offer

was made that, should such gifts be accepted, no name would be imposed upon them nor any change required in their church government or in any other way, only they would be counted in the World Union of Baptist Churches. A section of the brethren and of the meetings they belonged to was in favour of accepting this important help, but the greater number declined it, because, while they recognized and appreciated the love and generosity that prompted the gift, they felt that the acceptance of it would place them under an obligation, would alter their circumstances in a way that could not fail eventually to exercise an influence on their course, would tend to draw them away from their entire, manifest dependence on God, and would *give colour to the accusation that they represented a foreign religion and a foreign power ;* whereas they believed that the principles of Scripture are applicable to all countries alike and to all circumstances, as much to the poverty of Russia as to the wealth of America.

828 -
1930   The traveller through Central and Southern Europe cannot but be struck by the number of villages he passes, and may sometimes wonder what is going on in these groups of human dwellings, often so uncouth in appearance, differing so completely from the better known surroundings of the town dwellers.   They are often the scene of vivid spiritual experiences, and here also are many who are seriously affected by the importance of personal and corporate obedience to the Word of God.

In Hungary, Yugoslavia, Bulgaria, Roumania are numerous congregations of people who call themselves *"Nazarenes"*.* They live so quietly, so much to themselves, that they would hardly ever be heard of except for their constant conflict with the various Governments, due to their absolute refusal to bear arms.

Of themselves they write : "The Apostles preached repentance and faith; such as believed were added unto the people of the Lord. . . . Their brothers in the faith were to be found throughout all the centuries—here and there. . . . To-day there still exists a people—God's own—whose members are dispersed all over the world, living quietly

*Nazarenes in Jugoslavia" Apostolic Christian Publishing Co. Syra-
cuse N.Y., U.S.A.

and in seclusion, far away from politics, far away from the pleasures of the world. . . . Although they are not bound together by race, by origin, or by speech, nor by economic, political, or any other kind of bond, they are firmly united among themselves by a mighty spiritual bond, by divine love. . . . They too became members of this people, God's own, by a spiritual re-birth. . . . They are wedded to their Redeemer and Saviour, Jesus Christ, and they serve Him with soul and body, because He has bought them with His own blood from the world. . . His divine teaching is their guidance for life".

Continuing their account of themselves, they say: "The bright glory of Christ's teaching dimmed. . . . Then it was that God awakened in Switzerland, in the year 1828, a true and faithful witness in the person of the preacher S. H. Fröhlich, who entered into the 'new life in Christ' by his re-birth. . . . It was he who re-lit the candles with the bright light of the Gospel. On that account he was dismissed from his office or parsonage, in 1830. He began to preach the pure Gospel and brought together many believers in congregations. He evangelized from Switzerland up to the city of Strasburg, where he died in the year 1857, a true and faithful servant of the Lord. . . . The Jews called the Apostle Paul 'a ringleader of the sect of the Nazarenes' . . . the 'believers in Christ' are called 'Nazarenes' in Austria, in Hungary and in the Balkans, to this very day".

Born in Brugg, Aarau, in the year 1803, Samuel Heinrich Fröhlich studied theology in Zürich and Basle and became a Rationalist.* Unbelief led to sin and made him an opponent of the Moravian Brethren and of such as held Bible readings for the study of the Greek New Testament; indeed of all who aimed at spiritual reviving. But when about 22 years of age he was awakened; he now realized his unfitness for his calling as a preacher. He vowed faithfulness to God and endeavoured to overcome sin, yet only found himself involved the more in failure and misery. In the woods and on the mountains he prayed and cried to God for help, but found none, until he was able to look to Jesus and found peace in Him. In his father's house he prepared himself diligently for his examination. His

*"Einzelne Briefe und Betrachtungen aus dem Nachlasse von S. H. Fröhlich."

evangelical leanings displeased his examiners, and delayed his ordination, which, however, took place in 1827. During short periods in different parishes his study of the Scriptures led him into greater spiritual liberty. He was sent to a godless congregation in Leutweil and there his preaching of Christ crucified caused a revival to break out. This aroused the opposition of the clergy. He was now compelled, before delivering his sermons, to submit them to his church elders as well as to the surrounding clergy. These struck out all such passages as referred to man as being "dead in trespasses and sins", or justified only in Jesus Christ through faith. These teachings were bringing life and deliverance to burdened souls, but they were folly and stumbling to the wise. In teaching his catechists he received light as to baptism according to the New Testament. In spite of constant persecution he continued his labours for two years, till in 1830, with the support of the Government, the ecclesiastical authorities removed all the old religious books, replacing them by others of a rationalistic character. Refusing to accept these books, he was brought up before the authorities both for this offence and for other behaviour in which he had been displeasing to them. This resulted in his condemnation and deposition on the ground that he had acted contrary to law.

Two Hungarian journeymen locksmiths, Johann Denkel and another, in the course of their travels came from Budapest to Zürich, where they met Fröhlich and were converted and baptized. Returning to Budapest, Denkel was diligent in speaking to his fellow-workmen of the Gospel. Among those who believed was Ludwig Hencsey, who became a most active and successful worker, founding many congregations of the "Nazarenes". One whom he was early able to lead to Christ was a nobleman, Josef Kovacs, who corresponded with Fröhlich in Latin (1840). A widow, Anna Nipp, gave a room in her house in Budapest as the first meeting place. Hencsey wrote books explaining the principles of the faith, which, being copied out and distributed by the converts, were the means of adding many to their number (1840-1). A band went out from Budapest in different directions to carry the faith, the congregations spreading as far as the frontiers of Turkey; while in America also many were founded.

Wherever the Nazarenes are found they have acknowledged the constituted authorities and have served them loyally, but in respect of bearing arms and of taking oaths they have been inflexible in their refusal. Despite their willingness to serve in any non-combatant capacity, no consideration has been shown them by the military authorities. Moreover, their very numerical strength has but intensified the efforts to break down their opposition. They have been treated with great severity; always large numbers of them have been in prison, where many have spent the best part of their lives under wretched conditions, separated from their families and friends. Their patient submission as they have been brought into Court in batch after batch and condemned to long terms of imprisonment— seldom less than ten years—has won the admiration of many who do not share their convictions. Yet their martyrdom continues, many have been savagely ill-treated in addition to their imprisonment, and there are cases where, having almost served their term of punishment, they have been granted (without asking for it) a pardon, with restoration of their civil and military status, then immediately required to bear arms, and, upon their renewed refusal, been condemned to the full term of imprisonment over again, no account being taken of what they had already suffered.

Owing to his own experiences, Fröhlich wrote with unmeasured condemnation of the formal religion prevailing in the great Churches, Catholic and Protestant, and the Nazarenes generally are unsparing in their denunciation of what they believe to be contrary to the teaching of the New Testament. Among them a Lutheran church may be described as a "den of thieves", while many of them seem hardly to believe in the possibility of salvation outside their own circles. This exaggeration shows itself in Fröhlich's teaching.

Writing* on "The Mystery of Godliness and the Mystery of Iniquity" (1 Tim. 3. 16; 2 Thess. 2. 7), he says that what mankind now suffers under is not the result of Adam's transgression, which was put away by the death of Christ; but that on account of man's unbelief

* "Das Geheimniss der Gottseligkeit und das Geheimniss der Gottlosigkeit" S. H. Friölich, St. Gallen 1838.

towards Christ, Satan has been allowed to bring into the world a second deception and second fall, through which the members of the so-called Christian Church have come to count their Christianity as something they are born into, which they ground on their infant baptism and other forms, without being truly converted from sins and idols and the power of Satan. The imitated forms of Divine service and of piety, without power, are the second and worse deceit of Satan, which brings after it the second death. Only those called of God, who have made their calling and election sure through entire sanctification, are delivered from it.

These brethren, scattered over the wide valley and plains of the middle Danube and stretching far into the Balkans, are distinguished among their neighbours by their gravity and quiet diligence. Persecution has hammered them into a hardness of resistance not to be overcome, yet, in spite of a strain of hard legality, they exercise patient forbearance under harsh and unrighteous treatment, not resisting evil; and by the simplicity and Scriptural character of their worship and of their church life are a testimony to those around them.

CHAPTER XVI

Groves, Müller, Chapman

1825-1902

Churches formed in Dublin—A. N. Groves—Leaves with party for
Bagdad—Work begun—Plague and flood—Death of Mrs. Groves—
Arrival of helpers from England—Colonel Cotton—Removal of Groves
to India—Objects of his stay there—To bring missionary work back to
the New Testament pattern—To reunite the people of God—George
Müller—Henry Craik—Church formed at Bethesda Chapel, Bristol, to
carry out New Testament principles—Müller's visit to Germany—
Institutions and Orphanage carried on for the encouragement of faith in
God—Robert Chapman—J. H. Evans—Chapman's conversion—His
ministry in Barnstaple and travels—Circles accepting the Scriptures as
their guide.

IN the early part of the 19th century a number of people
were impressed by the importance as well as by the
possibility of a return to the teachings of Scripture, not
only in respect of questions of personal salvation and
conduct, but also as regards the order and testimony of the
churches.   A serious attempt was made to put such convictions into practice.*

Anthony Norris Groves, a dentist living in Plymouth,
was visiting Dublin in 1827 in connection with studies at
Trinity College.   In conversation with John Gifford
Bellett, a barrister and native of Dublin, with whom he
was associated in Bible study, Groves remarked that it
appeared to him from Scripture that believers meeting together as disciples of Christ were free to break bread together as their Lord had admonished them; and that, if they
were guided by the practice of the apostles they would set
apart every Lord's Day for thus remembering the
Lord's death and obeying His parting command.   Not long
afterwards they found a group of believers in Dublin who
were already meeting in this way.

One of the earliest members of this group was Edward
Cronin.   Originally a Roman Catholic, he had become
attached to the Independents.   Realizing the essential

*MSS. of J. G. Bellett and Ed. Cronin.
"A History of the Plymouth Brethren" W. Blair Neatby.

unity of the people of God, he was in the habit of taking the Lord's Supper from time to time with different bodies of Nonconformists.   Settling in Dublin, he found it was required of him that he should become definitely a member of one of them, otherwise he would not be allowed to break bread with any.   Seeing that this was a contradiction of the very unity he sought to recognize, Cronin refused com pliance, whereupon he was publicly denounced from one ol their pulpits.   Against this a protest was raised by one of the workers of the Bible Society and eventually he and Cronin began to meet in one of his rooms for prayer and the breaking of bread.   Others were added and they moved the meetings to Cronin's house, but soon afterwards (1829), their numbers increasing, Francis Hutchinson, who was one of them, lent them a large room in his house in Fitzwilliam Square.

Another such group was formed about the same time, also in Dublin.   About 1825 John Vesey Parnell (afterwards Lord Congleton) and two friends, being troubled by the fact that their fellowship with one another during the week was obscured by their separating on Sundays to their different denominations, tried to find some circle in which their differences of view on ecclesiastical points would no longer prevent the expression of their unity as children of God.   Failing to find any company such as they sought, and being clear that they needed no consecrated building nor ordained minister, they began to meet and break bread in one of their own rooms.   Shortly afterwards one of their number going out on a Sunday met a member of that circle where Bellett was, whom he knew as a Christian.   In a brief conversation they were struck by the fact that, though one in Christ, they were going different ways, and this led eventually to the bringing together of these two groups.   Groves had left for England, but Bellett and those with him had been joined by a young clergyman, John Nelson Darby.   These soon began to meet with the company in Francis Hutchinson's house, holding their meetings at such hours as did not interfere with any who might wish to attend the usual services at the churches or the dissenting chapels.

As their numbers increased it became inconvenient to have the meetings in a private house, so a large auction room in Aungier Street was taken, where the meetings were held and there was great joy in a sense of the Lord's presence and blessing. Cronin* writes of this time: "Oh the blessed seasons with my soul, which John Parnell, William Stokes and others knew, while moving the furniture aside and laying the simple table with its bread and wine on Saturday evenings, seasons of joy, never to be forgotten, for surely we had the Master's smile and sanction in the beginning of such a movement as this was!"

From time to time they found that companies of believers were meeting together in other parts of the British Isles and elsewhere, unknown to each other, believers on whose hearts and consciences it had been impressed that the Lord's people should return to a literal obedience to His Word, making that alone their guide, in so far as they understood it. There were also many individuals, who, as soon as they found that others were carrying out what they had, as yet, only desired, willingly associated themselves with them.

Anthony Norris Groves,† whose words in Dublin had proved so fruitful, though still quite a young man had prospered greatly in his profession. He was happily married, had three little children, a pleasant home in Exeter and a congenial circle of friends and relatives. Before his conversion, as a boy in his teens, he had felt that to be a missionary was the ideal way for a Christian, and when he was converted he devoted himself to the Lord with this in view. His young wife, however, who was converted about the same time and to whom he was devotedly attached, was opposed to any thought of their becoming missionaries, though she was of one mind with him in the desire to serve the Lord and they agreed together to give a tenth of their income and distribute it among the poor. This was soon increased to a quarter, and after a time they saw that they and all they had belonged to the Lord so gave up all idea of saving money or putting aside for their children, and, reducing expenses by simplifying their own manner of life in every way possible, they gave away all the rest.

*MS. Ed. Cronin.

†"Memoir of the late Anthony Norris Groves containing Extracts from his Letters and Journals" Compiled by his Widow 1856

Groves refrained from saying anything further to his wife of his unquenched desire for missionary work, seeing her set against it, but she had her own experiences, quickened by coming in contact with the poor and suffering in her distributions, and after some years she came independently to the conclusion which her husband had reached already.

Now it seemed to them that the right thing would be for him to be ordained and that they should go abroad in connection with the Church Missionary Society. It was with this in view that he went from time to time to Trinity College, Dublin, and on one of these occasions had the conversation with his friend Bellett which led to their meeting, with others, for the breaking of bread. On a later visit, his reading of the Scripture having shown him the liberty the Spirit gives for the ministry of the Word of God, he saw that there was no need for him to be ordained by the Church of England, and, speaking with Bellett on this he said: "This I doubt not is the mind of God concerning us—we should come together in all simplicity as disciples, not waiting on any pulpit or ministry, but trusting that the Lord would edify us together by ministering as He pleased and saw good from the midst of ourselves". Bellett relates: "At the moment he spoke these words, I was assured my soul had got the right idea, and that moment I remember as if it were but yesterday, and could point you out the place. It was the birthday of my mind . . . "

Still desiring to go abroad under the Church Missionary Society, Groves went to London to arrange for going as a layman, but finding that he would not be allowed to celebrate the Lord's Supper, even should no ordained minister be available, he withdrew his application. He had been baptized in Exeter, but when it was said to him: "Of course you must be a Baptist now you are baptized", he replied: "No, I desire to follow in all those things in which they follow Christ, but I would not, by joining one party, cut myself off from others".

In 1829 Groves and his wife, with their two boys of nine and ten, and Kitto, the boys' tutor (afterwards renowned as a Biblical scholar), as well as several others, set out and travelled by way of St. Petersburg and Tiflis to Bagdad. As their waggons traversed South Russia they met some of the Mennonite believers. Travelling through the mountainous country of Transcaucasia they saw in the distance, on the commanding summit of one of the countless hills, the well-built city of Shusha. They climbed the steep ascent and a large house, one of the first they came to, on the confines of the city, opened its doors to them and they were received by the missionaries of the Basle Missionary Society, Pfander and Count Zaremba, who did an important work in those parts until they were expelled from the country. Pfander accompanied the party to Bagdad and stayed with them there for a time, his experience and knowledge of languages enabling them to begin work there earlier than would otherwise have been possible. The needs of the journey were supplied in various ways and Groves writes: "I feel I am happy in having no system to support, in moving among either professing Christians or Mohammedans; to the one, a person so situated can truly say, I do not desire to bring you over to any church, but to the simple truth of God's Word, and to the others, we wish you to read the New Testament that you may learn to judge of God's truth, not by what you see in the churches around you, but by the Word of God itself".

The little household was established in Bagdad and the study of language begun, while the treatment of sick people gave access to many and a school was opened which prospered from the first. The Armenians were found accessible, and there were openings among some of the Jews and Syrians; Mohammedans were often hostile, but intercourse with some was possible.

"The two great objects of the Church in the latter days", Groves wrote, "seem to me to be the publication of the testimony of Jesus in all lands, and the calling out the sheep of Christ who may be imprisoned in all the Babylonish systems that are in the world".

The second year of their stay was entered upon with much to encourage, but rumours of war and plague were increasingly threatening, and when plague actually entered the city the question of leaving or remaining became urgent. Many were leaving, but considering the promising work begun, and the school, seeing also that a party of helpers on the way out f om England had already reached Aleppo, they decided to stay. The plague began to spread, crowds

who could get away fled, but the advance of a besieging
army cut off the retreat of many.   Water became
scarce and robbers took advantage of slackened authority
to pillage.   Rapidly the plague increased, and although
half the population had fled, among the 40,000 remaining
the mortality soon reached 2000 daily.   Then the river
rose and after days of anxious hope that it might yet
be stayed, the water began to trickle into the city.   Walls
were undermined and fell, and then a great inundation
swept away thousands of houses.   The plague-stricken
people were crowded into narrowed areas; food failed; in
a month 30,000 souls had perished in the utmost misery.
The harvest, ready to be reaped, was destroyed for 30 miles
round.   As to the little missionary household, their
hearts were rent at the sight of the indescribable
horrors going on around them, yet Groves was able to write
at this time: "the Lord has allowed us great peace, and
assured confidence in His loving care, and in the truth of
His promise, that our bread and our water shall be sure;
but certainly nothing but the service of such a Lord as He
is would keep me in the scenes which these countries do
exhibit, and I feel assured will, till the Lord has finished
His judgements on them for the contempt of the name,
nature and offices of the Son of God; yet I linger in the
hope that He has a remnant even among them, for whose
return these convulsions are preparing the way. . . . The
Lord has stopped the water just at the top of our street by
a little ledge of high ground, so that as yet we are dry;
and all free from the sword of the destroying angel".
Considering the ruin of the hopeful work begun, he wrote,
"it requires great confidence in God's love, and much
experience of it, for the soul to remain in peace, stayed on
Him, in a land of such changes, without even one of our
own nation near us, without means of escape in any direction; surrounded with the most desolating plague and
destructive flood, with scenes of misery forced upon the
attention which harrow up the feelings, and to which you
can administer no relief.   Even in this scene, however,
the Lord has kept us of His infinite mercy in personal quiet
and peace, trusting under the shadow of His Almighty
wing, and has enabled us daily to assemble in undiminished
numbers, when tens of thousands have been falling around

us. Neither is this all, for He has made us know why we stayed in this place, and why we were never allowed to feel it to be our path of duty to leave the post we were in".

The waters diminished; the virulence of the plague was spent. Then Mary, the wife and mother, the guide of the household, whose love and grace and unfailing faith had been a support on which all had leaned, sickened—as the anxious watchers soon realized—of the plague. Her husband and a faithful nurse cared for her. She had been entirely confident that they should stay in Bagdad, and now, faced with the prospect of leaving her husband and sons and the little baby born there, in such a place, she said: "I marvel at the Lord's dealings, but not more than at my own peace in such circumstances." She died. Her husband cried in mingled grief and worship: "How hard for the soul to see the object of its longest and best grounded earthly affections suffering without the power of affording relief, knowing too that a heavenly Father who has sent it can relieve it and yet seems to turn a deaf ear to one's cries; at the same time, I felt, in the depth of my soul's affections, that, notwithstanding all, He is a God of infinite love. Satan has sorely tried me, but the Lord has shown me, in the 22nd Psalm, a more wonderful cry *apparently* unheeded, and the Holy Ghost has given me the victory, and enabled me to acquiesce in my Father's will, though I now see not the end of His holy and blessed ways".

Then the baby was stricken and, in spite of her father's utmost devotion, was taken from them. He himself was the next to be attacked, and had the prospect of leaving his children desolate, but he recovered.

As plague and flood abated the enemy without advanced, the city was besieged and mob rule prevailed within. Groves' house was repeatedly attacked and robbed, but though unarmed and helpless, those in it suffered no bodily harm. Shells passed over the roof on which they slept and the building was struck by cannon balls. Violence prevailed in the streets, the children of the Christian population especially suffering abominable treatment. At last the city was taken; its captors behaved with unexpected moderation, so that quietness and order were restored.

In the summer of 1832 the long looked-for helpers from

England arrived. They were Dr. Cronin, now a widower, with his infant daughter and his mother, John Parnell and Francis W. Newman (whose brother, later, became the well-known Cardinal). Groves and all with him were greatly cheered by this arrival, and the whole of the increased company entered on a period, not only of activity in study and work, but of happy, helpful union and fellowship among themselves, and advanced into fuller knowledge of God and of holiness. They had all things common; on Fridays they fasted and prayed together. There was much study of the Word; conversions took place. These were times some of them could never forget and from which several, of different nationalities, dated the beginning of a new life in God.

Cronin's sister had been married to Parnell on the way out, at Aleppo, but had been quickly taken from him by death, and now her mother died also. In this same year Newman and Kitto went to England to seek further helpers, and the following year those in Bagdad were visited by Colonel Cotton,* whose engineering skill, and Christian care for the people of India, abolished the dreadful periodic famines of the Godaveri Delta and brought prosperity to its vast population. Groves went on with him to India, leaving the others for a time in Bagdad.

One object in going to India, Groves wrote, was "to become united more truly in heart with all the missionary band there, and show that, notwithstanding all differences, we are one in Christ; sympathizing in their sorrows, and rejoicing in their prosperity". The deep experiences through which he had passed made him peculiarly capable of this, also his remarkable and unaffected humility, which rendered him quick to see whatever was good in others, slow to condemn. Also his knowledge of Scripture and practical acquaintance with the work fitted him to give wise counsel, so that he did not merely travel praising all he saw, but could well point out possibilities of improvement. He saw so vividly the need of the vast multitudes that remain without the Gospel that he preferred almost any effort to reach them, however faulty, to none at all. Moreover he was hopeful that, if anywhere, it would be in a country outside of Christendom, such as India, that it

* "Gen. Sir Arthur T. Cotton His Life and Work" Lady Hope.

would first become possible for true believers to cast aside
their denominational differences and exhibit the essential
unity of the churches of God in obedience to the Scriptures
and in the forbearance of love. This would remove the
chief hindrance to the spread of the Gospel. It was a great
undertaking and worth attempting at any cost. Whether
in extensive travels all over the country, visiting many
missionaries of various confessions, or when he settled in
some particular district, the grace and power of Groves's
ministry, and his unselfish love, won many hearts and bore
abundant fruit in the lives and service of many. When,
however, it came to applying the principles of the Word to
persons and organizations that had in some ways departed
from them, opposition was aroused, and he suffered keenly
as his loving desire to serve was misunderstood by missionaries and societies and construed as criticism and affecta-
tion of superiority and as threatening the stability of
existing organizations.

His own words are: "How *slow* we are to learn really to
suffer, and to be *abased* with our dear Lord (Phil. 2. 3-10).
However, I think we are generally much more able to take
up cheerfully any measure of bodily or mental trial than
that which degrades us before the world. To see that *our
abasement is our glory*, and *our weakness our strength*, requires extraordinary faith: wherever I go, I perceive the
evil influence of contrary principles. I am persuaded that
not following our Lord, and going down among the people
we wish to serve, destroys all our real power; by remaining
above them, we have power, but it is earthly. O that the
Lord would raise up some to show us the way! When the
truth is impressed upon a person's mind in India, it seems
to seize it with a more powerful and tenacious grasp than
generally in England, people are often left with God's
word alone, the professedly religious circle being very
small, and thus the views they entertain are much more
scriptural. Never was there a time when it was more
important than now, to make every effort that they do not
rivet on this land the evils of ecclesiastical dominion, viz.,
the pride and earthliness under which the established
churches in Europe have groaned". Again he writes:
"Never was there a more important moment than the
present for India; up to this time everything in the Church

has been as free as our hearts could wish. Persons have been converted, either by reading God's Word, or through one another, and have drank the living waters wherever they could find them full and clear; but now the Church of England is seeking to extend its power, and the Independents and Methodists are seeking to enclose their little flocks.

My object in India is two-fold, to try to check the operation of these exclusive systems, by showing in the Christian Church they are not necessary for all that is *holy* and *moral*; and to try and impress upon every member of Christ's body that he has some ministry given him for the body's edification, and instead of depressing, encouraging each one to come forward and serve the Lord. I have it much at heart, should the Lord spare me, to form a Church on these principles; and my earnest desire is to re-model the whole plan of missionary operations, so as to bring them to the simple standard of God's Word. The encouragement the Lord has given me is great, beyond all I could have hoped; I cannot tell you how lovingly I have been received, not by one party only, but by all". On another occasion he writes: "The farther I go, the more I am convinced that the missionary labour of India, as carried on by Europeans, is altogether *above* the *natives*; nor do I see how any abiding impression can possibly be made, till they mix with them in a way that is not now attempted. When I think of this subject of caste, in connection with the humiliation of the Son of God, I see in it something most unseemly, most peculiarly unlike Christ. If He who is one with the Father in glory emptied Himself, and was sent in the likeness of sinful flesh, and became the friend of publicans and sinners, that He might raise them, it is truly hateful that one worm should refuse to eat with, or touch another worm, lest he become polluted. How strikingly the Lord's revelation to Peter reproves it all, 'what God hath cleansed that call thou not common'".

In making plans for living in India he says: "We purpose that our domestic arrangements should all be very simple and *very inexpensive*, and our plan strictly evangelical. Our great object will be to break down the odious barriers that pride has raised between natives and Europeans; to this end, it would be desirable for every evangelist to take with him wherever he went from two to six native catechists, with whom he might eat, drink, and sleep on his journeys, and to whom he might speak of the things of the kingdom, as he sat down and as he rose up, that they might in short be prepared for ministry in the way that our dear Master prepared His disciples, by line upon line, precept upon precept, here a little and there a little, as they could bear it, feeling from beginning to end, that our place is not to set others to do what we do not do ourselves, or to act on principles on which we do not, but that we are rather to be ensamples of everything we wish to see in our dear brethren. And I do not yet despair of seeing in India a church arise that shall be a little sanctuary in the cloudy and dark day that is coming on Christendom".

After visiting England, where he married again, Groves returned to India, bringing with him a missionary party, which included the brethren Bowden and Beer and their wives from Barnstaple, who began work in the populous Godaveri Delta. He himself settled in Madras where he was rejoined by the party he had left behind in Bagdad. Having long depended for his supplies on such gifts as the Lord sent through His servants, he felt that now, in Madras, the circumstances were such that it would be better for the testimony that he should follow the example of Paul, who was ready, according to circumstances, either to live from the gifts of the churches, or from his own labour and earn his own living. He therefore took up practice again as a dentist and was successful in this.

His efforts to help the different Missionary Societies led in time to his being opposed by some, excluded from their circles and spoken against as an enemy and a danger to the work. This he felt keenly and it was one reason for his leaving Madras and moving to Chittoor, which soon became a centre of activity and of blessing.

In order to encourage those engaged in the Lord's work to earn their living also, when possible, and those engaged in business to be active likewise in spiritual work, he took land, and carried on, first silk cultivation, afterwards sugar growing, thus giving occupation to many. At times this prospered, but there were also losses, and the acceptance of a loan offered on one occasion for extending the business involved him in much work and anxiety before it could be repaid.   A letter written to England at this period explains his purpose.

"That which renders your bounty doubly precious is, that it proves the continuance of your love to us individually, but above all, to the work of the Lord in these desolate and neglected lands.   I think we all feel an increasing interest in that plan of missions which we are now pursuing; either labouring ourselves, or being associated with those who profess some 'honest trade' . . . and also set an example to others that, by so doing they may support the weak. We have lately heard from several missionaries, who express the deepest interest in the prospect of our success.   That dear young native, by name Aroolappen, who went from us some months since, has, amid many discouragements, and many allurements, remained faithful to his purpose. He has determined to commence his labours in a populous neighbourhood, near the Pilney Hills, in the Madura district, a little south of Trichinopoly; and he has the prospect of being joined by a native brother, who is prepared to go forth to build, with the spade in the one hand and the sword in the other—the way in which the wall will, I believe, be built in these troublous times.   Dear Aroolappen has declined any *form* of salary, because the people, he says, would not cease to tell him that he preached because he was hired.   When he left me, I wished to settle something upon him monthly, as a remuneration for his labour in translating for us; but, unlike a native, he refused any stipulated sum.   The two others of whom I wrote, are an Englishman . . . and a native bookbinder, who are determined to pursue the same course".   Of the Englishman he writes further, "he is inured to the climate and can walk forty miles a day without fatigue.   He reads and writes Tamil and Telegoo freely, and gives up thirty-five rupees a month, a horse and a house, that he may do the work of God.   He goes through the Tamil and Telegoo country, in a little cart filled with books, tracts, and things for sale, preaching the gospel to the natives in their own tongues, as he passes on, and in English to all the soldiers in the military stations.   He has already been blessed to the conversion of two natives; one is . . . the bookbinder, the other, a servant of ours.   I assure you we all feel that, had we seen no other fruit of our labour than these two or three brethren, acting on these principles of service, we should have said, truly our labour has not been in vain in the Lord. I think, therefore, we may consider that, under God, our residence in India has been the means of setting up this mode of ministry among the native Christians and the heathen, and our continuance will be, I trust, by the grace of God, the means of establishing and extending it. Those who know the natives will, I am sure, feel with me, that this plan of missions, whereby the native himself is thrown *on God*, is calculated to develop that *individuality of character*, the absence of which has been so deeply deplored, and the remedy for which has so seldom been sought. The native naturally loves a provision and ease, and thereby he is kept in dependence on the creature: the European, on the other hand, loves to keep the native in subjection and himself in the place of rule. But, it must be obvious to all, if the native Churches be not strengthened by learning to lean on the Lord instead of man, the political changes of an hour may sweep away the present form of things, so far as it depends on Europeans, and leave not a trace behind. The late visit of Aroolappen to his family in Tinnevelly has led to the discussion of these principles among the immense body of labourers there; and though he has not taken up his residence among them, he is sufficiently near for them to observe both himself and the principles on which he is acting. Indeed we would commend these early buddings of the Spirit's power—for we trust they are such—to your very fervent prayers, that our brethren may be carried on in the spirit of real humility and dependence upon God. The fact that our position here puts pastoral work and fellowship on a simple Christian footing among the natives, is by no means the least important feature of our work. Until we came, no one but an ordained native was allowed to celebrate the Lord's Supper or to baptize; and when our Christian brethren Aroolappen and Andrew, partook of the Lord's Supper with the native Christians, it caused more stir and enquiry than you can imagine. The constant reference to *God's Word* has brought, and is bringing, the questions connected with ministry and Church government into a perfectly new position in the minds of many".

All this, however, did not prevent Groves from seeing

that there are those who at times are called to give their
whole time to the ministry of the Word, and he writes: "I
have no question but that those whom God has called to
minister should wait on their ministry and give themselves *wholly to it* . . . recognised pastors and teachers are
essential to the good order of all assemblies; and as such
required and commanded of God; and though I should not
object to unite with those who had them not, if it were the
result of the Lord's providence in not *giving* them any,
I should feel quite unable to join *personally* those who
reject them as unnecessary or unscriptural". For himself,
he said at this time: "It is much my desire, if the Lord
clears away difficulties, to give the rest of my short space
to an uninterrupted ministry". Writing of two members
of the Church of England who greatly helped the brethren
Bowden and Beer in their work in the Godaveri Delta, he
says: "Their system may be sectarian, but they are not so;
and it is ten times better to have to do with those who are
catholic in a sectarian system, than those who are sectarian
with no system".

Visiting England in 1853 he was taken ill and passed
away, suffering, but in peace, in the house of George Müller
in Bristol, at the age of 58.

Another who came to be impressed by the importance of
a literal obedience to the Scriptures was George Müller.*
He was a native of Prussia, born near Halberstadt, in 1805.
Although he studied for the ministry yet he grew up living
a sinful, profligate life and was even imprisoned on one
occasion for swindling. In a very unhappy state he was
taken by a friend, when he was twenty years old, to a
meeting in a private house in Halle where he heard the
Bible read. Though he had studied much this was new to
him; he was immediately and powerfully affected by it,
and it was not long before the love of Jesus to his soul and
the sufficiency of His atoning blood, won the response of
the love and faith of his heart. From the time of this crisis
he had much spiritual conflict, but his daily, regular habit
of reading the Scriptures and of prayer brought him into
a growing knowledge of the will of God.

He was very desirous of becoming a missionary to Jews

* "A Narrative of some of the Lord's Dealings with George Müller"

and was brought to England to study for such a position in the London Jews Society. Soon after reaching England he heard with delight of what A. N. Groves was doing in giving up a good income and going as a missionary to Persia, trusting in the Lord for the supply of his needs. Being sent to Teignmouth for his health he there met Henry Craik, who had been a member of the Groveses' household; this was the beginning of a lifelong friendship. Here he received further spiritual blessing, especially in seeing more clearly that the Word of God is the believer's only standard and the Holy Spirit his only teacher. Further light raised difficulties in his mind as to his connection with the Missionary Society and eventually by friendly agreement with the Committee this connection was severed. His reasons for leaving the Society were: he saw it was not according to Scripture that he should be ordained either in the Lutheran or Anglican Church; also that any such established Churches, being a mixture of the world and the true church, contain principles which must lead to departure from the Word of God, and the fact that they are establishments, prevents their altering their ways whatever fresh light they may receive from the Holy Scriptures. Also he had a conscientious objection to being directed by men in his missionary labours; as a servant of Christ he felt he ought to be guided by the Spirit as to time and place and though he loved the Jews he could not bind himself to work almost exclusively among them. A difficulty was that he had been some expense to the Society and was therefore under an obligation to it, but this matter he was able to arrange satisfactorily, the Society treating him with much consideration.

A further question was as to how his temporal needs could be supplied, but this did not trouble him, for he was able to rest on the Lord's promises, as in Matthew 7. 7, 8; 6. 25-34; John 14. 13, 14, and to see that if he really sought first the kingdom of God and His righteousness, these, his temporal supplies, would be added to him. At this time the minister of Ebenezer Chapel in Teignmouth having left, Müller was invited by the whole church of eighteen members to become their minister, at a salary of £55 a year, he accepted and ministered regularly among them, but also visited and preached in many places in the neighbourhood. He found his ministry was most effective when it took the form of expounding the Scriptures.

Listening one day to a conversation among three sisters in the Lord on the subject of baptism, he saw that, though he had always been a strong supporter of infant baptism, he had never seriously and prayerfully examined the Scriptures on the subject, so set himself to do so, and became convinced that the baptism of believers only, and that by immersion, is the teaching of Scripture. Many objections to his now carrying out this command presented themselves to his mind, but being assured that it was the Lord's will that he should act literally upon His commandments, he was baptized. Shortly after this he saw that, though it is not a command, yet the Apostles have given us the example of breaking bread every Lord's Day, also that it is according to Scripture that there should be liberty for the Holy Spirit to work through any of the brethren whom He pleases to use, so that all may benefit by the gifts which the Lord has bestowed among them. As these things were seen and considered by the church they were introduced into its practice.

The same year (1830) Müller married the sister of A. N. Groves, in whom he found a wife entirely of one mind and heart with himself in seeking to learn and carry out the will of God as revealed in the Scriptures. She was particularly concerned in the next steps which they took, for they saw now that it was not the right way for them that he should receive a fixed salary derived from pew rents and the regular contributions of members of the church, so this was given up. What actually cost them more than giving up the salary was the determination to act on a conclusion they had come to before God, that they should never ask for help, nor make known their needs to any man, but really go to the Lord and trust Him for the supply of all their needs. About the same time they received grace to act literally on the Lord's commandment: "Sell that ye have, and give alms." Writing more than fifty years later he said: "we do not in the least regret the step we then took. Our God also has, in His tender mercy, given us grace to abide in the same mind concerning the above

points, both as it regards principle and practice; and this
has been the means of letting us see the tender love and care
of our God over His children, even in the most minute
things, in a way in which we never experimentally knew
them before; and it has, in particular, made the Lord
known to us more fully than we knew Him before, *as a
prayer-hearing God*".

In 1832 the Müllers and Henry Craik removed to Bristol,
where the two brethren acted for a time as pastors of
Gideon Chapel, but they also rented Bethesda Chapel,
at first for a year only.   There one brother and four sisters
united with them in church fellowship "without any rules,
desiring" they said, "only to act as the Lord shall be
pleased to give us light through His word".   This church
grew steadily and was from the beginning very active in
good works.   After some five years a question arose which
caused them much searching of Scripture that they might
find a solution of it.   When the church was founded all its
members were baptized believers.   Then three sisters
applied for fellowship, as to whose faith and godliness there
could be no doubt, but they had not been baptized as
believers, nor, when the Scriptures were explained to them
did they see that this was the right course for them to take.
Most in the church, including Müller and Craik, thought
they should be received, but several could not conscien-
tiously receive unbaptized believers.   After much discussion of the Scriptures the number advocating refusal
was reduced to a few.   Some received help through the
counsel of Robert Chapman of Barnstaple, a man of such
saintly character, knowledge of the Word, and sound sense.
that he gained the respect of all who came in contact with
him.   He put the matter in this way: either unbaptized
believers come under the class of persons who walk disorderly, and in that case we ought to withdraw from them
(2 Thess. 3. 6); or they do not walk disorderly.   If a believer be walking disorderly we are not merely to withdraw
from him at the Lord's table, but our behaviour towards
him ought to be decidedly different from what it would be
were he not walking disorderly, *on all occasions* when we
may have intercourse with him or come in any way in
contact with him.   Now this is evidently not the case in
the conduct of baptized believers towards their unbaptized

fellow-believers. The Spirit does not suffer it to be so, but He witnesses that their not having been baptized does not necessarily imply that they are walking disorderly and hence there may be the most precious communion between baptized and unbaptized believers. The Spirit does not suffer us to refuse fellowship with them in prayer, in reading and searching the Scriptures, in social and intimate intercourse and in the Lord's work; and yet this ought to be the case were they walking disorderly. The conclusion was reached that "we ought to receive all whom Christ has received (Rom. 15. 7), irrespective of the measure of grace or knowledge which they have attained unto". A few left the church in connection with this, but most of them returned and there was never afterwards any difference on this subject.

Questions as to elders and as to church order and discipline came later to exercise the minds of the brethren, and there was long and careful examination of the Scriptures on these subjects. They came to see that the Lord Himself sets elders in every church in the office of rulers and teachers, and that this should continue now, in spite of the fallen state of the Church, as in Apostolic days. This does not imply that believers associated in church fellowship should elect elders according to their own will, but they should wait on God to raise up those who may be qualified for teaching and ruling in His church. These come into office by the appointment of the Holy Ghost, which is made known to those thus called and to those among whom they are to serve, by the secret call of the Spirit, by their possession of the requisite qualifications, and by the Lord's blessing on their labours. The saints are to acknowledge them and to submit to them in the Lord. Matters of discipline are to be finally settled in the presence of the church, being the act of the whole body. "As to the reception of brethren into fellowship, this is an act of simple obedience to the Lord both on the part of the elders and the whole church. We are bound and privileged to receive all those who make a credible profession of faith in Christ, according to that Scripture, 'Receive ye one another, as Christ also received us, to the glory of God'". These and other conclusions were not *rules* of the church, but expressed what the members had seen and purposed to act upon until they might receive further light from the Scripture. With regard to the Lord's Supper it was seen that "although we have no express command respecting the frequency of its observance, yet the example of the Apostles and of the first disciples would lead us to observe this ordinance every Lord's Day". "As in this ordinance we show forth our common participation in all the benefits of our Lord's death, and our union to Him and to each other, opportunity ought to be given for the exercise of the gifts of teaching or exhortation, and communion in prayer and praise. The manifestation of our common participation in each other's gifts cannot be fully given at such meetings, if the whole meeting is, necessarily, conducted by one individual. This mode of meeting does not however take off from those who have the gifts of teaching or exhortation, the *responsibility* of edifying the church, as opportunity may be offered".

Visiting Germany in 1843, George Müller spent some months, by their invitation, among a company who were glad to have his ministry, but would not allow him to break bread with them, when the time came, because he was willing to do so with Christians in the State Church, or who had not been baptized as believers. They even tried to get him to give an undertaking that he would never break bread with believers who, though baptized themselves, yet did not refuse fellowship with those who were not.

Commenting on these events, George Müller says: "These children of God had been right in considering believers' baptism to be Scriptural, and in separating from the state church. . . . But upon these two points they had laid *undue* stress. Though believers' baptism is the truth of God; though separation from state churches on the part of children of God who know that a church is 'a congregation of believers' is right, because they see in state churches nothing but the world mixed up with some true believers; yet, if these points are made too much of, if they are put out of their proper place, as if they were everything, then there must be spiritual loss suffered by those who do so. Nay, whatever parts of truth are made too much of, though they were even the most precious truths connected with our being risen in Christ or our heavenly calling, or prophecy, sooner or later those, who lay an *undue* stress upon *these parts* of truth, and thus make them too prominent, will be losers in their own souls, and, if they be teachers, they will injure those whom they teach. That was the case at Stuttgart. Baptism and separation from the state church had at last become almost everything to these dear brethren. 'We are the church. Truth is only to be found among us. All others are in error, and in Babylon'. These were the phrases used again and again by our brother . . .". "May God in mercy give and preserve to them and to me a lowly heart"!

The two brethren Craik and Müller felt strongly that every believer is bound, in one way or another, to help the cause of Christ, but that any means required for this should be asked for, not from men, especially not from those who are unconverted, but from the Lord Himself in believing prayer. In pursuance of this conviction they established in 1834 "The Scriptural Knowledge Institution for Home and Abroad", the object of which was to assist Day Schools, Sunday Schools and Adult Schools in which instruction is given on Scriptural lines; to circulate the Holy Scriptures, and to assist those missionaries whose proceedings appear to be most according to the Scriptures. Their reason for forming a new Institution when so many religious societies already existed was that, while they acknowledged the good done by these, there were some points where they could not with a good conscience unite with them. The end, they said, which these religious societies propose to themselves is the gradual improvement of the world until at last it will all be converted; whereas the teaching of Scripture is that the conversion of the world will not take place until the Lord's return, that in this present dispensation the world will rather get worse spiritually, but that the Lord is gathering out a people from among the nations. Further, these Societies have many connections with the world, so that by payment of a subscription an unconverted person may become a member; also the unconverted are often asked for money, and chairmen, patrons, and presidents are obtained by preference from among those who are wealthy and influential. These Societies also contract debts; all of which things are contrary both to the spirit and the letter of the New Testament.

They purposed, therefore, never to ask for money, though they would be free to accept it from any who gave it of their own accord; not to accept any unbeliever as a helper in managing or carrying on the affairs of the Institution; not to enlarge their sphere of work by going into debt, but in secret prayer to "carry the wants of the Institution to the Lord, and act according to the means that God shall give." From this small beginning, without any initial means, without advertisement, there flowed a constant stream of blessing, growing continually in volume. The poor were relieved, schools were established and carried on in various countries, large numbers of Scriptures were sold or given, help was sent to missionaries in many countries, and that in such a way as not to control them at all or to limit their liberty, but only to minister to their needs and those of the work they were doing. All these extensive and increasing activities were carried on in simple dependence on God. Again and again they were without funds either for the various needs they were ministering to or for their own personal necessities, but always in answer to prayer supplies were sent at the right time, so that their own faith in God and communion with Him were exercised and strengthened, while others, too, were encouraged in the path of faith.

In 1836 George Müller opened his first Orphan House, renting a house for a year in Wilson Street, Bristol, where he received 26 children. He states as his chief reasons for entering on this work: "(1) That God may be glorified, should He be pleased to furnish me with the means, in its being seen that it is not a vain thing to trust in Him; and that thus the faith of His children may be strengthened. (2) The spiritual welfare of fatherless and motherless children. (3) Their temporal welfare". Seeing that so many of the Lord's people are oppressed by cares and anxieties he desired to give visible, tangible proof that, in our day, God hears and answers prayer exactly as He ever did, and that if we trust Him and seek His glory He will supply our needs. He had himself been greatly helped by the example of Franke of Halle in Germany, who, in dependence on the living God alone, had built and carried on so large an Orphanage; and he felt sure that such a work in Bristol would be the best way of witnessing to the faithfulness of God in this country. All his expectations were more than realized. Though he was often reduced to the utmost extremity of need, yet the increasing number of orphans never lacked. The work was continued to his death in his 93rd year and since then his successors have carried it on in the same spirit. The great number of orphans received, of whom very many have been converted, the immense buildings erected, the vast sums of money received and employed—all provide a striking example of the prevailing power of the prayer of faith.

In 1837 George Müller published the first part of his book, "A Narrative of some of the Lord's Dealings with George Müller", a book which has exercised an extraordinary influence on the lives of a very great number of people, encouraging them in faith in God.

The Devonshire town of Barnstaple is connected with the name of Robert Cleaver Chapman,* who ministered the Word there for some seventy years and died there in 1902, close upon a hundred years old. He was born in Denmark (1803) of English parents and his mother, to whom he was deeply attached, exercised a great influence on him. While still living in Denmark he was taught by a French abbé, and afterwards went to school in Yorkshire. He developed pronounced literary interests and abilities, becoming also an excellent linguist. Attracted to the Bible at the age of sixteen, he made a careful study of the whole book, being greatly impressed by it. Devoting himself to law he became a solicitor, and did well in his profession.

At this time James Harrington Evans was preaching in London, in John Street Chapel, Bedford Row, which had been built for him by a friend. He had been a curate, but becoming converted by reading some sermons which his rector had lent him, he began, with earnest conviction, to preach justification by faith. This was the means both of the conversion of sinners and the reviving of believers, but was resented by his rector, who gave him notice to leave. He now came to have difficulties as to the baptism of infants, and perceived that the connection of Church and State prevented holy discipline in the Church. Accordingly he left the Church. Soon afterwards he and his wife were

*"Robert Cleaver Chapman of Barnstaple" W. H. Bennet.

baptized. Evans would not, however, become the pastor of a Baptist church, because that would have involved the refusal of church fellowship to many believers, among whom he thought there might well be better persons than himself. In John Street Chapel the Lord's Supper was celebrated every Sunday evening and those who proved themselves gifted in any way for the help and edification of the church were encouraged to make use of their gift.

It was into this church that, at about twenty years of age, Robert Chapman was brought. As he was walking one evening, in evening dress, near the chapel, one of the elders saw him and invited him to come in. This he did, and a few days afterwards he experienced the change of conversion. Describing this later he said: "Lord, I remember Thy dealings with me! When Thy hand at first arrested me, and Thy Spirit convinced me of sin, my cup was bitter with my guilt and the fruit of my doings . . . all was dreary winter within. Sick was I of the world, hating it as vexation of spirit, while yet I was unable and unwilling to cast it out. . . . In the good and set time Thou spakest to me, saying, 'This is the rest wherewith ye may cause the weary to rest, and this is the refreshing'. And how sweet Thy words, 'Son be of good cheer, thy sins be forgiven thee!' How precious the sight of the Lamb of God! and how glorious the robe of righteousness, hiding from the holy eye of my Judge all my sin and pollution! Then did the lame man leap as an hart, and the tongue of the dumb did sing. In Jesus crucified— in Thee my Lord, my soul found rest, and in the bosom of Thy love". He was baptized and associated with the congregation of believers in John Street.

These steps cost him many friends and brought on him the disapproval of relatives, but from the beginning of his new life he gave himself entirely to the following of Christ. The Scriptures became his increasing delight, he entered on a life of believing prayer, and was careful to occupy himself with the needs of the poor and such as were in trouble. He felt himself called of God to devote himself to the ministry of the Word; some said he would never make a preacher, but he replied: "my great aim will be to *live* Christ." He never married, and in 1832 he settled in Barnstaple, ministering the Word in Ebenezer Baptist Chape

Harrington Evans followed his course there with constant interest; saying of him: "He is one of my stars. I hold him to be one of the first men of the age. He has no ebbs or flows."

He disposed of all he possessed and lived in constant, immediate dependence on the Lord for the supply of his daily needs, giving away all he received beyond what was necessary for his own modest requirements. Of his early ministry in Barnstaple he wrote: "When I was invited to leave London and go to minister the Word of God in Ebenezer Chapel, then occupied by a community of Strict Baptists, I consented to do so, naming one condition only— that I should be quite free to teach all I found written in the Scriptures. This I continued to do for some time with blessing from the Lord. A brother who visited me in those days urged me to set aside the strict rule that none but baptized believers should be allowed to break bread. I replied that I could not force the consciences of my brethren and sisters; and I continued my ministry, patiently instructing them from the Word. I well knew at that time that I could have carried the point with a large majority, but I judged it to be more pleasing to God to toil on to bring all to one mind. A little time after that some Christians resident in Barnstaple, who held the strict views which we had by then abandoned, demanded that we should give up the use of the chapel. I carefully examined the Trust Deed, and found that in not one particular did we set aside its provisions. *Yet* we gave them the chapel, just as I should give my coat to a man who demanded it. You will not be surprised when I tell you that ere long the Lord gave us a much better chapel."

It was about this time that Robert Chapman made the acquaintance of George Muller and Henry Craik and also of some of those believers who in Dublin and elsewhere were endeavouring to carry out the Scriptures.

The two simple houses, 6 and 9 New Buildings, Barnstaple, where Robert Chapman and his friend William Hake lived in unbroken fellowship for twenty-seven years until the death of the latter in 1890, became a place of pilgrimage for people from all over the world, who came there for counsel and help in spiritual things.

Robert Chapman travelled in a number of countries. His

visits to Spain led several servants of the Lord to devote themselves to the work of the Gospel in that country, with fruitful result. The influence of his saintly life seems to have affected all who came into contact with him. When, years after his visits to Spain, others worked in that country, they found one instance after another of persons who had been converted and were maintaining a good testimony for Christ, the result of conversation with him. A traveller met an Englishman settled in business in one of the Black Sea ports in Roumania. They conversed of spiritual things, and the Englishman related how he had been religious before coming to Roumania, but now he had given it all up and was convinced that all who professed to be Christians were hypocrites, "but", he added, correcting himself, "I have met with one genuine Christian, he used often to walk through the place where I lived in Devonshire, his name was Robert Chapman".

The traditions and instructions of the Church's early days before the Scriptures were completed, have in the New Testament received a permanent form intended for the literal and continuous guidance, both of the individual saint and of the churches of God, and the endeavour to act in accordance with them has never ceased, even though at times only few have continued it. Some examples of this, in modern times, are the congregation in Edinburgh where the brothers Haldane worked, those assemblies in Dublin in which Groves, Cronin, Bellett, and others were concerned, the church in Bristol founded by Müller, Craik and those with them; the Mennonite Brethren in South Russia, and the Stundist gatherings in various parts of Russia. But these are only a few of many such movements in various countries, some limited to small groups, others extending to wide circles. In the most important principles they had strong spiritual affinity with those of the Baptist and Independent churches which resisted and remained unaffected by the popular Rationalism of the day.

CHAPTER XVII

Questions of Fellowship and of Inspiration

1830-1930

Meeting in Plymouth—Conditions in French Switzerland—Darby's visits—Development of his system—"The church in ruins"—August Rochat—Difference between Darby's teaching and that of brethren who took the New Testament as the pattern for the churches—Change from Congregational to Catholic principle—Spread of meetings—Letter from Groves to Darby—Suggestion of a central authority—Darby and Newton —Darby and the church at Bethesda, Bristol—Darby excludes all who would not join him in excluding the church at Bethesda—World-wide application of system of excluding churches—Churches which did not accept the exclusive system—Their influence in other circles—Churches on the New Testament pattern formed in many countries—Rationalism— Biblical Criticism—Increased circulation of the Scriptures.

A MEETING in Plymouth which had personal contacts with Dublin and with Bristol, early became influential, both by its numbers and by the striking gifts of some of its leaders and teachers. It was the importance of this meeting at that time which originated the name "Plymouth Brethren". Among its teachers the most eminent were Benjamin Wills Newton and J. N. Darby. The latter was connected with an assembly in London, but, devoting himself entirely to the ministry of the Word, travelled constantly and frequently ministered in Plymouth. Darby, unlike most of his associates, still taught infant baptism, though he had left the Church of England. His doctrine of it differed, however, from that of the Anglican Church, resembling rather that of Pelagius, who considered it as introducing the one baptized into a circle where he was capable of receiving the grace of God.

While F. W. Newman, once associated with A. N. Groves in Bagdad, became a powerful exponent of Rationalism, and his brother, John Henry Newman, became a chief leader of the Tractarian or Oxford movement through which the Anglo-Catholic revival in the Church of England was begun, John Nelson Darby passed through phases of development no less remarkable.

In 1838 he accepted an invitation to French Switzerland. Spiritual conditions there seemed favourable to revival. The ministers of the National Church had mostly been captured by the Rationalism of the day. This had led to the Free Church movement, which nevertheless had not wholly satisfied the desires of its adherents. A hundred years earlier Zinzendorf and his band of helpers had formed a considerable company of serious seekers and witnesses, and some traces of their work still persisted. In the neighbouring Jura mountains there still existed Scripturally founded assemblies of believers, persecuted formerly as Anabaptists. In Geneva, the fruits of Robert Haldane's Bible readings remained. The principal leaders of the Free Church movement there had been influenced by them and one result was visible in the assembly called "The New Church", which met from 1818 in Bourg de Four and later in the chapel of la Pélisserie. Other movements had taken or were taking place, both within and outside the National Church. That connected with S. H. Fröhlich had, from 1828, given rise to revival; Gaussen and Merle D'Aubigné had tried to bring back the National Church from Rationalism to the teachings of Calvin; others were combating the doctrine of Church and State and building up the Free Church, as Vinet, who with eight other theologians left the State Church in 1840, followed five years later by a large number of pastors.

In the midst of such excitement and change Darby with his great gifts found a ready ear. For some time he was associated with the church of Bourg de Four. His ministry was most acceptable as he spoke of the Lord's return, of the position of the Church, and of the believer as considered "in Christ", and as he expounded the prophetic Scriptures. His willingness to have fellowship with all believers irrespective of their church connections, attracted many. His meetings in Lausanne, which were largely attended and highly prized, gradually formed about him a special group —"the meeting"—where he further developed and formulated his particular views on the Church.

With regard to the various dispensations or different periods of God's dealings with men, Darby taught* that

* "Collected Writings of J. N. Darby" Edited by William Kelly. Ecclesiastical Vol. I.

each had failed from its beginning ". . . in every instance",
he says, "there was total and immediate failure as regards
man, however the patience of God might tolerate and carry
on by grace the dispensation in which man had thus failed
in the outset; and further . . . there is no instance of the
restoration of a dispensation afforded us, though there
might be partial revivals of it through faith".   Examples
given of these failures at the beginning of dispensations
are, Noah's drunkenness, Abram's going down into Egypt
and denying Sara, the making of the golden calf by the
people of Israel.

The same is asserted of the Church.   "There was",
Darby taught, "a moral departure from God in the bosom
of Christianity."   Even in the lifetime of Apostles the
"apostasy", "perilous times", "the last hour", "departure
from the faith", the working of the "mystery of iniquity",
were already present.   The Apostles failed to carry out the
Lord's commission to go into all the world and preach the
Gospel to every creature; and they remained in Jerusalem
when they should have fled from it.   A new Apostle, of the
Gentiles, was raised up to supplement their lack.   "Thus",
writes Darby, " . . . this dispensation as well as any other
failed and broke off in the very outset . . . it broke down in
the commencement—no sooner fully established than it
proved a failure."

He then asks whether believers are competent "in our
days, to form organized churches after the model, as they
suppose, of the primitive churches" and "whether the
forming of such bodies is agreeable to the will of God?"
His answer is "No", for "the church is in a state of ruin" ...
"the first departure is fatal and the ground of judgement"
... "the Scripture never recognizes a recovery from such a
state" . . . "It alters", he points out, "the whole position
of the soul to recognize that we live in an apostasy hasten-
ing to its final consummation, instead of a Church or dispensation which God is sustaining by His faithfulness of
grace".   In Scripture we see: "(1) The union of all the
children of God; (2) The union of all the children of God in
each locality; . . . this state of things, appearing in God's
word, has ceased to exist, and the question to be solved is
no other than this: How ought the Christian to judge and
act when a condition of things set before us in the word no

longer exists? You will say, 'he is to restore it'. Your
answer is itself one proof of the evil. It supposes that there
is power in ourselves. I would say, listen to the word and
obey it, as it applies to such a state of declension. Your
answer takes for granted two things: 1st, that it is according
to the will of God to re-establish the economy or dispensation on its original footing after it has failed; and, 2ndly,
that *you* are both able and authorized to restore it".

" . . . Before I can accede to your pretensions I must see,
not only that the Church was such in the beginning, but,
moreover, that it is according to God's will that it be
restored to its primitive glory; and, furthermore, that a
voluntary union of 'two or three' or two or three and twenty,
or several such bodies, are each of them entitled, in any
locality, to take the name of the Church of God, when that
Church originally was an assemblage of *all* believers in any
given locality. You must moreover, make it clear to me,
if you assume such a place, that you have so succeeded by
the gift and power of God in gathering together believers
that you can rightfully treat those who refuse to answer to
your call as schismatics, self-condemned, and strangers
to God's Church. And let me here dwell on a most important consideration, which they who are bent on making
churches have overlooked. They have had their thoughts so
fully engaged in their churches that they have almost lost
sight of the Church. "

"According to scripture the whole sum of the churches
here on earth compose the Church, at least the Church on
earth; and the Church in any given place was no other than
the regular association together of whatever formed part of
the entire body of the Church, that is to say, of *the complete
body of Christ here on earth*; and he who was not a member of
the Church in the place in which he dwelt, was no member
of Christ's Church at all. . . . " "The Church is in a state
of ruin . . . If the professing body is not in this state of
ruin, then I ask our dissenting brethren, Why have you
left it? If it be, then confess this ruin—this apostasy—
this departure from its primitive standing. . . . "

"How, then, will the Spirit work? What will be the
acting of such an one's faith? To acknowledge the ruin; to
have it present to his conscience, and to be humbled in
consequence. And shall we, who are guilty of this state

of things, pretend we have only to set about and remedy it?
No; the attempt would but prove that we are not humbled
thereby. Let us rather search in all humility what God
says to us in His word of such a condition of things; and let
us not, like foolish children who have broken a precious
vase, attempt to join together its broken fragments, and to
set it up in hopes to hide the damage from the notice of
others. "

"I press this argument on those who are endeavouring to
organize churches. If real churches exist, such persons are
not called on to make them. If, as they say, they did
exist at the beginning but have ceased to exist, in that case
the dispensation is in ruins, and in a condition of entire
departure from its original standing. They are undertaking in consequence thereof to set it up again. This
attempt is what they have to justify; otherwise the attempt
is without anything to warrant it. . . . To go about re-
making the Church and the churches on the footing on which
they stood at first is to acknowledge the fact of existing
failure without submitting ourselves to the witness of God,
as to His purposes with reference to such a state of ruin. . . .
The question before us is not whether such churches existed
at the period when the word of God was written; but
whether, after they have, by reason of man's sin, ceased
to exist, and believers have been scattered, those who have
undertaken the apostolic office of re-establishing them on
their original footing, and in so doing, to set up again the
entire dispensation, have really apprehended the Divine
will, and are endued with power to accomplish the task
they have taken upon themselves. . . . I am enquiring what
the word and the Spirit say of the state of the fallen
Church, instead of arrogating to myself a competency to
realize that which the Spirit has spoken of the first condition of the Church. "

"What I complain of is, that the thoughts of men have
been followed, and that which the Spirit has recorded as
having existed in the primitive Church has been imitated,
instead of searching for what the word and the Spirit have
declared concerning our present condition. . . . Obedience,
and not imitation of the Apostles, is our duty in such
circumstances. . . . When we are told that all the directions
for the churches are for all times and places, I venture to

ask if they are for times and places in which churches do not exist? and we are brought back to the enquiry—If the dispensation is in ruins who is to make churches? . . ."

"If I am asked what the children of God have to do in the present circumstances of the Church, my answer is very simple. They ought to meet in the unity of the body of Christ outside the world. . . . As regards details, take heed to the promise of the Lord 'Where two or three are gathered together in my name, there am I in the midst of them' (Matt. 18 20). That is what the heart needs that loves God and is tired of the world. Reckon upon that promise of the Lord, you, children of God, disciples of Jesus. If two or three of you meet together in His Name He will be there. It is there that God has put His Name, as of old in His temple at Jerusalem. You need nothing else but to meet together thus in faith. God is in your midst; you will see His glory. . . . Remember also, that when the disciples came together, it was to break bread. . . . If God sends us or raises up among us some one who can feed our souls, let us receive him with joy and thankfulness from God, according to the gift that has been vouchsafed to him. . . . Never make any regulations; the Holy Spirit will guide you. . . . As to discipline, remember that cutting off is the extreme resource. . . . To preserve the holiness of the Lord's table is a positive duty. . . . We owe it to Christ Himself. Cases may present themselves, where we repel with fear the manifestation of sin (Jude 23); but, on the other hand, beware of a judicial spirit, as of fire in your house. . . . ! 'Where two or three are gathered in my name, there am I in the midst of them'. If the whole corporate system has come to naught, I get back to certain unchangeable blessed principles from which all is derived. The very thing from which all springs, to which Christ has attached, not only His name, but His discipline—the power of binding and loosing—is the gathering together of the 'two' or 'three' ".

As to leaving an assembly, or setting up, as it is called, another table, Darby writes: "I am not so *afraid* of it as some other brethren, but I must explain my reasons. If such or such a meeting were the Church here, leaving it would be severing oneself from the assembly of God. But though wherever two or three are gathered together in

Christ's name He is in the midst, and the blessing and responsibility of the Church is, in a certain sense also, if any Christians now set up to be the Church, or did any formal act which pretended to it, I should leave them, as being a false pretension, and denying the very testimony to the state of ruin which God has called us to render. It would have ceased to be the table of the people and testimony of God, at least intelligently. . . . But, then, on the other hand, united testimony to the truth is the greatest possible blessing from on high. And I think that if anyone, through the flesh, separated from two or three walking godlily before God in the unity of the whole body of Christ, it would not merely be an act of schism, but he would necessarily deprive himself of the blessing of God's presence."

Among many in Switzerland who controverted Darby's views, one of the most distinguished both in character and ability was Auguste Rochat. He, referring to the expression, "the Church in ruins", showed that the Church as a united body cannot be in ruins though individuals may fall away. He pointed out that, while the Holy Scripture speaks of assemblies, it does not call the groups of believers living on the earth, separated from each other in different places, the Assembly or Church. Church, as general assembly, includes the believers of all times and places, those who are no longer living on the earth and those who are not yet born: the local assemblies are only bound together by love and brotherly fellowship. Darby taught that the Apostles alone, or their representatives, had had the right to choose or appoint elders in the church, but that in these days of apostasy those persons who are gifted by God for special service may be acknowledged, but not by any official designation. Rochat replied that there is no passage of Scripture that supports this but that on the contrary the assemblies had this right for they chose the men for certain offices in the church and placed them before the Apostles that they might acknowledge them and lay their hands on them. Rochat refused to accept Darby's expressions, "ruin", "apostasy", as applicable to the Church. An order of things cannot apostatize, only an individual can do this. The true Assembly never apostatizes. The Word of God never speaks of the apostasy of the Church.

Darby's theory of the immediate failure of each of the dispensations, and especially of "the ruin of the Church", and the deductions he drew from it, placed him, in principle, in opposition to all those who, throughout the Church's history, have either kept to the teachings and pattern of the New Testament, or have returned to those Scriptures as to a sure and abiding guide.

His view that the churches ceased to exist almost as soon as the Epistles written for their guidance had been completed, would render a great part of the New Testament inapplicable to present conditions.

His teaching abolishes the independence of congregations of believers and their immediate relations with the Lord, bringing in a body, introduction into which, or exclusion from which, by any part, is binding upon the whole; the Congregational principle exchanged for the Catholic.

Although he condemned the formation of churches, yet the gatherings of two or three or more which he commended exercised disciplinary powers, not only in their own local circle, but extending to the whole system of which they formed a part.

In spite of these limitations a great measure of spiritual power and blessing resulted from that part of Darby's teaching which revived truths contained in Scripture. He not only indicated the weakness of existing denominations, but his ministry stimulated faith in God and occupation with His Word, quickened the expectation of the Lord's return, with its sanctifying influences, and emphasized the liberty of the Spirit, who gives gifts according to His will through the various members of the body of Christ. Much spiritual blessing was experienced in the meetings. They spread rapidly, not only in Switzerland, but also in France and Belgium, Germany and Holland, Italy, and beyond.

They formed a close circle of communion among themselves, and this soon led to separation from many with whom Darby had formerly associated. About 60 members of the assembly of Bourg de Four separated from it (1842) and attached themselves to Darby's meetings, and in the Canton de Vaud many left the Free Church and took the same step.

Darby's development was looked upon as having dangerous tendencies, by some who still regarded him personally with undiminished love and respect, as is seen from a letter written to him in 1836 by Groves, on leaving again for India after a visit to England.* He wrote: " . . . I wish you to feel assured that nothing has estranged my heart from you, or lowered my confidence in your being still animated by the same enlarged and generous purposes that once so won and riveted me; and though I feel you have departed from those principles by which you once hoped to have effected them, and are in principle returning to the city from whence you departed, still my soul so reposes in the truth of your heart to God that I feel it needs but a step or two to advance and you will see all the evils of the systems from which you profess to be separated, to spring up among yourselves. You will not discover this so much from the workings of your own soul as by the spirit of those who have been nurtured up from the beginning, in the system they are taught to feel the only tolerable one; that not having been led like you, and some of those earliest connected with you, through deep experimental suffering and sorrow, they are little acquainted with the real truth that may exist amidst inconceivable darkness; there will be little pity and little sympathy with such, and your union daily becoming one of doctrine and opinion more than light and love, your government will become—unseen perhaps, and unexpressed, yet—one wherein, overwhelmingly, is felt the authority of *men*; you will be known more by what you witness against than what you witness for, and practically this will prove that you witness against all but yourselves. . . . It has been asserted . . . that I have changed my principles; all I can say is, that as far as I know what those principles were, in which I gloried on first discovering them in the word of God, I now glory in them ten times more since I have experienced their applicability to all the various and perplexing circumstances of the present state of the church; allowing you to give every individual, and collection of individuals, the standing *God* gives them, without identifying yourselves with any of their evils. I ever understood our principles of communion to be the possession of the common life . . . of the

*"Memoir of the late Anthony Norris Groves containing Extracts from his Letters and Journals" Compiled by his Widow, 1856.

family of God . . . these were our early thoughts and are my most matured ones. The transition your little bodies have undergone, in no longer standing forth the witnesses for the glorious and simple *truth*, so much as standing forth witnesses against all that they judge error, have lowered them in my apprehension from heaven to earth. . . . What I mean is, that then, all our thoughts were conversant about how we might *ourselves* most effectually manifest forth that life we have received by Jesus (knowing that that alone could be as the Shepherd's voice to the living children) and where we might find that life in others; and when we were persuaded we had found it, bidding them, on the Divine claim of this common life (whether their thoughts on other matters were narrow or enlarged) to come and share with us, in the fellowship of the common Spirit, in the worship of our common Head; and as Christ had received them, so would we to the glory of God the Father; and farther, that we were free, within the limits of truth, to share with them in *part*, though we could not in *all*, their services. . . . I would *infinitely rather bear with all their evils*, than *separate* from *their good* . . . feeling assured in my own heart, that your enlarged and generous spirit, so richly taught of the Lord, will one day burst again those bands, which narrower minds than yours have encircled you with, and come forth again, rather anxious to advance all the living members of the living Head into the stature of men, than to be encircled by any little bodies, however numerous, that own you for their founder . . . ".

That the idea of a central authority for the meetings was considered, is indicated in a letter from Wigram, one of Darby's closest adherents, in which he asks the question, regarding meetings in London:* "How are meetings for communion of saints in these parts to be regulated? Would it be for the glory of the Lord and the increase of testimony to have one central meeting, the common responsibility of all within reach, and as many meetings subordinate to it as grace might vouchsafe? or to hold it to be better to allow the meetings to grow up as they may without connexion and dependent upon the energy of individuals only?"

Returning in 1845 from a visit to the Continent, Darby went to Plymouth to deal with conditions there which he

* "A History of the Plymouth Brethren" W. Blair Neatby.

judged to be unsatisfactory because of the influence and teaching of Newton. There had long been divergence between these two able men. They differed in their views on dispensational truth and on prophecy and on points of church order. There had been no little controversy both by word and pen and a party spirit had grown up. Darby's visit brought matters to a crisis. At the close of the meeting one Sunday morning he announced his intention to "quit the assembly" and some weeks later he began to break bread in Plymouth with his supporters apart from the original assembly. About two years after this some MS. notes— taken by a hearer—of an address given some time before by Newton, came into the hands of one of Darby's sympathizers. It contained comments on the Psalms, and Darby and his friends maintained that in these comments, Newton, explaining their typical application to Christ, had taught unorthodox doctrine with regard to the nature of the sufferings of Christ during His life on earth, and on the cross. The notes were published without reference to Newton in regard to their accuracy; their unorthodox character was pointed out, deductions were drawn and a charge of heresy fastened upon him. Newton, while repudiating the doctrine deduced from these notes, and affirming his firm, unquestioning belief in Christ as truly God and truly man, untouched by sin, admitted having used expressions from which wrong conclusions could legitimately be drawn. He therefore published *A State-ment and Acknowledgment respecting Certain Doctrinal Errors*, in which he confessed his error, acknowledging it as sin, and withdrew all statements, in print or otherwise, in which it could be found, expressed his grief at having injured any and prayed that the Lord would not only pardon him but also counteract any evil effects. This acknowledgment made no impression on Newton's accusers, who continued with unabated zeal to connect him with the heresy he denied.

When the division took place in Plymouth, the church at Bethesda Chapel, Bristol, where Müller and Craik were, took no side in the controversy, but acknowledged as fellow-believers those in both meetings.

In 1848 two brethren from the meeting in Plymouth which Darby had excommunicated, visited Bristol, where they were in the habit on such occasions of breaking bread at Bethesda. They were carefully examined as to their soundness in doctrine and freedom from the error attributed to Newton. All being satisfied as to this, they were received as they formerly had been. Darby now required that the church at Bethesda should judge the question of Plymouth, which they declined to do, on the ground that it was not a question that affected them, that they were not competent to judge a church, and that it would be harmful to introduce discussions on such a topic. Eventually, owing to pressure also from within, the question was considered, and a letter written stating "that no one defending, maintaining or upholding Mr. Newton's views or tracts should be received into communion", but, they continued: "Supposing the author of the tracts were fundamentally heretical, this would not warrant us in rejecting those who came from under his teaching, until we were satisfied that they had understood and imbibed views essentially subversive of foundation-truth . . . " Darby then wrote: "I feel bound to present to you the case of Bethesda. It involves to my mind the whole question of association with brethren, and for this very simple reason, that if there is incapacity to keep out that which has been recognized as the work and power of Satan, and to guard the beloved sheep of Christ against it—if brethren are incapable of this service to Christ, then they ought not to be in any way owned as a body to whom such service is confided: their gatherings would be really a trap laid to ensnare the sheep. . . . I do not . . . desire in the smallest degree to diminish the respect and value which any may feel personally for the brethren Craik and Müller, on the grounds of that in which they have honoured God by faith . . . but I do call upon brethren by their faithfulness to Christ, and love to the souls of those dear to Him, in faithfulness to set up a barrier against this evil. Woe be to them if they love the brethren Müller and Craik or their own ease more than the souls of saints dear to Christ! And I plainly urge upon them that to receive anyone from Bethesda (unless in any exceptional case of ignorance of what has passed) is opening the door now to the infection of the abominable evil from which at so much painful cost we have been delivered. *It has been formally and deliberately admitted*

*at Bethesda under the plea of not investigating it (itself a
principle which refuses to watch against roots of bitterness),
and really palliated. And if this be admitted by receiving
persons from Bethesda, those doing so are morally identified
with the evil, for the body so acting is corporately responsible
for the evil they admit. If brethren think they can admit
those who subvert the person and glory of Christ, and principles which have led to so much untruth and dishonesty, it
is well they should say so, that those who cannot may know
what to do.* . . . For my own part, I should neither go to
Bethesda in its present state, nor while in that state go
where persons from it were knowingly admitted. . . . "

Thus the church at Bethesda was excommunicated and
all who might have fellowship with it. The ostensible
ground was that of false doctrine, but this doctrine was never
held by any at Bethesda. The real reason was that, while
the church at Bethesda continued to do what Darby himself
had done at the first, that is, to maintain the independence
of each congregation and its right to receive any individual
whom it had reason to believe was born again and sound in
faith and conduct, Darby had shifted from that ground and
adopted the "catholic" position of an organized body of
churches, excluding all outside their own circle, and subject
to one central authority, in this case himself and the
meeting in London with which he was associated. Fellowship ceased to be based on life, rejection of Bethesda was
also obligatory. No faith or godliness could atone for
refusal to condemn Bethesda.

Even Darby's marvellous influence could not impose
this great change on all, but, by untiring propaganda, a
large number of churches were induced to accept as a
necessary test of fellowship the condemnation of the
church at Bethesda on account of a doctrine never held by
it. By dint of constant repetition this circle of churches
came to believe, in all sincerity, that Bethesda had been
cut off for holding Newton's error, an error which he himself had repudiated, and which the church at Bethesda had
never entertained. So consistently was this system carried
out that Negro brethren in the West Indies had to judge the
Bethesda question, and Swiss peasants in their Alpine
villages were obliged to examine the errors attributed to
Newton and condemn them.

Such a system could not fail to lead to further divisions. Even in Darby's lifetime, several such took place, the parties taking different sides excluding each other as rigorously as they had unitedly excluded Groves and Müller.

Those churches which did not follow Darby continued their endeavour to carry out the principles of Scripture. They varied in many ways, but as they did not believe in the right of one church to cut off another their differences did not necessitate division. Some of them, standing in fear of the criticisms of the followers of Darby (often called "Exclusives") became, in varying degrees, exclusive themselves, but others maintained fellowship with all saints. Though persistently calumniated and rejected by those who had separated from them, they did not cease to include these in the number of those whom they were willing to receive, recognizing them as brethren. Robert Chapman expressed their attitude toward them when, refusing to use the odious name "Exclusive", he called them "Brethren dearly beloved and longed for", and described them as "Those brethren whose consciences lead them to refuse my fellowship and to deprive me of theirs".

The churches which, with Chapman, maintained the original ground of fellowship were often called "Open Brethren", but while there must always have been some individuals and some churches among them which were sectarian at heart and so deserved a sectarian name, for there is an ever-present danger in any spiritual movement that it may crystallize into a sect, yet there remained many who might rightly claim every name that unites, while disclaiming every name that divides the Lord's people. They maintained an active Gospel testimony, reaching out also into most parts of the world.

The influence of this movement has been important beyond the limits of the meetings more particularly associated with it. In face of the great prevalence of Rationalism, and its having captured to so large an extent the Theological Colleges, the pulpits of the principal Nonconformist bodies, and of a considerable section of the Church of England, these meetings have maintained absolute loyalty to the Scriptures as inspired by God and have defended this conviction with an ability and zeal that makes them valuable allies of the numerous believers who, in their different circles, suffer under those of their ministers and clergy who have no such faith.

Movements of a similar character, that is, of believers meeting in accordance with the New Testament teaching and example, are to be found in many parts of the world. They are free from the historic developments of ritual or organization that have drawn so many away from the pattern, and their simplicity makes them adaptable to all varieties of men and conditions. They do not publish, nor even compile, statistics, nor do they depend on publicity or appeals for help for carrying on their testimony, so that they are little known in the world, even in the religious world, and this gives their work a quiet effectiveness, the value of which is especially seen when they come into circumstances of persecution. Such circles are continually being formed in our day among every kind of people, they contain in themselves the power for carrying the Word of Life farther afield, and go on increasing. Their histories are constantly reminiscent of the Book of the Acts, those who go among some of them—and none can know them all—see that their works are like those of their Lord, "if they should be written every one . . . even the world itself could not contain the books that should be written".

Attention has been drawn to persons and to churches that have accepted the Scriptures as a Divine Revelation, suited and sufficient to show the way of personal salvation and conduct as well as to guide the churches of those who believe in regard to their order and their testimony.

It has been seen how a clerical body arose which gradually assumed dominion and developed a system of Ritualism which became the relentless enemy of those who continued to act upon the teaching of the Scriptures.

A different form of attack upon the Scriptures, which may be described as Rationalism, was developed in the 19th century. Rationalism set aside Revelation, assuming the sufficiency of the mind, or Reason, to enable man to find out truth and to attain to the highest good.

The unprecedented progress made in scientific knowledge not only gave valuable insight into the works of God in

Creation, but also stirred in some minds a desire to explain creation apart from God. This made it necessary to prove that the account of the Creation given in the book of Genesis did not spring from Divine inspiration, but from the ignorance of men, who, living before us, were presumed to have known less than we do. As fresh discoveries were made in the illimitable field of Nature, theories were founded upon them which were said to be incompatible with the Genesis history and therefore to prove it incorrect. As further facts came to light new theories had to be formed, each displacing its predecessor, yet each in turn accepted on the authority of the learning of the men of science who promulgated it. The "Origin of Species" published by Charles Darwin in 1859 is an important landmark in this development of thought.

Those who accepted the view that there had been no creation, of necessity lost the knowledge of the Creator. This involved the loss of all revealed knowledge, for the revelation of God through the Scriptures begins with Creation as the work of God, without which there could have been no Fall of His creature, Man; and neither need nor possibility of man's Redemption. Consequently, the new theories evolved from the minds of men discarded the Scripture teaching of the Fall, replacing it by constantly changing theories of the development of man from a lower form of life. The experience of Salvation and the hope of Redemption became incredible on the basis of these teachings, and whatever vague promises might be held out to the race, the individual was left without hope.

Although in the minds of the multitude evolution has replaced God the Creator, so that many trace their ancestry from beasts rather than from God, and are ignorant of God as their Redeemer, yet not all, even among those recognized as the most eminent men of science, have followed this teaching. It would not be correct to say that increase of knowledge of the facts of Nature necessarily leads to disbelief in God or in the Scriptures. Many have found that the more they have learned of the works of God in Creation the more they have appreciated the consonance of this revelation with that contained in the Scriptures. Indeed, the assertion so often and so eagerly made that no modern, intelligent, educated man can believe the Scriptures, is without foundation. It is not a fact that the more people know the less they believe, nor yet that the more ignorant they are the more faith they possess.

Rationalism is largely due to the failure to recognize that man is not only mind, but mind and heart, and that the mind always serves the heart. The heart, which is the character, will, and affections, and is the seat of experience, uses in its service the mind, with its intelligence and reasoning powers. The heart of the natural man uses his mind in order to justify his unbelief in God and in Scripture by finding countless reasons for complaint against God, and contradictions and errors in the Scriptures; but if this same man has an experience which brings him to see his sinful state, his need of salvation, and Christ is revealed to him, then his heart—that is, his will and affections—are captured; they go out to Christ in faith as Saviour and Lord, and the Divine and Eternal Life is communicated to him, as it is written: "that whosoever believeth in Him should not perish, but have eternal life" (John 3. 15). With that in his mind, though neither more nor less capable, intelligent and instructed than before, enters into the service of a changed heart, finding truth and beauty and revelation in the very Scriptures which it formerly despised, and discovering in the ways of God constant reason for thanksgiving and worship. Saul the persecutor, changed to Paul the apostle is a striking illustration of this.

Another line of attack upon the Scriptures, also developed chiefly in the 19th century, took the form of Biblical Criticism. This, like the investigations of Science, is in itself good, but Rationalism pushed it into erroneous theories. The critical examination of the text of Scripture, including the study of the ancient manuscripts, has been of the utmost value, correcting errors and exhibiting more fully the content, force, and meaning of the written Word.

The "Higher Criticism," taking into account the historical, geographical, and other outward circumstances under which the different books were written, examining also their internal literary character, and deducing from all these what may be learned as to their date and authorship, has brought much of interest to light. Here again, however, the rationalistic method, the examination of the Scriptures apart from God, leaving out of account the inspiration of the Holy Spirit working through the human authors and in conjunction with them, has led to strange and varying theories.

The Scriptures were given to the world through a chosen instrument, the people of Israel. Moses and the Prophets spoke by the Word of the Lord, and the different books containing their utterances, whether Law, Histories, Psalms, or Prophecies, were preserved by the Jewish people with a care and tenacity of which no other race would have been capable. Christ and the Apostles accepted and used the Old Testament to the full as the Word of God, completing it by the addition of the New Testament. In all times this Book, or Bible, has been accepted as divinely inspired, and by its working in the hearts and lives of men has proved its Divine power. There have always been those who denied its claims, but it was reserved for the 19th century to see so far-reaching a development of this denial.

Ritualism had long taught a development which added to Scripture and involved departure from it, but Rationalism, taking from it, has the effect of undermining it and destroying its credibility.

One of the earlier of the more striking developments of the Higher Criticism was founded on the use of different names for God in the book of Genesis. From these differences it was argued that the book must be the work of different authors. Much ingenuity was then displayed in dividing this, and subsequently other books, into the different authorships, various critics having their varying schemes. Under this process the personality of Moses was obscured, and it soon became the fashion to deny the existence of Abraham and of other characters described in the earlier Scriptures, representing them as mythical personages, the product of legends concerning several heroes attached to one imaginary man. Further and more rapid progress was made on these lines when Eduard Reuss (1834) put forward a theory that the books of the Law were written after those of the Prophets, and the Psalms later still. This supposition gave rise to much speculation and fitting of the various parts of the Old Testament into the newly devised scheme. At the same time the New Testament miracles were rejected as impossible, and it was laboriously explained how the narration of them grew up out of misunderstandings and legendary accretions. The Gospel history was reconstructed; Renan's "Vie de Jesus" and the "Leben Jesu" of Strauss had a considerable vogue for a time. Criticism ran riot. The mere fact that anything was affirmed in the Bible was almost considered as a reason for doubting its truth. Such extremes led to a certain amount of reaction; much that had been rejected was readmitted. Archaeological research revealed the historical exactitude of much that had been pronounced fabulous.

The increasing occupation of many with the Scriptures, which these conflicts aroused, brought out more than ever their treasures of truth and wisdom. All the time they continued to be the means of bringing salvation to sinners of every sort.

As Ritualism owed it to the clergy that it became effectual as a means of keeping sinners from the Saviour, so Rationalism is indebted for its wide prevalence to-day, and its power to hold multitudes in unbelief, to the fact that it laid hold of the ministerial and theological mind, and seemed to make those who adopted it the intellectual leaders of the people. Its conquest of the theological colleges and training institutions for the ministry has been little short of complete, so that the spiritual guides of the people lead their often unwilling flocks where there is no pasture, showing them that they can no longer be considered intellectual, nor even intelligent, unless they accept the supposed proofs that there is no divinely inspired revelation, and consequently no Creator; no Son of God who for the sake of sinners became Man and, for us men, vanquished sin and death and opened the way of return to God. The Rationalist teaching has reduced Him to a good man, often mistaken, though a pattern for our imitation. Promises that these doctrines would bring about universal peace, prosperity and brotherhood, have been woefully belied by war and preparation for war, by strike and bankruptcy. The hope and expectation of the Lord's coming to reign are lost to those who do not know Who it was who came to suffer.

Among many who resisted this teaching and continued to use the Scriptures with a power and effect which demonstrated the truth of their claim to be the inspired Word of God, none was more eminent than Charles Haddon Spurgeon. When sixteen years of age (1850) he was converted and received among the Baptists. Immediately he began to witness for Christ, and a year later, setting aside any conventional theological preparation, became pastor of a Baptist church. His preaching even then was with such spiritual power that increasing numbers were attracted to hear him. No available building was sufficient for such a preacher, so the Metropolitan Tabernacle was built to seat 6000 people, and there he not only preached the Gospel regularly throughout his lifetime, but expounded the Scriptures and took his part, with his great gifts and with unspoiled humility, in the building up of a church on New Testament principles, from which streams of life flowed to innumerable souls. In preaching, Spurgeon adhered closely to the Scriptures, which he applied with genuine sympathy and emotion to his hearers, pointing his message with endless apt illustration and with a pungent humour that never failed. His sermons were as effectual when read as when heard; they were published as soon as preached, and their circulation was immense, continuing after his death. Feeling strongly the hindrance to the Gospel caused by the doctrine of Baptismal Regeneration, he took the bold course of preaching and publishing a sermon on the subject, which exposed him to attack from the large number of Protestant and Evangelical bodies which hold it. The conflict aroused led him a year later to withdraw from the "Evangelical Alliance." As Biblical criticism developed along the line of undermining faith in the inspiration of the Scriptures and came increasingly to influence the "Baptist Union," Spurgeon withdrew from that association also (1887). This step cost him friends and involved him in controversy, but put heart into many who were in danger of doubting the foundations of their faith, and, in difficult days, encouraged that justification of the truth of Scripture which was soon to be so strongly reinforced by the further discoveries of both ancient historical and modern scientific research.

At the same time, the Scriptures were never so widely

circulated, nor so much read as now, and their call to repentance and faith is as effectual as ever it was. The British and Foreign Bible Society, with others, not only continues, but continues to increase its translations and sales. Its colporteurs press in growing numbers into ever-widening spheres. New translations open up the treasures of the Word to the most remote peoples. If among some favoured peoples the gift of the free reading of the Scriptures, so dearly bought by the blood of their ancestors, is neglected, there are those, later called, who are pressing into the places of the first.

It has been reserved for the twentieth century to experience an unexampled acceleration in the course of events. As an avalanche begins its slow movement, which, from being almost imperceptible, gains in speed until it comes down with overwhelming power, so the slow development of earlier years has become the rushing torrent of our time. The powers hidden in the air are being uncovered—"And God said Let there be a firmament" (Gen. 1. 6), and for long men were content to breathe it, but now it is found to be the carrier of light and heat and electricity, and of sound, so that the voice speaking may be heard round the world—and by millions of listeners. Its mass carries mighty machines and that at incredible speeds, so that distance diminishes and all the world is bound together. The structure and qualities of material things are examined and found to contain complexities of form and action of unimaginable variety. In the midst of such wonders human intelligence has been quickened and knowledge has been put to uses good and bad, all of which tend to speed the pace at which our age presses on to its consummation. In this great stream of history the Scriptures remain unchanged and are found to be equally applicable to all the changing conditions of life. Those who walk in the obedience of faith, whether gathered in churches or scattered through the world, find that this compass always points to Christ, of Whom it is testified: "All things were made by Him," and Whom God sent into the world "that the world should be saved through Him."

Those churches which still make the Scriptures their guide and pattern, and endeavour to act according to this rule, are entirely free from Rationalism, as they have always been from Ritualism.   They therefore form a bulwark against unbelief and provide a refuge for souls seeking where they may act in obedience to the Word of God in fellowship with those like-minded.   Their increase and their spread into many countries, as well as the fact that fresh churches keep arising spontaneously in parts where the Bible penetrates, is of the greatest importance.   It is also to be anticipated that, as many of the different denominations depart farther from the faith, there will be Christians among them who will find themselves obliged to do as so many have done before them, that is, form churches of those that believe, to carry out the teachings of the Word themselves and preach the saving Gospel to others.   Members of the clergy have often been leaders in revivals following on some return to the principles of the Word of God, and this may be so again.   Huss the chaplain, Luther the monk, Spener and Franke, both Lutheran pastors, and the Church of England clergymen, John and Charles Wesley, with George Whitefield, are but a few examples.   The training and experience of such men become especially valuable when once they are freed from the fetters which hinder the obedience of faith.

CHAPTER XVIII

Conclusions

Can churches still follow New Testament teaching and example?—
Various answers—Ritualistic churches—Rationalism—Reformers—Mystics and others—Evangelical Revival—Brethren who throughout all the
centuries have made the New Testament their guide—Spread of the
Gospel—Foreign Missions—Revival through return to the teachings of
Scripture—Every Christian a missionary, each church a missionary
society—Difference between a church and a mission station—Difference
between an institution and a church—Unity of the churches and spread
of the Gospel—New Testament churches among all people on the same
basis—Conclusion.

THE Church Question, that is to say, the question
whether we can, and should, continue to carry out
the New Testament teaching and example as to the ordering
of churches, has been answered in various ways:—

1. The theory of "development" would make it unde-
sirable to do so, because, as is claimed by the ritualistic
churches, such as the Church of Rome, the Greek Orthodox
Church, and others like them, something better than
that which was practised in the beginning has been
attained, and the Scriptures have been modified, or even
supplanted, by tradition.

2. Rationalism gives the same answer, looking upon it
as retrogression to go back to the original pattern, since
it denies that the Scriptures provide an abiding authority.

3. Reformers of existing churches have tried to effect
a compromise, returning in part, but not altogether, to
the acknowledged pattern, as Luther, Spener, and others.

4. Some have abandoned the attempt, as the Mystics,
who devoted themselves instead to the attainment of personal holiness and communion with God, examples of
whom are Molinos, Madame Guyon, and Tersteegen; and
the Friends, who set aside the outward ordinances of
baptism and the Lord's Supper, and occupied themselves
rather with the testimony of the inner Light than with the
outward Scriptures; others, as Darby and his followers,
repudiated the obligation and replaced it by a witness to
"the ruin of the Church".

5. Evangelical Revival set it aside as unimportant, concentrating on the conversion of sinners and organizing what seemed suitable to meet practical needs, as Wesley's Methodist Societies, or the Salvation Army.

6. But there have in all times been brethren who have answered "yes" to the Question though they have been called by many names, Cathars, Novatians, Paulicians, Bogomils, Albigenses, Waldenses, Lollards, Anabaptists, Mennonites, Stundists and others innumerable, many congregations also of Baptists and Independents, and assemblies of Brethren; they have been one in their endeavour to act upon the New Testament and to follow the example of the New Testament churches.

Closely connected with the former question is another— Is it possible to-day to preach the Gospel as at the beginning and might not a much more rapid spread of the Gospel result from so doing? Indeed, the question enlarges and presses itself upon us—Is it not *only* by a return to the Scriptures that the unity of the children of God can be manifested and the evangelization of the world be accomplished?

In the beginning of the Gospel there was no distinction between "home" and "foreign" work. Gradually the spontaneous spread of the churches, irrespective of country and nationality, was modified by the change from primitive Apostolic churches to the organization that developed from these, and "missions" began to be sent out representing the central authority that sent them. As organized Christian denominations multiplied, missions to other lands increased, each preaching Christ, but representing also its own particular scheme and development of Christianity, thus introducing among the heathen that confusion of conflicting sects from which Christendom suffers. The original way was not dependent upon material wealth but on the power of the Holy Spirit, and was always connected with poverty. The methods that have developed are expensive, because the gifts of the Holy Spirit, who dwells in the newest believer and supplies the needs for testimony of the least company of disciples, are not recognized, a "Mission Station" being established to supply all needs. This has to be supported, and it becomes necessary to appeal for money at the "home base" or, where this is thought unworthy of faith, some reliance is placed for the awakening of interest in the work on the publication of moving incidents or distressing needs. In this way, too, the direction and support of the work "abroad" being largely in the hands of those "at home", or their representatives, it remains an alien institution in the land where it is carried on and the spread of the Gospel is impeded to an incalculable degree.

Following Christ and denying self may well include readiness to sever the most cherished ties that bind us to our different denominational organizations, and to find means of practising genuine fellowship with all the Lord's people, exercising that forbearance with one another which our present weakness would necessitate. If we ourselves kept the teachings of Scripture we might then put it into the hands of men of all nations and by precept and example show them that it is given for them as much as for us, in the sure belief that God would keep and guide them, and give them their place as independent churches and their inheritance among the saints.

We do not know what gifts the Holy Spirit may awaken in places outside the scope of modern missionary activities and in circumstances manifestly beyond our power to control. The persecuted Russian churches have experiences beyond ours and a zeal and devotion is quickened among them to which most professing Christians in easier circumstances are strangers; it may well be that in their midst miracles of unity and testimony will be wrought such as we have failed to accomplish. Out of the heathen world leaders may be raised up, so filled with the Spirit that they will be able to leave behind both the divisions and the wealth of European and American Missions and will see conversions and the growth of churches of God among their own people, churches which may indeed have to learn from mistakes of their own, but will be free from ours. With God nothing is impossible, He might call, even out of Islam, submissive, devoted disciples of Christ whom He could use in His service among that people. All this does not leave out of account the value, beyond price, of the devotion and service that have so long flowed, and still flow, through Missionary Societies and Institutions, to the world, but it envisages the multitudes that are unreached (and will remain unreached at the present rate of progress), pointing out the one way of revival, which is a return to the way of the Word.

God is manifested in Christ by the Holy Spirit as the Lover, Seeker, Saviour and Keeper of lost mankind. There is no revelation more affecting than this, that God is of such a nature that the misery of fallen man has constrained Him to lay aside His heavenly glory, to become Man, to bear all our sin and more than all our sorrow, and by death vanquish death and give to dying sinners Eternal and Divine Life. Every one who by faith receives this Life is under the same necessity as He from whom he derives it, so that, on this account, every Christian is naturally a missionary. He hears in his soul as an impelling command, the words: "Go ye into all the world and preach the Gospel to every creature". In the New Testament there is no distinction between clergy and laity, all the saints are priests; so also there is no distinction between missionaries and non-missionaries, every believer is "sent", or has a "mission", to be a witness for Christ in the world. The formation of a separate missionary class, grouped in missionary societies, supported by special mission funds, working through mission stations, though it has accomplished so much, is dearly bought while it contents the vast bulk of Christians to be non-missionaries and dims the vision of every saint as, in every circumstance, wholly the Lord's, and devoted first and last to His service. The aim of the Gospel is the conversion of sinners into saints, and the gathering of these as churches. Since each member of a church is called to be a missionary, or witness for Christ, each church is a "missionary society", a society of persons who are collectively engaged in the testimony of the Gospel.

The difference between a mission station and a church is that a mission station, with the missionary society of which it is a branch, is the centre to which the natives of the country in which it is look for guidance and supplies. A church, on the other hand, in the New Testament sense of the word, is, from the moment of its beginning, when two or three are gathered in the Name of the Lord Jesus, on the same foundation as the oldest established church, having the same Centre, the same principles. Different it is true in gift and experience, it is yet partaker of the same Grace, and draws its supplies from the same Source. Moreover, it is the most suitable instrument for the furtherance of the Gospel among the people from which it has been called, and with whose thoughts, language, customs and needs, its members have perfect acquaintance. A mission station may be of great value, but should never be made the centre around which a church gathers: that centre is Jesus Christ.

There is also a difference between a church and an Institution, such as a hospital or school. These may be of the utmost value, commending the Gospel, gaining the confidence of the people; but if a hospital or school, of foreign origin, comes to be regarded as the centre around which the church is gathered, and upon which it depends, such a church cannot develop according to the New Testament pattern. It remains a foreign religion dependent on supplies from abroad. It may even develop a system of salaried "native evangelists", destructive of dependence upon God, hindering growth in learning to know Him.

Scripture does not lead us to expect that the Gospel will prevail so as to bring about the conversion of the world; on the contrary we are taught to look for increasing departure from God, bringing terrible judgements upon all the earth. The return of the Lord Jesus Christ in glory is the hope set before the Church. Awaiting that great event we remember the Lord's last prayer for His disciples:

"That they all may be one. . . .
That the world may believe that Thou hast sent Me."

These two things, the unity of the people of God, and the making known of the Saviour in the world, are the desire of all who are in communion with the Lord. The history of the Church shows that revival comes through return to obedience to the Word of God. This prayer of the Lord is certainly promise also; it will be accomplished as He prayed. Doubtless the full accomplishment of it will be when He comes, but it may be that the last great revival will be a foreshadowing, even here on earth, of that which is shortly to come to pass both in heaven and on earth.

When the disciples of the Lord repent and forsake ways that are ways of departure from His Word, and gather as churches in immediate dependence upon Him, free from the bondage of human federations and organizations, and free to receive all who belong to Him, they will experience His sufficiency, as those did who went before them in this path; being delivered, on the one hand, from fellowship with unbelievers, and, on the other, from separation from fellow-saints.

Moreover, in taking the Gospel to people of all nations and races, they will apprehend that the whole Word of God is for others as well as for themselves; that all who believe are brought into the same relationship to Him, and that no difference of nationality can affect the standing of a church in the sight of God. The work of the Spirit in all will manifest the truth that Peter had learned when he said:

"God, which knoweth the hearts, bare them witness, giving them the Holy Ghost, even as He did unto us;

And put no difference between us and them,

purifying their hearts by faith. . . .

we believe that through the grace of the Lord Jesus Christ we shall be saved even as they. "

As we review the long path already traversed by the Pilgrim Church, certain salient points appear. Rising above the mass of detail, so poignant at the time to those whose lives made it up, they rightly claim attention, for they turn the experience of the way that lies behind into guidance for the track that stretches before.

One is that the Pilgrim Church has possessed in the Scriptures a safe and sufficient guide for all the way from Pentecost to the present time, and has the assurance that it will suffice until that lamp shining in a dark place shall pale before the glory of the appearing of Him Who is the Living Word (2 Peter 1. 19).

A second is that the Pilgrim Church is separate from the World; though in it is not of it. It never becomes an earthly institution. Though a witness to the world and a blessing in it, yet, since the world which crucified Christ does not change, and the disciple is content to be as his Master, the pilgrims still exhort one another with the words: "Let us go forth therefore unto Him *without the camp*, bearing His reproach. For here have we no continuing city, but we seek one to come" (Heb. 13. 13, 14).

A third is that the Church is One. In so far as we know ourselves to be members of the Pilgrim Church we acknowledge as our fellow-pilgrims all who tread the Way of Life. Passing differences, however keen at the time, grow dim as we view the whole pilgrimage spread out before us. In deepest humility as we think of the littleness of our own part, and with heartfelt delight in our fellows, we claim them as such. Their sufferings are ours, their testimony ours, because their Saviour, Leader, Lord and Hope is ours. By enlightening of the Holy Spirit we have learned, with them, to rejoice with the Father when He says: "This is My beloved Son, in whom I am well pleased" (Matt. 3. 17). With them, too, we rejoice in the prospect of that day when the Son will present to Himself "a glorious church, not having spot, or wrinkle, or any such thing" (Eph. 5. 27).

Index

Aarau, 343.

Aberdeen, 299.

Achaia, 68; name given to Mananalis, 52.

Afrahat, Persian, author of "Homilies", 70-71.

Agrippa of Nettesheim, 212.

Ainsworth, Henry, 243, 245.

Albi, 87, 88.

ALBIGENSES, connections with Bogomils, 62, 65, 87; country devastated, 88, 89, 185, 233, 395.

Alefeld, Count, 193.

Aleppo, 351, 354.

Alexander I, Czar of Russia, 325, 327.

Alexander II, Czar of Russia, 329.

Alexander III, Pope, 93, 96.

Alexander VI, Pope, 131.

Alexandria, 9, 10, 21, 74, 324.

Alexius, Byzantine Emperor, 58-59.

Alexius, St., 92.

Alfonso, King of Aragon, 96.

Alleghany Mountains, 305.

Allen, William, 326.

Alsace, 105, 270.

Altona, 268.

Alzey, 166.

Ambrose, Bishop of Milan, 24, 37, 99.

AMERICAN BAPTIST MISSIONARY SOCIETY, 341.

Amiens, 256.

Amsterdam, 138; church of exiles in, 243-244; 245, 262; Labadie in, 265-268.

Amurath, Sultan, 325.

ANABAPTISTS, 112, 153 et seq; 197-199, 200-201, 203-207, 229, 243, 247, 283, 373, 395.

Ancyra, 56.

Andrew, Indian believer, 359.

Angrogne, 217, 219

Anthony, a negro, 276.

Anthony, hermit in Egypt, 31.

Anthony the Good, Duke, 214.

ANTI-BURGERS, 299.

Antichrist, 140, 282; Vaudois MS., 220.

Antioch, 43, 74, 314.

Antioch in Pisidia, 5.

Antwerp, 236.

APOCRYPHA, 22, 38.

APOSTLES, WALDENSIAN, 99-100, 102, 109.

APOSTOLIC SUCCESSION, teaching of Priscillian, 40; among Waldenses, 99; Marsiglio of Padua, 103; United Brethren, 130; Brush Run, 308.

Apulia, 217.

Aquinas, Thomas, 105.

Aquitaine, Louis son of Charlemagne king of, 49; Aquitania, fourth century reformation in, 36.

Aragon, 96.

Ararat, Mount, 44.

ARIAN, bishops appointed, 21; Government persecutes Catholics, 21; ARIANS, 86, 90.

ARIANISM, long remained state religion in northern kingdoms, 22; denies Divinity of Jesus Christ, 30; and Unitarianism, 224.

Arius, 21, 70, 86.

Armenia, primitive churches in, 42, 44; first country to make Christianity state religion, 43; 45, 65.

ARMINIANISM, 243, 244, 293.

Arminius, Jacobus, 243-244.

ARNALDISTAE, 97.

Arndt, 282.

Arnold, Gottfried, life and writings, 279-280.

Arnold, Henri, 92.

Aroolappen, 358, 359.

ASCETICISM, of Marcionites, 14; of hermits, 31; use of a by Priscillian, 37, 39; of Bogomils misrepresented, 59; excessive, 113.

Athanasius, 21-22, 70.

Athos, Mount, 324.

Aubigné, Merle d', 303, 373.

Augsburg, 110, 157; Denck in, 160-161; "martyrs' conference" held in, 162, 165.

Augusta, John, 132-134.

Augustine, conversion and teaching, 24-28, 99, 112, 116, 119, 132, 243.

Augustine, missionary to England, 35-36.
Australia, 317.
AUTHORISED VERSION, 248.
Avignon, 213.
Avila, 37.

Baanes, 51, 52.
Babinot, 222.
Babylon, 16; spiritual, 137, 190, 232.
Baden, 164.
Badly, Thomas, 122.
Baedeker, Dr., 331.
Bagdad, 79, 81, 84, 325; Groves in, 350-354, 357, 372.
Bahram V, king of Persia, 74
Ball, John 121.
Bamburgh, 258.
BAN, title of Bosnian rulers, 61, 62, 63, 64.
BAPTISM, of believers, 8; of infants, 8-9, 43, 145; change of teaching concerning, 9; regeneration by *b*, 9, 145; delayed by British monks until evidence of faith given, 35; of Priscillian, 36; description of *b* in "Key of Truth", 53; of infants, brought the world into the church, 54; of Jesus, 55; 87; among Waldenses, 99; 108; of believers at Reichenau and Lhota, 130; in relation to the church question, 147-148; Luther on, 148; believers baptized, 153; of believers, punished by death, 154, 165; 156; by Hubmeyer, 157, 161; 164, 166; of children made compulsory, 169; of believers punished by drowning, 169; source of endurance of Anabaptists, 171; question as to salvation of children, 172; of infants cannot be proved from Scripture, 173; believers baptized, to be drowned, 173; in Tyrol, 176; 180; of adults made obligatory in Münster, 181; similarity c outward *b* does not establish fellowship, 185; Snyder beheaded for renewing his, 186; Menno and infant, 186-187; teaching of Scripture on, 187; corrupted *b*, 188; true *b*, 189; Menno begins to baptize, 191; Pilgram Marbeck on, 194-196; edict against, 197; 198; Schwenck-

feld on, 203, 204, 207; of a child in Paris and results, 228; difference between Independents and Baptists, 239; of infants in the Church of England, 246-247; not practised by the Friends, 253; not the ground of fellowship, 254; 263; James Haldane on, 301; Robert Haldane and, 303; Campbell and, 306, 309; Mennonite, 319; among Mennonite Brethren, 321; liberty of, 323; among Stundists, 325-326, 328, 338; Oncken on, 340; Fröhlich and, 344, 346; Müller on, 362, 363, 365, 366; Evans on, 368, 369; Chapman on, 370; Darby and, 372; Spurgeon on, 391-392; the Friends and, 394.
BAPTISMAL REGENERATION, 391-392.
BAPTISTS, called Anabaptists, 161; in Strassburg, 162; hymns, 165; imprisoned and put to death, 165; Schwenckfeld and the, 203, 204, 206; churches in London, 239; persecuted, 240; views on civil power, 245, 247, 248; 249; conflict renewed, 253; in Russia, 335-336; connections with other bodies, 371; 395; AMERICAN, 309-311, 313, 314-315, 341; GERMAN, spread to Russia, 328; churches formed, 338; in Russia, 341.
BAPTIST UNION, 392.
BARBE, title of Vaudois elders, 217; visit Reformers, 218; 219.
Barcochebas, 4.
Barnabas, 5, 43.
Barnstaple, 357, 363, 368, 369, 370.
Barrowe, 240.
Bartholomew, St., massacre of, 230, 280.
Basil, Bogomil elder, 58-59.
Basil I, Byzantine Emperor, 56.
Basle, 106, 109; Council of, 126, 128; Bible-study and printing in, 156; 158, 162-163, 216; Vaudois Barbes come to, 217; Mission, 326, 351; 224, 343.
Bastille, 279.
BATTLES, Kossovo, 64; Lipan, 126; Mühlberg, 133; White Mountain, 135; 214.
Baxter, Richard, 253.
Beaufort, 233.

Beccles, 123.

Beda, Noël, 210, 212.

Bedford, Church in, 254.

Beer, George, 357, 360.

BEGHARD, 101, 105, 106, 107, 111.

BEGHINE, 101, 105, 106.

BELGIAN CONFESSION, 262, 263.

Bellett, John Gifford, 347, 348, 350, 371.

Benedict of Nursia, 32.

Benedict, caves of St., 222.

Bentinck family, 339.

Bernard of Clairvaux, 32, 86, 99.

Bernard of Cluny, 32.

Berleburg, 280, 281; BIBLE, 281, 283; 282.

Berlin, 272, 276, 340.

Bern, 169, 302.

Berquin, Louis de, 210, 212, 215.

Berthelsdorf, 273, 274, 275.

Bethesda Chapel, Bristol, 363-365, 382-384.

Bethlehem, 67, 69, 324.

Beziers, 89.

BIBLICAL CRITICISM, 14, 388, 392.

Biel (Bienne), 169.

Bjelopolje, 62.

Blaurock, 168, 169, 170.

Blois, 226.

Bockelson, Jan (John of Leyden), 180-184.

Boehler, Peter, 276, 277, 289.

BOGOMILI (BOGOMILS), meaning of name, 57-58 and n-57-58; early opinions of, 59-60; misrepresented by enemies, 60; many churches of b in Bosnia, 61; intercourse with believers in other countries, 62; attacked by Pope and king of Hungary, 63-64; inquisition established in Bosnia, 63; accept Turkish help, 64; Turks capture Bosnia, 65; tombstones, 65-66.

BOGOMOLICI, 57n.

BOHEMIAN BRETHREN (see Unitas Fratrum, Moravian Church), 136, 276, 284, 293.

BOHEMIAN CHARTER, 135

Böhmerwald, 112.

Bohnekämper, 326.

BOLSHEVIK, 325, 337, 338, 392.

Bona, 25.

Boniface, led Roman missionary system against British, 36.

Boniface VIII, Pope, 102.

Boniface IX, Pope, 111.

BOOKS, First Epistle of Clement to the Corinthians, 7; Hexapla (Origen), 10; Antitheses (Marcion), 14; Confessions, 24-25, City of God, 25 (Augustine); Heliand, 36; Priscillian's works, 38-40; Koran, 50, 56; Key of Truth (tr. Conybeare), 52, 53-55; Homilies of Afrahat, 70; The Bazaar of Heraclides of Damascus (Nestorius, tr. Bethune-Baker), 75-77; Commentary on the Epistle to the Galatians (Claudius), 91; Defensor Pacis (Marsiglio), 102-103; History of Tauler's Conversion, 108; Nine Rocks, 108-109; Greek New Testament (Erasmus), 114; The Kingdom of God, 118, Of the Truth of Holy Scripture, 119 (Wycliff); The Net of Faith (Cheltschizki), 127-129; The Labyrinth of the World and the Paradise of the Heart, 136, The Testament of the Dying Mother, 136-137, The Voice of Mourning, 138, One Thing Needful, 138-140 (Comenius); Imitation of Christ (à Kempis), 141; Address to the Nobility of the German Nation on the Liberty of the Christian Man, 143, Babylonian Captivity of the Church, 143 (Luther); Spiritual Exercises (Loyola), 150; translation of the Prophets (Denck and Hetzer), 162; Vermanung, etc. (Marbeck), 194 and n-196; Of the New Pamphlet of the Baptist Brethren, etc. (Schwenckfeld), 207; reply to above (Marbeck), 207; Lives of the Saints (Le Fèvre), 209; Noble Lesson, Catechism, Antichrist (Vaudois MSS.), 220; The Institutes of the Christian Religion (Calvin), 224; A Booke which sheweth the Life and Manners of all true Christians etc., 239-240; A Treatise of Reformation without Tarrying for Anie (Browne), 240; Ecclesiastical Polity (Hooker), 241-243; Book of Common Prayer, 253; Saints' Everlasting Rest (Baxter), 253-254; Pilgrim's Progress (Bunyan), 254; The discernment of a true church etc. (Labadie), 261; Eukleria (van Schürman), 266, 268; Spiritual

Guide (Molinos), 279; First Love, that is a True Picture of the First Christians etc., 279-280, Impartial History of the Churches and Heretics etc., 280 (Gottfried Arnold); Marburg Bible, 281; Berleburg Bible, 281; The Mystery of Godliness and the Mystery of Iniquity (Fröhlich), 345-346; Narrative of some of the Lord's dealings with George Müller, 368; Origin of Species (Darwin), 387; Vie de Jésus (Renan), 390; Leben Jesu (Strauss), 390.

Bordeaux, 37, 255, 256.

Bosna river, 64.

Boston, 249.

Bowden, William, 357, 360.

Bradford, 277.

Braga, 37.

Brandenburg, 110, 232, 237, 272.

Brandhuber, Wolfgang, 170.

BREAKING OF BREAD (see LORD'S SUPPER), 9, 168, Schwenckfeld on, 204, 207; in caves of St. Benedict, 222; in Herford, 268; Stundists, 326, 328, 333; liberty for, 347, 349, 350; Müller, 362; Darby, 377, 382, 383.

Bremen, 268.

BRETHREN, 111, 395.

BRETHREN OF THE COMMON LIFE, 141-142.

Briconnet, Bishop of Meaux, 209, 211, 214, 256.

Bristol, 290; open-air preaching, Whitefield and Wesley, 291; 360, 363; Müller's Orphanage opened, 367, 371, 372, 382.

BRITISH AND FOREIGN BIBLE SOCIETY, 325, 327, 348, 392.

BRITISH MUSEUM, ix, 82, 324.

Browne, Robert, 239-240.

BROWNISTS, 239, 243.

Brueys, Pierre de, 85.

Brugg, 343.

Brush Run, 308, 309.

Bucer, 161, 162, 187, 196, 199, 215.

Buckinghamshire, 123.

Budapest, 344.

Buddha, 16; BUDDHISM, 16, 79.

Buffalo Creek, 309.

BUILDINGS, no special *b* required for meetings, 3; missionary villages, 35; simple houses and rooms, 46; to receive relics and in honour of martyrs, consecrated to Virgin or saints, 46; Bogomil meetings held in any house or in plain meeting rooms, 61; meetings in private houses forbidden by Synod of Seleucia, 73; de Brueys taught useless to build churches, 85; Waldensian meeting rooms, 100; cathedrals, 104.

BULGARIAN CATHOLICS or PAVLICANI, 60-61.

BULGARIANS, name given to believers, 57n, 60, 85.

Bunyan, John, 254.

Burdigala, former name of Bordeaux, 37.

Bury St. Edmunds, 240.

Caesaraugusta, former name of Saragossa, 37.

Caesarea, 316.

Calabria, 217, 218.

CALIXTINES, see UTRAQUISTS, 125.

CALVINISM, CALVINISTS, 225, 243-244, 246, 293, 313.

Calvin, Jean, 92, 151; in Poitiers, 221; in Geneva, 224-225; on elders, 228; 243, 246, 256, 257, 373.

Cambridge, 235, 250.

CAMERONIANS, 299.

CAMISARD, CAMISARD WAR, 233.

Campbell, Alexander, 307-310, 314, 315.

Campbell, Thomas, 305-309, 314, 315.

CAMPBELLITES, 316.

Cane Ridge, 311, 313, 314.

Canisius, 151, 199.

CANON OF SCRIPTURE, 7, 22, 38.

Canterbury, 36, 122.

Capito, 161, 162, 179, 196, 215, 216.

Carbeas, 55.

Cardiff, 286.

Carey, William, 295-297.

Carl, Dr., 282.

Carniola, 63.

Carolina, North, 310.

Carthage, 10, 12-13, 28.

Casimir, Count, 280, 282.

CATECHISM, in various languages, 141; 220; RACOVIAN, 225.

CATHARS, name given to Christians who adhered to Scripture, 15, 62, 85, 89, 97, 395.

Cathay, former name for China, 81

Catherine de Medici, 229, 230.

Catherine II, Empress of Russia, 318.

CATHOLIKOS, title of bishop of Seleucia, 69; moved to Bagdad, 79; 83, 84.

Caucasus, 319, 326, 327, 330, 334, 335.

Cavalier, Jean, 233.

Celestinus, 27, 28.

Cennick, 277-278.

Cevennes mountains, 232, 233, 280.

Chaistellain, Jean, 212, 214.

CHALDEANS, see NESTORIANS, 79.

Chambéry, 222.

Chanforans, conference between Vaudois and Reformers, 219.

Chapman, Robert Cleaver, 363, 368-371, 385.

Charlemagne, Emperor, 49.

Charles IV, Emperor, 110.

Charles V, Emperor, 133, 154, 165, 172, 174, 214.

Charles I, king of England, 324.

Charles of Žerotín, 134, 136.

Chayla, Abbé du, 233.

Cheltschizki, Peter, "The Net of Faith," 127-129; 129.

Chittoor, 357.

CHRISTIAN ASSOCIATION OF WASHINGTON, 306, 308.

CHRISTIAN BRETHREN, 236.

CHRISTIAN CONNECTION, 314.

CHRISTIANS, 310, 311, 314.

Christian VI, king of Denmark, 276.

CHRIST'S PAUPERS, 101.

Chortitza, district and river, 319.

Chrysocheir, 55-56.

Chrysostom, 99.

CHURCH AND STATE, associated under Constantine, 20; union repudiated by Christians faithful to Scripture, 20; church fails to save the state by union with it, 23, 29; forcible conversions, 34; many disciples consider union contrary to the Lord's teaching, 41; unite in Armenia, 43; unite in restoring image worship, 48; churches uninfluenced by union of, 89; 99; Marsiglio of Padua on, 102-103; relations defined by cities, 104; Luther adopts principle of, 145; Calvin introduces into Geneva, 224; Church of England, 237; Gottfried Arnold on, 280; Evans, 368.

CHURCHES OF CHRIST, 316.

CHURCHES OF THE DESERT, 233, 234.

CHURCHES UNDER THE CROSS, 233.

CHURCH MISSIONARY SOCIETY, 297, 350.

CHURCH OF ENGLAND, established, 237; development of, 239; defended by Hooker, 241-243; nonconformity punished, 243; character of, 246-247; Act of Uniformity, 253; Societies within the, 277; Groves on ordination, 350; in India, 356; unsectarian members of, 360; Darby and the, 372; Anglican, Anglo-Catholic, 372; influenced by Rationalism, 385, 391; influence of clergy, 393.

Citeaux, 32.

Claudius, Bishop of Turin, 49-50, 91.

Clement, elder of church in Rome, 7-8.

Clement VII, Pope, 100-101.

Cluny, 32, 86.

Cobham, Lord (Sir John Oldcastle), 122.

Coccejus, 262.

Coct, Anemond de, 215.

CODEX ALEXANDRINUS, 324.

Colet, John, 113-114, 115.

Coligny, Admiral, 229, 230.

Cologne, church and martyrs in, 96; Walther burnt, 104-105; Eckart and Tauler in, 106, 107; meetings and persecutions, 197-199; Hermann v. Wied, 151, 199; 235.

Columba, 34.

Comenius, Jan Amos, life and writings, 136-140, 273, 275.

COMMUNITIES, in Egypt, 31; in Italy, 32; Columban settlements, 32; of Bohemian Brethren, 132, 134; in Moravia, 178-179; Labadists, 265-269; Groves, 354.

COMMUNITY OF GOODS, Hubmeyer on, 156; in Münster, 181; see COMMUNITIES.

Comnena, Anna, 58-59.

COMPACTS OF BASLE, 126.

Condé, Prince of, 230.

CONFERENCE, of overseers, 9; at St. Félix de Caraman, 87; Waldensian, 100; in Moravia, 157; martyrs', 162; of brethren in Baden, 164; Wesleyan Methodist, 294.

CONGREGATIONALISTS (see INDE-
PENDENTS), 239, 310.
CONSISTORIUM, 261, 263.
Constance, Council of, 123-125;
157.
Constantine, Byzantine Emperor,
son of Leo the Isaurian, 48, 57.
Constantine Chrysomalus, writer,
condemned for Bogomil doctrine,
60.
Constantine, Emperor (the Great),
15; edict of Milan, 18; church
and state associated, 20-21; 22,
41, 43, 46, 62, 69, 72, 83, 89,
280, 314.
Constantine Pogonatus, Byzantine
Emperor, 45.
Constantine Silvanus, Paulican
elder, 45-46, 51, 52.
Constantinople, 23, 24, 33, 34, 46,
47, 48, 52, 54, 56, 57; Basil
burnt, 58; 60; capture of, 64;
74, 77, 87, 113, 324, 325.
Constantius, Byzantine Emperor,
21.
CONTINENTAL SOCIETY, 339.
CONVERSIONS, Augustine, 25; Priscillian, 36; Constantine Silvanus, 45; Simeon Titus, 46;
Sergius, 51; Peter Waldo, 92;
Francis of Assisi, 94; Suso, 106;
Luther, 116; Loyola, 150; Hub-
meyer, 155; Menno Simon, 189;
Farel, 209; Louis de Berquin,
210; Anna Maria van Schürman,
266; Franke, 272; Hutton, 276-
277; William Wroth, 286; John
Wesley, 289; Charles Wesley,
289; Wüst, 320; Oncken, 339;
Fröhlich, 343; George Müller,
360; Robert Chapman, 369.
Corinth, 7, 103.
Cornelius, Bishop of Rome, 15.
Cosmas, 59.
Cotton, Colonel (Gen. Sir Arthur),
354.
COUNCILS, Nicaea, Nicene creed
framed, 21, 70, 72; first six
general, 22; on Pelagianism,
28; Frankfurt, on images, 49;
Second of Nicaea, 49; at Ephesus, Nestorius condemned, 74;
Lombers, trial of heretics, 87;
Toulouse, inquisition made permanent institution, 89; third
Lateran, refused application to
preach of "Poor Men of Lyons"-
93; Tours, Waldenses con-

demned, 96; Constance, Huss
and Jerome burnt, 123-125;
Basle, treaty with Hussites,
126; Speyer, protest of Refor-
mers, 146; about "Anabaptist"
movement, 154.
COUNTER REFORMATION, 149-152.
COUNTESS OF HUNTINGDON'S CON-
NEXION, 293.
COURALT, 226.
Court, Antoine, 234.
COVENANT, SCOTTISH, 248.
Coverdale, Miles, 238.
Cowling Castle, 122.
Cradock, Walter, 286.
Craik, Henry, 361, 363, 370, 371,
382, 383.
Cranmer, Archbishop, 237.
CREEDS, 21, 22.
Cremona, Archbishop received
Papal authority to extirpate
Vaudois in the valleys, 101.
Crete, 324.
Crimea, 319.
Croatia, 63.
Crocus, Richard, 157.
Cromwell, Oliver, 248.
Cronin, Edward, 347, 349, 354.
Cross Creek, 310.
CRUSADES, 33, 88.
Cyril, Bishop of Alexandria, 74.
Cyril, Byzantine missionary, 57,
323.
CYRILLIC ALPHABET, 323.

Dadaz, Étienne, 303.
Dalmatia, 61, 63, 87.
Daniel of Valence, 219, 220.
Darby, John Nelson, 348; life and
teaching, 372-385; 394.
Darbye, John, 238.
Darwin, Charles, 387.
Dauphiny, 85, 209, 215, 217, 232,
233.
David, Christian, 273,274, 275, 277.
David, Metropolitan of Nestorian
bishoprics in China, 78.
David of Augsburg, inquisitor, 93,
97.
Dax, Leonhard, 177.
DEACONS, 308.
DECIAN PERSECUTION, 10.
DEFENDERS, name of Board for
carrying out terms of Bohemian
Charter, 135.
Delft Haven, 245.
Demetrius, Bishop of Alexandria,
10.

Denck, Hans, 157, and life teaching, 158-163.
Denkel, Johann, 344.
D'Esch, 213, 214.
Deventer, school at, 141.
Devonshire, 368, 371.
DIASPORA, JEWISH, 3, 4.
DIET, of Worms, 143; of Speyer, 146.
Dijon, 218.
DIOCESES, (see PARISHES), 68, 96.
Diognetus, EPISTLE TO, 16-17.
DISCIPLES, 316.
DISSENTERS, 233, 253.
Divara, 183, 184.
Dnieper, river, 319.
Dober, Leonard, 276.
Doboj, rocks of, 64.
Dominic, 89.
DOMINICANS, 63; inquisition established, 89; 95, 96-97, 106, 150, 151.
DONATISTS, 15-16, 20-21, 26, 31.
Donatus, 16.
Dordrecht, Labadie expelled from Reformed Church, 264.
DRAGONNADES, 231, 232, 233.
Drayton-in-the-Clay, 249.
Dresden, 126, 272.
Drucker, Thomas von Imbroek, 198.
DUALISM, 13, 16.
Dublin, 347, 348, 349, 350, 370, 371, 372.
Dulignon, 259, 266, 268, 269.
Duprat, 210.

East Anglia, 122.
Eckart, Master, 106, 108.
EDICT, of Milan, 18, 22; St. James, 131-132, 134; Speyer, 154, 165; Lyons, 154; Duke Johann of Cleve, 197; Nantes, 230, 231; revocation of, 231, 232, 233; of Toleration (in Russia), 335-336.
Edinburgh, 300, 371.
EDINBURGH BIBLE SOCIETY, 339.
EDUCATION, in monasteries, 33; by British monks, 35; Waldenses, 100; Beghards, 101; Bohemian Brethren, 131; Comenius, 136, 138; Brethren of the Common Life, 141-142; 286.
Edward VI, king of England, 239.
Ekaterinoslav, 319.
ELDERS, of church at Ephesus, 8; the same as presbyters, 8; description of ordination in "Key

of Truth", 53-54; guides of churches in Bosnia, 61; from Bosnia and Provence consult together, 62; church at Kunwald elects, 129; recognized in churches of brethren, 155; dangerous service, 173; many put to death, 179; appointed in church in Paris, 228; attend Synods, 228; in church in Middelburg, 264; at Brush Run, 308; of churches in Russia banished, 336; in Bristol, 364.
Eliot, John, 249.
Elizabeth, Princess, Abbess of Herford, 267-268.
Elizabeth, Queen of England, 239, 243, 244, 247.
Epaphroditus, name adopted by Paulician elder Joseph, 52.
Ephesus, 8, 55, 56.
Epirus, 68.
EPISCOPALIAN, 247, 248.
Erasmus, 114-115, 141, 143-145, 158, 199, 216.
ERASTIANISM, 237.
Erfurt, 116, 272.
Errett, Isaac, 316-317.
ESTABLISHED CHURCH OF SCOTLAND, 298-299.
Étaples, 208.
Euchrotia, 37.
Eunomius, EUNOMIANS, 86.
Euphrates, river and valley, 44, 45, 68.
Eusebius, 67.
Euthymius, 59.
EVANGELIC, title given to Vaudois, 92; EVANGELICAL, title of church in Middelburg, 264.
EVANGELICAL ALLIANCE, 392.
EVANGELICAL CHRISTIANS, 355, 336, 341.
EVANGELISTS, 308.
Evans, James Harrington, 368-370.
Evesham, 122.
EXCLUSIVES, 385.
Exeter, 349, 350.
Ezra, 4.

Faber, Bishop, 169.
Fabian, Papal inquisitor in Bosnia, 63.
Farel, Guillaume, 209-211, 212, 215; in Neuchâtel, 216-217; visits the valleys, 219-220; 221, 224-225.

Felicitas, **13**.

Félix de Caraman, St., 87.

Fénélon, Archbishop, 279.

Ferdinand and Isabella, 150.

Ferdinand I (house of Hapsburg), king of Bohemia, Emperor, 132; exiles the brethren, 133; burns Hubmeyer, 157-158; compels magistrates to persecute, 174; burns Huter, 175-176; burns Mändl, 176-178; 206.

Ferdinand II, king of Bohemia, battle of the White mountain, execution of Hussite noblemen, 135.

Feret, 225.

Fetter Lane, **293**.

Fèvre, Le, Jacques, 208-210, 212, 215, 216, 221, 256.

Fisher, Dr., 115.

Florence, 113-114.

Fox, Christopher and Mary, **249**.

Fox, George, 249-253.

Francis of Assisi, 94-95, 96, 283.

Francis I, king of France, 91, 115, 209, 214, 226-228.

FRANCISCANS, 63, 81, 94-96, 101, 105, 211, 213.

Franecke, University, 258, 259.

Franke, August Hermann, 272-273, 367, 393.

Frankfurt, 49, 93, Spener in, 270-271; 272.

Frederick, king of Bohemia, 135.

FREE CHURCH (ÉGLISE LIBRE, Switzerland), 373, 379.

FREE SPIRIT, BRETHREN AND SISTERS OF THE, 112-113.

Freiburg, 155.

FRENCH CONFESSION, 262.

Fresenburg, 193.

FRIARS, 82, 95, 114.

Friend of God from the Oberland, 109-110.

FRIENDS OF GOD, meaning of name 'Bogomil', 58, 65; name of Waldensian Apostles, 100; Tauler takes the name, 107; in distress, 109; meeting in mountains, 110.

FRIENDS, SOCIETY OF, 251-253, 326-327, 391, 394.

Fröhlich, Samuel Heinrich, 343-346, 373.

Froment, Antoine, 216, 223, 303.

Fuller, Andrew, 296, 297.

Fulneck, in Moravia, 136, 273; in Yorkshire, 277.

Gainsborough, 244.

Gallen, St., 160, 161, 169.

Gap, 209, 212, 215.

Gascony, 85.

Gaussen, 303, 373.

Gemadius, Patriarch, **60**.

Genesios, 51, 52.

Geneva, 220; Froment in, 223; Calvin in, 224-225; 228; Labadie in, 257, 259, 262; Haldane in, 302-303; 304, 373.

Genghis Khan, 79.

Genoa, 110.

Georg, Duke of Saxony, 144.

Georgen, St., 175.

Georges, Barbe from Calabria, **218**.

Georgia, 288, 289, 290.

Gilles, St., 85.

Giwargis, 80.

GLAGOLITIC CHARACTER, 66, 323.

Glasgow, 307.

Gloucester, 290.

GNOSTIC, GNOSTICISM, 6, 14, 16, 37, 38.

Godaveri Delta, 354, 357, 360.

Gomersal, 277.

Gonin, Martin, 217, 218, 219.

Gonthier, 303.

GOOD MEN, title given to believers, 87.

Görlitz, 273.

Görz, 170.

GOSPELLERS, 229.

Grand Cham, Emperor of the Tartars, 81.

Granson, 216, 218.

Gratian, Roman Emperor, 37.

Grebel, Konrad, 168, 169.

Gregory, Magistros, 52, 53.

Gregory of Narek, 59.

Gregory the Patriarch, 129, 130.

Gregory I, Pope, 35.

Gregory IX, Pope, 97.

Grellet, Étienne de, **326**.

Grenoble, 209, 233, 234.

Groote, Gerhard, 141-142.

Groves, Anthony Norris, 347-348; journey to and stay in Bagdad, 349-354; in India, missionary principles, 354-360; 361, 371, 372; letter to Darby, 380-381; 385.

Groves, Mary, 349-353.

Guerin, Jean, 303.

Guers, 303.

GUILDS, 103-104, 154.

Guise, Duke of, 230.

Guyenne, 256.

Guyon, Madame de la Mothe, 279, 280, 281, 394.

Hake William, 370.
Halberstadt, 360.
Haldane, James Alexander, 297-302, 307, 371, 373.
Haldane, Robert, 297-301; in Geneva, 302-304; 307, 371, 373.
Halifax, 277.
Halle, Franke in, 272-273; 274, 283, 360, 367.
Hamburg, 213, 236; Oncken in, 338, 339, 340.
Hapsburg, House of, 132.
Harding, Stephen, of Citeaux, 32.
Harris, Howel, 286-287.
Hausschein (Œcolampadius), 163.
Hegius, Alexander, 141.
Heidelberg, 166, 259.
Helena, 46.
HELIAND, alliterative Saxon Epic, 36.
Helwys, Thomas, 245.
Hencsey, Ludwig, 344.
HENRICIANS, 86.
Henri the Deacon, 86.
Henry IV, king of England, 117, 122.
Henry V, king of England, 122.
Henry VI, king of England, 123.
Henry VIII, king of England, 115, 237.
Henry IV, of Navarre, king of France, 230.
Herat, 78.
HERESY, measures taken against gnostic, 6; Marcion, 14-15; Augustine advocates use of force against, 26-27; Gnostic, 37; Bernard of Clairvaux on, 86; Alsace full of, 105; Eckart cited for, 106; sufferings for, 111; legislation in England against, 122; England absolved by Pope, 239.
HERETICS, bodies called, 11; Christians faithful to Scripture called, 20, 42; burnt by Byzantine Emperor Justinian II, 46; protest against image worship, 50; in Asia Minor and Bulgaria accused of sin and hypocrisy, 59; Pavlicani described as, 61; Paulicians described as, 61; not to be tolerated in Bosnia, 62; imaginary heretical Pope, 62; one of them becomes inquisitor,

62; Pope incites Ban of Bosnia to exterminate, 63; ordered by Pope to be banished from south of France, 88; testimony of Reinerius, 90; numerous and active, 96; executions of, 97; enumerated, 97; persecuted in Waldensian valleys, 100-101; in Beghard houses, 101; accused of disobedience to the Church, 105; thought to be subdued, 111; 120; first to be burnt in England, 122; no obligation to keep faith with, 124; "nest" burnt, 136; hymn book of, 142; persecuted for centuries, 154; publish books in Basle, 156; to be punished, 168; killed by soldiers without trial, 171; 192; Schwenckfeld, 206; Wycliffite, 239.

Herford, 268.
Hermann V, Archbishop of Cologne, 151, 199.
HERMITS, 31; Hermit of Livry, 211, 215.
Herrnhut, 274; in England, 277; 289.
HIGHER CRITICISM, 388-390.
Hippo, see Bona, 25.
Hiuan Tsung, Chineses Emperor, 79.
Hochenau, Hochmann von, 282, 283.
Hoffman, 283.
Holbeck, 277.
Holstein, 193.
HOLY SYNOD, 325, 328, 329; regulations for exterminating Stundists, 334.
Hooker Richard, 241-243.
HOUSEHOLD CHURCH, 265.
Hubmeyer, Dr. Balthazar, 155-158, 161, 203.
HUGUENOTS, 229-232.
Hulava, Jakob, 130.
Huntingdon, Countess of, 291, 293; CONNEXION, 293
Huss, John (Jan Hus), 123-125, 126, 132, 393.
HUSSITES, 65, 132, 135.
HUSSITE WAR, 125-126.
Hut, Hans, 157, 203.
Hutchinson, Francis, 348.
Huter Jakob, 170, 175-176.
HUTIST BAPTISTS, 203, 204.
Hutton, James, 276-277.
Hy, see Iona, 34.
Hydatius, 37, 40.

HYMNS, Bernard of Clairvaux, 32; taught by British monks, 35; written among Bohemian brethren, 131; in Latin, taught at Brethren's schools, 141-142; hymn book published in Ulm, 142; 161; written in times of persecution, 165; Isaac Watts, 254; Charles Wesley, 292; Malan, 303.

ICONOCLAST, ICONOCLASTIC, 48, 49, 50.

Ignatius, 8.

IMAGES, Christians refuse divine honours to, 18; believers in Asia Minor refuse worship of, 45; relics and pictures become objects of veneration and of worship, 46, 47; campaign of Leo the Isaurian against, 47; John of Damascus defends worship of, 47-48; Theodora persecutes those opposed to the use of, 50; unsuccessful attempts at forcible suppression of worship of, 52; condemned in "Key of Truth," 54; not found among Mohammedans, 56; brought by Nestorian missionaries to China, 79; of Tartars, 81; in Nestorian churches in China, 82.

INDEPENDENTS, 239, 240, 247, 248, 249, 253, 356, 371, 395.

INFANTS, 27-28, 172, 372.

INFIRMARY, 101.

Ingham, Benjamin, 277.

Ingoldstadt, 155.

Innocent I, Pope, 28.

Innocent III, Pope, 62, 88-89, 94, 100.

Innocent VIII, Pope, 101.

Innocent XI, Pope, 279.

Innsbruck, Kirschner burnt, 170; Huter burnt, 175-176; Mändl burnt, 176-178.

INQUISITION, established in Bosnia, 63; in south of France, 89; made permanent institution, 89; Loyola and the, 150-151; Molinos, 279; 392; red, 338.

INQUISITORS, Reniero Sacconi, 62, 92; Fabian in Bosnia, 63; sent to Waldensian valleys, 100-101; to examine books, 106; sent by Pope and Charles V into the Empire, 110; sent by Boniface IX, 111; Peter Pilichdorf, 111.

INSCRIPTIONS, Madras and Kattayam in Travancore, 78; Chinese and Syriac, Si-ngan-fu, 78; Turkish and Syriac, Issyk-kul, 80.

INSPIRATION, 200, 387-390.

Iona, Isle of, (Hy), 32, 34.

Irak, 78.

Irenaeus, 8.

Irene, 48.

Irkutsk, 331.

Isaak, Bishop, 71-73.

Isabeau, la belle, 232.

ISLAM, religion founded by Mohammed, 50; threatens Europe, 63; continued conflict, 64; Bosnians subjugated to, 66; Nestorians scattered or absorbed by, 79; Christendom and heathen powers to combine against, 79; efforts to gain Mongol khans, 81.

Israel, George, 133.

Issyk-kul, 80.

Istria, 63.

Jacob, Henry, 245.

Jakoubek, 126, 127.

James I, king of England, 135, 244.

James II, king of England, 252.

Jean of Molines, 219, 220.

JEDNOTA BRATRSKA, 130.

Jerome, 27, 38n.

Jerome of Prague, 111, 123, 125.

Jerusalem, Gospel first preached at, 3; destruction of, 7; relics from 46; Gospel spread from, 67; 151, 178; spiritual, 190; 255, 269, 316, 374, 377.

JESUITS, 81, 107, 134, 135, 151, 199, 231, 255, 256, 279, 325.

Johann, Duke of Cleve, etc., 197.

John, Martyr in Strassburg, 97.

John of Damascus, 47-48.

Johnson, Francis, 243, 245.

Jones, Abner, 311.

Jones, Griffith, 286.

Jordan, pool near Tabor (Bohemia), 125.

Joseph (Epaphroditus), 51, 52.

JOSEPINI, 97.

Judaea, 4.

JUDAISM, 6, 13, 14.

Julia (Nestorian), 80.

Julian, Bishop of Eclanum, 28.

Julius II, Pope, 114, 115.

Jungbunzlau, 133.

Jura mountains, 373.

Jurieu Pierre, 232.

JUSTIFICATION BY FAITH, taught by Clement, 8; preached by British monks, 35; experience of Luther, 116; revived among Bohemian brethren, 131; taught by Luther, 145; Denck on, 158; balancing doctrine, 163.

Justinian II, Byzantine Emperor, 46.

Justus, adopted son of Constantine Silvanus, 46.

Ju-tê-a (Judaea), 82.

Kambaluk (Pekin), 78.

Kascha, Jagub (Jakov Deljakovitch), 327.

Kashgar, 78.

Kempis, Thomas à, 141, 282.

Kent, 35.

Kentucky, 311, 313.

Kettering, 296.

Khorasan, 78.

Kibossa, 45, 46; called Macedonia, 52.

Kiev, 323.

Kingswood, 290.

Kirkwall, 299.

Kirschner, Michael, 170.

Kitto, 350, 354.

Klausen, 170, 176.

Köbner, Julius, 340.

Königsberg, 133.

KORAN, 50, 56.

Kossovo, battle of, 64.

Kotorsko, 66.

Kovacs, Josef, 344.

Krajek, Konrad, 133.

Kreuznach, 166.

Krishna, Pal, 297.

Kulin, Ban of Bosnia, 61-64.

Kunewald (Moravia), 274.

Kunwald (Bohemia), 129, 130.

Labadie, Jean de, 255-270.

LABADISTS, 269, 284.

Lambert, François, 213.

La Minerve, 89.

Langegger, Hansen, 170.

Langenmantel, Eitelhans, 161, 165.

Languedoc, 85, 88, 232.

Laodicea, 52, 281.

Lausanne, 234, 373.

Leade, Jane, 281.

LEAGUE, WARS OF THE, 230-231.

Leclerc, Pierre and Jean, 211; Jean, 212, 213-214.

Leeds, 277.

Leeuwarden, 186.

Lehmann, Gottfried Wilhelm, 340.

Lenz, Paul, 178.

Leo III, the Isaurian, Byzantine Emperor, 47, 48, 52.

Leo IV, Byzantine Emperor, grandson of Leo the Isaurian, 48.

Leo the Armenian, Byzantine Emperor, 52.

Leo X, Pope, 115.

Leonhard, Count, 157.

Leonidas, 10.

LEONISTS, 90.

Leupold, Hans, 165.

Leutweil, 344.

Leyden (Holland), 245, 262; John of (see Bockelson), 180, 183, 184.

Lhota, 130, 153.

Lichtenstein, Hans von, 157.

Liebich, Jörg, 176.

Liegnitz, 205.

Linz, 170.

Lipan, battle of, 126.

Lissa (Lesno), 136.

LITERATURE, Catholic, preserved, that of Dissidents destroyed, 11; attraction of classic, 36; of believers in Asia Minor destroyed, 44; of Bogomils destroyed, 65; called "heretical," destroyed, 105-106, 123; renaissance, 113; Kralitz Bible basis of Czech, 134; of those called "Anabaptists", destroyed, 153-154, 164; used to confound different lines of teaching, 184.

Lititz, 129.

"Little Prophets," 232.

Livry, forest of, 211.

Llangeitho, 287.

Llanvachery, 286.

Llanvaches, 286.

Lodensteyn, Jodocus van, 258, 259, 260.

LOLLARDS, 36, 105, 111; name, 117; 122, 185, 235, 239, 395.

Lombardy, 96.

London, 82, 114; congregations of believers in, 122; 123, 236-237; church in, 239; 257; Teelinck, in, 258; Peter Boehler in, 276, John Wesley in, 289; revival in, 290; J. H. Evans preaches in, 368; J. N. Darby in, 372; meetings in, 381.

LONDON JEWS SOCIETY, 361.

LONDON MISSIONARY SOCIETY, 82, 297.

LORD'S COMING, THE EXPECTATION OF, 12, 283, 373, 379.

LORD'S SUPPER, THE (see BREAKING OF BREAD), change of meaning attached to, 9; Priscillian objects to taking L.S. with worldly persons, 38-39; given to unbelievers, 43; view attributed to Bogomils, 59; among Waldenses, 99; taken by "Friends of God" in the mountains, 110; taken at Tabor by Hussites, 125; liberty to take, admitted at Council of Basle, 126; in relation to the church question, 147; 164; in Zürich, 168; in Münster, 181; understood by Menno from Scripture, 187; corrupted, 188; true, 189; Pilgrim Marbeck on, 194, 196; desecrated, 199; Schwenckfeld on, 200; discontinued by Schwenckfeld and by Lutheran clergy in Liegnitz, 205, 206; in Pau, 221; at Pré l'Evêque, 223; and the Mass, 226; in Church of England, 247; not observed by the Friends, 253; Labadie and, 256, 263, 265; Spener abstains from, 271; in Edinburgh, 300, 301; in Geneva, 303; 307; at Brush Run, 308; Mennonites and, 321; liberty to take, 323; Oncken and, 340; Cronin and, 348; A. N. Groves and, 350; natives of India and, 359; in Bristol, 365; J. H. Evans and, 369; set aside by the Friends, 394.

Lorraine, 214, 217.

LOT, THE, 276.

Louis, king of Aquitaine, later Emperor, 49.

Louis XIV, king of France, 231, 233, 257, 279.

Louis XVI, king of France, 234.

Loyola, Ignatius, 150-151.

Lübeck, 272.

Lucas, Cyril, 324-325.

Ludwig of Bavaria, Emperor, 102, 104, 106, 110.

Lukas of Prague, 131, 132.

Lusitania (Portugal), fourth century reformation in, 36, 37.

Luther, Dr. Martin, 92, 112; found by Staupitz in Erfurt, 116; and the Bohemian brethren, 132; life and work, 142-149; 157, 172, 179, 184, 186, 199; and Schwenckfeld, 200, 201; 209, 212, 213, 218, 221, 235, 246, 393, 394.

LUTHERAN CHURCH, formation of, 145, 147; Luther's opinion of, 148-149; alarmed at spread of the brethren, 154; requirements for unity of, 160; 196, 199, 205; persecutes Schwenckfeld, 206; 246, 270; Pietist Societies within the, 272; and Moravians, 275-276; 283, 284, 391, 393.

Lutterworth, 118, 121.

Lyons, Irenaeus bishop of, 8; Peter Waldo of, 92; expulsion of Poor Men of, 93; edict against brethren, 154.

Macedonia, name given to Kibossa, 52; early preaching of Gospel in, 68.

Mâcon, Jean de, 228.

Madras, 78, 357.

Madura District, 358.

MAGI, 69, 73.

Mainz, 104, 111, 113.

Malan César, 303.

Mananalis, 52; called Achaia, 52

Mändl, Hans, 176-178.

Mani, 16, 43, 57, 59, 70, 86.

MANICHAEISM, Gnostic religion 16; attracts Augustine, 24; denies God as Creator, 29; attracts Priscillian, 36; Priscillian accused of, 37, 38; opposed by Pricsillian, 39; primitive churches accused of, 43; no trace of m among them, 43; attributed to believers, 55; but incredible, 56, 57; 85, 86, 87, 90.

Manresa, 150.

Manz, Felix, 168, 169.

Marbeck, Pilgram, 194-196; life, 196; 207.

MARBURG BIBLE, 281.

Marcion, 13-15, 70.

MARCIONITES, 13-14.

Marcus Aurelius, Roman Emperor, 12.

Margaret of Valois, 209, 214, 215; Queen of Navarre, 221.

Marguerite, daughter of Catherine de Medici, 230.

Maria, believer, in Russia, 332.

Marseilles, 95.

Marsiglio of Padua, 102-103.
Martin, Bishop of Tours, 37, 40.
Martin V, Pope, 124.
Martinitz, 135.
MARTYRS : Peter, 7; Paul, 7;
Polycarp, 8; Leonidas, 10; Ori-
gen, 10; Perpetua, 13; Felicitas,
13; Fabian, 15; Novatian, 15;
Boniface, 36; Priscillian, 37;
Euchrotia, 37; Constantine Sil-
vanus, 46; Simeon Titus, 46;
Basil, 58; Pierre de Brueys, 85;
Henri the Deacon, 86; John, in
Strassburg, 97; Walther in Co-,
logne, 105; William Sawtre, 122;
Thomas Badly, 122; Lord Cob-
ham, 122; Huss, 124-125;
Jerome of Prague, 125; Jakob
Hulava, 130; Hubmeyer, 158;
his wife, 158; Sattler, 164; his
wife, 165; Leupold, 165; Langenmantel, 165; Blaurock, 170;
Langegger, 170; Kirschner, 170;
girl of sixteen, 170; Spittelmeyer, 170; Brandhuber, 170;
Huter, 176; Ulrich Müllner,
176; Hans Mändl, 178; Snyder,
186; Thomas Drucker von Imbroek, 198; Matthias Zerfass,
198-199; Jean Leclerc, 213-214;
Chastellain, 214; Schuch, 214;
the Hermit of Livry, 215; Pierre
Masson, 218; Vernou, 222; Servetus, 225; Louise Mouïin, 233;
Jacques Roger, 234; Tyndale,
237; Barrowe, 240; Greenwood,
240; Penry, 240.
Maruta, Bishop, 71-73.
Mary, Queen of England, 239.
Mary, the Lord's mother, build-
ings dedicated to, 46; wor-
shipped as "our Lady", 47;
worship of the Virgin, 54; the
Lord's mother, 55; teaching of
Theodore of Mompsuestia, and
of Nestorius, 74; dedication of
Loyola to, 150.
MASS, re-introduced into Bosnia,
62; Menno's doubts, 186; 222;
Placards, 226; refused, 232.
Masson, Pierre, 217, 218.
Matthias of Kunwald, 130.
Matthys, Jan, 180-182.
Maxmillia, 12.
Maxmillian, king of Bohemia, 134.
Maximus, Emperor, 37.
Mayflower, the 246.
Mazarin, 231.

Meaux, 209, 210, 211, 212, 214.
Mecca, 50.
Medici, 115, 229, 230.
Meijer, Ludwig, 262.
Mejanel, 303.
Melanchthon, 149, 184, 199, 227.
Melville (Vassilij Ivanovitch), 327.
Menno, Simon, 185-193, 318.
MENNONITE BRETHREN, 321-322,
371.
MENNONITES, 112; name, 186; 244,
260; in Russia, 318-322, 326,
337, 351, 395.
Menuret, 259, 266, 267.
Merandol, 217.
Merswin, Rulman, 108, 109, 110.
Merv, 78.
Mesopotamia, 67, 68.
METHODIST NEW CONNEXION, 294.
METHODISTS, 287, et seq., 310, 313,
320, 356, 391.
METHODIST SOCIETIES, 293, 395.
Methodius, 57, 310.
Metropolitan Tabernacle, 391.
Metz, 96, 212, 213, 214.
Meyer, Jörg, 176.
Michael III, Byzantine Emperor,
48, 55.
Middelburg, 258; Labadie in,
260-265.
Middle Kingdom, 78.
Milan, Edict of, 18; Ambrose
bishop of, 24; Augustine con-
verted in, 25; protest of Am-
brose, 37; 110.
Miletus, 8.
Ming Dynasty, 82.
MINISTRY, 264, 270-271, 301, 350,
362.
Minoslav, Prince of the Herze-
govina, 61.
Mirandola, 219.
Mirfield, 277.
Mohammed, 50.
Mohammed II, captures Constan-
tinople, 64.
MOHAMMEDANISM, 21, 24, 50, 55,
56, 57, 61, 64, 66, 79.
Molines, Jean of, 219, 220.
Molinos, Miguel de, 279, 394.
Möllenbecker, Heinrich, 183.
MONASTICISM, Pachomius in Egypt,
31; Benedictine monasteries, 32;
development of monastic orders,
32-33; Irish and Scottish monks
in England, 35; Benedictine
monks land in Kent, 35; 40, 50,
284.

Mongols, 78, **79**, 81, 82.

Monica, 24, 25.

Monod, Adolph, 303.

MONTANISTS, 11, 12, 13, 31.

Montanus, 12.

Montauban, 257, 262, 303.

Monte Corvimo, John of, 81-82.

Montserrat, 150.

MORAVIAN CHURCH, 136-137, 274; in England, 276, 277, 278; 282, 293, 320, 343.

More, Sir Thomas, 115, 236.

Morel, Georges, 217, 218.

Morrison, Robert, 82.

Moulin, Louise, 233

Moulton, 295.

Mount Pleasant, 305, 308.

Mühlberg, battle of, 133.

Müller, tried in Zürich, 167-168.

Müller, George, 360-368, 370, 371, 372, 383, 385.

Müllner, Ulrich, 176.

Münster, events in, 179-184, 185, 189, 190, 203, 338.

Müntzer, 203.

Murrhard, 307.

Muschag, 60.

MYSTERIES, of heathen religions, 6; of Gnostic sects, 14.

MYSTICS, 87, 116, 145, 150-151, 171, 255, 271, 279; aims of the, 284, 394.

Naarden, 262.

NAMES, see Cathars, Puritans, Novatians, Priscillianists, Paulicians, Thonraks, Bogomils, Bulgarians, Patarenes, Albigenses, Nazarenes, Nestorians, Petrobrussians, Henricians, Good Men, Poor Men of Lyons, Waldenses, Vaudois, Evangelic, Spirituali, Passagini, Josepini, Arnaldistae, Speronistae, Weavers, Beghards, Beghines, Brethren, The Poor in Life, Apostles, Schwestrionen, The Poor, Hussites, Taborites, Utraquists, Calixtines, Bohemian Brethren, Jednota Bratrská, Unitas Fratrum, Anabaptists, Mennonites, Mennonite Brethren, Lollards, Wycliffites, Picards, Corner-Preachers (192), Deceivers (192), Heretics, Bush Preachers (199), Sectaries (199), Hutists, Gospellers, Those of the Religion (229), Huguenots, Independents,

Congregationalists, **Baptists**, Brownists, Presbyterians, Particular Baptists, Quakers, Friends, Evangelical (264), Pietists, Spenerites, Quietists, Moravians, Methodists, Stonettes, Campbellites, Disciples, Churches of Christ, Stundists, Evangelical Christians, Plymouth Brethren, **Exclusives**, Open Brethren.

Nancy, 214.

Nantes, Edict of, 230, 231; Revocation of, 231, 233.

Narbonne, Inquisition established, 89.

NATIONAL (or) STATE CHURCH, 147, 148, 202, 248; Mennonites become, 319; Württemberg, 320: Swiss, 373.

Navarre, 221; Henry, king of, 230

NAZARENE, name given to Christians in Persian Empire, **69**; name taken by Christians in Central Europe, 342-346.

Neander, 282.

Neff, Félix, 303.

Nelson, John, 291.

NEO-PLATONISM, 36.

NESTORIANS, 75-84, 86.

Nestorius, 74-77, 86.

Neuchâtel, Farel in, 216-217, 220-221, 225; contrasted with Geneva, 223.

Neuhoffnung, 320.

Neunkirchen, 320.

Newman, Francis W., 354, 372.

Newman, John Henry (Cardinal), 354, 372.

Newton, Benjamin Wills, 372, 382, 383, 384.

New York, 269, 307.

Nicaea, First General Council of, 21; Second, 49; 56, 70, 72.

Nicomedia, 56.

NIHILISTS, 329.

Nikolaus, 126.

Nikolsburg, 157.

Nîmes, 50.

Ninoslav, 63.

Nipp, Anna, 344.

Nitschmann, 274; David, 276.

NONCONFORMISTS, ACT OF UNIFORMITY, 253.

Norfolk, 122, 123.

Northampton, 295.

Norwich, 244.

Novatian, 10, 11, 15.

NOVATIANS, 15, 395.
Novgorod, 323.
Numidia, 24.
NUNNERIES, 33.
Nûremberg, Poor Men of Lyons driven from, 93; burnings in, 111; Denck expelled from, 158-159; Spittelmeyer martyred, 170
Nursia, 32

Odenbach, Johann, 166-167
Odessa, 326.
Œcolampadius (Hausschein), 163, 216; visit from Vaudois, 217-218.
Oldcastle, Sir John (Lord Cobham) 122.
OLD CATHOLIC CHURCH, 10.
Olivetan, 220, 223, 224.
Olopun, 78-79.
Ohio, 313.
Omsk, 332.
Oncken, Johann Gerhard, 338-341.
OPEN BRETHREN, 385.
Orange (also Prince of, William of), 257, 258, 262, 318, 339.
Orbe, 216, 221.
ORDINATION, 309.
Origen, 9-10.
Orkney Islands, 299.
Osiander, 158-159.
Ossett, 277.
Ostrog, 323.
Ostrorog, 133.
Oude Kloster, 187.
OVERSEERS, 8, 9, 309.
Owens, John, 254.
Oxford, Colet in, 113-114; Wycliff, 117, 118, 121; Jerome of Prague, 123; Tyndale, 235; 238, 250; Holy Club, 287, 372.

Pachomius, 31.
Packington, 236-237.
Padua, 102.
Pag-Mangku, 80.
Palatinate (Pfalz), 259.
Palmyra, 68.
Papa ben Aggai, 68-69, 83.
Paris, 102, 106, 168; Le Fèvre in, 208-209; 212; Hermit of Livry burnt, 215; 220, 221; the Placards in, 225-228; church formed in, 228; 229; massacre of St. Bartholomew, 230; 302.
Parnell, John Vesey (Lord Congleton), 348, 349, 354.

PARTICULAR BAPTISTS, 245, 295.
Pasak, 80.
Paschkov, Vassilij Alexandrovitch (Colonel), 328.
Paslovatz Hill, 66.
PASSAGINI, 97.
Passau, 96.
PATARENES, name given to believers, 61, 85, 97.
Pau, 221.
PAULICIANS, name given to primitive churches in Asia Minor, 43; descended from Apostolic churches, 44; Constantine and Simeon, 45-46; denounce idolatry, 47; Sembat and Sergius, 51; persecution, 52-53; doctrines found in "Key of Truth", 53-55; Carbeas and Chrysocheir, 55-56; many removed to Europe, 57; innocent of wicked practices attributed to them, 60; 89, 185, 283, 395.
Pavanne, Jacques, 211.
Pavia, battle of, 214.
PEASANT REVOLT, 121.
PEASANTS' WAR, 143, 203.
Pekin (Kambaluc), 78.
PELAGIANISM, 28-29, 30.
Pelagius, 27-28, 243, 359.
Pelagius Alvarus, 105.
Pélisserie, La, 303, 373.
Pennsylvania, 305.
Penry, 240.
"PERFECT", THE, 87-88, 99-100, 129.
Perpetua, 13.
Peter, Bulgarian Czar, 57n.
Peter, Nestorian Commentator, 80.
Petersburg, St., 326, 327, 328, 329, 350.
PETROBRUSSIANS, 86.
Pfander, 351.
Philadelphia, 305, 309.
PHILADELPHIAN INVITATION, 282, 284.
PHILADELPHIAN SOCIETIES, 278-283.
Philip, chosen by the church, 103.
Philippi, name given to church in Asia Minor, 52.
Phrygia, 12.
Picardy, 208, 210, 256.
PICARDS, name given to believers, 172, 206.
Piedmont, 89, 91, 92.
PIETIST, 271; societies within the Lutheran Church, 272; 273, 274, 284; in Russia, 319, 320, 338.

Pilichdorf, Peter, 90-91, 111.

Pilney Hills, 358.

Pingjum, 186.

PLACARDS, in Meaux, 212; in Paris and France, 226-228.

Plymouth, Pilgrim Fathers sail from, 246; 347, 372, 381.

PLYMOUTH BRETHREN, 372.

Pobiedonostsef, 329, 334, 335.

Poitiers, 221, 222.

POLISH BRETHREN, 225.

Polycarp, 8.

POMAKS, 61.

Pomerania, 110.

Pontus, 13.

POOR, churches set apart money for relief of the, 61-62, 100, 131, 221, 223; individual care for the, 92, 101, 110, 121, 272, 349, 367, 369.

POOR MEN OF LYONS, 93, 97.

POOR, THE, name of Dissenters, 111.

Prague, Jerome and Huss, 123; 126, 127, 129; exiles from, 133; end of Hussites, 135.

Pré l'Evêque, 223, 303.

PRESBYTERIANISM, introduced into France, 228; 240, 245, 247; established religion of Scotland, 247; 248; efforts to establish in England, 248; 249; Baxter, 253; differs from Congregationalism, 260; in America, 305, 306, 308, 311, 313; 314, 391.

PRIMITIVE METHODISTS, 294.

Prisca, 12.

Priscillian, life of, 36-37; martyrdom, 37; writings discovered, 38; teaching, 38-40.

PRISCILLIANISTS, 37-38, 40.

Pritchard, Rees, 286.

PRIVYE CHURCH IN LONDON, 240.

PROTESTANT, name given to Reformers at Diet of Speyer, 146; 225, 239, 247.

Province, 62, 63, 85; devastated by Papal Crusade, 88, 89; 96, 105, 217.

Pseudo-Reimer, 99.

Pskov, 323.

Pudsey, 277.

PURITAN (CATHAR), 15, 247, 248.

Pyt, 303.

QUAKERS, 252, 253, 268.

QUIETISTS, 271, 279.

RACOVIAN CATECHISM, 225.

Radstock, Lord, 327.

Raleigh, Sir Walter, 239.

RATIONALISM, in Holland, 262; a persecuting power, 338; 339, 343, 372, 373, 385; development of, 386-388; 389, 390, 391, 394.

Raymond VI, Count of Toulouse, 88.

REDSTONE BAPTIST ASSOCIATION, 309-310.

REFORMED CHURCH, 199, 202, 228 et seq., 256 et seq.

REFORMERS, 314-315.

Regensburg, 155.

Reichenau, 130.

RELIEF SYNOD, 299.

RENAISSANCE, 113, 154.

Reniero Sacconi (Reinerius), 62, 90, 92.

REPUBLICAN METHODISTS, 310.

Reublin, Wilhelm, 156, 157.

Reuchlin, 114.

Reuss, Eduard, 389.

Richelieu, Cardinal, 231.

Riedenau, 320.

RITUALISM, 386, 389, 390, 392, 394.

Rive Noble, 219.

Robinson, John, 244-246.

Roch, Friedrich, 283.

Rochat Auguste, 378.

Rochelle, la, 231.

Rogatitza, 66.

Roger, Jacques, 233-234.

Rome, 5-7, 15; Constantine, 18; Sylvester, 20, 23; taken by Alaric, 24; 27, 28, 32, 34, 35, 40, 48, 61, 64, 77, 82, 94. 114.

Rorenco, Marco Aurelio, 91.

Roth, Friedrich, 161n.

Rothe, Johann Andreae, 273-275.

Rothman, Bernard, 179-183.

Rottenburg, 164-165.

Rotterdam, 114.

Roussel, Arnaud and Gérard, 210; Gérard, 215, 221, 256.

Rowlands, Daniel, 287.

Rudolph II, Emperor, 134.

RUNCARIANS, 90.

Rüscher, Hubert, 181.

Rysbroeck, Jan van, 141-142.

SABBATH, 5.

Sabellius, SABELLIANS, 86.

SACERDOTALISM, 30-31.

SACRAMENT, SACRAMENTS, salvation by means of, 26; tyrannical use of, 31; Priscillian on the, 39, 40; of the Mass re-introduced into Bosnia, 62; Nestorian belief in salvation through the, 84; Luther on the, 148-149; Menno's use of, 191; of the altar, 198; Schwenckfeld on, 202; Labadie on, 263; Moravians and, 276.

SALVATION ARMY, 395.

Salzburg, 170.

Samarcand, 16, 33, 78, 81.

Sapor II, Persian king, 69.

Saragossa, 37.

Sarajevo, 66.

Sardis, 281.

Sarkis (Sergius), 51.

Sattler, Michael, 164-165.

Saunier, 219-220.

Savoy, Savoie, 91, 222.

Sawtre, William, 122.

Saxony, 237, 273, 274, 276.

Schäfer, 273, 275.

Scharlinger, Jörg, 175.

Schepss, Georg, 38.

SCHOOLS, British missionary, 35; Bohemian Brethren's, 131; of Brethren of the Common Life, 141.

Schuch, 214.

Schürman, Anna Maria van, 258, 259, 266-269.

Schwenckfeld, Kaspar von, 179; teaching, 200-207; 274.

SCHWESTRIONEN, 11.

Scott, Walter, 315-316.

Scrooby Manor House, 244.

Sears, Professor, 340.

SECEDERS, 305, 307.

SECTARIANISM, 197.

Selucia-Ctesiphon, 69, 71, 83, 84.

Sembat, 51.

SEPARATIST CHURCH, 320.

Sergius (Sarkis), 51.

Serre, Du, 232.

Serrières, 216, 217.

Servetus, 225, 302.

Seyon, river, 216.

Shliha, 80.

Shusha, 351.

Siberia, 33, 319, 321, 327; believers exiled to, 330-332, 335, 336.

Sicily, 103.

Siena, 225.

Sigismund, king of Hungary, 64.

Silesia, 200, 205.

Sillian, 175.

Silvanus, 45, 51.

Simeon Titus, 45-46.

Simon de Montfort, 88-89.

Sinope, 13.

Sixtus V, Pope, 108.

SLAV, old Church language, 322, 323.

Slavonia, 63.

Slawata, 135.

SMALCALD LEAGUE, 133, 146, 180.

Smith Elias, 311.

Smithfield, 122.

Smyrna 8.,

Smyth, John, 244, 245.

Snyder Sicke, 186.

SOCINIANISM, 224, 225.

Solaro, 219.

Soltania, Archbishop of, 81.

Sophia, St., church in Constantinople, 48.

Sorbonne, Paris University, 214

South Carolina, 276.

Sozini, Lelio and Faustus, 225.

Spalatin, 132.

Spalato, 61.

Spangenberg, 277.

Speedwell, ship, 245, 246.

Spener, Philip Jakob, 258; life and work, 270-272, 279, 394.

SPENERITE, 271.

SPERONISTAE, 97.

SPIRITUALI, 95.

Spittelmeyer, Ambrosius, 170.

SPRINGFIELD PRESBYTERY, 313, 314.

Spurgeon, Charles Haddon, 391-392.

Staupitz, Johann von, discovers Luther, 116; 132, 142; warns Luther, 146.

Steier, 111.

Steinach, 176.

Stephen, chosen by the church, 103; 204.

Stilling, Jnug, 283.

Stokes, William, 349.

Stone, Barton Warren, 311-314, 315.

Stonettes, 316.

Strassburg, Waldenses burnt, 96-97; a centre of the brethren, 104; heretical literature destroyed, 105; Master Eckart, 106; Tauler, 106-107; Rulman Merswin, 108; 109, 110; document describing the brethren, 111-112; Denck, 161-162; 164, 179; Pilgram Marbeck, 196; refuge of fugitives from France, 215, 216; visit of

Vaudois Barbes, 218; 224; Fröhlich, 343.

STUNDISTS, name, 325; 326; decree for suppressing, 334; 371, 395.

Sturm, to Melanchthon, 227.

Stylites, Simeon, 31.

Suffolk, congregations of believers, 123.

SUNDAY SCHOOL, 299, 339.

Surinam, 269.

Suso, 106, 108, 109.

Sylvester, Bishop in Rome in time of Constantine, 20, 90, 91, 99, 130.

SYNAGOGUE, 3-5, 67.

SYNOD, at Rome excommunicates Novatian, 15; at Caesaraugusta, 37; at Burdigala condemns Priscillianists, 37; at Treves approves sentence on Priscillian, 37; at Braga confirms execution of Priscillianists, 37; at Constantinople condemns Bogomil teaching, 60; deposes bishops as Bogomils, 60; at Seleucia organizes Eastern churches, 71-73; Nestorian quadrennial s, 78; Seleucia, 83; Amsterdam, Leyden, Vlissingen, 262; Naarden, 262-263; Dordrecht, Labadie expelled from Reformed Church, 264; of Established Church of Scotland, of Antiburgers, Relief, condemns unlicensed preaching, 298-299; Philadelphia, 305; Pittsburg, 308; Lexington, 313; at Bethlehem, opposes reform, 324-325; Holy s. opposes spread of Scriptures, 325; persecutes believers, 328, 329, 330; issues decree for suppression of Stundists, 334-335.

SYNODS, introduced into French churches, 228, Provincial and National, 228; restored by Jacques Roger, 234; refused by Independents, 260; adopted by Reformed Church in Holland, 260; condemned by Labadie, 263; Alexander Campbell and, 307.

Tabor, 125.

TABORITES, 125, 126.

Take, 80.

Tamerlane, 81.

Tartary, 78.

Ta Ts'in, 78, 79, 82.

Tauler, Dr. Johannes, 106, 107, 108, 109, 116, 142, 282.

Tauris, Tabriz, 81.

Taurus Mountains, 45, 47, 54, 65, 74, 90.

Teelinck, Willem, 258-260.

Teignmouth, 361.

Temple, destroyed, 4.

Tennessee, 313.

Tephrice, 55, 56.

Tepl, 112, 113.

Tersteegen, Gerhard, 283, 394.

TERTIARIES or THIRD ORDER, 94-95.

Tertullian, condemns infant baptism, enjoins liberty in religion, 9; becoming Montanist separates from Catholic body, 13; two or three form a church, 13; opposes Marcion, 13.

Te Tsung, Chinese Emperor, 78.

Tetzel, 142.

Theodora, re-establishes images, 48; persecutes the brethren, 50; 52, 55.

Theodore of Mopsuestia, 74.

Theodosius 11, Byzantine Emperor, 74.

Theophilus, Byzantine Emperor, 48.

THIRTY YEARS' WAR, 136, 193, 270.

THONRAK, name given to primitive churches in Asia Minor, 43; doctrine found in "Key of Truth", 53-55; opinions about, 59-60.

Thrace, 57.

Thuringia, 111.

Tiflis, 334, 350.

Timotheus, name adopted by Genesios, 51-52.

Timur, see Tamerlane, 81.

Tinnevelly, 359.

Titus, name adopted by Simeon, Paulican elder, 46, 51.

Toeltschig, 274, 277.

Tolouse, 87; Raymond VI, Count of, 88; Council of, 89, 96, 222.

Tours, Martin, bishop of, 37; council at, 96.

Toussaint, Pierre, 213, 214.

TRACTARIAN MOVEMENT, 372.

TRADITION, not necessary for guidance of churches, 22.

Transcaucasia, 335, 351.

TRANSLATIONS OF THE BIBLE, Septuagint, Hebrew into Greek, 4; in monasteries, 33; by British monks, 35; Nestorian, into Sogdianese, 78; 79; Franciscan into language of Cathay, 82; Robert Morrison, Bible into Chinese, 82; Roman Catholic missionary, Latin into Chinese, 82; in use in Metz in German, 96; New Testament into early German, 112; Erasmus, Greek New Testament with Latin, 114; Wycliff, into English, 118; effect of English *t*, 121; into Czech, Kralitz Bible, 134; Luther into German, 143; Denck and Hetzer, the Prophets into German, 162; Le Fèvre, New Testament and Psalms into French, 210; Olivetan, Bible into French, 220, 223; Tyndale into English, 235-237; Authorised Version influenced by Tyndale's, 236; Coverdale, into English, 238; Tyndale's forbidden, 238; Authorized Version into English, 248; Eliot, into an Indian language, 249; into German, Marburg Bible, 281; into German, Berleburg Bible, 281; Cyril, part of New Testament into old Russian, 323; Yaroslav, parts of Bible into Little Russian, 323; Archbishop of Novgorod, Bible into Russian, 323; into Russian, 327; 392.

TRANSUBSTANTIATION, denied by Wycliff, 118; Thomas Badly burnt for denying, 122.

Transylvania, 225.

Trebizond, 55.

Treves (Trier), 37, 104.

Trichinopoly, 358.

Trier, see Treves, 37.

Tübingen, University, 320.

Turin, Claudius, bishop of, 49, 50, 91.

Turkestan, 80, 319.

Tvrtko, Bosnian Ban, becomes king, 64.

Tyn church, Prague, 129, 135.

Tyndale, William, 235-238.

Tyre, 10.

Tyrol, entrance of Gospel into, 170; magistrate defend themselves against charge of laxity in persecution, 174; many baptized

by Mändl, 176; Marbeck a native of, 196.

UNITARIANISM, opposed by Calvin, 224; permitted in Poland and Transylvania, 225.

UNITAS FRATRUM, UNITED BRETHREN, name of brethren in Bohemia, 130; John Augusta, 132; effort to make the U.F. into National Church of Bohemia, 134; signed Bohemian National Protestant Confession, 135; catechism, 141.

Urumia, 83.

UTRAQUISTS (CALIXTINES), religious party in Bohemia, 125; acknowledged by Pope as National Church of Bohemia, 126; archbishop preaches in Prague, 129; pastor at Kunwald, 129; take part in persecution of brethren, 132; membership made obligatory, 132, 133; joined by John Augusta, 134.

Utrecht, 259, 262.

Valnagin, 216.

Val de Ruz, 216.

Valence, Daniel of, 219, 220; 233.

Vallenses, Alpine valleys, 93.

Varel, Duchy of, 339

Vaud, Canton de, 379

VAUDOIS (see WALDENSES), name given to believers in Alpine valleys, 89; return to their valleys, 92; successors of fugitives in time of Paul, 92; meet Reformers, 217-219.

Veere or Ter Veere, 264, 265.

Vernou, Jean, evangelist in France, 222.

Véron, evangelist in France, 222

Vienna, 158, 168.

Vilvoord, 237.

Vinet, 373.

Virginia, 310.

Vivier, du, 304.

Vlissingen (Flushing), 262.

Voet, Gisbert, 258-260, 267.

Volga, river, 23, 319.

Vuktchitch, Stefan, Prince of Herzegovina, protects Bogomils, 64.

VULGATE, Latin translation of Bible by Jerome, 38n, 112.

WALDENSES, see VAUDOIS, connection with Bogomils, 65; with Albigenses, 88; name given to believers in Alpine valleys, 89; same as Leonists, 91; not founded by Claudius of Turin, 91; spread of, 96-97; doctrines and practices of, 97-101; prepared the way for Hussite movement, 123; connected with Wycliff and Huss, 124; teaching in Bohemia, 126; some come to Kunwald, 129; baptism of believers by immersion common among, 130; connections in Bohemia and in Austria, 130; always maintained first Christian principles, 130; catechism in various languages, 141; 172, 185; meet Reformers, 217, 219, 247, 259, 283, 381.

Waldo, Peter, of Lyons, life, 92-94; organises preachers, the "Poor Men of Lyons", 93; connection with Waldenses, 93-94; compared with Francis of Assisi, 96; later results of work, 154.

Waldshut, 155.

Wallis, Mrs., 296.

Waltha Castle, 268, 269.

Walther, martyred in Cologne, 105.

Wandsworth, 247.

Warham, Archbishop, 115.

Wartburg, castle where Luther translated the New Testament, 143.

Washington, 305, 306, 307, 308.

Watteville, de, 274, 275.

Watts, Isaac, 254.

WEAVERS, name given to believers, 103.

Wenzel of Budowa, 134-135.

WESLEYAN, 293.

WESLEYAN METHODIST MISSIONARY SOCIETY, 297.

Wesley, Charles, 287-292, 393.

Wesley, John, 277, 278; life and work, 287-295; 393, 395.

Wesley, Susanna, 287-288.

West Indies, 276, 384.

Westminster, 248; CONFESSION, 249.

Westphalia, Peace of, 136; 280.

Whitefield, George, 278, 287; life and work, 290-293; 393.

White Mountain, Battle of the, 135, 273, 275.

White Sea, 336.

Wied, Hermann von, Archbishop Elector of Cologne, 151, 199.

Wieuwerd, 268, 269.

Wigram, 381.

Winserbaum, prison in Hamburg, 340.

Witmarsum, 187.

Witt, Jan de, 265.

Wittenberg, Bohemian brethren receive news from, 132; Luther nails Theses on church door, 142; burns Papal Bull, 143; 158, 161; theologians press persecution of Anabaptists, 165; 196, 213.

Wittgenstein, 280, 282.

Wolzogen, Ludwig, 262.

WOMEN, martyrs in Rome, 7; mother of Origen, 9-10; Prisca, Maximillia, 12; Perpetua, Felicitas, 13; Monica, 24, 25; Euchrotia, 37; Helena, 46; Irene, 48; Theodora, 48, 50, 52; Mary the Lord's mother, 46, 47, 54, 55, 74, 150; wife of Hubmeyer, 158; wife of Sattler, 165; Divara, 183, 184; wife of Thomas Drucker von Imbroek, 198; Margaret of Valois, 209-210; mother of Pierre and Jean Leclerc, 211, 212; wife of François Lambert, 213; Catherine de Medici, 229; Marguerite, wife of Henry of Navarre, 230; Louise Moulin, 233; Queen Mary, 239; Queen Elizabeth, 239, 243, etc.; Anna Maria van Schürman, 266; Princess Elizabeth, Abbess of Herford, 267-268; Jane Leade, 281; Susanna Wesley, 287-288; Mrs. Wallis, 296; Catherine II, Empress of Russia, 318; Maria, Russian believer, 332; Anna Nipp, 344; Mary Groves, 349-353; wife of George Müller, 362; wife of J. H. Evans, 368-369; mother of R. Chapman, 368.

WORKHOUSES, 101.

Worms, Luther before Papal authorities, 143; Denck in, 162; large congregation of believers, 165.

Wroth, William, 286.

Würtemberg, 282, 319, 320, 338.

Wüst, Eduard Hugo Otto, 320, 321.

Wüstenfelde, 193.

Wu Tsung, Chinese Emperor, 79.

Wycliff, John, life and teaching, 117-121; influence on Jerome of

Prague, 123; writings burnt in Prague, 123; doctrine discussed at Constance, 124; books published in Basle, 156.
WYCLIFFITES, name given to followers of Wycliff's teaching, 121; numerous in England, 122.
Wyke, 277.
Wyllyams, Robert, shepherd, 238.

Xavier, Francis, 151.

Yabh-alaha III, Chinese Catholikos of Syrian Church, 79.
Yaroslav, 323.
Yezdegerd I, Persian king, 71-74.
Yezdegerd II, Persian king, 74.
Yorkshire, 277, 368.
Yvon, 259, 265, 266, 268, 269.

Zacharius, Paulician, elder, 51, 52.
Zaremba, Count, 351.
Zeisberger, 274.
Zerfass, Matthias, 198, 199.
Žerotín, 134, 136.
Zimisces, John, Byzantine Emperor, 57.

Zinzendorf, Count, life and work, 273-277; 282, 283, 284, 289, 373.
Zittau, Zinzendorf, finds document in, 275.
Žižka, Jan, 125-127.
Zoroaster, 16, 69.
ZOROASTRIANISM, 69.
Zozimus, Pope, reinstates and then excommunicates Pelagius, 28.
Zuma, 80.
Zürich, Reublin expelled from, 156; Hubmeyer imprisoned in, 157; influence of Zwingli in, 157, 167; 161; brethren in, 168; public baptisms in, 168; persecution in, 169; conflict on subject of baptism, 173; 209, 216, 343-344.
Zwingli, Ulrich, disputation with Hubmeyer, 157; 161, 162; introduces State Church system, 167; relations with the brethren, 168; baptism, 168; criticised by Blaurock, 169; conflict on baptism, 173; 216, 221.
ZWINGLIAN CHURCH, 205-206.

NOTES